What sports Hall of Fame in Fort Lauderdale, Florida has inducted these members: Benjamin Franklin, Julius Caesar, and Winston Churchill? (See "Lesser-Known Sports Halls of Fame," page 110)

What major-league team mascot was suspended for throwing a Nerf ball at an umpire? (See "17 of the Most Notorious Disqualifications and Suspensions," page 168)

Who was the woman who:
a) struck out Babe Ruth and Lou Gehrig?
b) was the first woman to compete in the Indianapolis 500?
c) was the first woman judge for a heavyweight
title fight?
(See "Women Competing with, and Against, Men," page 201)

What basketball player impersonated a family member in a phone call to his team's front office to say the player had missed a practice because of "a slight death in the family?" (See "The Half-Dozen Worst Excuses in Sports History for Not Performing Well—Or at All," page 217)

Why do the Detroit Red Wings wait for an octopus to be tossed onto the ice before the start of every Red Wings playoff series? (See 7 Sports Superstitions and Jinxes, page 397)

What 83-year-old man won an Olympic medal for ski jumping? (See "1 Athlete Who Simply Waited Long Enough," page 425)

THE ULTIMATE BOOK OF SPORTS LISTS

THE
ULTIMATE
BOOK OF
SPORTS
LISTS

ANDREW POSTMAN
and LARRY STONE

BANTAM BOOKS
NEW YORK • TORONTO • LONDON • SYDNEY • AUCKLAND

THE ULTIMATE BOOK OF SPORTS LISTS
A Bantam Book / December 1990

ISBN 0-553-28540-8

Published simultaneously in the United States and Canada

Bantam Books are published by Bantam Books, a division of Bantam Doubleday Dell Publishing Group, Inc. Its trademark, consisting of the words "Bantam Books" and the portrayal of a rooster, is Registered in U.S. Patent and Trademark Office and in other countries. Marca Registrada. Bantam Books, 666 Fifth Avenue, New York, New York 10103.

PRINTED IN THE UNITED STATES OF AMERICA

OPM   0 9 8 7 6 5 4 3 2 1

DEDICATION

For my grandmothers, Faye
and Bea, with love.

A.P.

To the "Babe Ruth of Families," Mom, Dad, Esther, and
Judy; and to my new "Family
of the Century," Lisa and
Jessica.

L.S.

ACKNOWLEDGMENTS

We would like to thank Elaine Markson, our agent, and Tom Dyja, our editor, for their assistance.

We would also like to thank Lisa Stone and Shelley Postman for their extraordinary help. We appreciate the contributions of Jay Rosen, Henry Ferris, and David Holtz.

Finally, we wish to acknowledge our gratitude for several especially useful sources: the members of the Society for American Baseball Research (S.A.B.R.) and the fine articles included in their yearly *Baseball Research Journals; The Hockey Encyclopedia* by Stan Fischler and Shirley Walton Fischler; *The Kentucky Derby: The First 100 Years* by Peter Chew; and David Wallechinsky's *The Complete Book of the Olympics,* an enormously comprehensive and compelling history of the Olympic Games.

CONTENTS

Patsies . . . 9 of the Friendliest Rivalries . . . The Most
Dominant Tandems in Sports . . . 5 Three-Headed Mon-
sters . . . Take That!: 9 Exercises in Sports One-upmanship
and Revenge . . . 10 Memorable Nicknames of Teams
. . . And 10 Parts of Teams . . . And 10 Fan Clusters
. . . An Embarrassment of Riches . . . Just a Few of the
Most Frustrated Athletes and Teams of All Time . . . 14
of the Most Utterly Dominant Teams and Countries in
Sports History . . .

8 SEX AND DEATH

Killed in the Line of Duty . . . Repellent Sex Crimes
Involving America's Team: Your Dallas Cowboys . . .
Similarly Repellent Sex Crimes Involving America's
Putative Embodiment of Evil: The Oakland/Los Angeles
Raiders . . . Athletes Involved in Murder . . . Women Com-
peting with, and Against, Men . . . The Most Notable
Suicides in Sports . . . New York Giants Who Have
Been Diagnosed with Cancer Since the Team Moved to
New Jersey in 1976 . . . 9 Individual Sports Figures
Killed in Air Crashes . . . 9 Teams Killed in Air Crashes
. . . Homosexuality in Sports . . . 19 of the Strangest Ail-
ments, Freakiest Injuries, and Weirdest Deaths . . . Sexism
in Sports . . . 13 Athletes Who Died from War . . .

9 OFF THE FIELD, AND EXTRACURRICULAR ACTIVITY

The Half Dozen Most Legitimate Excuses in Sports
History for Not Performing Well—or at All . . . The Half
Dozen Worst Excuses in Sports History for Not Per-
forming Well—or at All . . . The Worst Excuse for Not
Allowing Someone to Perform . . . No Excuse, Period
. . . Los Angeles Dodgers in 1960s TV Sit-Coms . . . 6
Things with Wings or Tails That Made an Impact . . . A
Dozen Golf Tournaments That Are, or Were, Named
for Show-Business People . . . 3 Very Stupid Questions
. . . And 6 Very Snappy Answers . . . The World's
Most Famous Lineup . . . The Most Memorable Trades
in Sports . . . Cocky and Good: The Most Famous
Boasts . . . 10 Examples of Language Abuse by People

9 Noted Examples of Not Giving It Your All... Ironmen... 6 Weird Hybrid Sporting Events... The Most Notable Falls in Sports... 13 Heralded Upsets... Running Away with It: A Few of the Most Memorable Routs of All Time...

Lesser-Known Siblings... Winning Is Thicker Than Blood or Marriage... It's My Ball, So I'll Make the Rules: 6 Examples of Favoritism and Nepotism in Sports... Athletic Mothers and Mothers-to-Be... Giving Birth to Sports... The Best Sports Pedigrees... 6 Happy Families... Oedipal Triumphs and Families That Compete Against Each Other... 15 Famous Athletic Marriages ... More Athletic Siblings...

Déjà Vu: 17 of the Most Haunting Cases... What If...?... The Most Famous Quotations in Sports History... 10 Non-Immortals Who Had a Nose for Historical Occasions... And 1 Immortal Who Had a Nose for Historical Occasions... "The Game of the Century"... 14 Who Followed in the Steps of Legends... 12 Immortalized Athletes... Debunking 11 Sports Myths... The Most Compelling Firsts in Sports... And Just a Few Best Lasts... It's Appropriate... 9 Possibly Overlooked Moments That Signaled a Major Change in Sports... 7 Very Good Athletes We'll Remember Primarily for Their Misfortunes...

If You Think They're Good, You Should See the **Third**-String: The Greatest Plan B's in Sports... Models of Perfection... 10 of the Most Utterly Dominating Individuals in Sports History... It Should Have Been Enough: Great Performances Overshadowed by Even Better Performances... The Homages That Ruth Built... The Best Innovators and Pioneers in Sports... Innovations Named for Their Innovators... Just a Few of Wayne Gretzky's NHL Records... The Greatest Multisport

Talents . . . Staying Power . . . Staying Power II: Sports Figures Who Excelled When They Were Young and Excelled When They Were Not So Young . . . That Missing Something: 22 Greats and the Milestones They Never Achieved That You'd Think They Would Have . . . Living Legends . . . Beyond 60 + 714: Some Lesser-Known Facts About, and Records Held by, Babe Ruth . . . Chronic Winners: Ridiculously Successful Sports Figures . . . Overshadowed: The 23 Most Prominent—That Is, Neglected—Second Bananas of All Time . . . 10 Great Coaches and Mentors . . .

15 CURIOSITIES 391

One Dozen of the Stupidest Ideas in Sports . . . The Most Notable Draft Oddities . . . 13 Examples of Bad Timing, Rotten Luck, and Generally Bad Karma . . . 7 Sports Superstitions and Jinxes . . . Huh?: A Dozen Sports Things We Simply Don't Understand . . . 10 Great Sports Ironies . . . 24 Facts That You Might Easily Have Forgotten or Never Knew . . . 10 Things in Sports That You'll Rarely, If Ever, See . . . 20 of the Most Unusual College Mascots . . . The Most Ingrained Misnomers in Sports . . . Notable League Commissioners and Assorted Executives . . . Intriguing Team Owners . . . Serious Trivia: 39 Things Worth Knowing, Late at Night, in a Bar . . .

16 THE ENDS 415

Memorable Victory Celebrations . . . The Most Notable and Unusual Retired Numbers . . . Ending with a Flourish, Closing with a Rush: The Greatest Finales . . . Going Out with a Thud: The Sorriest Finishes in Sport . . . If at First . . . : Athletes Whose Perseverance Happily Paid Off . . . 1 Athlete Whose Perseverance Unhappily Paid Off . . . 1 Athlete Who Simply Waited Long Enough . . . I Shoulda Stood in Bed: At Least 5 Reasons to Stay Retired . . . The Most Memorable Farewells . . . It Ain't Over . . . It Ain't Over . . . It's Over! It's Over! . . . Let's Pretend It Never Happened: 22 Greats Who Finished Their Careers on Unholy Ground . . . Athletic Careers That Were Cut Short . . . And One **Race** That Was Cut

Short . . . Perfection Undone . . . Going Out on Top: Sports Figures Who Got Out Before the Cheers Turned to Boos . . . The 11 Most Unfulfilling Celebrations . . .

A List of 10 Empty Lists . . .

INTRODUCTION

You never make love with just one person, Freud said, but at least four. Or maybe it was Danny Ozark who said it. Either way, the sentiment applies not only to the parental attachments and emotional baggage that we bring to relationships but, of course, to sports statistics. A real student of the back pages never sees just a number, but a number that means a dozen different things. A baseball team with a seemingly forgettable 81-81 record may elicit several reactions: if only they'd played as well on Astroturf as they had on grass; or, how could they hit so poorly against right-handed pitching and yet tee off like that on lefties?; or, 81-81's a moral victory with such a young pitching staff (or, 81-81's a disgrace with that payroll).

We found ourselves doing this all the time. We'd watch our favorite NBA power forward go crazy in the third quarter and score 21 points with four minutes still to go in the period and inevitably we'd start to wonder, What's the record for a quarter? (33, George Gervin, 1978, second quarter, San Antonio at New Orleans.) For a half? (59, Wilt Chamberlain, 1962, second half, Philadelphia vs. New York at Hershey, Pennsylvania.) For his team? For that arena? For his family?

The questions would multiply until they got so out of hand that either we had to call in the police or find some place to put the overflow.

Lists.

As fans and writers, we had been to hundreds of contests, seen countless on-screen graphics, read and heard miles of words and numbers and tales about the athletes involved. We saw each game or fight or race or match as a story, one that had a narrative clarity and a resolution unlike most of life. Each game was a battle, each season a war. To us, sports was history on speed. And, frankly, we had become overwhelmed by it. The time had come for some mental spring cleaning. We'd been reduced to vessels filled with unconnected, if often intriguing, facts and statistics about sports, and there seemed no end to the supply. We could only guess at the damage that ESPN was wreaking on America. We were becoming increasingly cranky at home and at the office. Perhaps it was chronic-fatigue syndrome.

We needed to move toward places of less clutter. If we could only find somewhere to neatly put all of the statistical and anecdotal flotsam that had collected in our heads over the years, perhaps we would be able to get on with our lives, start families or continue them, maybe even begin reading those Russians that we kept putting off.

One summer day we began making lists of things about sports. We made up a list of golf tournaments named for celebrities, a list of the best streaks in sports, a list of athletes killed in the line of duty. It was habit-forming, this list thing. We made up a list of the most dominating individuals, of notable uniform numbers, of defunct leagues. No longer would we ever have to think about the World Football League; we had found a place to store for eternity all our knowledge about it. Bye-bye, Jim Kiick. So long, Birmingham Americans and Jacksonville Sharks.

We made up a list of relocated teams that had won world championships, and one of moments where politics interfered with competition. Athletes with glasses, and examples of favoritism in sports. We were collating what we knew about sports not by RBIs or career rushing yardage or plus/minus ratings but by what we believed were at least as compelling criteria: tendencies, styles, curiosities.

Soon, we started to order everything—nicknames, routs, places, numbers, quotations, Chinese food. Before we knew it, the man was there with the spare ribs and we only had enough to give him a small tip. We made more lists. Multisport athletes, notable substitutes. Trophies that they play for in college football rivalries. It was getting late. We were getting hungry again. Our heads were clearing.

Over the next several months, we made more and more lists—memorable trades, unusual draftees, athletes who caused rule changes. As we put the information into neat little piles, our minds became freer. We could re-member the name of our best friend when we were five, recall a donut that we had once dipped into a cup of milk at an aunt's house. We made some more lists—women competing with men, the most precocious athletes, the worst debuts. Our minds were emptying. Suddenly there was the outline of Grandpapa's face, and we were only two when he died! Just a few more lists—great team nicknames, famous second bananas in sports, the best examples of home field advantage.

Autumn had given way to winter, winter to spring. We had written a whole book made up of nothing but lists that organized everything we ever knew about sports. We felt eerily liberated. No longer were we dazed by the wave of sports information that had knocked us over early in life and kept us in the undertow ever since. As a matter of fact, to celebrate, we drove to the beach. We looked out at the horizon, and somehow everything seemed possible and new. We had unburdened ourselves of disorder and randomness and team ERA's.

We walked down to the surf, splashed some water on our faces. We heard a small voice. It was Ralph Kiner. A sunbather we hadn't noticed before was watching the Mets game on a little television under a beach umbrella. The Padres had just gone out in order and Kiner was segueing into the between-innings commercial. "We'll be back after this word from Manufacturers Hangover," he said.

Yogi lives, Casey lives. We had heard too many comments like Kiner's not to honor it, do something with it, find a place to keep it. So we would make another list—Language Abuse by Sports Figures. We walked back to the car with heads bowed. Perhaps our book was not done. Perhaps, in a sense, it never would be.

Andrew Postman
Larry Stone

1
PERSONALITY AND STYLE

THE 17 STRONGEST REACTIONS IN SPORTS HISTORY

■ Elizabeth Ryan, holder of a then-record 19 Wimbledon titles, had said that she did not want to live to see her record broken. The day before Billie Jean King had a chance to break the record, Ryan collapsed on the grounds of Wimbledon and died that night. The next day, King won the women's doubles title and broke Ryan's record.

■ Joseph Guillemot of France vomited on Finland's Paavo Nurmi as they crossed the finish line in the Olympic 10,000m race in 1920.

■ *Washington Post* sportswriter Tony Kornheiser wrote an article that parodied the trouble that Bolivia was having raising money to send a contingent to the 1984 Los Angeles Olympics. A national spokesman said that the country took offense at the article, and that the article played a part in Bolivia's decision ultimately to not attend the Games.

■ In July 1950, eight Uruguayans reportedly died of heart attacks as a result of their country's unexpected World Cup victory over Brazil.

■ During the McCarthy era and the "Red Scare," the Cincinnati Reds changed their name to the Redlegs. The baseball team changed its name back to the Reds in 1960.

■ When the distance of Bob Beamon's world-record long

jump was announced at the 1968 Olympics, he sank to the ground with what doctors described as a cataplectic seizure, caused by emotional excitement.

■ Boxer Alexis Arguello punched Cornelius Boza-Edwards with such force that Boza-Edwards lost control of his bodily functions and soiled his trunks.

■ While flying in a small plane that he had chartered from Detroit to Buffalo on September 17, 1935, outfielder Len Koenecke, recently released by the Brooklyn Dodgers, went berserk and tried to wrest control of the plane from the pilot. Koenecke was clubbed to death with a fire extinguisher by the pilot. Koenecke was reported to have been despondent over his release.

■ At the 1964 Olympics, Elvira Ozolina of the Soviet Union was so anguished about finishing fifth in the javelin—she was the defending champion and world record holder—that she punished herself by getting her head shaved. All the members of the Japanese wrestling team had their heads shaved after performing poorly at the 1960 Olympics.

■ Basketball star Spencer Haywood admitted in a *People* magazine article on June 13, 1988 that he had plotted to kill Los Angeles Lakers coach Paul Westhead after Westhead had suspended him during the 1979–80 NBA Finals. Haywood said that he and two friends planned to sabotage Westhead's car. Haywood's mother eventually talked her son out of it.

■ San Diego Chargers football coach Harland Svare was so convinced that Oakland Raiders owner Al Davis had bugged the visiting locker room at Oakland Coliseum that Svare started screaming at a light bulb.

■ In the modern pentathlon at the 1968 Olympics, Hans-Jurgen Todt of West Germany attacked his horse after it had balked three times at one obstacle.

■ CBS anchorman Dan Rather, upset that the broadcast of the U.S. Open tennis tournament had run into his news

2

telecast, walked off the set on September 11, 1987. The CBS screen was blank for six minutes.

■ In October 1977, in a Colombian second-division soccer match, Santa Rosa de Cabal left-winger Libardo Zuniga replaced an injured goalie in an important league game and made several spectacular saves. Near the end of the game, an opposing striker, enraged by Zuniga's success in goal, ran up and kicked him full force in the groin. Zuniga died within moments, and the striker was arrested and charged with murder.

■ On May 29, 1882, National League umpire James L. Hickey called out Cleveland outfielder John Richmond for going outside the baseline while running to first base on a walk.

■ In a double dose of strong reaction, heavyweight Bob Fitzsimmons protested violently when he was disqualified in his 1896 non-title fight with Tom Sharkey. Finally, referee Wyatt Earp—of "O.K. Corral" fame—drew his gun on Fitzsimmons.

■ "Gorgeous Gussie" Moran caused a sensation at Wimbledon in 1949 by wearing lace panties designed by Ted Tinling. The All-England Club committee ruled that the panties were "unnecessarily attracting the eye to the sexual area," and terminated Tinling's services as an umpire for 20 years.

HELLO IN THERE? IS ANYBODY HOME?: 10 TALES OF PEOPLE WITHOUT A CLUE

■ The Russian contingent showed up late for the military rifle team competition at the 1908 Olympics because they were operating on the Julian calendar rather than the

3

customary Gregorian calendar. Twelve days separated the two calendars.

■ Boston Celtics announcer Johnny Most visited team doctor Thomas Silva to complain of deafness in 1987. Silva extracted a TV earplug which had been lodged in Most's ear for a year and a half.

■ At the 1896 Olympics, many fencing judges, unschooled in the sport, thought that a fencer earned points if he *received* a hit.

■ In the third round of the 1983 Canadian Open, golfer Andy Bean used the grip of his putter to knock in a two-inch putt on the 15th hole. He was penalized two strokes. He finished the tournament two strokes behind the winner.

■ One more installment from the let's-see-how-hard-we-can-make-it-on-ourselves tradition: 1988 Tour de France champion Pedro Delgado of Spain began defense of his title by showing up 2 minutes and 40 seconds late to the starting line of the 1989 Tour. He finished the opening prologue 2:54 behind the leader. After 33 days, he ended up in third place, 3:34 behind the winner.

■ In a 1917 World Series game, Chicago White Sox pitcher Red Faber attempted to steal third base while a teammate was already occupying it.

■ American Emerson Spencer, the world-record holder in the 400m run (47.0 seconds) in 1928, made only the Olympic relay team. At the Olympic trials for the individual 400m, Spencer thought he was in a heat race and did not run at full speed. It was actually the final, and he did not qualify.

■ At the 1948 Olympics, one judge awarded a gymnast a score of 13.1.

■ On the fifth hole of the final round of the 1970 British Open, Lee Trevino shot for the wrong flag. Trevino, who started the day with a three-stroke lead, bogeyed the hole and finished tied for third.

■ After losing money gambling, Cuban Felix Carvajal had to hitchhike to St. Louis for the 1904 Olympics. He arrived at the starting line for the marathon wearing heavy street shoes, long trousers, a long-sleeved shirt, and a beret.

THE UNLV BASKETBALL TEAM AND 7 OTHER ATHLETES WHO WOULD KNOW HOW TO THROW A GREAT PARTY

Some athletes sense that extraordinary times—on the field or off—demand extraordinary measures, and the way to publicly celebrate something special is to raise their game, get a hit, perform with authority. Outfielder Jimmy Piersall had the idea—sort of—when, on the occasion of his 100th career home run, he ran around the bases backward (not in reverse order, mind you, but backward, facing home plate as he headed for first base).

The following athletes did not do anything as radical as that; indeed, they stayed fully engaged in the game—perhaps even more so than usual. And maybe that is precisely what enabled them to perform in such a way that punctuated what was already a special occasion.

■ On April 22, 1970, before a game against the San Diego Padres at Shea Stadium, New York Mets pitcher Tom Seaver was presented with his first Cy Young Award, for the 1969 season. To mark the occasion, he took the mound and tied one major league record by striking out 19 batters in a nine-inning game, and set another record by striking out 10 batters in a row—the last 10 he faced. He won the game, 2-1.

■ On September 10, 1963, Stan Musial, in his first at-bat after becoming a grandfather, hit a home run off of Glen Hobbie.

◼ In an October 18, 1924 game against Michigan to dedicate the University of Illinois' new Memorial Stadium, Illini running back Red Grange had one of the greatest days in college football history. He returned the opening kickoff for a 95-yard touchdown, then scored on runs of 67, 56, and 44 yards, all in the first 11 minutes of the game. He later scored a fifth touchdown, threw for a sixth, and accounted for 402 total yards.

◼ American Pete Herman got married the morning of his 1917 world bantamweight title bout with Frankie Burns. That night, Herman won the fight.

◼ Cincinnati Red Johnny Vander Meer pitched the second of his consecutive no-hitters—a feat unmatched in major league history—in the first night game in Ebbets Field history, June 15, 1938.

◼ Kansas City Royals pitcher Bret Saberhagen shut out the St. Louis Cardinals 11-0 in Game 7 of the 1985 World Series and won the Series MVP Award the night after he became a father.

◼ Philadelphia Phillies pitcher Jim Bunning was the father of six children when he took the mound against the New York Mets on June 21, Father's Day, 1964. He pitched a perfect game.

◼ For University of Nevada–Las Vegas coach Jerry Tarkanian's 600th coaching victory on January 2, 1985, his team defeated Utah, 142-140, in triple overtime, the highest-scoring game up to that time in the history of major college basketball.

5 INSTANCES OF LOW SELF-ESTEEM FROM THE ANNALS OF SPORT

◼ In 1980, Oakland Athletics owner Charlie Finley submitted a salary arbitration offer of $58,000 for infielder Mike Edwards. Edwards submitted a salary demand of $50,000.

■ New York Yankees star Lou Gehrig, doing a live radio endorsement for a cereal called "Huskies," was asked, "To what do you owe your strength and conditioning?" By accident—and instinct—Gehrig replied, "Wheaties." Gehrig was apologetic afterward and tried to refuse compensation, but the "Huskies" people insisted on paying him.

■ The Gaelic Athletic Association, the ruling body of the not very widely played sport of hurling, states among its laws that those who play and officiate hurling are prohibited to play, watch, or encourage soccer, rugby, cricket, and hockey.

■ San Francisco Giants shortstop Johnnie LeMaster was booed so often that he once wore "Boo" on his jersey instead of his name.

■ For the countries that boycotted the 1984 Los Angeles Games, Berlin held the "Alternative Olympics."

Honorable mention:
Former Chicago Bears running back Gale Sayers, whose autobiography is entitled *I Am Third*.

SOME UNORTHODOX TECHNIQUES THAT WORKED

■ Rick Barry shot free throws underhanded. At 90 percent, he is the most accurate free-throw shooter in NBA history. (The technique alone does not guarantee success: Wilt Chamberlain shot free throws underhanded, too, and was a career 51 percent shooter).

■ Harold Connolly wore ballet shoes for better footing in the finals of the 1956 Olympic hammer-throw competition, which he won.

■ Washington Redskins placekicker Mark Moseley, who once made a record 23 consecutive field goals, wore five pairs of socks on his kicking foot.

■ In the 1930s, golfer Leo Diegel used a putting style in which his left hand was inverted and his elbows were held out. Sam Snead putted croquet-style, a method that was later banned.

■ 5,000m former world record holder Zola Budd, American pole vaulter Desha McNeal Beamer, placekickers Tony Franklin and Rich Karlis, and India's national field hockey team all competed barefoot.

■ New York and later San Francisco Giants outfielder Willie Mays popularized the basket catch, and his teammate, pitcher Juan Marichal, the high leg kick.

■ Rather than clear the hurdles in the steeplechase in traditional fashion, 1968 Olympic gold medalist Amos Biwott of Kenya hopped over them.

■ The arc of Jamaal Wilkes's jump shot began over his shoulder and almost behind his head. He was a career 50 percent shooter from the field.

■ New York Giant Mel Ott high-stepped into his swing, as did Japanese baseball great Sadaharu Oh. Ott hit 511 home runs, and Oh 868.

■ To keep loose, Canadian Earl Thomson, gold medalist in the 1920 Olympic 110m hurdles, tied his legs to the bed before going to sleep so that he could not curl up and cramp.

11 SCENES OF HUMILIATION

■ In Lewiston, Maine, on May 25, 1965 singer Robert Goulet forgot the words to the National Anthem at the second Muhammad Ali–Sonny Liston fight.

■ Oakland Athletics utility infielder Mike Andrews was "fired" by team owner Charlie Finley during the 1973 World Series after Andrews made two costly errors against the New York Mets in the 12th inning of Game 2. Finley announced that he was deactivating Andrews and tried to place him on the disabled list with a shoulder injury, and even got Andrews to sign a statement saying that he was hurt. Baseball commissioner Bowie Kuhn stepped in and ordered Andrews reinstated.

■ In 1960, half-miler Wym Essajas became the first person ever to represent Surinam in the Olympics. He was given the wrong starting time for his heat and was resting when he should have been running. He went home without competing.

■ Bernice Gera umpired a game between Geneva and Auburn in the New York–Penn League on June 24, 1972, but, after making a controversial call and ejecting a manager, she resigned in tears before the second game of the doubleheader.

■ Greek Spiridon Belokas took third place in the 1896 Olympic marathon in Athens but fourth-place finisher Gyula Kellner of Hungary protested that Belokas had ridden part of the way in a carriage. Belokas confessed to the charge. In punishment, he was stripped of both his medal and his shirt.

■ During her second-round match against Billie Jean King at Wimbledon in 1979, the breasts of 18-year-old American Linda Siegel popped out of her low-cut tennis dress. The picture made the British tabloids.

9

■ After getting swept 8-0, 8-0, and 9-2 in the season's opening series in Los Angeles, the 1974 San Diego Padres were trailing the Houston Astros 9-2 in the middle of the eighth inning of their fourth game—their home opener—when Padres owner Ray Kroc publicly dressed them down. Kroc grabbed the public-address microphone and announced to the fans, "I've never seen such stupid ball playing in my life."

■ At the 1988 Olympic trials, David Patrick finished the 400m hurdle race and took off on a joyful victory lap after a TV cameraman handed him a flag and congratulated him for finishing third. In fact, Patrick had finished fourth, and thus just missed earning a spot on the Olympic team. "I don't know who gave me the flag," Patrick said afterward, "but I'm going to look for him."

■ Ewa Klobukowska of Poland, the 100m bronze medalist in 1964, was barred from international competition on September 15, 1967, when she failed a sex chromosome test.

■ In June 1940, the Cleveland Indian players petitioned the team owner to fire manager Ossie Vitt. They later withdrew their demand but Vitt was let go at the end of the season.

■ Australian tennis star Margaret Court was embarrassed on national television on Mother's Day, 1973, when aging hustler and former tennis great Bobby Riggs beat her in straight sets.

TRIUMPH OVER PAIN AND ADVERSITY: THE MOST COURAGEOUS AND INSPIRING ATHLETES

Images of athletes who have gone beyond pain, fatigue, and anguish to perform—and perform extraordinarily—

are among the most vivid in sports. For many, the most excruciating such image may be that of Shun Fujimoto, the Japanese gymnast in the 1976 Olympics who dismounted from the rings with a broken leg that he had told no one about. He scored an astonishing 9.7 on the exercise, dislocated his knee on the dismount, and finally received medical attention and withdrew. Had Fujimoto withdrawn earlier, the Japanese team would have been out of the running for a team medal; with his help, they won the gold. For anyone who saw him land on his dismount—wobbly at first, then wincing to steady himself—the image is ineradicable.

Other images of athletes rising above their pain to perform in big games, or memories of them returning to their sports after debilitating injuries, are compelling. There is Ken Venturi playing 36 holes in 100-degree heat, despite near exhaustion that required medical treatment, to win the 1964 U.S. Open in what some have called "the most courageous round of golf ever played." There is New York Knicks center Willis Reed, on horribly battered knees, hobbling out to the Madison Square Garden floor to take his place as starter in Game 7 of the 1970 NBA Finals against the Los Angeles Lakers, and leading the team to the title more by inspiration than by any concrete contributions (he scored only two baskets, in the opening moments of the game). There is Gabriele Andersen-Scheiss, the Swiss runner, suffering heat prostration at the end of the 1984 Olympic marathon, waving off medical assistance, and, staggering and weaving, finishing the final quarter-mile lap in 5 minutes and 44 seconds, good for 37th place. Of even more recent vintage is Jim Abbott, born with only one hand, blossoming into a formidable starting pitcher for the California Angels without a day of minor league experience; and Michael Chang, who, despite severe leg cramps that eventually forced him to serve underhand, upset Ivan Lendl in the 1989 French Open semifinals, on his way to becoming the first American in 34 years, and the youngest male ever, to win the French Open men's title.

Here, then, are some of the most memorable examples of athletes overcoming adversity.

11

■ Tim Tam finished second in the Belmont in 1958 after fracturing the sesamoid bone in his right leg while passing the quarter pole.

■ When he was seven, future Hall of Fame pitcher Mordecai "Three Finger" Brown caught his right hand in a corn grinder, lost most of his forefinger, and crushed his middle finger. He was a third baseman until he found that his mangled hand helped his curveball.

■ Olympic equestrian competitor Konrad Freiherr von Wangenheim of Germany suffered a broken collarbone when he was thrown from his horse during the steeple-chase portion of the two-day team event in 1936, but to keep the German team from being disqualified, he remounted and finished the remaining 32 obstacles without a fault. The next day, he arrived in a sling, which he removed for the jumping competition. Again, he was thrown from his horse, got back on, and again finished without a fault, helping Germany to win the gold.

■ In 1953, 3½ months after undergoing an emergency colostomy for cancer, Babe Didrickson Zaharias was back on the women's golf tour, finishing third in a tournament. The next year, she won the U.S. Open by 12 strokes. (The cancer eventually returned and she died September 17, 1956, at age 42.)

■ Karoly Varga of Hungary won an Olympic gold medal in shooting in 1980 despite breaking his shooting hand two days before the competition.

■ Jockey Ricky Frazier broke his neck, fractured his skull, and was partly paralyzed when his horse fell during a 1984 race. Frazier came back to be a top rider.

■ Swimmer Steven Genter was second to Mark Spitz in the Olympic 200m freestyle in 1972 despite surgery for a partially collapsed lung while in Munich. He was released from the hospital a day before the race.

■ Hugh "One Arm" Daily pitched for six years in the majors (1882–87) despite having lost his arm below his elbow in a fireworks accident. One-armed Pete Gray, an outfielder, was the 1944 MVP for Memphis of the Southern Association, batting .333 with five home runs, and played in 77 games for the St. Louis Browns in 1945.

■ Kenny Walker's father died just before the 1989 NBA All-Star Game, to which the New York Knick had been invited to compete in the Slam Dunk competition. Walker wanted to withdraw from the competition but his mother told him to go and do well for his father. In an upset, Walker won the event.

■ Hubert Green won the 1977 U.S. Open despite a death threat. The threat was relayed to him during the final round but he decided to continue playing. He made a three-foot putt on the 18th hole to beat Lou Graham.

■ New Zealand's Neroli Fairhall was the first paraplegic Olympian. She competed in the 1984 archery competition seated in a wheelchair and finished 35th. Fairhall was paralyzed from the waist down in a motorcycle accident.

■ Dawn Fraser of Australia, who in 1962 became the first woman to swim under a minute in the 100m freestyle competition, was in a March 1964 car accident that killed her mother, knocked her sister unconscious, and chipped Dawn's vertebrae. Her neck was in a plaster cast for six weeks. She went on to win her third consecutive gold medal in the 100m freestyle seven months later.

■ Jeff Blatnick, who was diagnosed with Hodgkin's disease in 1980, won a 1984 Olympic wrestling gold.

■ Champion distance runner Glenn Cunningham's leg was severely burned in a fire when he was eight years old.

■ Alice Marble fainted on court at the 1933 French championships, was rushed to the hospital, and was diagnosed as having tuberculosis. She came back to win the U.S. Championships four times.

■ On the day that the Czechoslovakian gymnastics team began competition at the 1948 Olympics, teammate Eliska Misakova died of infantile paralysis. The Czechs went on to win the gold. (The flag raised for the medal ceremony was bordered with black ribbon.)

■ Ben Hogan nearly died on February 2, 1949 in a Texas car accident that caused him multiple injuries and hospitalized him for a month. Hobbling badly, he captained the U.S.'s victorious Ryder Cup team in England later that year and in January 1950 entered the Los Angeles Open and tied for first with Sam Snead. A month later, Hogan won the U.S. Open in a playoff. Hogan won five majors after his accident.

■ Weightlifter Tommy Kono, who set 21 world records in four different weight classes and won two Olympic gold medals, spent part of his youth in the Tule Lake detention camp for Japanese-Americans.

■ Doug Herland, coxswain for the U.S. bronze medal pair-oared shell crew in 1984, suffered from osteogenesis imperfecta (brittle-bone disease). He was 4'9", 103 pounds, and had been born with broken hips, broken ribs, and a broken collarbone.

■ American cyclist Greg LeMond, 1986 Tour de France winner, was accidently shot and nearly killed by his brother-in-law while they were turkey hunting in April of 1987. LeMond returned to win the Tour de France in 1989.

14

■ Assault won the 1946 Triple Crown despite a permanently deformed foot.

■ Ildiko Ujlaki-Rejto, gold medalist in the 1964 women's foil competition, was born deaf. Her coaches gave her instructions written on pieces of paper.

■ George Eyser, gold medalist in the parallel bars and vault in 1904, had a wooden leg. He won two silvers in the pommel horse and combined, and a bronze in the horizontal bar.

■ Pitcher Lou Brissie lost his leg in World War II, and wore an artificial leg from his knee down. He returned to the major leagues and posted marks of 14-10 in 1948, and 16-11 in 1949, and played until 1953.

■ Harry Greb, world middleweight champion, was blind in one eye.

17 EXAMPLES OF EXTRAORDINARY LACK OF INSIGHT

■ In 1950, Boston Celtics coach Red Auerbach passed up choosing Holy Cross star Bob Cousy, calling him a "local yokel." Celtics owner Walter Brown later picked Cousy's name out of a hat in a special dispersal draft, and Auerbach was "stuck" with Cousy. Cousy became the starting point guard and, along with Bill Russell, helped to create an NBA dynasty.

■ Buddy Parker quit as the Detroit Lions coach during the 1957 training camp because he was not hopeful about his team's chances for success. Four months later, the Lions, now coached by George Wilson, beat the Cleveland Browns, 59-14, for the NFL title.

■ In 1935, Chicago Cubs owner Philip Wrigley called night baseball "just a fad, a passing fancy."

■ In 1875, when Matthew Webb, the first person to swim the English Channel, was honored by the city of Dover, the mayor proclaimed, "In the future history of the world, I don't believe that any such feat will be performed by anyone else." Swimmers have successfully crossed the English Channel about 270 times since.

■ Baseball lore is filled with stories of spectacularly near-sighted trades. Babe Ruth had led the Boston Red Sox to three pennants in five-plus years when Harry Frazee, the Sox owner, sold him to the New York Yankees for $125,000 and a $300,000 loan to Frazee. The next year, 1920, Babe hit 54 home runs; the Sox as a team hit 22. Ruth would lead the Yankees to seven pennants. Boston would not win another one for 28 years.

The Cincinnati Reds shipped Frank Robinson to the Baltimore Orioles before the 1966 season, writing him off as "an old thirty." In his first year with the Orioles, he won the American League Triple Crown, led his team to the pennant and victory in the World Series, and was named American League MVP. The best player that the Reds received in return for Robinson was pitcher Milt Pappas.

After 2½ years, the Chicago Cubs had seen enough of outfielder Lou Brock to trade him to the St. Louis Cardinals in June of 1964. Brock batted .348 the rest of the year, played 15 more years after that, helped the Cardinals to win three pennants and two World Series, and stole a major league record 938 bases. He entered the Hall of Fame in 1985.

■ When the AAFC champion Cleveland Browns were absorbed into the NFL in 1950, most around the NFL, believed that the competition in the other league was far inferior and were certain that the Browns would be humiliated. The Browns won the NFL title in their first year, and made the title game in each of their first six.

■ Jim Brown was chosen sixth in the NFL draft, after having been fifth in the Heisman Trophy voting.

■ In the late 1940s, University of Kentucky basketball coach Adolph Rupp, commenting on the wave of point-shaving and other scandals in the college game, said, "They couldn't touch my boys with a ten-foot pole." Soon after, it was discovered that some Wildcat players had been involved in game-fixing.

■ In 1956, Bart Starr was not drafted until the 17th round, by the Green Bay Packers. He went on to win more championships than any NFL quarterback before or since, and was elected to the Hall of Fame. The sports-scouting community showed a similar lack of insight about future All-Star first baseman Don Mattingly, who wasn't picked until the 19th round of the 1979 amateur baseball draft, and San Francisco 49ers quarterback Joe Montana, owner of four Super Bowl rings and the highest efficiency rating of any quarterback in NFL history, who was the 82nd pick (third round) in the 1979 draft.

■ Steve Largent, the eventual all-time leader in pass receptions, was cut by the Houston Oilers.

■ Italy's Giovanni Benvenuti won the Val Barker Trophy for the most stylish boxer at the 1960 Games, the same Olympics in which a young fighter named Cassius Clay fought and won a gold medal.

■ In a model example of teammates watching and learning from each other's mistakes, Toronto Blue Jay Barry Bonnell was picked off first base by Baltimore Orioles pitcher Tippy Martinez in an August 24, 1983 game. Blue Jay Dave Collins was walked and Martinez picked him off first base. Blue Jay Willie Upshaw got an infield hit and Martinez picked him off first base.

■ Before the 1973 Kentucky Derby, alleged betting expert

Jimmy "The Greek" Snyder said, "I don't know why, but I don't like Secretariat."

QUICK STUDIES:
7 ATHLETES WHO LEARNED FAST

This list is dedicated to Dave Stapleton, an infielder for the Boston Red Sox in the 1980s, who was decidedly *not* a quick study. Stapleton spent seven years in the major leagues, and every year his batting average declined: .321, .285, .264, .247, .231, .227, and .128.

■ American Elizabeth Ryan and Frenchwoman Suzanne Lenglen lost their first doubles match together, and then never again. They won six Wimbledon titles together.

■ Lenglen was apparently a slightly quicker learner than Ryan: the first time the two faced each other in singles, Ryan beat Lenglen, and then never again. Lenglen won their next 36 singles matches.

■ Suffering from a severe gallbladder infection during the 1968 Olympics, Kenya's Kipchoge Keino still entered the 1,500m, the 5,000m, and the 10,000m competitions. During the 10,000m, he was leading with two laps to go when he collapsed. A stretcher was brought out but Keino got up and finished the race. Four days later, he ran in the 5,000m and took second place. In his final race, the 1,500m, he took the gold in Olympic record time.

■ On April 23, 1944, Boston Braves pitcher Jim Tobin pitched a one-hitter. Four days later, against the Brooklyn Dodgers, he pitched a no-hitter.

■ In Secretariat's record-breaking Kentucky Derby (1:592/5)

in 1973, each of his quarter mile splits was faster than the preceding one.

■ In just the second marathon of her life, Joan Benoit won the 1979 Boston Marathon, setting an American record (2:35:15) in doing so.

■ At St. Andrews in 1921, in the third round of Bobby Jones's first appearance at the British Open, Jones picked up his ball in frustration and tore up his card. In each of his other three appearances in the tourney, he won the title.

WHAT DO I HAVE TO DO TO GET A MENU AROUND HERE?: 8 RESPECTABLE ACHIEVEMENTS THAT WERE TREATED WITHOUT MUCH RESPECT

■ In 1933, Philadelphia Phillies outfielder Chuck Klein won the Triple Crown. In the off-season, he was traded to the Chicago Cubs.

■ In 1935, when Jesse Owens set or tied six world records, the Sullivan Award, given by the AAU to the best amateur American athlete, was won by golfer Lawson Little. In 1936, when Owens won four Olympic gold medals, the award was won by Glenn Morris, the Olympic decathlon champion. President Franklin Roosevelt did not invite Owens to the White House or send him a letter of congratulations after his Olympic performance.

■ In 1953, Kurt Nielson was unseeded when he made his mark on the tennis world by earning a spot in the Wimbledon finals. Two years later, in 1955, he again made the finals— and again he had to do so as an unseeded player.

■ In 1941, the season in which he hit .406, Ted Williams did not win the American League MVP. This is explainable in part by the fact that the player who beat him out, Joe DiMaggio, enjoyed a 56-game hitting streak that season. In 1942, Williams came back to win the Triple Crown—and this time the MVP Award went to New York Yankees second baseman Joe Gordon, who batted .322 with 18 home runs, and led the league in striking out (Williams had twice as many homers, 34 more RBIs, and batted .356). In 1947, Williams again won the Triple Crown, becoming only the second player in history to do it twice. The MVP Award that year went to Joe DiMaggio.

■ The only other man besides Ted Williams to win two Triple Crowns, Rogers Hornsby, fared no better. He was traded to the New York Giants following the 1926 season, in which he played *and* managed the St. Louis Cardinals to victory in the World Series.

■ The WBC took away Marvin Hagler's world middleweight title after he outpointed Roberto Duran in their thrilling 1983 fight because the contest had been 15 rounds and not the WBC's new required distance of 12 rounds.

■ Bill Madlock, four-time batting title winner, never started in an All-Star Game and was traded by the Chicago Cubs to the San Francisco Giants in 1976 after winning his second consecutive batting championship.

■ In 1989, four days after Dan Simrell became the winningest coach in University of Toledo football history, he was fired.

AMBIDEXTERITY

■ At one Olympics only, the 1912 Stockholm Games, shot putters, and discus and javelin throwers made one throw with the left hand, one with the right, and the greatest aggregate total won. (The standard one-handed competition in each event was also held that year.)

■ Beverly Baker Fleitz, a 1955 Wimbledon finalist, switched her racket from one hand to another so that her only groundstroke was a forehand.

■ Natural right-hander Elton "Icebox" Chamberlain became a southpaw for two innings in an 18-6 victory for Louisville of the American Association, on May 10, 1888. He pitched the last two innings left-handed, giving up four hits and no runs.

■ In a July 18, 1882 American Association game against Baltimore, Louisville pitcher Tony Mullane, a right-hander, pitched left-handed in the fourth inning to Baltimore's left-handed hitters, retiring them all.
    Mullane's entry in *The Baseball Encyclopedia* reads: "BB TB" ("Bats Both, Throws Both")

■ A third ambidextrous pitcher of the 19th century was Larry Corcoran of Chicago, who was forced by a blister on his right index finger to throw left-handed on June 16, 1884. He had less success than Chamberlain and Mullane. Chicago lost, 20-9.

■ Philadelphia Warrior Joe Fulks, who scored 63 points in one 1949 basketball game—especially impressive for that low-scoring era—took jump shots with either hand.

■ In his day, Gordie Howe was the only ambidextrous player in the NHL.

■ 1955 Grand Slammer Maureen "Mo" Connolly, a natural lefty, became a right-handed tennis player after she was informed by her coach, Eleanor "Teach" Tennant, that no left-hander in this century had won a top women's singles championship.

THE MOST EFFICIENT AND RESOURCEFUL ATHLETES AND TEAMS OF ALL TIME

◼ In the seventh inning of an April 22, 1959 game against the Kansas City Athletics, the Chicago White Sox scored 11 runs on one base hit. The Sox were the beneficiaries of 10 walks, three errors, and one hit batter.

◼ In their 49-0 win over Stanford in the 1902 Rose Bowl, Michigan played the same 11 men the whole game.

◼ Dean Stone was the winning pitcher in the 1954 All-Star Game without retiring a batter. He entered the game in the eighth inning and threw out Red Schoendienst trying to steal home. The American League then scored three times in the bottom of the inning—the pinch hitter for Stone hit a home run—and a reliever pitched the ninth to preserve Stone's victory.

◼ After winning the 10,000m walk at the 1912 Olympics, Canadian George Goulding sent a telegram to his wife that read, "Won—George."

◼ In the 1920–21 seasons, Larry Gardner of the Cleveland Indians knocked in 233 runs with just six home runs. In 1928, Pie Traynor of the Pittsburgh Pirates had 124 RBIs and only three homers.

◼ "Cactus" Gavvy Cravath won the 1919 home run title with only 214 at-bats.

◼ Detroit Lions wide receiver Mark Nichols co-owned a limousine service that carried his teammates to and from home games.

■ Only nine Cincinnati Reds batted in the 1976 World Series, which they swept from the New York Yankees.

■ After his first six completions against the University of New Mexico on October 27, 1967, UTEP quarterback Brooks Dawson had thrown six touchdowns.

■ John Russell, the Philadelphia Phillies part-time outfielder in the 1980s, married Gail Clements, the left field ball girl.

■ For the 1946 British Open, German prisoners of war were used to clear the rough before the tournament.

■ In the 1963 World Series, the Los Angeles Dodgers used only four pitchers. In the 1928 Series, the New York Yankees used just three pitchers. In the 1910 Series, the Philadelphia Athletics used two pitchers. Each of those three teams won the Series.

■ In Game 6 of the 1977 World Series, New York Yankees star Reggie Jackson took only three swings. He homered each time. (The last swing he took in Game 5 also produced a homer.)

THE MOST EFFICIENT BASEBALL PLAYER OF ALL TIME— AND WE MEAN THAT IN A BAD WAY

■ In his last two at-bats in Game 5 of the 1920 World Series, Brooklyn Dodgers pitcher Clarence Mitchell accounted for five outs by hitting into a triple play and a double play.

20 PROMINENT BESPECTACLED SPORTS FIGURES

1. George Mikan, Minneapolis Laker center.
2. Billie Jean King, tennis player.
3. Chick Hafey, the first bespectacled player to make it to the Baseball Hall of Fame. He will soon be joined by...
4. ...Reggie Jackson, baseball player.
5. Chuck Muncie, running back.
6. Hale Irwin, three-time U.S. Open–winning golfer.
7. Martina Navratilova, tennis player. She eventually switched to contact lenses.
8. Ryne Duren, pitcher.
9. Jaroslav Drobny, tennis player.
10. Bob Griese, Miami Dolphin quarterback.
11. Richie Allen, baseball player.
12. Matti Jarvinen, 1932 javelin gold medalist.
13. Kurt Rambis (nicknamed "Clark Kent"), basketball forward.
14. Dom DiMaggio, baseball player.
15. Laurent Fignon, two-time Tour de France winner.
16. Clint Courtney, first bespectacled catcher, 1951.
17. Livio Berruti, 1960 Olympic 200m champion.
18. Kent Tekulve, relief pitcher.
19. Ingrid Kristiansen, Norway's world champion distance runner.
20. Eddie Rommel, first bespectacled umpire, 1956.

25 OF THE BEST MOMENTS OF INTEGRITY, HUMANITY, AND CLASS

◙ After hockey's Lady Byng Trophy—the award given annually for gentlemanly play—had been won in 1935 by

New York Rangers center Frank Boucher for the seventh time in eight years, he was given the trophy to keep, and Lady Byng had another one struck.

■ Bobby Joe Morrow, a devout Christian who won the 100m in the 1956 Olympics, would not try to anticipate the starter's pistol with a "rolling start" because he felt it was unsportsmanlike.

■ In the 1953 Walker Cup competition between the United States and Great Britain, American James Jackson was found to have 16 clubs, which called for immediate disqualification. The British, captained by Tony Duncan, refused to accept such a victory, and modified the penalty to a loss of two holes. (America went on to win.)

■ When it was discovered that 1932 U.S. Olympic sprinter Ralph Metcalfe, who had finished a disappointing third in the 200m, had dug his starting holes a few feet behind the other runners—through no fault of his own—he was offered a rerun. Metcalfe probably could have moved up to at least the silver medal but he declined, not wishing to jeopardize the American sweep in the event.

■ New York Yankees manager Dick Howser was pressured by owner George Steinbrenner to fire his friend and third-base coach Mike Ferraro, after Ferraro waved Yankees second baseman Willie Randolph home in Game 2 of the 1980 American League playoffs and Randolph was thrown out. Howser had refused to carry out Steinbrenner's wish, and was eventually forced out with Ferraro. (A poignant footnote: When Howser stepped down as the Kansas City Royals manager six years later to have a brain tumor removed, Ferraro took over for him as interim manager.)

■ Several members of the 1919 Chicago White Sox—who are known more familiarly as the Black Sox—were not on the take, and performed admirably in the World Series against the Cincinnati Reds, despite less-than-sterling support from the rest of the team. Pitcher Dickie Kerr won two games—a three-hit, 3-0 shutout and a 10-inning, 5-4 win—and compiled a 1.42 ERA in 19 innings. Other "clean" members of the team included Manager Kid Gleason, Eddie Collins, Red Faber, and Ray Schalk.

◼ The University of Nebraska football team could have kicked an extra point for the tie in the final moments of the 1984 Orange Bowl with the University of Miami and thus preserve its #1 ranking and the national championship, but the Cornhuskers elected to try to prove that they were the best by going for a two-point conversion. (The conversion failed, and Miami won the game, 31-30, and the national title.)

◼ Mario Lemieux was credited with a goal and six assists in the Pittsburgh Penguins' 7-5 win over the Los Angeles Kings on February 13, 1988. A seven-point game would have been a Penguins team record, but Lemieux told officials that he did not deserve the final assist. A review showed that he was right, and the assist was credited to Doug Bodger.

◼ Swede Hugo Weislander and Norwegian Ferdinand Bie, runners-up to Jim Thorpe in the 1912 decathlon and pentathlon, respectively, were offered his first-place medals after Thorpe was stripped of them for having earned $25 a week playing minor league baseball in 1909 and 1910. Weislander and Bie both refused to accept the gold medals.

◼ Race car driver Whitey Gerken stopped his vehicle during a 1970 race at the Indianapolis Fairgrounds to pull an unconscious opponent, Jack Bowsher, from his overturned car. "Why not?" Gerkin said. "I wasn't running well, anyway."

◼ During a barrage (fence-off) in the 1932 Olympics, Heather Guinness of Great Britain informed officials of two touches against her that they had missed, which turned out to be the margin of victory for the gold medal by Ellen Preis of Austria.

■ In 1986, Jan Kemp, an English professor at the University of Georgia, blew the whistle on academic fraud and preferential treatment to football players at the school, at the cost of her job. (She later sued the school for firing her and won the case.)

■ In a 100-km Olympic cycling race in 1896, Leon Flameng of France stopped and waited while the bike of his opponent, G. Kolettis of Greece, was repaired.

■ In the midst of trying to qualify for the 1988 LPGA Tucson Open, Mary Bea Porter jumped a fence to give CPR to a three-year-old boy who had been pulled out of a swimming pool, where he had been found face down. Porter revived him. She returned to the golf course, bogeyed two of the next three holes, and missed the cut but LPGA members signed a petition to include Porter in the tournament.

■ India had a chance to win its first-ever Davis Cup in 1974 but defaulted to its opponents in the finals, South Africa, to protest apartheid.

■ In the 1928 Olympic 100m hurdle finals, South Africa's Syd Atkinson, who had finished a close second in 1924, drew the inside lane, which had been chewed up by rain. Teammate George Weightman-Smith, who had set a world record in the semifinals, offered to switch lanes with Atkinson, who declined. Weightman-Smith insisted, Atkinson finally accepted, and he ended up winning the gold medal. Weightman-Smith took fifth.

■ Pam McGee, a basketball All-America from the University of Southern California, made the 1984 Olympic team while her sister, Paula, also a USC All-America, did not. After helping the United States to win, Pam gave her gold medal to Paula.

■ Russian Viktor Tsibulenko lent his steel javelin to Egil Danielson of Norway in 1956, and Danielson got off a world record throw to win the Olympic gold. Tsibulenko took third.

■ It is not true that nice guys finish last. The 1971–72 and 1984–85 Los Angeles Lakers, both of whom won NBA titles, had only seven players foul out of games all season, the second-lowest total in NBA history.

■ In 1968, the Cuban team that finished second in the 4x100m relay mailed their silver medals to Stokely Carmichael in support of the cause of U.S. blacks.

■ In Havana, Cuba, on April 5, 1915, heavyweight champion Jack Johnson, losing badly to challenger Jess Willard, motioned his wife over to the ring before the 26th round and told her to leave the arena so that she would not have to see him get knocked out.

■ While in first place by a stroke, Greg Norman disqualified himself from the $625,000 Daikyo Palm Meadows Cup in Brisbane, Australia, in January 1990. Norman said that he had inadvertently taken illegal relief—moving his ball when he wasn't allowed—on a drive into the water in the first round and only later overheard that such a gesture was outside the rules. Norman had shot 66 in the first round and a course record 63 in the second round before withdrawing.

■ Lucien Duquesne of France pulled out Paavo Nurmi when he fell into the first water jump in a steeplechase heat in the 1928 Olympics. Nurmi reciprocated by pacing Duquesne the rest of the way.

■ In 1987, Oakland Athletics rookie Mark McGwire, with 49 home runs, passed up the final game of the season —and a chance to become the first major league rookie ever to hit 50 home runs in a season so that he could witness the birth of his son, Matthew.

■ Before their second run on the two-man bobsled in 1964, British pair Anthony Nash and Robin Dixon discovered that an axle bolt had broken off of their sled. Eight-time world champion Eugenio Monti removed a bolt from his own sled and gave it to them, helping Nash and Dixon to win the gold. Monti's Italian team took the bronze.

IT'S JUST A GAME, PEOPLE

By now, every sports columnist in America has devoted much ink decrying the fact that sport is no longer sport but a business, cold as any other. And they're right. There's too much lucre involved for anyone not to see it. Sadly, with the tremendous pressure to win on players, coaches, and owners, one of the basic satisfactions of sport—simply having fun—seems to have suffered. Just listen to the hardened talk of any holdout-threatening phenom two weeks before training camp. Money must mean a great deal to anyone who, at the peak of his physical powers, threatens to sit out a year and wait to be paid uninsultingly enormous sums of cash, rather than play and receive simply very large sums of it.

Pitcher Lefty Gomez once called timeout while he was on the mound during a game to watch a plane fly overhead. We like that story.

Here are some others who have understood that it is, after all, just a game.

■ Frenchman Jules Goux, winner of the 1913 Indianapolis 500, drank chilled champagne during pit stops.

■ In September of 1989, Jamaican sprinter Linford Christie won a 100m race in London wearing a running suit designed to look like a James Bond–style dinner jacket with bow tie.

■ On the last day of the 1952 season, St. Louis Cardinals outfielder Stan Musial and Chicago Cubs outfielder Frankie Baumholtz, one and two in the National League batting race, faced each other—literally. Musial came in from center field to pitch once to Baumholtz. Baumholtz, a lefty, batted right-handed against Musial, who had been a pitcher in the minor leagues. Baumholtz grounded to the third baseman, who made an error on the play. Musial then returned to the outfield. (Musial won the batting title.)

■ In a 1985 game against the San Antonio Spurs, Quintin Dailey of the Chicago Bulls had the ballboy order a pizza during the game. Dailey ate it on the bench at the end of the third quarter.

■ In 1950, the St. Louis Browns held a champagne celebration after their 55th win, which meant that they could not lose 100 games that year. (The season then was 154 games long.)

■ In the 1989 season, Portland State held a contest asking their fans to send in plays for the football team. When the team was about to run the play that won the contest, the coach waved a white towel to let the fans know. The winning playcaller received $10 for every yard that the play gained, $20 per yard if the play went for a touchdown.

■ During long matches, Jack Crawford, a tennis star of the 1930s, liked to have a pot of tea, with milk and sugar, at the umpire's bench. He would relax with a cigarette during the interval after the third set.

THE DOZEN GENTLEST
COLLEGE MASCOTS

The team mascots of most schools are robust or snarling or generally excitable creatures: Lions, Gators, Buffalo, a Wolfpack here and there. Presumably, such nicknames inspire the school's athletic teams—in other words, its football team—collectively to take on the personality of a junkyard dog. If the school doesn't go in for animals, you'd probably be right to guess that its mascot name was something that sounded angry or destructive— Boilermakers, Fighting Irish, Hurricanes.

Other teams—some might say more self-motivated

ones—do not require the yoke of an aggressive nickname to carry out their duties on the field, and in fact may perform more adeptly using a gentle nickname, the better to lull their opponents into a sense of complacency. The Saltillo Serape Makers of the Mexican Baseball League is such a team. The Chattanooga Choo Choos of baseball's Negro League was another.

More follow, from the college ranks.

New York University Violets
Whittier (California) Poets
Centenary (Louisiana) Gentlemen
St. Joseph's (Maine) Monks
Heidelberg (Ohio) Student Princes
St. Mary of the Woods (Indiana) Woodsies
University of Pennsylvania Quakers
St. Bonaventure (New Jersey) Bonnies
Whitman (Washington) Missionaries
University of New England (Maine) Pilgrims
Thomas Jefferson (Pennsylvania) Medics
Boston University Terriers

5 INSTANCES OF PERSONS WHO TOOK BASEBALL OR SOCCER TOO SERIOUSLY

■ On May 31, 1949, Charley Lupica, a fan of the seventh-place Cleveland Indians, held a vigil on the platform of a flagpole, vowing not to relinquish his perch until the team took over first place. They did not, rising only to fourth place, and Lupica was finally persuaded to come down after 117 days.

■ For the 1982 World Cup, the Kuwait team president offered $200,000 per man for a victory over the French. (The French won, 4-1.)

■ In 1889, M.H. Davidson, the owner-manager of the Louisville club in the American Association, fined one player $25 for a bobble and a wild throw, another one $25 for stupid baserunning, and then told the team that everyone would be fined $25 each if they did not win the next day. (The two fined players and four others went on strike, and the replacement players helped Louisville establish a major league record of 26 consecutive losses.)

■ During a pre-Olympic soccer match between Peru and Argentina on May 24, 1964, a riot broke out in which 328 people were killed and over 500 were injured.

■ On the bottom of one tombstone in a Chicago-area Jewish cemetery is written, in Yiddish, "The Cubs Stink."

ADDING INSULT TO INJURY

■ On April 12, 1988, Cal Ripken, Sr., had just returned from the courthouse, where he had pleaded guilty to a charge of driving while intoxicated, when he received the news that he had been fired as manager of the Baltimore Orioles.

■ The California Golden Bears not only embarrassed Stanford in 1982 with perhaps the most dramatic game-ending play in the history of football—the famous five-lateral kickoff return for the winning touchdown that came to be known simply as "The Play"—but they did so with only 10 men on the field.

The Dallas Cowboys also had only 10 men on the field in the 1983 game when running back Tony Dorsett set an NFL record with a 99-yard run from scrimmage against the Minnesota Vikings.

■ Brett Jennings of Lingleville, Texas, so overpowered the Santo High School baseball team on April 28, 1986, that in only seven innings he struck out 24 batters. Three strikeout victims reached first base on dropped third strikes.

■ Toward the end of the worst rout in NFL history, the Chicago Bears' 73-0 destruction of the Washington Redskins in the 1940 title game, officials asked the Bears not to kick extra points after touchdowns but to run or pass for them, because so many balls had already been lost in the stands.

■ In the 1926 PGA, Walter Hagen beat Leo Diegel in the match-play final by five and three strokes. On one hole, Diegel's ball finished under Hagen's parked car.

■ Not long after invading Afghanistan, the Soviet Union beat them in team handball at the "Friendly Army Tournament" in Miskolc, Hungary, by a margin of 86-2, the highest score ever in an international handball match.

■ Not only did Australian cyclist Phil Anderson lap several competitors in the final portion of a 1986 race in New York City, but he then drifted behind them to improve his time. (Anderson ignored repeated warnings to break from the pack, and was fined $5,000 by the U.S. Pro Cycling Federation.)

THE ULTIMATE ATHLETE, FROM HEAD TO TOE

If someone were to create a monster made up of sports history's most renowned body parts—not always the *best* parts, mind you, but the most renowned—the blueprint might look something like this:

■ The brown SKIN of Brooklyn Dodger Jackie Robinson, who broke baseball's color barrier.

■ The electrified HAIR of boxing promoter Don King or the tenuously anchored HAIRPIECE of sportscaster Howard Cosell.

■ The STEEL PLATE that is allegedly lodged in Chicago Cubs manager Don Zimmer's skull.

■ The considerable BRAINS of UCLA basketball coach John Wooden. "The Wizard of Westwood."

■ The prominent EARS of American League pitcher Don Mossi.

■ The watchful EYES of hockey legend Wayne Gretzky, whose peripheral vision tested 30 percent better than average.

■ The immediately apparent NOSE of American League slugger Ken "Hawk" Harrelson.

■ The handlebar MUSTACHE of many of the 1970s Oakland Athletics, "The Mustache Gang."

■ The ever-moving MOUTH of major league manager Leo "The Lip" Durocher.

■ The infrequent TEETH of Philadelphia Flyer Bobby Clarke.

■ The ever-searching TONGUE of Chicago Bull Michael Jordan.

■ The nonexistent NECK of 5'6", 165-pound major leaguer Walt "No-Neck" Williams.

■ The pumped-up SHOULDERS of seven-time Mr. Universe, Arnold Schwarzenegger.

■ The massive ARMS of Cincinnati Reds slugger Ted Kluszewski.

■ The sharp ELBOWS of once and current Detroit Piston "Bad Boys" Rick Mahorn and Bill Laimbeer.

■ The powerful WRISTS of home run champion Hank Aaron.

■ The notoriously sticky HANDS of Oakland Raiders defensive back Lester Hayes.

■ The scarce FINGERS of Hall of Fame pitcher Mordecai "Three Finger" Brown.

■ The flamboyantly painted FINGERNAILS of sprinter Florence Griffith Joyner.

■ The chiseled CHEST of heavyweight Ken Norton.

■ The HEART of Italian marathoner Dorando Pietri, who nearly collapsed five times before finishing the 1908 Olympic marathon.

■ The unswerving NERVE of New York Jets quarterback Joe Namath.

■ The once-jiggling BELLY of Los Angeles Dodgers manager Tommy Lasorda.

■ The ample GLUTEUS MAXIMUS of Soviet weightlifter Vassily Alexeyev.

■ The elegant PELVIS of lithe Romanian gymnast Nadia Comaneci.

■ The muscular THIGHS of speedskater Eric Heiden.

■ The ravaged KNEES of Chicago Bear Dan Hampton, who has undergone 11 operations on them.

■ The stupendous FEET of basketball center Bob Lanier, who needs size-22 shoes to cover them.

THE ULTIMATE GETUP, FROM HAT TO SOLE

The only thing more unnerving than watching this monster rise from the table would be to take it shopping. And as long as it's going shopping, it might as well wear the most renowned clothes and use the most renowned accessories from the sports world, including the following:

■ The baseball CAP of hitting star Harry "The Hat" Walker, who took it off and put it back on after each pitch.

■ The cotton HEADBAND of tennis great Bjorn Borg.

■ The outer-space GOGGLES of basketball legend Kareem Abdul-Jabbar; or,

■ The sinister SHADES of quarterback Jim McMahon.

■ The attention-garnering EARRING of punk linebacker Brian Bosworth.

■ The loud SPORT JACKET of broadcaster Lindsey Nelson, which would cover the . . .

■ . . . even louder, lucky SWEATER of St. John's University basketball coach, Lou Carnesecca.

■ The sleeveless SHIRT of Ted Kluszewski, the only shirt that will cover those massive arms. (Refer back to the monster's blueprint.)

36

■ The gray T-SHIRT that New York Knicks center Patrick Ewing wore under his jersey at Georgetown University.

■ The denim SHORTS of tennis player Andre Agassi.

■ The white SHOES of football speedster Billy "White Shoes" Johnson.

Walking down the street toward the arena, the monster would dab its brow with the white TOWEL of UNLV basketball coach Jerry Tarkanian (and perhaps chew on it), puff on the CIGAR of basketball whiz Red Auerbach, and maybe, only then, pleased with its outfit, would crack the 10,000-watt SMILE of Los Angeles Laker Magic Johnson.

STEADY AS THEY GO: CONSISTENCY

To call an athlete consistent is usually to compliment him—he puts out the same, presumably full, effort in every game, and his level of performance does not waver all that much from one day to the next. He may do the usual great things each time out—score in double figures, pitch at least seven good innings, carry the ball 20 times for 100 yards. Or he may just give you a workmanlike effort—four or five rebounds in limited minutes, a couple of first downs on third-and-inches.

Ultimately, to call an athlete consistent is to know what to expect of him or her. Here are some of the best examples.

■ Golfer Densmore Shute won the 1933 British Open with rounds of 73, 73, 73, and 73.

■ Jimmie Foxx hit 30 or more home runs for 12 consecutive years. Hank Aaron hit 20 or more home runs for 20 consecutive years. Foxx and Lou Gehrig both drove in 100 or more runs for 13 consecutive years.

■ From the 1950–51 through the 1954–55 seasons, Hall of Fame goaltender Terry Sawchuck had a goals-against average of between 1.90 and 1.99.

■ In the 1971–72 season, the Los Angeles Lakers committed 1,636 fouls. The following season, they again committed 1,636 fouls.

■ In 1968, the steady and unspectacular Jan Jansen of Holland became the first cyclist to win the Tour de France without having worn the yellow jersey during the race.

■ Warren Spahn won 20 games a record 13 times, but never won more than 23.

■ For the six seasons from 1944–45 to 1949–50, NHL defenseman Bill Quackenbush had the following assist totals: 21, 21, 22, 22, 23, and 25.

■ In 1983, New York Mets outfielder Mookie Wilson hit .276. In 1984, he hit .276. In 1985, he hit .276. (Wilson was highly erratic before that: in 1981, he hit .271 and in 1982, .279.)

■ Don Sutton struck out at least 100 batters for 21 consecutive seasons.

■ From 1962 to 1981, Jack Nicklaus played 80 majors and made the top 10 in 60 of them. In 42 of them, he was in the top three.

■ NHL goalie Eddie Giacomin's regular season goals-against average was 2.82. His playoff goals-against average was 2.82.

2
NUMBERS AND STATISTICS

THE MOST STARTLING (POSITIVE) ABERRATIONS

For one game or season, the following athletes performed strangely better than they did in the rest of their careers.

■ Atlanta Brave Davey Johnson hit 43 home runs in 1973. He never hit more than 18 in any of his other 12 seasons.

■ Running back Charles White rushed for an NFL-leading 1,374 yards in 1987, four yards fewer than his combined total for the seven previous seasons.

■ Broker's Tip won the 1933 Kentucky Derby. He had never won a race before and would never win one again.

■ Wilt Chamberlain, a 51-percent career free-throw shooter, made 28-of-32 free throws—88 percent—and set the record for most free throws made in a game on the night that he scored 100 points.

■ In 1912, Pittsburgh Pirate Owen Wilson set the major league record of 36 triples. He had no more than 14 in any other year.

■ Francisco Fernandez Ochoa of Spain won the Olympic slalom gold medal in 1972, despite never before finishing higher than sixth in an international meet.
Austria's Leonhard Stock won the 1980 Olympic down-

hill gold. He was an alternate and had never won a World Cup downhill race.

◼ Ali Haji-Sheikh set an NFL record with 35 field goals as a New York Giant rookie in 1983, then never kicked more than 17 in any other season.

◼ Bumpus Jones (career 2-4 record) pitched a no-hitter, as did George Davis (7-10) and Mike Warren (9-13).

◼ The U.S. Open has seen several middle-of-the-pack golfers suddenly flourish, if only for that moment. Janet Alex Anderson's only career win was the 1982 U.S. Open. The next year, she shot 82 and missed the cut. Unknown Jack Fleck beat Ben Hogan in a playoff in the 1955 Open, preventing Hogan from winning his fifth Open. Fleck, a municipal-course pro from Iowa, made two birdies on the final two regulation holes to tie Hogan. And although Orville Moody was a familiar figure on the PGA Tour, the only win of his career before joining the Seniors circuit was the 1969 U.S. Open.

◼ Lee Fogolin, an NHL defenseman for 13 years, scored 13 goals in 1980–81, and no more than five in any other season.

◼ On July 18, 1948, Pat Seerey became one of the rare major leaguers to hit four home runs in one game—but he hit just eight more after that, and had only 86 in his career.

◼ Unknown Paul Pilgrim won the 400m and 800m in the 1906 Interim Olympic Games. He never again won a major race.

◼ In 1942, Johnny Beazley won 21 games. In his whole major league career, he won 31 games.

◼ Oakland Athletics catcher Gene Tenace was a .251 career hitter, then batted .348 with four home runs and nine runs batted in in the 1972 World Series, then returned to being a .239 hitter for the rest of his career.

◼ Before 1989, when they lost their first-round NCAA

tournament game to Siena, Stanford University's basketball team had made only one NCAA tournament appearance, in 1942. They won the national title that year.

◼ Detroit Tiger Norm Cash hit .361 to win the 1961 American League batting title. In his other 16 years in the league, he never hit more than .286.

Tito Francona, a lifetime .272 hitter, hit .363 in 1959.

◼ Don Woods rushed for 1,162 as a San Diego Charger rookie in 1974. The next-best season total for his seven-year career was 514 yards.

◼ Detroit Tigers pitcher Dave Wickersham won 19 games in 1964 but never more than 12 in any other year.

Pitcher Monte Weaver won 22 games for the 1932 Washington Senators, the only time he won more than 12 in a season.

◼ Fred Odwell hit one home run in 1904, then nine in 1905 to win the National League homer title, then no more.

◼ To win the only professional tennis tournament of his career, the 1981 Seiko Classic in Tokyo, Vince van Patten beat John McEnroe, Vitas Gerulaitis, Jose-Luis Clerc and, in the final, Mark Edmondson. Van Patten's next-best success was reaching the quarterfinals of a tournament in Tel Aviv.

AND A FEW MORE STARTLING
(NEGATIVE) ABERRATIONS

◼ Joe Sewell of the Cleveland Indians struck out twice against Chicago White Sox pitcher Pat Caraway in one game on May 26, 1930. That may not seem like a lot for most players but it was for Sewell, the hardest man to strike out in the history of baseball. He did not strike out again for the rest of that season, and in his 14-year career, he fanned once every 63 at-bats (114 strikeouts in 7,132 at-bats).

■ On April 26, 1931, New York Yankee Lou Gehrig, one of the most alert baseball players ever, passed a teammate on the basepaths and lost credit for the home run that he had hit. That year, Gehrig and teammate Babe Ruth tied for the home run crown with 46.

■ Nap Lajoie, one of the greatest players and fielders of all time, was once charged with five errors in a game. Brooks Robinson, the most brilliant third baseman of his era, made three errors in a game against the Oakland Athletics. It was the only time that happened in his career. And the record for most errors in a World Series, six, used to be held by baseball legend Honus Wagner.

THE TIDIEST STATISTICS IN SPORTS

Something about the statistician—or the accountant—in all of us that loves numbers that end in a zero. There's something precise about it, something clean. In 1927, heavyweight Gene Tunney earned $990,445 for beating Jack Dempsey, but Tunney was paid with a $1 million check and then wrote his own check to make up the difference.

The following people did not fudge their numbers to look neat. It just happened that way.

■ Joe Gordon played 1,000 games with the New York Yankees and had 1,000 hits.

■ In his NBA career, basketball star Elvin Hayes played exactly 50,000 minutes.

■ Wide receiver Lionel Taylor had 100 catches for the AFL's Denver Broncos in 1961.

■ The career of Pittsburgh Pirate Roberto Clemente was cut short by a plane crash. He died with exactly 3,000 hits.

■ Gregg Pruitt rushed for exactly 1,000 yards for the Cleveland Browns in 1976, as did the Los Angeles Rams' Willie Ellison in 1971, and the Miami Dolphins' Mercury Morris in 1972. (Morris had 991 yards at season's end but in reviewing game film, NFL commissioner Pete Rozelle found a nine-yard error, bringing Morris up to exactly 1,000 yards.)

■ Billy Goodman and Enos Slaughter each had a career batting average of .300.

■ In 1964, Northern Dancer ran the Kentucky Derby in precisely 2:00.0, the only time that has ever happened in the Derby.

■ Richard Petty won his 200th NASCAR race on July 4, 1984, in the Pepsi Firecracker 400 in Daytona Beach. He has not won another NASCAR race in over six years and counting.

THE MOST MEMORABLE UNIFORM NUMBERS

An athlete's uniform number may signify a number of things: he plays a certain position, such as lineman, and thus can wear a number only within a narrow range; it's the number he's worn since Pee Wee League; it was the last clean jersey in the locker room when he joined the team.

This list is about uniform numbers that carried a more compelling significance than that, and who wore them.

■ *100*, by University of Kansas senior placekicker Bill Bell. Bell wore #12 in his sophomore and junior seasons, during which he scored exactly 100 points. Kansas coach Pepper Rodgers received NCAA permission for Bell to exceed the two-digit uniform number limit in his final year, 1969, which was also college football's 100th anniversary.

■ *100*, by West Virginia University placekicker Chuck Kinder in 1963, to commemorate the Mountain State's centennial.

■ *99*, by Willie Crawford of the Oakland Athletics in 1977. It is the highest number ever worn in baseball.

■ *96*, by major league pitcher Bill Voiselle, whose hometown was Ninety-Six, South Carolina.

■ *85*, by NHL forward Petr Klima to commemorate 1985, the year he defected from Czechoslovakia.

■ *72*, by Carlton Fisk of the Chicago White Sox, to represent the turnaround in his career—hence, he chose the reverse of the #27 he wore with the Boston Red Sox.

■ *50*, by New York Mets pitcher Sid Fernandez, in honor of his native Hawaii, the 50th state in the Union.

■ *42*, by Dave Henderson of the Oakland Athletics, because it was the number worn by Jackie Robinson, whose courage opened the way for all black players in the major leagues.

■ *31*, by no Buffalo Bill ever. The Bills have never issued #31 because it was the number worn by the Buffalo player on the club's letterhead from the 1960s, when the Bills were in the AFL.

■ *25*, by Miami Dolphin Louis Oliver, to remind him of the disappointing position that he was selected in the first round of the 1989 NFL draft, after unsubstantiated drug rumors about Oliver, the country's top collegiate safety, circulated on draft day.

■ *17*, by Carlos May, who was born on May 17, and thus is the only known major leaguer whose uniform displayed his birthdate.

■ *17*, by Andy Messersmith of the Atlanta Braves, because Braves owner Ted Turner saw a chance to promote simultaneously his star pitcher and his station, WTBS, Channel 17.

■ ɼ (a backward 7), worn by John Neves, a minor league baseball player whose name spelled backward is "seven."

■ *4*, worn by Houston Rocket Rick Barry for road games.

■ *2*, worn by Houston Rocket Rick Barry for home games.

■ *1/8*, by Eddie Gaedel, the 3'11" midget hired by St. Louis Browns owner Bill Veeck to take one major league at-bat. (Gaedel walked on four pitches.)

■ *0*, by Al Oliver, in 1978, when he was with the Texas Rangers. It is the lowest uniform number ever worn in baseball. 0, as well as 00, has been worn by others, including Oddibe McDowell and Jeffrey Leonard.

■ *00*, by Oakland Raiders center Jim Otto, to commemorate the beginning and end of his last name.

■ *?*, by Max Patkin, a veteran entertainer and clown at minor league baseball games (seen in the movie *Bull Durham*).

MISLEADING TALLIES:
THE STORIES BEHIND 6 SCORES

Given little more than the final score, a fan can often tell a great deal about a game—how it progressed, whether it was exciting (no matter how you cut it, no 6-0, 6-0, 6-0 tennis match is exciting), maybe even make an educated stab at who did what—for example, if you hear that your team was involved in a high-scoring affair at Wrigley and you know that the wind was blowing out, you can't help but instinctively add a homer or two to your slugger's total before you even bother with the box score.

If you imagined a pat scenario for any of the following scores, you'd be wrong.

■ On September 24, 1967, the St. Louis Cardinals beat the Pittsburgh Steelers, 28-14. However, the Cardinals did *not* score four touchdowns; 21 of their points were the result of a record seven field goals by kicker Jim Bakken.

■ In the first round of the Ginny women's tennis tournament in Richmond, Virginia, on September 25, 1984, Vicki Nelson defeated Jean Hepner, 6-4, 7-6. It was simply a straight set affair—as well as the longest match in duration ever played, lasting 6 hours and 31 minutes, not counting intermissions and interruptions. The match included one rally of 643 shots, and the final tiebreaker game lasted *one hour and 47 minutes*.

■ In the 1964 NFL title game, the Cleveland Browns clobbered the Baltimore Colts, 27-0. But it was a much closer game than that; the halftime score, in fact, was 0-0.

■ On August 23, 1961, a baseball version of that NFL title game occurred. The San Francisco Giants destroyed the Cincinnati Reds, 14-0. After eight innings, however, the Giants were only leading 2-0.

46

◾ In a 1970 game against Florence State University, Russell Thompson of Birmingham Southern State College scored 25 points. Oddly enough, however, Thompson did not make a single field goal. He was 25 for 27 from the foul line.

◾ In the 1929 World Series, the Chicago Cubs lost Game 4 in a thriller, 10-8. Sadly for Cub fans, their team had been running away with the game all along, leading 8-0 in the seventh inning.

SOFT ACCOMPLISHMENTS

Some feats are remarkable on the face of them, and then seem even more so if you know the surrounding circumstances. Roger Bannister's breaking of the four-minute mile was one of the great athletic achievements of the century; yet it is more impressive still when you consider that Bannister had to contend with, according to reports in the *New York Times*, "a 15mph crosswind during the race and gusts [that] reached 25mph just before the event began." Al Geiberger's PGA record score of 59 for 18 holes was accomplished in 1977, on the 7,249-yard Colonial Country Club Course in Memphis, the longest course played on the U.S. tour that year.

This is not about especially impressive records. The listed feats of the following athletes are commendable at first glance. But once we consider the competition against whom the feat was registered, or the fortunate circumstances that facilitated it, or what the athlete's peers have achieved—or could achieve—when trying to accomplish the same thing under different conditions, we see that these accomplishments were really not so spectacular.

◾ Czechoslovakia's Jan Kodes won the 1973 Wimbledon title after 79 members of the Association of Tennis Profes-

47

sionals, including 13 of the 16 seeded players, boycotted the tournament to protest the suspension of Yugoslav Nikki Pilic for not playing Davis Cup.

■ In 1983, Montreal Expos pitcher David Palmer threw a rain-shortened five-inning perfect game against the St. Louis Cardinals.

■ Soviet Anatoly Parfenov won the 1956 Olympic Greco-Roman super heavyweight wrestling gold medal in rousing fashion: he lost his opening match, but a Soviet protest was upheld; he lost his second-round match; he won by forfeit in the third round; and he received a bye in the fourth. In the fifth round, he had his only undisputed win, a decision.

■ New York Met Howard Johnson holds the all-time National League record for most home runs in a season by a switch hitter, with 36. The American League record is 54, by Mickey Mantle in 1961.

■ The St. Louis Browns won their only pennant in 1944, a year when the major leagues were depleted by the war.

■ Because of the 1982 NFL strike and the revised playoff format, the Cleveland Browns and Detroit Lions both made the playoffs with 4-5 records.

■ In 1930, Max Schmeling became the first boxer to win the heavyweight title on a foul (over Jack Sharkey).

■ Oliver Kirk won Olympic gold medals in both the featherweight and bantamweight divisions in 1904 though he had only one bout in each.

■ Because of the disqualification of one American quarter-miler from the 1908 Olympic 400m competition, and the ensuing protests of two others, Britain's Wyndham Halswelle won the gold medal by running alone in the final.

■ Anthony Allen set a Washington Redskins team record with 255 receiving yards in a 1987 strike game.

◧ In 1922, Mike Collins, a fight manager who was also publisher of a weekly called *The Boxing Blade*, invented a new division, the light welterweights, and held a competition among his readers to determine who should be the division's first champion. Not surprisingly, the winner of the poll was one of Collins's own fighters, Myron "Pinkie" Mitchell. Mitchell kept the title for four years without defending it. When he finally *did* defend it, on September 21, 1926, he lost a 10-round decision to Mushy Callahan.

◧ Because of the liberal NHL playoff system and the traditionally weak competition in the Norris Division, the Toronto Maple Leafs made the playoffs in each of the three seasons from 1985–86 to 1987–88. Their cumulative record over that span was 78-139-23.

◧ In an NBA game on November 22, 1950, the high scorer for Fort Wayne, John Oldham, had five points.

◧ In 1984, Brigham Young University finished 13-0 and won the national championship. None of their wins, including a Holiday Bowl victory over Michigan, came against teams that finished in the final Top 20.

BEAMONESQUE ACHIEVEMENTS

The word "Beamonesque" has entered the vocabulary of sports historians to mean a feat so dramatically superior to its predecessors that it cannot be sufficiently appreciated except to be called, well, "Beamonesque."

American Bob Beamon astounded the world when he won the long jump at the 1968 Olympics with his record 29'2½" leap, a standard that has stood now for over 20 years. It is not that Beamon wasn't a world-class jumper before that day; he was. It is not that a world record jump at those Games couldn't have been anticipated; it was, what with the thin air of high-altitude Mexico City. What was astounding about the jump was that Beamon became not only the first human to clear 29 feet but also the first to clear 28 feet. In fact, the first 28 foot-long jump would not occur for 12 more years, until the 1980 Olympics, when Lutz Dombrowski did it. To put Beamon's feat further into perspective: his jump increased the world record by 21¾ inches, while in the 33 years before that, since Jesse Owens's jump of 26'8¼" in 1935, the record had increased by 8½ inches.

The following achievements reveal a level of proficiency that only one person or team has achieved, for a brief period or over a career. Because these feats may not be as "pure" as those in track and field, circumstances might have facilitated the achievement—for example, a team played a weak schedule, or the prevailing rules favored a player's style. But we still believe that they deserve the high distinction of Beamonesqueness.

■ American Mary T. Meagher is swimming's Bob Beamon. On August 13, 1981, she swam the 100m butterfly in 57.93 seconds. No woman has yet gone under 59 seconds. The second-fastest time through 1989 was Kristin Otto's 59.00 in Seoul on September 23, 1988. Meagher has 6 of the fastest 10 times in the 100m butterfly.

In the 200m butterfly, Meagher holds the world record of 2:05.96, set August 16, 1981. Her second-best time is 2:06.09, and she owns all 10 of the fastest times in the event. The best time by another woman swimmer is Cornelia Polit's 2:07.82, in 1983.

■ In 1984, Miami Dolphins quarterback Dan Marino passed for 48 touchdowns, breaking the old mark of 36 held by Y.A. Tittle and George Blanda.

■ LSU basketball star Pete Maravich holds the Division I scoring average record of 44.2 points per game (1968–70). Notre Dame's Austin Carr is a distant second with 34.6 points per game (1969–71).

■ Connie Mack, who owned the Philadelphia Athletics, was a manager for 53 years, including 3 years as player-manager. He managed 20 years longer than the next person, John McGraw, who was a major league skipper for 33 years.

■ In January of 1914, speedskater Oscar Mathisen of Norway set a record in the 1,500m (2:17.4 seconds) that stood for 23 years, when it was broken by Michael Staksrud's 2:14.9. Only twice was Mathisen's performance bettered in the 38 years from 1914–52.

■ Through the 1989 season, Nolan Ryan had pitched 199 games in which he struck out 10 or more batters. Sandy Koufax is next with 97 such games.

■ New York Yankee Babe Ruth inaugurated the lively-ball era in 1920 with 54 home runs. George Sisler was the runner-up with 19.
    In 1927, Ruth's Yankees hit 158 home runs—102 more than the second-best team. That year, the Boston Red Sox hit five home runs all year at Fenway Park, their home; Ruth himself hit eight at Fenway, and teammate Lou Gehrig hit six.

■ Cornelius "Dutch" Warmerdam pole-vaulted 15 feet or more 43 times between 1940 and 1944. No one else cleared the height until 1951. When he retired, Warmerdam's best vault was nine inches higher than anyone else's. His world record of 15'7¾", set on May 23, 1942, remained until April 27, 1957, when Bob Gutowski broke it.

■ In 1962, Los Angeles Dodger Maury Wills led the National League with 104 stolen bases. His teammate, Willie Davis, was next with 32.

■ Romanian high-jumper Iolanda Balas set 14 world records from 1958–66, the most for any athlete in a single event, and was the first woman to clear six feet. She had done that in 46 different meets before another woman, Michele Brown of Australia, cleared it.

■ In 1971, Montreal Expo Rusty Staub was second in

getting hit by pitches with nine. Ron Hunt, his teammate, led the league with 50.

■ Wayne Gretzky broke Gordie Howe's NHL career scoring record in his 11th season. Howe played in the NHL for 26 years.

■ Jim Thorpe's world record score in the 1912 decathlon, 700 points more than the runner-up, was so high that it would have won the silver medal in the 1948 Games.

6 FAMOUS RECORDS AND THE RECORDS THAT THEY BROKE

■ Roger Maris's 61 home runs in a season broke Babe Ruth's 60, which broke Ruth's own record of 59, which broke Ruth's record of 54, which broke Ruth's record of 29, which broke Ned Williamson's record of 27.

■ Wilt Chamberlain's 100 points in a game broke his own record of 78, set earlier in the season, December 8, 1961.

■ Joe DiMaggio's 56-game hitting streak broke Wee Willie Keeler's 44-game streak in 1897.

■ New Orlean Saint Tom Dempsey's 63-yard field goal in 1970 broke Baltimore Colt Bert Rechichar's 56-yarder in 1953.

■ Orel Hershiser's 59-consecutive-innings scoreless streak broke Don Drysdale's 58-innings streak, which broke Walter Johnson's 55⅔-innings streak.

■ In 1924, Jim Bottomley drove in 12 runs in one game to break Wilbert Robertson's record of 11, set in 1892. Ironically, Robertson was managing the opposing team that day and got to see in person his record broken.

WHEN IT RAINS, IT POURS

Success breeds success. An athlete or team overcomes some psychological or physical barrier and suddenly he or she is confident that the barrier no longer exists. The best example of this might be that of the four-minute mile. Before Roger Bannister crossed that threshold in 1954, it was widely believed to be physically impossible. By the end of 1957, 16 other runners had also broken the four-minute mile.

Then again, some things just come in bunches.

■ At the 1976 Montreal Games, Romanian Nadia Comaneci became the first Olympic gymnast ever to receive a perfect score of 10—and she got seven of them.

■ In his six years with the Baltimore Orioles, Frank Robinson hit only two grand slams—and they came in consecutive at-bats at Washington, on June 26, 1970.

■ Fred Dryer holds the NFL record for most safeties in a game, two, and they are the only ones of his career.

■ Before the 1986 postseason, no major league team had ever come back from more than two runs down in the ninth inning to win a playoff or World Series game. In the space of 21 hours, it happened twice during the American League playoffs and once in the National League playoffs.

■ Eddie Collins is the only player in the 20th century to steal six bases in a game, and he did it twice in less than two weeks in 1912, on September 11 and 22.

■ Before 1987, Don Mattingly had never before hit a grand slam. That season, he hit six, a major league record.

■ In 29 seasons under head coach Tom Landry, the Dallas Cowboys were shut out twice. In the first season under Jimmy Johnson, they were shut out three times.

■ Only three batters hit balls during regulation games into the Polo Grounds center-field bleachers—and the second and third, Lou Brock and Hank Aaron, did it on consecutive days in 1962, June 17 and 18.

■ Through the middle of the 1989 NFL season, Cincinnati Bengals running back James Brooks had not fumbled for 38 consecutive games. In his next seven games, he fumbled seven times.

■ The Tampa Bay Buccaneers lost the first 26 games in their history, the longest losing streak in NFL history. They broke the skein by winning the next-to-last game of the 1977 season. They liked that so much that they won the next week, too.

■ In the 14-year period from 1935–48 there were six horseracing Triple Crown winners, then none until decades later, when Secretariat (1973), Seattle Slew (1977), and Affirmed (1978) each took the Crown in a six-year period.

■ On May 30, 1927, Chicago Cubs shortstop James Cooney pulled off an unassisted triple play. The next day, Detroit Tigers first baseman John Neun duplicated the feat. In the entire history of baseball, there have been eight unassisted triple plays.

6-4-3: NUMBERS THAT SPEAK FOR THEMSELVES

Certain numbers have an intrinsic significance for certain sports: 7 (touchdown with extra point) for football;

15-30-40 (the game score) for tennis; 60'6" (the distance from the mound to the plate) in baseball.

Other numbers are representative of a certain aptitude: 3,000 (career hits) or 40-40 (homers and steals in a season) in baseball; 19 (feet) in pole vaulting; 300 (a perfect game) for bowling.

And then there are numbers that, pure and simple, mean something to sports fans, statistically-minded fans, because the numbers are not just that but a shorthand for a longer story: of a player, a season, a game, a moment.

Here are some of the most cherished numbers in baseball, and a few more from elsewhere. Although these numbers are eloquent by themselves, we will provide a minimum of parenthetical commentary.

Baseball

- 714 and 755 (Babe and Hank)

- 60 and 61 (Babe and Roger)

- 2,130 (Lou)

- .406 (Ted)

- 511 (Cy)

- 4,191 and 4,256 (Ty and Pete)

- 383 (Ryan's Express)

- 190 (Hack)

- 1.12 (Bob G.)

- 116-36 (Chicago Cubs)

- 1919 (Black Sox)

Basketball

- 50.4 (Wilt)

- 88 (UCLA)

- 69-13 (LA)

Football

- 73-0 (Bears and Redskins)
- 2,105 (Eric D.)

Golf

- 59 (Al)

Tennis

- 1-6,7-5,6-3,6-7(16-18),8-6 (five in a row)

Track and Field

- 29'2½" (Bob)
- 9.92 (without steroids)
- 9.79 (with steroids)

IT HAPPENED BUT ONCE: 29 OF THE MOST MEMORABLE "ONLYS" IN SPORT

Science tells us that in most cases, if something happens once, it could happen again. Secretariat is currently the only horse ever to break two minutes for the Kentucky Derby (1:59 2/5 in 1973) but in time another will do it and break Big Red's hold on that distinction. The discus is the only men's track and field event in which a world record has not been set at the Olympics, but after 1992 that may no longer be true.

There are other singular achievements, however, that cannot be ravaged by time: Ken Williams of the St. Louis Browns will always be the only non-Yankee to win an

American League home run title in the 1920s. And chances are that CCNY will remain the only team to win the NCAA and the NIT basketball tournaments in the same year (1950, beating Bradley in both finals) since schools today compete in either one or the other tournament, not both.

What follows is a collection of "onlys" that were true at the time of this writing.

■ Gallant Fox is the only Triple Crown winner (1930) to sire another Triple Crown winner (Omaha, the 1935 winner).

■ Eddie Arcaro is the only jockey to ride two Triple Crown winners. He won on Whirlaway in 1941 and Citation in 1948.

■ Red Auerbach is the only pro basketball coach to win more than 1,000 games. His record is 1,037-548, including playoffs, in the NBA and BAA.

■ Jack Nicklaus is the only golfer to win all four majors, plus the U.S. Amateur.

■ Dave Krieg is the only alumnus of Milton College to play in the NFL, and he should remain that way. The school is now defunct.

■ Brazil is the only nation to qualify for and take part in all 14 World Cups.

■ England is the only country to participate in every Summer and Winter Olympics since the Games began in the modern era.

■ Comedian Lenny Bruce claimed that the only baseball game he ever attended was Game 7 of the 1960 World Series (the Bill Mazeroski home run game).

■ Archie Griffin of Ohio State is the only football collegian to win the Heisman Trophy twice (1974 and 1975).

■ Don Shula is the only coach to lead two different teams

to the Super Bowl—Baltimore (in 1969) and Miami (in 1972, 1973, 1974, 1983, and 1985).

■ Johnny Mize is the only lefty in the National League to hit 50 home runs in a season (51 in 1947).

■ American Harold Osborn is the only Olympian to win the decathlon and an individual event (the high jump). He accomplished this at the 1924 Paris Games.

■ The only track and field world record set at the 1984 Los Angeles Olympics was in the men's 4x100m relay (37.83 seconds), by the United States.

■ Jim Clark of Great Britain is the only race car driver to win the Indianapolis 500 and the World Driving Championship in the same year (1965).

■ Mel Stottlemyre balked only once in his career. He faced 10,972 batters.

■ Sugar Ray Robinson failed to go the distance only once in 201 pro fights, against Joey Maxim in 1952. Tiring in intense heat, Robinson retired at the end of the 13th round.

■ The Miami Dolphins are the only Super Bowl team to have gone a whole game without scoring a touchdown—Super Bowl VI, which they lost, 24-3, to the Dallas Cowboys.

■ The 1932 Yankees are the only team since the turn of the century to go the entire season without being shut out.

■ Buck Shaw's 1960 Eagles are the only team to beat Vince Lombardi's Packers in a playoff game, winning 17-13. Lombardi won the other nine playoff games in which his teams appeared.

■ Green Bay Packer Jim Taylor is the only running back to beat Cleveland Brown Jim Brown for the rushing title (in 1962) during Brown's career (1957 to 1965).

■ Bob Meusel was the only Yankee to hit more home runs during a given season in the 1920s than Babe Ruth. Meusel outhomered Ruth 33-25 in 1925.

■ There was only one fan on hand to watch Washington State play a football game against San Jose State, on November 12, 1955.

■ Roger Maris won only one home run title (in 1961), though in his case that would seem enough.

■ Joe Kuharich is the only Notre Dame football coach not to have a winning record. He was 17-23 from 1959 to 1962.

■ Martina Navratilova's only loss in 87 matches in 1983 was to Kathy Horvath at the French Open, 6-4, 0-6, 6-3.

■ Hall of Famer George Hainsworth is the only NHL goalie to register a season goals-against average of under 1.00 (0.98 in 1928–29).

■ The Chicago Cubs are the only National League team not to have posted a winning record against the 1962 Mets.

■ Pee Wee Reese is the only player to appear in every Brooklyn Dodgers–New York Yankees World Series game.

■ At 67, Sam Snead beat his age in the 1979 Quad Cities Open, the only PGA player ever to do so.

BABE RUTH SLEPT HERE:
A FEW NOTABLE HITTING
ACHIEVEMENTS BY PITCHERS

■ Louisville's Guy Hecker is the only major league pitcher to win a batting title. He hit .342 to lead the American

Association in 1886. Hecker started 49 games, going 27-23 (including relief), and also played 22 games at first base and 17 in the outfield.

■ The oldest man to hit a major league home run is 46-year-old Jack Quinn, a pitcher for the Philadelphia Athletics, who hit the last of his eight career homers in 1930.

■ In 1973, Philadelphia Phillies pitcher Ken Brett hit home runs in four consecutive games, on June 9, 13, 18, and 23.

■ Red Lucas, a National League pitcher in the 1920s and 1930s, is sixth on the all-time pinch-hitting list (through 1989).

■ Tony Cloninger, a starting pitcher for the Milwaukee Braves, is the only National Leaguer ever to hit two grand slams in one game. He did it against the San Francisco Giants on July 3, 1966. He hit 5 of his 11 career home runs that year.

■ On April 21, 1898, Philadelphia pitcher Bill Duggleby hit a grand slam in his first major league at-bat.

CLOSE BUT NO CIGAR:
ATHLETES WHO BARELY MISSED
RECORDS AND VICTORIES

■ Frank Hunter twice came within three games of winning the U.S. Open but lost in five-set finals, first to Henri Cochet in 1928, then to Bill Tilden in 1929.

■ In the second Indianapolis 500, in 1912, Ralph DePalma, driving a Mercedes, took the lead 10 miles into the race, and led by 10 miles with six laps to go when his connecting rod snapped and the engine blew. Rather than stopping to fix it, DePalma tried to sputter home, slowing to 20 miles per hour. Finally, on the home stretch of the 199th lap, his car died. DePalma and his mechanic tried to push the car to the finish line but could not do it. Joe Dawson passed them to win.

■ On December 10, 1972, St. Louis Cardinals quarterback Jim Hart threw a 98-yard pass completion to Bobby Moore that, astonishingly, did not go for a touchdown.

■ American Micki King was leading the 1968 Olympics springboard diving competition after 8 of 10 dives. She broke her arm on her penultimate dive, costing her the gold medal. (She took her last dive and finished fourth.)

■ Right-hander Charlie Ferguson won 99 games pitching for the National League Philadelphia team from 1884–87. Before he had a chance to win his 100th game, he died of typhoid fever on April 29, 1888, at the start of the new season.

■ St. Bonaventure's basketball team was going for its 100th straight home win when Niagara beat them, 87-77, in February of 1961.

■ Sam Rice retired with 2,987 hits—the most of anyone *not* with 3,000 hits.

In 1929, Lefty O'Doul hit .398—the closest anyone has gotten without hitting .400. One more hit would have brought O'Doul to .400. (Harry Heilmann also hit .398 one year but in another year he hit .403.)

■ Roy Face was 18-1 in 1959.

■ Basketball star Anne Donovan, the 1983 Naismith College Player of the Year, played in 136 games at Old Dominion and scored 2,719 points, for a career scoring average of 19.9926 points per game. Although that rounds off to 20 points per game, she would have hit it exactly had she scored one more point.

■ In 1986, Toronto Blue Jays relief pitcher Mark Eichhorn posted a 1.72 ERA but was five innings short of being considered for the ERA title that he would have won.

■ In 1939 and 1940, Johnny Mize won two of three categories for the Triple Crown.

■ American Fred Lorz almost got away with victory in the 1904 Olympic marathon. He was standing for a photograph with Alice Roosevelt, Teddy's daughter, and was ready to receive the gold medal when he was found out. Lorz had quit running 9 miles into the race, hitched a car ride for 11 miles, and then began to run again. Lorz was given a lifetime ban by the AAU. (He was reinstated later and won the 1905 Boston Marathon.)

HIGH HEAT

The need for speed runs deep in many sports—not only to move one's self faster, but also to send the ball of choice hurtling through space at ever-dizzying velocities. To throw a ball very fast earns one admiration and, particularly in baseball, some compelling, if curious, descriptions. A good fastball has variously been described as smoke, high heat, the hard cheese, having mustard on it; a pitcher who throws such a ball is airing it out or bringing it.

The following is a list of the top recorded speeds of various balls and other moving bodies, in miles per hour.

■ A jai alai pelota: 188

■ A golf ball driven off a tee: 170

■ A tennis serve*:
by Bill Tilden   163.6

by Colin Dibley	148
by Jeff Southwick	141
by Steve Denton	138
by Scott Carnahan	137

(*depending on how it was measured)

- A Gordie Howe slapshot: 118.3

- A ping pong ball: 105.6

- A Nolan Ryan or Goose Gossage fastball: 103

- A Frisbee (by Alan Bonopane): 74

- Bill Johnson skiing (1984 Olympic downhill): 64.95

- A cheetah running: 63

- A horse running: 43

- A greyhound running: 42

- A Sugar Ray Robinson punch: 35

- Eric Heiden speedskating: 31

- Ben Johnson and Carl Lewis running (during the fastest 10m interval of the 1988 Olympic 100m final): 26.95

- Matt Biondi swimming: 5.05

And one extremely slow speed:

- A rope in tug-of-war, an Olympic sport from 1900 to 1920: 0.00084 (averaged)

18 STATISTICAL QUIRKS, COINCIDENCES, AND INTRIGUES

- From 1949 to 1958, the New York Yankees reached 100 victories just once, in 1954—the only season in that stretch that they did *not* win the American League pennant. That year, the Cleveland Indians won an American League record 111 games. In each of the other nine years, the Yankees won the pennant with a victory total numbering in the nineties.

■ In the 1950 season, Pittsburgh Pirates infielder Pete Castiglione made one error as a first baseman, two as a second baseman, three as a third baseman, and four as a shortstop.

■ All of the New York Mets runs in a 16-4 win over the Houston Astros on July 27, 1985, were unearned. Houston made five errors in the game.

■ Harry Heilmann won the American League batting title every other year from 1921–27.

■ Of Hank Aaron's four home run titles, three were won with a total of 44, which was also his uniform number.

■ O. J. Simpson and Marcus Allen each starred at running back at the University of Southern California, each won a Heisman Trophy, and each gained 697 yards in his rookie NFL season.

■ In the 1962 World Series, the New York Yankees won Games 1, 3, 5, and 7, and the San Francisco Giants took Games 2, 4, and 6.
    Checkerboard wins have also marked the 1909 World Series, and the NBA Finals in 1952, 1954, 1960, 1970, and 1974.

■ In 1953, twins Johnny and Eddie O'Brien each appeared in 89 games for the Pittsburgh Pirates, as rookie infielders.

■ The fewest yards gained rushing in an NFL or AFL game is minus 53, by the Detroit Lions in 1943. The fewest yards gained passing in a game is minus 53, by the Denver Broncos in 1967.

◾ Eddie Mathews and Hank Aaron, Braves' teammates for over a decade, hit their 500th homers on July 14, one year apart.

◾ Through the 1990 World Cup, England was the only country in the world to win the competition *once*.

◾ The two times that Babe Ruth hit three home runs in a World Series game were in Game 4 of the 1926 Series at Sportsman's Park in St. Louis, and Game 4 of the 1928 Series, at Sportsman's Park.

◾ From 1972–80, the Super Bowl was won by a team whose starting quarterback wore #12.

◾ Billy Herman played in four World Series, in three-year intervals—1932, 1935, 1938, and 1941.

◾ From 1973–79, the worst regular season record the Washington Bullets compiled was their 44-38 in 1977–78— and that was the year that they won their only NBA title.

◾ The all-time record attendance for Chicago's Comiskey Park, set on May 20, 1973 for a doubleheader between the White Sox and the Minnesota Twins, is 55,555.

◾ In 1975, the University of California football team gained 2,522 yards rushing and 2,522 yards passing.

◾ During his record 56-game hitting streak in 1941, Joe DiMaggio collected 56 singles and scored 56 runs.

3
CHANGE

10 OCCASIONS THAT WERE NOT A SIGN OF THINGS TO COME

■ In his first major league at-bat, New York Giants pitcher Hoyt Wilhelm hit a home run. (He hit no more for the rest of his 21-year career.)

■ The U.S.A. advanced to the semifinals of the first World Cup, in 1930. (They have not been back to the semifinals since, and in 1990 qualified for the Cup competition for the first time since 1950.)

■ On October 7, 1916, the Cumberland College football team's first play of the game was a rush that gained a respectable three yards. (It was their biggest rushing gain of the whole afternoon and they lost 222-0 to Georgia Tech, the worst rout in major college football history.)

■ An American was the first to hold the official world ski jumping record, in 1924. (No American has held it since.)

■ The Chicago Cubs showed promise of a dynasty when they won back-to-back World Series in 1907 and 1908. (They have not won one since.)

■ The Cubs' American League soulmates, the Boston Red Sox, were also dynasty-bound when they went 4-for-4 in World Series play in a seven-year span during the 1910s. (They have not won another one, and are 0-for-4 in Series play since then.)

■ Jockey Eddie Arcaro lost his first 250 races. (He went on to win two Triple Crowns, five Kentucky Derbies, six Belmonts, six Preaknesses, and a total of almost 5,000 races.)

■ On September 17, 1967, the New Orleans Saints scored a touchdown on the opening kickoff of their first regular season game of their first NFL season. (They went on to lose that game to the Los Angeles Rams, and then have 20 consecutive losing seasons.)

■ In his first NFL game, Chicago Bear Walter Payton carried the ball eight times for a total of zero yards. (He went on to become the all-time leading rusher in NFL history.)

■ Mike Parrott of the Seattle Mariners won on Opening Day, 1980. (He finished the season with a record of 1-16.)

THERE'S GOOD NEWS AND THERE'S BAD NEWS: HAPPY ACHIEVEMENTS DEFLATED BY LESS HAPPY ONES

An athlete may win the battle but lose the war; will perform spectacularly and end up with nothing to show for it; will achieve success on the field and, off the field, have it taken away.

The good news surrounding the following events was doused by bad news that was at least as, and usually more, profound.

■ The USFL won its pivotal antitrust suit against the NFL in 1986. The new league had asked for $1,690,000,000 in treble damages; they were awarded $1, tripled to $3. The league disbanded.

■ On the 1956 day that he pitched his World Series perfect game, New York Yankee Don Larsen was notified that his estranged wife, Vivian, had filed a court action seeking to withhold his Series money. She charged that Larsen was delinquent in his support payments.

■ On September 15, 1969, St. Louis Cardinals pitcher Steve Carlton set a record for a nine-inning game by striking out 19 New York Mets, including outfielder Ron Swoboda twice. In each of Swoboda's other two at-bats, however, he hit a two-run homer, and the Mets beat Carlton, 4-3.

■ Ram's Horn finished in the money in the 1905 Kentucky Derby, taking third place. It might have been a distinguished finish except that only three horses ran in the Derby that year.

■ In 1966, American balloonist Nicholas Plantanida set the unofficial altitude record—23.45 miles—but died during the attempt.

■ On August 6, 1926, American Gertrude Ederle became the first woman to swim the English Channel. Her world record time of 14 hours, 31 minutes was two hours faster than the men's record. Tragically, she became deaf as a result of her Channel swim.

■ In 1977, Larry Biittner, an outfielder-infielder, once got to pitch an inning for the Chicago Cubs. He struck out the side, but also gave up six runs, for a lifetime ERA of 54.00.

■ The Gordon Gin Company has a standing offer, until the year 2000, to award $1 million to any athlete who wins two U.S. Opens. Unfortunately, the Gordon Gin Company means tennis's U.S. Open *and* golf's U.S. Open.

■ The 1960 New York Yankees recorded a team batting

average of .338, the highest ever for a World Series, outscored their opponents, the Pittsburgh Pirates, 55-27, and outhit them 91-60—and lost. (Looked at another way, the 1960 Pirates recorded a team ERA of 7.11—the third-worst ever in a World Series—and won.)

■ The Boston Bruins were 17-0-2 against the Philadelphia Flyers in their previous 19 meetings at Boston Garden and had the home ice advantage for the 1974 Stanley Cup finals—and lost. The 1988 New York Mets were 10-1 against the Los Angeles Dodgers during the regular season, and lost to them in the National League Championship Series.

■ The longest known tennis point ever played took 51½ minutes, in a match between 11-year-olds Cari Hagey and Collette Kavanaugh at the 1977 Anaheim junior championships. Kavanaugh won the point but lost the match.

■ Michael Jordan's 63 points against the Boston Celtics in Game 2 of the first round of the 1986 playoffs set a postseason record, but his Chicago Bulls were still swept in three games.

■ On April 23, 1964, Ken Johnson of the Houston Colt .45s became the first pitcher in history to throw a nine-inning complete game no-hitter and lose. He was beaten, 1-0, by the Cincinnati Reds.

■ "Shoeless" Joe Jackson hit a robust .382 in 1920. However, it was his last year in baseball because he was banned for life for taking part in helping to fix the 1919 World Series.

■ Johnny Gross won his super middleweight bout over Mike Caminiti in May 1989, but lapsed into a coma an hour later and died on January 28, 1990.

THERE'S BAD NEWS AND THERE'S GOOD NEWS: NOT-SO-HAPPY MOMENTS OFFSET BY SOMEWHAT HAPPIER ONES

■ In 1969, Penny Tweedy lost a coin flip for the right to choose the first foal of Bold Ruler. In compensation, Tweedy was given the first choice the following year. She picked a foal named Secretariat.

■ In 1903, the Pittsburgh Pirates lost the World Series to the Boston Red Sox but received more money per player ($1,316) than the winners ($1,182) because the Pirate owner gave his share to the team.

■ The embarrassing record for the fewest field goals made (207) in a seven-game NBA Final is held by Syracuse in the 1955 series against Fort Wayne. Syracuse still won the title.

■ On Thanksgiving 1942, Boston College's undefeated football team was heavily favored to beat Holy Cross at Fenway Park. In a stunning upset, Holy Cross crushed BC 55-12. In no mood to celebrate, the Eagles canceled their postgame party at the Cocoanut Grove nightclub. They ended up missing a massive fire that broke out at the club that night and took the lives of 491 people.

■ In 1982, Rickey Henderson was caught stealing a major league record 42 times. However, this was overshadowed by his more significant feat, stealing a major league record 130 bases.

■ Tom Okker lost the men's singles final of the 1968 U.S. Open to Arthur Ashe. However, Ashe was an amateur at the time and thus could receive no prize money, so Okker got the first-place check of $14,000.

■ New York Yankees pitcher Whitey Ford lost more World Series games than anyone else, but he also won more than anyone else. Overall, he was 10-8 and had a Series ERA of

2.71. Similarly, Nolan Ryan has the record for issuing the most career walks but also the most career strikeouts, and Cy Young holds the record for most career losses (313) but, more significantly, most wins (511).

■ Jacqueline Pung had the lowest total in the 1957 U.S. Open but signed a scorecard that stated incorrectly that she had gotten a five at the fourth hole, not a six. While her total score was correct, Pung was disqualified. The sympathetic members of Winged Foot took up a collection for Pung that eventually totaled more than $3,000. The first-prize check for winning the Open was $1,800.

■ In 1981, the Detroit Pistons lost the coin flip for the #1 pick to the Dallas Mavericks. With the first pick, Dallas chose Mark Aguirre. With the second pick, the Pistons chose Isiah Thomas.

■ Lars Hall of Sweden won the Olympic modern pentathlon in 1952 when the horse he drew turned up lame, and the substitute he was given turned out to be the best horse in Finland.

■ Here is perhaps the finest example of an athlete losing the battle and winning the war—almost literally: after boxer Eugene Criqui of France was struck in the jaw by a German bullet during World War I, a silver plate was attached to the shattered bone. After the war, the plate actually helped Criqui resist punches and he went on to win the world welterweight title.

FINALLY, THERE'S GOOD NEWS AND THERE'S BAD NEWS—AND THEN THERE'S GOOD NEWS ONCE AGAIN

■ When the 1962 AFL title game between the Dallas Texans and the Houston Oilers went into overtime, Dallas won the coin toss. In a moment of paramount stupidity, they proceeded to give up both the ball and the wind.

Dallas still won.

CHANGING NAMES

Cassius Clay and Lew Alcindor are the two most prominent American athletes to have changed their names, retitling themselves Muhammad Ali and Kareem Abdul-Jabbar, respectively, when they became Black Muslims. Athletes have changed their names for religious and other reasons—self-promotion, peace of mind, to honor someone else. Many other things in the realm of sport—institutions, prizes, even sports themselves—have changed their names.

◼ Boxer Marvin Hagler officially changed his name to Marvelous Marvin Hagler.

◼ Cornelius McGillicuddy was the given name of Philadelphia Athletics owner and manager Connie Mack.

◼ Los Angeles Laker Michael Thompson had the spelling of his first name legally changed to Mychal.

◼ Basketball star Walt Hazzard became Mahdi Abdul-Rahman after he graduated from UCLA. He later changed his name back to Walt Hazzard.

◼ Lexington, a great thoroughbred racehorse and sire from the late 1800's, was originally named Darley, after the Darley Arabian, one of the three original sires of all modern thoroughbreds. After racing under the name Darley as a three-year-old, the horse was purchased under the

72

condition that his name be changed to Lexington, for Lexington, Kentucky.

■ After 1935, the Downtown Athletic Club Trophy was renamed the Heisman Trophy. (Jay Berwanger, the award's first recipient, was the only one to win the Downtown Athletic Club Trophy.)

■ Andre Rouisimoff and Terry Bollea became, respectively, Andre the Giant and Hulk Hogan, professional wrestlers.

■ Oakland Athletics owner Charlie O. Finley wanted star pitcher Vida Blue to change his first name to "True." Blue refused and told Finley that if he liked the name so much, he should call himself True O. Finley.

■ Miami Dolphins wide receiver Mark Duper went to court in 1985 and changed his name to Mark Super Duper.

■ Stanford University's athletic teams, called the Indians since 1930, were renamed the Cardinal in 1972 because of protests by Native Americans.

■ Tennis player Richard Raskind changed his name to Renee Richards after his sex change operation. In her first women's tournament—the La Jolla Championships—before her previous identity was discovered, she played under the name Renee Clark.

■ The New York Jets used to be called the New York Titans, the New England Patriots were the Boston Patriots, the California Angels were the Los Angeles Angels, and the New York Yankees were the New York Highlanders.

■ Philadelphia 76er gunner and playground legend Lloyd Free changed his name to World B. Free.

■ In 1957, Oklahoma A&M became Oklahoma State. In 1967, Texas Western, whose basketball team won the NCAA finals the year before, became the University of Texas El Paso (UTEP).

⬛ The father of Olympic cross-country skier Bill Koch, exasperated with mispronunciations of his name, had it legally changed to Frederick Coke Is It.

⬛ Before it opened in 1965, the Houston Astrodome was called Harris County Domed Stadium. The Astros themselves were called the Colt .45s from 1962–65.

⬛ Golfer Phil McGleno changed his name in 1978, combining the nickname of a friend and his mother's maiden name, to arrive at Mac O'Grady.

⬛ Tennis used to be known as lawn tennis. Before that, it was *sphairistike*.

⬛ Heavyweight champion Jack Dempsey, born William Harrison Dempsey, started fighting in 1914 under the name Kid Blackie.

⬛ With the addition of Arizona and Arizona State in 1978, the Pacific-8 became the Pacific-10 (Pac-10).

⬛ Notre Dame's athletic teams used to be known as the Catholics and later the Ramblers. They officially became the Fighting Irish in 1927.

⬛ When José Gonzalez was traded in 1985 from the St. Louis Cardinals to the San Francisco Giants in the Jack Clark deal, Gonzalez decided to use his mother's maiden name and became José Uribe. He has come to be known as the genuine "player to be named later."

19 OF THE MOST DRAMATIC TURNAROUNDS AND COMEBACKS

⬛ In 1978–79, the Boston Celtics were 29-53. In June of

1979, they signed Larry Bird. In their next season, they were 61-21.

■ In 1916, the football team from tiny Centre (Danville, Kentucky) College lost 68-0 to the University of Kentucky. In 1917, Centre came back and won 3-0.

■ Heavyweight Henry Cooper of England lost the first three title fights of his career, for the British, Commonwealth, and European titles. He later won all three.

■ In 1928, the New York Giants were 4-7-2. In 1929, with the University of Michigan's great star, Benny Friedman, at quarterback, the Giants went 13-1-1.

■ Evonne Goolagong lost in the first round of the 1970 Wimbledon. The next year, she won the tournament.

■ At the other extreme, Manuel Santana won Wimbledon in 1966, but was beaten in the first round the following year by Charlie Pasarell. Santana is the only champion to have been eliminated so unceremoniously.

■ A few weeks before the U.S. Olympic hockey team upset the Soviets at the 1980 Olympics, the U.S.S.R. beat the Americans by seven goals.

■ Italy's Paolo Rossi scored three goals in the 1982 World Cup semifinals, and six goals overall. Only nine weeks earlier, he was still serving a multiple-year suspension by the Italian Football Federation for a 1980 betting scandal (though he'd been found not guilty by the Italian courts).

■ Walter Johnson won Game 7 of the 1924 World Series. In the 1925 World Series, he lost Game 7.

■ Bobby Lowe of Boston's National League team was 0-for-6 in the first game of a May 30, 1894 doubleheader. In the second game, he hit four home runs.

■ Dave Schultz, the chief Philadelphia Flyers goon of the first half of the 1970s, became the commissioner of the

Atlantic Coast Hockey League and tried to rid the league of fighting.

■ In 1939, Stanford University's football team lost every conference game. They hired a new head coach, Clark Shaughnessy, who experimented with a T-formation. Stanford responded with an unbeaten season and a Rose Bowl win over Nebraska, and helped to popularize the T-formation.

■ Between 1930 and 1939, the St. Louis Browns drew an average of 115,000 fans per year. When the franchise moved to Baltimore in 1954, the team's attendance in the first year almost topped the total for that entire decade in St. Louis.

■ Martin Gison of the Philippines, who finished fourth in the small-bore rifle (prone) competition at the 1936 Olympics, survived the Bataan death march in World War II and competed again in 1948.

■ Dale Ellis averaged 8.2 points per game in three seasons with the Dallas Mavericks. In 1986, he was traded to the Seattle Supersonics and in his first season there averaged 24.9 points a game.

■ Al Singer won the lightweight boxing title with a first-round (1:46) knockout of Sammy Mandell on July 17, 1930. Singer lost the lightweight title on November 14, 1930, in a first-round knockout by Tony Canzoneri (1:06).

■ American diver Bruce Kimball was known as "The Comeback Kid" because he almost died as a result of a 1981 automobile accident with a drunk driver but recovered to win the 1984 Olympic silver medal in platform diving. In 1988, Kimball killed two teenagers in Florida while driving drunk. He was sentenced to 17 years in prison.

■ After clinching the Eastern League pennant in mid-

August of 1884, the Wilmington Quicksteps replaced Philadelphia in the Union Association. They proceeded to compile the worst record in the history of the major leagues.

■ In 1833, Irish heavyweight champion Simon Byrne demolished Sandy McKay, who died from the beating. Three years later, Byrne died as a result of his 98-round beating at the hands of English Champion James "Deaf" Burke.

2 GRADUAL TURNAROUNDS

■ The Detroit Pistons ushered in the 1980s with a then-NBA record losing streak of 21 games, and saw the decade out with their first NBA championship.

■ In their first season, 1962, the New York Mets compiled the worst record in 20th century baseball, 40-120. At decade's end, the Mets won 100 regular season games and the World Series.

1 EXCRUCIATINGLY GRADUAL TURNAROUND

■ In 1883, the Philadelphia Phillies, in their first season in the National League, were last with a 17-81 record, while Baltimore was last in the American Association at 28-68. One hundred years later, in 1983, Baltimore beat the Phillies in the World Series.

DEFUNCT OLYMPIC EVENTS

Ancient Olympic competitions tested not only athletic skills but creative, intellectual, and rhetorical powers as well. Poetry, music, and eloquence were just three of the "events" contested at the ancient Games.

The modern-day Games are supposedly devoted to testing athletic prowess exclusively, though many surprising events have found their way onto the Olympic docket, primarily in the earliest Games—in Athens in 1896, Paris in 1900, St. Louis in 1904, and Athens again, site of the Interim Olympic Games in 1906. The following events have since been removed from the Olympic program, often after one appearance and usually with good reason.

■ Live pigeon shooting (1900). This is the only event in Olympic history in which animals were killed intentionally. Leon de Lunden of Belgium won the gold medal, with 21 birds killed, one more than Frenchman Maurice Faure bagged.

■ A 100m freestyle swim that was only open to members of the Greek navy (1896).

■ Tug-of-war (1900–20). In 1908, after a humiliating first-round loss to the British, the Americans protested that the British had used illegal spiked boots. When the protest was disallowed, the Americans withdrew.

■ Croquet (1900).

■ Dueling pistols (1906).

■ Plunge for distance (1904).

■ Skeleton (1928, 1948). This event was held only when the Olympics were staged in St. Moritz, Switzerland. The competitor rode a heavy sled headfirst and steered by shifting his weight and dragging his feet. American John

Heaton took the silver medal in the skeleton both times, 20 years apart.

■ Underwater swimming (1900).

■ The standing broad jump (1900–12).

■ The standing long jump (1900–12).

■ The standing triple jump (1900 and 1904).

■ Motor boating (1908).

RULES AND CONVENTIONS THAT CHANGED

■ For the first two years of the Indianapolis 500, cars lined up in the order that their entries were received. In 1914, a drawing was held. In 1915, cars lined up for the first time in order of qualifying speed.

■ The Preakness used to be scheduled before the Kentucky Derby.

■ In 1903, and from 1919 to 1921, the World Series was a best-of-nine games affair.

■ In the first Rose Bowl in 1902, a touchdown counted for five points, field goals five points, and conversions one point. The game was played on a 110-yard field at Tournament Park.

■ In 1893, the distance from the mound to home plate was extended from 50 feet to its present distance, 60′6″.

■ Until the 1915–16 season, it was against the rules for a

basketball player to shoot off the dribble. In 1923–24, the designated foul shooter was eliminated; after that, a fouled player had to shoot his own foul shots.

■ In 1920, all "freak" pitches, including the spitball, were outlawed, though pitchers who relied on that pitch and were already in the major leagues—and *only* they—were allowed to continue throwing the pitch.

■ Golf's U.S. Open used to conclude with a double round of 36 holes.

■ Until 1953–54, if an NBA player committed three personal fouls in a quarter, he had to sit out the remainder of the period.

■ The winner of a running race used to be the first person to cross the line; now, the winner is the first person to reach the finish line. In the 1932 Olympic 100m, American sprinter Ralph Metcalfe finished in a dead heat with teammate Eddie Tolan, but a split second later, pictures showed that Tolan's chest had crossed the line while Metcalfe's had not yet done so. Tolan won the gold medal, Metcalfe the silver. Under the current rules, they would have shared the gold.

■ There is now an age limit in Olympic gymnastics competition requiring that men be at least 16 years of age, and women at least 15. Had this rule been in effect in 1976, Nadia Comaneci would not have been deemed old enough to compete.

■ Before baseball adopted the nine-inning-game rule in 1857, the first one to score 21 runs was the winner.

■ Until 1937, there was a jump ball after every basket in NCAA play. The National Basketball League did away with the jump ball after every basket in the 1939–40 season.

■ In 19th-century baseball, runners were credited with a stolen base if they went from first to third on a single, and walks were counted as hits when computing batting average.

▪ Wimbledon, the U.S. Championships, and the Davis Cup all used a Challenge Round. The winner of the Challenge Round would face the defending champion to determine the next champion. The America's Cup sailing competition still uses the Challenge method.

▪ The PGA tournament used to be match play.

▪ On December 26, 1985, the European Parliament was petitioned to ban the increasingly popular sport of "dwarf throwing."

ALICE IN WONDERLAND MEETS THE SPORTS WORLD: 11 MIRROR IMAGES AND THINGS IN REVERSE

▪ Ma Chin-shan of Taiwan, who competed in pistol shooting at the 1964 Tokyo Olympics, asked to return to mainland China to live with his parents. He is the only Olympic athlete ever to defect *to* a communist country.

▪ The greatest number of interceptions quarterback Sammy Baugh threw in a single game was four. As a defensive back, Baugh is co-holder of the NFL record for interceptions in a single game, with four.

▪ The heart of Frenchman Joseph Guillemot, the 5,000m champion at the 1920 Olympics, was located on the right side of his chest.

▪ The McKeever twins, Mike and Marlin, were all-conference football players for USC in 1959. Mike wore uniform #68, and Marlin wore #86.

■ In 1963, at 23 years and two months, Jack Nicklaus became the youngest golfer to win the Masters (until Seve Ballesteros usurped that distinction in 1980). In 1986, when he was 46, Nicklaus became the oldest player to win the Masters.

■ St. Louis Cardinals pitcher Bob Gibson lost his first World Series decision, won his next seven, and then lost his last decision.

■ Boxer Nelson Azumah changed his name to Azumah Nelson.

■ In 1976, Don Gullett pitched the opening game of the World Series against the New York Yankees. The following year, he pitched the opening game of the Series *for* the Yankees.

■ Many trapshooters use alcohol or tranquilizers to slow their heart rates and steady their hands. Paul Cerutti, 65, a trapshooter from Monaco, was disqualified at the 1976 Olympics for taking amphetamines.

■ In May of 1931, Swiss Auguste Piccard and a companion became the first humans to reach the stratosphere when they ballooned to 51,961 feet over Augsburg, Germany. In January of 1960, Piccard's son, Jacques, and a companion, in a bathyscope, reached the record depth of 6.78 miles in the Pacific Ocean, southwest of Guam.

■ "Australian doubles" is what Americans call it when tennis partners, on serve, both stand on the server's half of the court. "Americans doubles" is what Australians call it when tennis partners, on serve, both stand on the server's half of the court.

11 COMMONLY FLOUTED BASEBALL RULES

Although the game of baseball is structure incarnate, its rule book a Baedeker that speaks to virtually every on-field occasion, the game conducts itself with a degree of elasticity. Umpires, for instance, routinely allow the "phantom" double play, in which the shortstop makes the relay to first base and avoids colliding with the oncoming runner—both without actually touching second base. Third-base coaches who stray from the coaching box to wave a player home or hold him up may literally be breaking Rule 4.05.b.2, but a commentary in the book of *Official Baseball Rules* (published by *The Sporting News*, 1989 Edition) suggests that there is no need to enforce this rule strictly unless the opposing manager complains. And while Rule 2.00 does its best to define the strike zone, God knows that no two umpires call the same one. Ask any player.

Various edicts from the rule book are commonly ignored by players, coaches, and umpires—sometimes with good reason, sometimes with malice aforethought.

■ From Rule 3.09: "Players of opposing teams shall not fraternize at any time while in uniform."

■ Rule 3.02: "No player shall intentionally discolor or damage the ball by rubbing it with soil, rosin, paraffin, licorice, sand-paper, emery-paper or other foreign substance."

■ From Rule 8.04: "When the bases are unoccupied, the pitcher shall deliver the ball to the batter within 20 seconds after he receives the ball. Each time the pitcher delays the game by violating this rule, the umpire shall call 'Ball.'"

■ From Rule 3.01.e: "After a home run is hit out of the playing grounds, the umpire shall not deliver a new ball to the pitcher or the catcher until the batter hitting the home run has crossed the plate."

■ From Rule 3.17: "Players on the disabled list are permitted to participate in pre-game activity and sit on the bench during a game but may not take part in any activity during the game such as... bench-jockeying."

■ From Rule 1.10.a: "The bat shall be one piece of solid wood."

■ From Rule 6.02.b: "Umpires may grant a hitter's request for 'Time' once he is in the batter's box, but the umpire should eliminate hitters walking out of the batter's box without reason. If umpires are not lenient, batters will understand that they are in the batter's box and they must remain there until the ball is pitched."

■ From Rule 9.05 (General Instructions to Umpires): "Umpires, on the field, should not indulge in conversation with players... and do not talk to the coach [in the coaching box] on duty."

■ From Rule 5.09.e: "When... a foul ball is not caught ... the umpire shall not put [a new] ball in play until all runners have retouched their bases."

■ From Rule 9.05 (General Instructions to Umpires): "You no doubt are going to make mistakes, but never attempt to 'even up' after having made one."

■ From Rule 8.02.d: "To pitch at a batter's head is unsportsmanlike and highly dangerous. It should be—and is—condemned by everybody."

IT MAKES NO DIFFERENCE TO THEM: SPORTS FIGURES UNFLUSTERED BY A CHANGE IN CIRCUMSTANCES

■ Ethiopia's Abebe Bikila won the 1960 marathon running barefoot. He defended his title in 1964 running in shoes and socks.

■ In 1929, Notre Dame's new football stadium was under construction, so the team played no games at home. They went 9-0.

■ As a junior at Illinois, Andy Phillips was an All-America basketball player in 1943. Phillips then spent three years in the Marine Corps. He returned for his senior year in 1946–47 and again was an All-America.

■ Irina Rodnina of the U.S.S.R. won four skating pairs titles with Aleksei Ulanov, from 1969–72, then six more with her husband, Aleksandr Zaitsev, from 1973–78.

■ Between 1960 and 1965, Australian tennis star Roy Emerson won six successive French Open doubles titles with five different partners.

Françoise Durr of France was runner-up in six Wimbledon doubles finals with five partners.

■ Playing in an afternoon game for the New York Mets on August 4, 1982, Joel Youngblood got a single off of Chicago Cubs pitcher Ferguson Jenkins. During the game, Youngblood was traded to the Montreal Expos. He flew to Philadelphia, and that evening got a single off of Philadelphia Phillies pitcher Steve Carlton.

■ Tennis partners Adrian Quist and Frank Bromwich won the Australian men's doubles titles from 1938–40. The tournament was then suspended for five years for World

War II. When it resumed, Quist and Bromwich won five more doubles titles.

■ Where the following major leaguers played had no effect on their power. They each hit exactly the same number of career home runs at home as they did on the road:

Wally Berger, 121 at home (mostly Braves Field), 121 away;

Willie Jones, 95 at home (mostly Connie Mack Stadium), 95 away;

Charles Gehringer, 92 at home (mostly Briggs Stadium), 92 away.

■ Moses Malone won the NBA's MVP Award with the Houston Rockets in 1981–82. He was traded to the Philadelphia 76ers the following year and again won the MVP Award.

■ Despite not having their star first baseman Lou Gehrig in the lineup for the first time in 2,130 consecutive games, the New York Yankee juggernaut went out and crushed the Detroit Tigers, 22-2, on May 2, 1939, and Gehrig's replacement, Babe Dahlgren, hit a home run.

■ Boxer Craig Bodzianowski won a 10-round decision over Francis Sargent. Bodzianowski was later involved in a motorcycle accident and lost part of his leg. With an artificial leg, Bodzianowski continued his boxing career. On December 14, 1985, he once again faced Sargent and this time knocked him out in the second round.

■ In a 1912 football game against Army, Carlisle's Jim Thorpe scored on a 92-yard run that was called back on a penalty. On the next play, Thorpe scored on a 97-yard run.

■ In 1974, baseball commissioner Bowie Kuhn banned New York Yankees owner George Steinbrenner from baseball for a year for making illegal contributions to Richard Nixon's presidential campaign. Steinbrenner adapted to his new situation by blistering the team on tape recorder and then making manager Bill Virdon play it for the team.

2 ATHLETES WHO SHOULD HAVE BEEN MORE FLUSTERED BY A CHANGE IN CIRCUMSTANCES

■ In 1984, Puerto Rico pulled out of the 4x400m relay finals when it learned that Margaret de Jesus, who was not a team member, had substituted for her twin sister, Madeline de Jesus, in the qualifying heat. Madeline had injured herself in the long jump.

ATHLETES WHO HELPED LEAD TO RULE CHANGES

■ In 1910, Washington Senator Germany Schaefer "stole" first base. With a runner on third, Schaefer, on first, stole second to try to draw a throw. When the catcher did not throw, Schaefer ran back to first. (He would steal second again, this time drawing a throw and allowing the runner to score from third.) A new rule, 7.08.i, was instituted to prevent stealing of a previously-held base.

■ In the 1949 British Open, runner-up Harry Bradshaw's drive on the fifth hole of the second round wound up in a broken bottle. He had to play it as it lay, but the incident led to a change in the golf rules.

■ In college and pro basketball, the dominance of certain big men has caused several significant new rules. St. John's All-America center Harry Boykoff, George Mikan, Wilt Chamberlain, Bill Russell, and Lew Alcindor, to name a few, each helped to inspire crucial changes, including defensive and offensive goaltending, establishing the three-second rule, widening the lane, and a "no-dunk" rule in college (since revoked).

■ The ability of Maurice "The Rocket" Richard and the Montreal Canadiens in the 1950s to score routinely several goals during the power play inspired the 1956 rule change in which the power play, on a minor penalty, would not continue if a goal was scored by the team with the man advantage.

■ Ilie Nastase's on-court behavior helped cause the Association of Tennis Professionals to institute a code of conduct.

■ Tommy McCarthy perfected the ploy of letting an infield fly drop with runners on first and second base and fewer than two outs, and then starting a double play. This led to the infield fly rule.

■ St. Louis Cardinal Conrad Dobler's play led to a rule change stating that an offensive lineman could not reach over his head with his arms. This was designed to prevent, among other things, the "throat block."

■ The presence of Dummy Hoy, a deaf major leaguer who played in the late 19th century, prompted umpires to begin using hand signals for their calls.

■ On November 21, 1953, Notre Dame's football team, which became known as the "Fainting Irish," twice faked injuries to stop the clock. Rules were changed to prevent feigned injuries.

■ The NFL's "taunting rule" prohibiting prolonged, excessive, or premeditated celebrations was spurred by the sack dances of New York Jets defensive end Mark Gastineau.

A ROLLERCOASTER RIDE

Most durable athletes are known for their ability to look victory and defeat straight in the eye and treat them equally. Some athletes have needed to overdevelop this capacity because they have experienced the highs and lows of sport in particularly dramatic fashion. Minor league left-handed pitcher Steve Dalkowski was legendary for his blazing fastball, averaging 15 strikeouts per nine innings in his first five seasons in professional baseball. Unfortunately, he was just as legendary for his terrible control and averaged 17 walks per nine innings. Arm problems in 1963 slowed him down and he never made it to the major leagues.

Here are some of the more schizophrenic moments and teams and players from the sports world.

■ In 1972–73, the Philadelphia 76ers recorded the worst season record in NBA history, 9-73. Six years before, the team recorded what was at the time the best NBA record ever, 68-13. (The 1971–72 Los Angeles Lakers were 69-13.) Leroy Ellis and John Q. Trapp played on both the best (1971–72 Lakers) and worst (1972–73 Philadelphia) teams in NBA history.

■ In his collegiate debut in 1969, University of Florida quarterback John Reaves threw for five touchdowns, an NCAA record for a first game. Six weeks later, Reaves threw for nine interceptions, a record for most interceptions in a game. His NFL counterpart, Chicago Cardinals quarterback Jim Hardy, threw for a record eight interceptions on September 24, 1950, and the next week passed for six touchdowns, his career high.

■ One competitor at the 1960 Portland City Amateur golf tournament missed his first tee shot, then hit another one in the lake, and on his third tee shot got a hole-in-one.

■ In the 1927 singles final of the Cannes championship between French tennis stars Henri Cochet and Jacques Brugnon, Cochet lost the first set badly, 6-1. He won the next two sets easily, 6-1, 6-0. He lost the fourth set badly, 6-1. He won the fifth and final set easily, 6-0.

■ In 1983, Pat Corrales was fired while managing a first-place team, the Philadelphia Phillies, and rehired to take over a last-place team, the Cleveland Indians.

■ On September 14, 1986, San Francisco Giant Bob Brenly tied a major league record by committing four errors in one inning, then hit two home runs, one in the bottom of the ninth inning, to help win the game, 7-6.

■ Tom Brown played outfield and first base in 61 games for the last-place Washington Senators in 1963, and played safety for the Green Bay Packers in their two Super Bowl victories.

■ Philadelphia Phillie Mike Schmidt had a club-high .467 batting average in the 1983 National League Championship Series, and a club-low .050 in the World Series.

■ In 1983, Lamarr Hoyt led the majors in wins with 24. The next year he tied for the major league lead in losses. Steve Carlton accomplished this feat in the National League, leading in wins in 1972, with 27, and in losses the following year, with 20.

■ The 1954 Cleveland Indians set an American League record for most wins in the regular season (111), and then got swept by the New York Giants in the World Series.

The 1988–9 Los Angeles Lakers set an NBA record for consecutive playoff wins by sweeping their first three opponents, and then got swept in the finals by the Detroit Pistons.

The St. Louis Blues swept the Philadelphia Flyers and Los Angeles Kings in 1969, then got swept in the Stanley Cup finals by the Montreal Canadiens.

■ Casey Stengel managed the New York Yankees when they became the only franchise to win five world championships in a row, and won a record 10 pennants with them. He also managed the worst team in modern baseball history, the 1962 Mets, and finished his career with three last-place finishes. He retired in 1965, with the Mets again in last place.

■ In college football bowl games from 1967–74, the University of Alabama under coach Paul "Bear" Bryant was 0-7-1. In their next—and his last—eight bowl games, they were 7-1.

■ The Cleveland Indians are the only team in history to have a winning season (1986) between two 100-loss seasons (1985, 1987).

■ When NBC tennis broadcaster Bud Collins was coach of the Brandeis University tennis team, one of his players was future radical Yippie leader Abbie Hoffman, whom Collins claimed was one of the most conservative baseliners ever.

■ Hall of Famer Red Ruffing spent several years with the second-division Boston Red Sox, where he compiled season records of 9-18, 6-15, 5-13, 10-25, and 9-22, and then with the perennially contending New York Yankees, where he compiled season records of 18-7, 19-11, 20-12, 20-7, 21-7, 21-7, 15-6, 14-7. . . .

■ Buff Donelli simultaneously coached a football team from the college ranks, Duquesne University, and from the NFL, the Pittsburgh Steelers, for one month in the 1941 season. Duquesne went undefeated, while the Steelers did not win a game under Donelli.

■ Linebacker Larry Ball and defensive lineman Maulty Moore both played for the 1972 Miami Dolphins (17-0) and the 1976 Tampa Bay Buccaneers (0-14).

■ In the 1972 Olympic Nordic combined event, Japan's

Hideki Nakano of Japan finished first in the ski jump and last in the 15km race. (He finished in 13th place overall.)

THE 19 MOST INTRIGUING DEFUNCT LEAGUES

If you lived through the past two decades and never heard of the International Boxing League or Major League Rodeo, it doesn't mean that you weren't paying attention. Neither league was a groundbreaking idea; neither is around any more. But they are not alone in the dead league office. Here are some of the more unusual, and even briefly successful, professional sports leagues that are no longer.

- **All-American Girls Professional Baseball League**, 1943–54.
  Notable players: first basewoman Dottie Kamenshek (called a major league-caliber fielder by New York Yankee Wally Pipp); Sophie Kurys (stole 201 bases in 1946). Jimmie Foxx was the manager of the Fort Wayne Daisies.
  Innovations: Athletes were sent to charm school during spring training; professional chaperones were hired; use of a ball sized between a baseball and a softball.
  Final championship: The Kalamazoo Lassies defeated the Fort Wayne Daisies, September 5, 1954.

- **International Track Association**, 1973–76.
  Notable athletes: Jim Ryun, Ben Jipcho, Brian Oldfield, Bob Beamon, Dave Wottle, Kip Keino, Bob Seagren, Wyomia Tyus.
  Innovations: Pacer lights on the inside of the track; co-ed 30-yard dashes; athletes wore singlets with corporate sponsors.
  Final championship: None.

■ **World Football League**, 1974–75; the league disbanded October 22, 1975, 10 weeks into its second season.

Notable players: Larry Csonka, Jim Kiick, Paul Warfield, Danny White, Anthony Davis.

Innovations: The "action point": after a touchdown, which was worth seven points, the ball was placed on the 2½-yard line, from where a run or a pass produced the action point (worth one point).

Final championship: The Birmingham Americans defeated the Florida Blazers, 22-21, in the World Bowl in Birmingham, Alabama, on December 5, 1974. Because the Birmingham team was in arrears, their uniforms were confiscated by the sheriff's department after the game.

■ **Players League**, major league baseball, 1890.

Notable players: Monte Ward, Old Hoss Radbourne, Ed Delahanty, Pete Browning, Charles Comiskey, Hugh Duffy.

Innovations: Players were part team owners and were to have shared in the profits, had there been any.

Champion: Boston, with an 81-48 record, was five games ahead of Brooklyn.

■ **Federal League**, major league baseball, 1914–15.

Notable players: Eddie Plank, Mordecai "Three Finger" Brown, Chief Bender, Joe Tinker, Edd Roush.

Innovations: Wrigley Field (known then as Weeghman Field) was built for the Federal League's Chicago Whales.

Final champion: Chicago, with an 86-66 record, finished percentage points ahead of St. Louis, at 87-67.

■ **World Team Tennis**, 1974–78.

Notable players: Billie Jean King, Ken Rosewall, Chris Evert, Jimmy Connors, Bjorn Borg, Martina Navratilova.

Innovations: The term "love" was eliminated; use of a four-point, no-ad scoring system; replacements allowed at any time; crowds were encouraged to be rowdy.

Final championship: The Los Angeles Strings defeated the Boston Lobsters three games to one in a best-of-five series that ended September 21, 1978.

■ **National Bowling League**, 1961–62.

Notable players: Carmen Salvino, Buzz Fazio, Tony Lindemann, Bud Horn, Bill Bunetta, Steve Nagy, Joe Joseph, Billy Golembiewski.

Innovations: There were two ways a player could score: by winning a match, and by earning bonus points for his score (e.g., a score of 210-219 earned one point; 220-229 earned two points, etc.; a 300 earned 10 points). Also, there was a wild-card substitution rule: when a player was faced with a shot that he was not sure of, the team captain could call in a "specialist" to roll for him—for instance, a lefty for a righty when pins were standing on the right side.

Final championship: The Detroit Thunderbirds defeated the Twin Cities Skippers three games to none in a best-of-five series that ended May 6, 1962, in Allen Park, Michigan.

■ **American Basketball Association**, 1967–76.

Notable players: Julius Erving, Moses Malone, George Gervin, Dan Issel, Artis Gilmore, Billy Cunningham, Rick Barry.

Innovations: A red, white, and blue ball; the three-point basket.

Final championship: The New York Nets defeated the Denver Nuggets, 112-106, May 13, 1976, taking the series four games to two. The Nets, Nuggets, Indiana Pacers, and San Antonio Spurs were accepted into the NBA.

■ **All-American Football Conference**, 1946–49.

Notable players: Lou Groza, Marion Motley, Otto Graham, Frankie Albert.

Final championship: The Cleveland Browns defeated the San Francisco 49ers, 21-7, on December 11,

1949, at Cleveland. Cleveland, San Francisco, and the Baltimore Colts were accepted into the NFL for the 1950 season.

■ **International Volleyball Association**, 1975–79.

Notable players: Mary Jo Peppler (1964 U.S. Olympian), Scott English (former NBA-ABA forward), Eileen Clancy (4'10", 90 pounds), Stan Gosciniak (league MVP).

Innovations: A Mexican franchise (the El Paso–Juarez Sol); men and women playing together (two of six players were required to be women); "designated switchers" (one man and one woman who could change positions on each point).

■ **World Hockey Association**, 1972–79.

Notable players: Bobby Hull, Gordie Howe, Derek Sanderson, Gerry Cheevers, Bernie Parent, Wayne Gretzky.

Innovations: No reserve clause; no option clauses in players' contracts.

Final championship: The Winnipeg Jets defeated the Edmonton Oilers 7-3 on May 20, 1979, to win the AVCO World Cup. Edmonton, Winnipeg, the Quebec Nordiques, and the Hartford Whalers were admitted into the NHL.

■ **North American Soccer League**, 1968–85.

The league was formed by the merger of the National Professional Soccer League and the United States Soccer Association. In 1971, three foreign clubs—Portuguesa of Brazil, Lanerossi-Vicenza of Italy, and Apollo of Greece—joined to compete against league members in cup competition, the results of which were included in league standings.

Notable players: Pelé, Giorgio Chinaglia, Franz Beckenbauer, Carlos Alberto, Kyle Rote, Jr., Shep Messing.

Innovations: The "shoot-out" tiebreaking procedure; abolition of the 107-year-old FIFA offsides rule: the league changed the demarcation from the midfield line to a line 35 yards from the opponent's goal.

Final championship: The Chicago Sting defeated the Toronto Blizzard, on October 13, 1984.

■ **United States Football League**, 1983–86.
   Notable players: Doug Flutie, Steve Young, Herschel Walker, Jim Kelly, Mike Rozier.
   Innovations: Spring schedule; instant replay for officiating.
   Final championship: The Baltimore Stars defeated the Oakland Invaders, 28-24, on July 14, 1985, at Giants Stadium, in East Rutherford, New Jersey.

■ **Women's Basketball League**, 1978–81.
   The league peaked with 14 teams, and finished with 8. In 1979–80, all 14 teams had male head coaches.
   Notable players: Nancy Lieberman, Ann Meyers, Molly "Machine Gun" Bolin, who scored 55 points in one game.
   Notable coaches: Butch van Breda Kolff, Larry Costello, Dean Meminger.
   Final championship: The Nebraska Wranglers defeated the Dallas Diamonds, 99-90, on April 20, 1981, at the Omaha Civic Auditorium, to take the best-of-five series.

■ **American Professional Slo-Pitch League**, slow-pitch softball, 1977–79.
   Notable players: Norm Cash, Jim Northup, Joe Pepitone, Benny Holt (who won the league's 1977 Triple Crown with 89 homers, 187 RBIs and a .690 batting average).
   Innovations: A deader ball was used in the final season to curb the offense of the Detroit Caesars, who had won the first two World Series; to lower scores, the base paths were extended to 70 feet, and the distance down the foul lines was made a minimum of 300 feet. Also, the first foul after two strikes meant a strikeout.

■ **American Football League**, 1960–69.
> Notable players: Joe Namath, Lance Alworth, Jim Otto, George Blanda, Nick Buoniconti, Billy Cannon, Jack Kemp.
>
> Innovations: Two-point conversions after touchdowns; players' names were displayed on the backs of their jerseys; the official time was determined by the scoreboard clock and not, as in the NFL, by an on-field official.
>
> Final championship: The Kansas City Chiefs defeated the Oakland Raiders, 17-7, on January 4, 1970. The Chiefs went on to upset the Minnesota Vikings, 23-7, in Super Bowl IV. All ten AFL teams were merged into the NFL.

■ **National Professional Golf League**, 1972.
> Notable players: Billy Casper, Sam Snead, Dow Finsterwald.
>
> Final championship: None was ever played.

■ **International Women's Professional Softball Association**, fast-pitch softball, 1976–77.
> Notable players: Joan Joyce (co-founder, along with Billie Jean King, and star pitcher), Rosie Black (who toured with a team called "The Queen and Her Maids").
>
> Innovations: Pitchers could not appear in consecutive games, a rule adopted mainly because of Joyce's prowess; use of a yellow ball and yellow bases.

■ **Intercontinental Football League**, which was announced in June of 1974 by NFL commissioner Pete Rozelle but never came into being. The league was to be made up of six teams and begin play in the spring of 1975. The six designated teams would have been: the Istanbul Conquerors; the Rome Gladiators; the Vienna Lippizaners; the Munich Lions; the West Berlin Bears; and the Barcelona Almovogeres.

HOW TIMES HAVE CHANGED:
8 FORMERLY COMMON THINGS THAT HAVE FADED INTO MEMORY

■ *The preeminence of the Olympics over war.* When an Olympic Games began in ancient times, wars were suspended for the duration of the competition. Today, the opposite is true: because of World War I, no Olympics were held in 1916; because of World War II, there were no Games in 1940 or 1944.

■ *Grass-court tennis tournaments.* There is only one professional grass-court tennis tournament still played in the United States, at Newport Casino in Rhode Island.

■ *Fights ending in a "no-decision."* In the early 20th century, fighters would routinely record as many as 50 to 100 no-decisions during their career. Middleweight champion Harry Greb, for example, won 112 fights, lost 8, drew 3, and registered 170 no-decisions.

■ *American shotputting supremacy.* The United States has won 15 Olympic gold medals in the event, swept the medals seven times, and held the world record from 1934 to 1976. But America has not won a shotputting gold medal since then.

■ *Rampant basketball violence.* In its early days, the professional game was so reckless that wire cages (hence the name "cagers") were built around courts to protect fans from violence. There was no out-of-bounds, the ball was always in play, players were routinely gashed by wire, and blood on the court was not uncommon. In Pennsylvania coal towns, miners would heat nails with their lamps and throw them at referees and opposing players. Some officials carried guns. The cage was eliminated in 1929.

■ *Pitchers hurling an entire doubleheader.* The last player to pitch two complete-game wins in one day was Dutch Levsen for the Cleveland Indians, on August 28, 1926.

■ *Nonastronomical prices paid for the Olympics.* CBS paid $50,000 for the rights to the 1960 Winter Olympics at Squaw Valley. For the 1992 Winter Olympics at Albertville, France, CBS paid $243 million. NBC paid $401 million for the 1992 Barcelona Summer Olympics.

■ *Greek athletic prowess.* As the birthplace of the ancient Olympics, Greece naturally dominated those Games and even as recently as 1896, when the first modern Olympics were held in Athens, Greece performed admirably, winning 10 golds and 47 total medals. Since 1924, Greeks have won just 11 medals at Summer Olympics, and only two golds.

ET PLUS ÇA CHANGE...: 4 EXAMPLES THAT SOME THINGS NEVER CHANGE

■ Roman Emperor Theodosius canceled the ancient Olympics in 392 A.D. in part because riots had broken out over charges made by Greek athletes that some of their Roman competitors were professionals.

■ The Carnegie Report in the late 1920s blasted football administrators for serious abuses. In 1929, a financial scandal involving the University of Iowa's All-America halfback Willis Glasgow led to the Hawkeyes' being suspended by their conference for a year, the first time that had happened.

■ University of Oklahoma wide receiver Lance Rentzel was declared ineligible for the 1965 Gator Bowl for having signed a professional contract.

■ Paavo Nurmi, the great Finnish distance runner, was suspended one week before the 1932 Olympic marathon for taking money beyond his expenses on an exhibition tour.

99

4
PLACES

HOME AWAY FROM HOME

Although the home field advantage in sports can rarely be underestimated, some teams have ventured forth, willingly, to use another site as their surrogate home. Other teams have temporarily had to move because of unusual circumstances. And circumstance has also forced events to relocate from their usual site to a home away from home.

■ A section of the Philadelphia Spectrum blew off in March of 1968. The resident NHL Flyers played their final seven regular season home games at Madison Square Garden in New York City, Maple Leaf Garden in Toronto, and Le Colisée in Quebec. The Spectrum roof was fixed by the time the playoffs began.

■ Man O' War, perhaps the greatest Kentucky-bred thoroughbred ever, never raced at a track in the state of Kentucky.

■ During the 1971–72 NBA season, the Houston Rockets played home games at six different sites: 21 at Hofheinz Pavilion, 8 at Astrohall, 6 at the Astrodome, 3 in San Antonio, 2 in Waco, and 1 in El Paso.

■ Because of fears of a Japanese sneak attack on the West Coast, the 1942 Rose Bowl game—to be played less than a month after the attack on Pearl Harbor—was moved from Pasadena to Durham, North Carolina. Oregon State beat Duke, 20-16.

■ The AFL All-Star game in 1965 was moved from New Orleans because black players protested widespread discrimination in the city. The game was played the following week in Houston.

■ In 1957, the Brooklyn Dodgers, who played at Ebbets Field, hosted 15 games in Jersey City's Roosevelt Stadium. Don Drysdale pitched his first career shutout there.

■ The Boston Celtics have played three home games a year at the Hartford Civic Center since 1981–82. (Before that, the number of games they played there varied.)

■ At the last minute, the 1957 British Open was moved from Muirfield to St. Andrews because of a gas shortage caused by the Suez Canal crisis.

■ At the 1956 Melbourne Olympics, the equestrian events were held separately in Stockholm, Sweden, because of Australian quarantine laws.

■ In 1914, the Boston Braves played their home World Series games at Fenway Park, home of the Red Sox, because the Braves' new park was not ready. The next two years, the Braves let the Red Sox use Braves Field in the World Series because it had a larger capacity than Fenway.

■ As heavyweight champion, American George Foreman never fought in the United States. His title defenses were made in Kingston, Jamaica; Tokyo, Japan; Caracas, Venezuela; and Kinshasa, Zaire.

■ In 1968 and 1969, the Chicago White Sox played 20 home games at Milwaukee's County Stadium.

■ In the 1968 Davis Cup, Rhodesia faced Sweden at a private club in France to stay clear of anti-apartheid demonstrations in Sweden.

■ The New York Yankees used Shea Stadium as their home from 1974–75, while Yankee Stadium was being renovated.

■ In 1950, the Stanley Cup finalist New York Rangers were bumped from Madison Square Garden by the incoming circus. They played Games 2 and 3 against the Detroit Red Wings in Toronto's Maple Leaf Garden—the first time since 1920, when Ottawa faced Seattle in the finals, that two teams battled for the Stanley Cup without a local team's being involved. Detroit hosted the last four games of the series. The Rangers lost in seven—gamely, it must be said, considering that they played not one of the seven contests at home.

Special "Home Away from Home" Honor:
■ Gaston Chevrolet, whose brother Louis founded the car company, won the 1920 Indianapolis 500 driving a Monroe.

THE MOST DRAMATIC EXAMPLES OF
HOME FIELD ADVANTAGE

In 1908, the Spaulding basketball guide said that home court advantage was "easily worth 15 points to the home team." That was quite telling, since the average margin of victory in games then was 15 points.

Playing on familiar ground, with supportive fans—and, on occasion, sympathetic officiating—makes for a serious competitive edge. Teams have even been known to accentuate the advantage, at times unethically. The visiting locker room at the Boston Garden is notoriously overheated, while the visitors' bench at the Montreal Forum used to be across the ice from the penalty box, thus keeping the enemy team from making player changes after returning to equal strength as quickly as the Canadiens could. The Jersey Knights (formerly the New York Raiders and the New York Golden Blades) of the defunct World Hockey Association played in New Jersey's Cherry Hill Arena, which had no showers in the visiting dressing room. Their opponents dressed in a motel two miles away.

The following offers a sampling of what "home field" may mean.

■ Only three times in 13 World Cup competitions through 1986 has a country from outside the host continent won the Cup—and on two of those occasions, a South American team won in Mexico. Five times, the host country has won the cup: Uruguay in 1930; Italy in 1934; England in 1966; West Germany in 1974; and Argentina in 1978. The host country has gone to the Cup semifinals or beyond eight times.

■ At the 1984 Los Angeles Olympics, 37 of the 38 fights that involved U.S. boxers and that went the full three rounds were decided in favor of Americans. Redzep Redzepovski of Yugoslavia, silver medalist in the flyweight division, said, "As long as an American is standing on his feet for three rounds it is hard to get a decision over him."

■ The golfers that defeated the American team at Prairie Dunes, Kansas, for the 1986 Curtis Cup, became the first British team to win the Curtis, Walker, or Ryder Cup on American soil.

■ Japan had won only one Winter Olympic medal before the 1972 Games in Sapporo, Japan, where they swept the 70m ski jump competition.

■ The University of Kentucky basketball team lost at home on January 2, 1943, and not again until January 8, 1955—a streak of 130 home wins.

■ Golfer Larry Mize of Augusta, Georgia, won the Masters in 1987.

■ In 1955, the Detroit Red Wings beat Montreal four games to three for the Stanley Cup. While the series sounds as if it were competitive, the home team won every game, and no game had a margin of under two goals.

In the 1987 World Series, the Minnesota Twins beat

the St. Louis Cardinals four games to three, with the home team winning every game.

■ From 1985–86 through 1986–87, the Boston Celtics were 79-3 in regular season home games.

■ The Arizona State football team won four of the first five Fiesta Bowls, in 1971, 1972, 1973, and 1975. The site of the Bowl was Sun Devil Stadium, Arizona State's home field.

■ Notre Dame did not lose a home football game from 1906–27.

■ During the 1981–82 NHL season, the New York Islanders were 33-3-4 at Nassau Coliseum.

■ Two of the three times that the Winter Olympics have been held in the United States, the American hockey team has won the gold medal. Those two golds are the only ones that the U.S. hockey team has won.

■ The University of Kansas basketball team won the 1988 NCAA final in Kansas City. North Carolina State won the 1974 title game, played at Greensboro, North Carolina. In 1968 and 1972, the Final Four was held in Los Angeles, and both titles were won by UCLA. In 1950, CCNY won the title game in New York.

■ "Cobb's Lake" was the area of dirt in front of Tiger Stadium's home plate that was kept wet by groundskeepers to slow down Ty Cobb's bunts and cause infielders to slip while fielding them.

Philadelphia's Connie Mack Stadium sported "Ashburn Ridge" to help speedy Richie Ashburn with his bunts down the third-base line. Similarly, the chalk along the baselines at Dodger Stadium was kept notoriously high to help Maury Wills's bunts stay fair, while the infield at Candlestick Park, home of the Dodgers' rivals, the San Francisco Giants, was kept muddy when the Dodgers were in town to slow Wills down on the bases.

■ Although they were not at home, African distance runners, who train at altitude, must have felt that way at the 1968 Olympics in Mexico City, a high-altitude city, as they dominated the distance races.

■ Chris Evert, the "touring professional" for Amelia Island, Florida, went almost five years without losing a set in tournament play there, until Carling Bassett beat her in 1983.

■ The San Francisco 49ers won Super Bowl XIX at Stanford University's football stadium in Palo Alto, 20 miles south of San Francisco.

■ Some baseball parks are easier to hit home runs in than others, but perhaps no player in the history of the game took greater advantage of the friendly confines of home than Ken Williams of the St. Louis Browns. He hit 142 of his round-trippers at home, most of them at Sportsman's Park, and only 54 on the road. (Elston Howard, on the other hand, hit only 54 home runs at home, mostly at Yankee Stadium, and 113 on the road.)

■ Amateur Francis Ouimet, 20, stunned the golf world by beating Harry Vardon and Ted Ray in an 18-hole playoff to win the 1913 U.S. Open at the Brookline Country Club in Massachusetts. Ouimet grew up across the street from the club.

■ Every game of the 1916 New York Giants' major league record 26-game winning streak was played at the Polo Grounds, their home field.

IT MUST BE SOMETHING IN THE WATER: PLACES IN THE WORLD THAT GROW ATHLETES

It may be due to the weather or the facilities, the coaching or the tradition; but whatever it is, certain places just have it. Some towns and schools and teams in America and beyond have produced an uncanny number of good athletes. We know that Oklahoma and USC grow running backs, the University of Miami and BYU quarterbacks, New York City basketball players, the Philadelphia Flyers goons, the Los Angeles Dodgers pitchers, Czechoslovakia tennis players. Why these spots are so fertile is often explainable—for instance, a coach knows how to take good athletes and turn them into great ones; or the appearance of one great athlete makes others want to flock to his school, or to master his specialty; or it's simply the mutual confidence that athletes develop around each other, making everyone better; or maybe again it's none of these, and just coincidence.

Whatever.

■ San Pedro de Macoris, a town of 100,000 in the Dominican Republic, has produced major league shortstops Alfredo Griffin, Tony Fernandez, Damaso Garcia, and Rafael Ramirez; 15 other major leaguers including Juan Samuel, George Bell, Joaquin Andujar, Julio Franco, and Pedro Guerrero; and more than 100 minor leaguers.

■ The soccer team of Hartwick College (1990 enrollment: 1,565) has spawned more than two dozen All-Americas and over 40 players who have gone on to play professionally and for the U.S. National and Olympic teams.

■ World-class distance runners Kipwambok (Henry) Rono, Kip Keino, and Mike Boit are all members of the Nandi, a subgroup of the Kalenjin tribe in Kenya.

■ The Miami (Ohio) College football team has included among its coaching and playing ranks the following coaching legends: Ara Parseghian, Red Blaik, Paul Brown, Woody Hayes, Carm Cozza, John Pont, Sid Gillman, and Weeb Ewbank.

■ In 1976, Guy Drut became the first person from a non-English-speaking country to win the Olympic high hurdles. Drut was born on the same street as Michel Jazy, France's last track and field medalist.

■ Eddie Murray, probably the premier American League first baseman of the 1980s, and Ozzie Smith, the premier National League shortstop of the 1980s, were high school teammates at Locke High School in Los Angeles, California.

New York Mets outfielders Cleon Jones and Tommie Agee were high school teammates at Country Training High School in Mobile, Alabama.

Herb Score and Dick Brown of Lake Worth, Florida, later became battery mates for the Cleveland Indians.

Waxahachie (Texas) High School produced four future major leaguers in one year: Paul Richards, Art Shires, Belv Bean, and Jimmy Adair.

Four other high schools have each had four future big leaguers on their team at one time: Roosevelt (St. Louis, Missouri) High School and Washington High School of Los Angeles in the 1930s, Beaumont High School in St. Louis in the 1940s, and Compton (California) High School in the 1970s.

■ In the 1950s, Australia produced tennis greats Rod Laver, Roy Emerson, Ken Rosewall, Frank Sedgman, Lew Hoad, Rex Hartwig, Mervyn Rose, Mal Anderson, Ashley Cooper, Fred Stolle, John Newcombe, and Tony Roche.

■ Martin's Ferry, Ohio, and its sister villages have produced the following sports stars: Lou and Alex Groza, Bill Mazeroski, John Havlicek, Olympic wrestler Bobby Douglas, NFL linebacker Bill Jobko, and Phil and Joe Niekro.

■ Basketball players from DeMatha High School in Hyattsville, Maryland include Adrian Dantley, Dereck Whittenberg, Adrian Branch, Sidney Lowe, Danny Ferry, Kenny Carr, Bennie Bolton, Sid Catlett, Hawkeye Whitney, and CBS announcer James Brown.

■ Gabby Hartnett and Nap Lajoie, both Hall of Famers, were born in Woonsocket, Rhode Island.

■ Tom Landry and Vince Lombardi were assistants together on the New York Giants coaching staff, 1954–58.

■ Baseball players from Hillsborough High School in Tampa, Florida include Dwight Gooden, Gary Sheffield, Floyd Youmans (who transferred to Fontana, California in his senior year), Mike Heath, Vance Lovelace, and José Alvarez.

■ A special mention goes not to a place but to a year—1982—whose senior class produced the following crop of future NFL quarterbacks: Dan Marino from the University of Pittsburgh, John Elway from Stanford, Jim Kelly from Miami, Ken O'Brien from Cal-Davis, Tony Eason from Illinois, and Todd Blackledge from Penn State.

■ The University of Indiana basketball team in 1975 produced eight players who went into the NBA—and that does not include Larry Bird, who quit the team and left the school.

■ The 1937 Newark Bears, perhaps the best minor league team in baseball history, won the International League championship with a 109-43 record. Of the 17 regular players, 16 eventually made it to the major leagues, including 9 the following year.

■ Al Arbour and Scotty Bowman each coached the 1970–71 St. Louis Blues. After leaving that post, they would, between them, win nine Stanley Cups in the next 12 years.

■ In the 1940s and 1950s, Calumet Farms was likened to the New York Yankees' Murderers Row: among the horses that came from there were Citation, Armed, Faultless, Wistful, Bewitch, Fervent, Two Lea, Ponder, Coaltown, and Whirlaway. Between 1932 and 1972, Calumet horses won 2,199 races, 456 of those stakes.

■ Undefeated heavyweight world champion Rocky Marciano and once-defeated middleweight world champion Marvin Hagler were both from Brockton, Massachusetts.

■ Olympic gold medalist skiers Egon Zimmerman, Orthmar Scheider, and Trude Beiser all came from Lech, Austria, a hamlet of fewer than 200 people, which had been converted to a ski resort following World War II.

IT REALLY MUST BE SOMETHING IN THE WATER

In the late 1980s, Minnesota Vikings Tommy Kramer, Rich Gannon, Issiac Holt, Hassan Jones, Tim Newton, Ray Berry, Steve Jordan, and Keith Millard were all charged with Driving While Intoxicated.

10 ATHLETES WHO SHOULD BE FROM SOMEPLACE ELSE

A baby is about to be named when suddenly, in the next room, a dish drops, the phone rings, perhaps there is a crash of lightning, someone panics, and everything goes a little crazy...and a mistake that cannot be revoked is made. The person is misnamed. A great American woman fencer goes through life as Vincent Bradford, while an NHL defenseman must sign his name as Carol Vadnais—a world turned upside down. Such mistakes even occur years into adulthood. How did the PR director of Japanese baseball's Pacific League, Kazuo Ito, get the nickname "Pancho"? What is wrong with this picture?

■ Oskar Schmid, professional basketball player and leading scorer in the 1988 Summer Olympics: Brazil

■ Rob de Castella, world-class marathoner and winner of the 1986 Boston Marathon: Australia

- Gabriela Sabatini, world-class tennis player: Argentina

- Nelli Kim, 1976 and 1980 Olympic gymnast: U.S.S.R.

- Socrates, World Cup soccer forward: Brazil

- George Bell, Toronto Blue Jay outfielder: Dominican Republic

- Greg LeMond, two-time Tour de France winner: U.S.A.

- Yolanda Chen, long-jumper: U.S.S.R.

- Emerson Fittipaldi, auto racer: Brazil

- Pancho Villa, boxer: Philippines

Special recognition is also due the following Davis Cup tennis players: Bob Falkenburg and Tom Koch, both of whom played for Brazil, and Martin Mulligan, who played, naturally, for Italy.

LESSER-KNOWN SPORTS HALLS OF FAME

"Cooperstown" has become shorthand for the National Baseball Hall of Fame and Museum, situated in Cooperstown, New York, 70 miles west of Albany, and the most widely known and frequently visited sports hall of fame in America. Other popular halls include the Naismith Memorial Basketball Hall of Fame in Springfield, Massachusetts, the Pro Football Hall of Fame in Canton, Ohio, and the International Tennis Hall of Fame and Museum in Newport, Rhode Island.

Dotted about our country and elsewhere, however, are shrines that celebrate lesser sports, athletes from different ethnic groups, and specific competitions. Certain of these institutions have enshrined some surprising members.

■ U.S. Croquet Hall of Fame, in Palm Beach Gardens, Florida.
   Notable enshrinees: Harpo Marx, Samuel Goldwyn, George S. Kaufman, Richard Rodgers, Alexander Woollcott, Gig Young, Louis Jordan.

■ Hall of Fame of the Trotter, in Goshen, New York.
   Notable enshrinees: Leland Stanford, founder of Stanford University and a prominent horse breeder; drivers Stanley Dancer, Billy Haughton; horses Dan Patch, Hambletonian.

■ International Jewish Sports Hall of Fame, in Netanya, Israel.
   Notable enshrinees: Sandy Koufax, Mark Spitz, Hank Greenberg, Benny Leonard, Sid Luckman, Mel Allen, Red Auerbach.

■ American Museum of Fly Fishing, in Manchester, Vermont.
   Board member: Baseball Hall of Famer Ted Williams.

■ International Swimming Hall of Fame, in Fort Lauderdale, Florida.
   Notable enshrinees: Benjamin Franklin, who was an avid swimmer; Julius Caesar, Winston Churchill.

■ National Softball Hall of Fame and Museum, in Oklahoma City, Oklahoma.
   Notable enshrinee: Joan Joyce.

■ The Muskegon Area Sports Hall of Fame, in Muskegon, Michigan.
   Notable enshrinees: Earl Morrall, Bennie Oosterbaan.

■ Fredonia College Sports Hall of Fame, in Fredonia, New York.

Notable enshrinee: Neil Postman, former basketball star and father of the author.

◼ National Italian American Sports Hall of Fame, in Arlington Heights, Illinois.
  Notable enshrinees: Joe DiMaggio, Vince Lombardi, Mario Andretti, Rocky Marciano.

◼ Mexican Professional Baseball Hall of Fame (Salón de la Fama), in Monterrey, Mexico.
  Notable enshrinees: Roy Campanella and Josh Gibson, who played in the Mexican leagues while the color barrier still existed in the major leagues.

◼ National Polish American Sports Hall of Fame and Museum, in Detroit, Michigan.
  Notable enshrinee: Stan Musial was their first inductee.

◼ Women's Sports Foundation International Hall of Fame in New York, New York.
  Notable enshrinees: Billie Jean King, Chris Evert, Peggy Fleming, Olga Korbut, Janet Guthrie.

RELOCATED TEAMS THAT WON MAJOR CHAMPIONSHIPS

Football

◼ The Baltimore Colts won the Super Bowl in 1971. They moved to Indianapolis in 1984.

◼ The Oakland Raiders won in 1977 and 1981. They moved to Los Angeles in 1982.

Baseball

■ The New York Giants won the World Series in 1905, 1921, 1922, 1933, and 1954. They moved to San Francisco in 1958.

■ The Philadelphia Athletics won in 1910, 1911, 1913, 1929, and 1930. They moved to Kansas City in 1955.

■ The Boston Braves won in 1914. They moved to Milwaukee in 1953.

■ The Washington Senators won in 1924. They moved to Minnesota in 1961.

■ The Brooklyn Dodgers won in 1955. They moved to Los Angeles in 1958.

■ The Milwaukee Braves won in 1957. They moved to Atlanta in 1966.

Basketball

■ The Philadelphia Warriors won the NBA title in 1947 and 1956. They moved to San Francisco in 1962.

■ The Minneapolis Lakers won in 1949, 1950, 1952, 1953, and 1954. They moved to Los Angeles in 1960.

■ The Rochester Royals won in 1951. They moved to Cincinnati in 1958.

■ The Syracuse Nationals won in 1955. They moved to Philadelphia in 1963.

■ The St. Louis Hawks won in 1958. They moved to Atlanta in 1968.

(The Baltimore Bullets won in 1948. They moved—but not very far—to Landover, Maryland, in 1973.)

Hockey

■ The Ottawa Senators won the Stanley Cup in 1920, 1921, 1923, and 1927. They moved to St. Louis in 1933, and folded after a year.

YOU CAN GO HOME AGAIN

■ Willie McCovey left the San Francisco Giants in 1974 and played for the San Diego Padres from 1974–76 and the Oakland Athletics, later in 1976. He returned to the Giants in 1977 for his final four years.

■ Lee Mazzilli, Brooklyn-born and a New York City favorite, started his career with the Mets, was traded to the Texas Rangers, then later to the Pittsburgh Pirates (with a pitstop in between to play for New York's other baseball team, the Yankees), and then returned to the Mets, where he delivered two crucial World Series pinch hits to help them win the championship in 1986.

■ Maury Wills was traded by the Los Angeles Dodgers to the Pittsburgh Pirates in 1967, went to the Montreal Expos in 1969, and in midseason was traded back to the Dodgers, where he finished his career.

■ Fran Tarkenton started his career as quarterback with the Minnesota Vikings, was traded to the New York Giants where he played for five years, and then finished his career with the Vikings.

■ In the last part of his career, Lloyd Waner played for the Boston Braves (1941), Cincinnati Reds (1941), Phila-

114

delphia Phillies (1942), Brooklyn Dodgers (1944), and finally the Pittsburgh Pirates (1944–45), the team with which he had played the first 15 years of his career.

■ Don Bunce, quarterback for Stanford's 1972 Rose Bowl team, became one of Stanford's team physicians.

■ Phil Niekro came back to the Atlanta Braves for one last start in 1987. Niekro played his first 20 years with the Braves before making stops with the New York Yankees (1984–85), the Cleveland Indians (1986–87), and the Toronto Blue Jays (1987).

■ At Hollywood Park in the 1970s, the great thoroughbred Affirmed once ran off by himself, setting off a frantic search. He was finally discovered back in his stall, which he had found among 2,244 others.

ATHLETES WITHOUT A HOME

Some athletes and places were made for each other—Casey Stengel and New York City, for instance: Casey wore the uniforms of all four New York teams in existence during his baseball career—as player for the New York Giants and Brooklyn Dodgers, and as manager of the Yankees and Mets. Pete Rose, a native of Cincinnati, found fame and fortune in his backyard, and Kent Hrbek, from Minneapolis, did not have to move far when he made it to the bigs with the Twins.

Others are not so lucky. They may never find a place that they can call home. Or, they find a home but it's one far from the place where they began.

■ At the turn of the century, Tacks Latimer had a five-year major league career, and each year he played with a different team.

■ German Bernard Trautmann, an outstanding soccer player, was taken prisoner of war by the British during World War II. After the war, Trautmann remained in England and became a star goalie for the Manchester City club in the English Soccer League.

■ Jaroslav Drobny played under four different nationalities. He was born in Prague and first classified as a Czech. After the Nazi invasion of Czechoslovakia, Drobny was listed in 1939 as being from Bohemia-Moravia. From 1946–48 Drobny was Czech again, but in 1949 he became a naturalized Egyptian. In 1960, he was given British citizenship.

■ Goaltender Gary "Suitcase" Smith was traded or moved 11 times in 15 years in the NHL and WHA.

■ In 1976, James Gilkes of Guyana, who had won the Pan-Am Games 200m, was kept out of the Olympics by his country's boycott. The International Olympic Committee turned down his appeal to compete under the Olympic flag.

■ On January 16, 1905, outfielder Frank Huelsman went from the Boston Red Sox to the Washington Senators, the sixth time he was traded or loaned in eight months.

■ Tennis player Bettina Bunge was born in Switzerland, lived for 14 years in Peru, moved to Florida and then to Monaco.

■ Major leaguer Glenn Hubbard was born in West Germany and played Little League in Taiwan.

■ Tom Owens played for the following professional basketball teams: Memphis, Carolina, St. Louis, Memphis again, Kentucky, Indiana, and San Antonio of the ABA; and Houston, Portland, Indiana again, and Detroit of the NBA.

■ Football coaching legend John Heisman led teams at

Oberlin, Akron, Auburn, Clemson, Pennsylvania, Washington and Jefferson, Rice, and Georgia Tech—the only one of those schools at which he stayed for as long as six years.

■ The successful and peripatetic Larry Brown, basketball's John Heisman, has coached the ABA's Carolina (1972–74) and Denver (1974–79) teams; UCLA (1979–81); the New York Nets (1981–83); the University of Kansas (1983–88); and the San Antonio Spurs (beginning in the 1988–89 season).

■ Because of liberal college eligibility rules during World War II, football end Barney Poole played for Mississippi in 1942, North Carolina in 1943, Army in 1944–46, and Mississippi again in 1947–48.

THE 25 MOST HALLOWED PIECES OF REAL ESTATE IN SPORTS

Without much trouble, most fans could come up with legitimate substitutions—Waveland Avenue behind Wrigley Field, Pauley Pavilion, the streets of Monte Carlo where the Grand Prix is contested, Boston Garden, the Cresta Run at St. Moritz, Forest Hills, the swimming pool in Mission Viejo, California, the Rose Bowl—for items in the following list. Some may disagree with our choices, and bother about the holy ground that we ignored, or the sports that we failed even to represent.

So be it. We have chosen the 25 sites or venues (and, where appropriate, the most hallowed part of that site) from today and yesterday—some of which no longer exist as they once did—that have taken firmest hold in the collective consciousness of American and world fandom.

■ Yankee Stadium's home plate, the pitching mound, and the fenced-off shrine behind left-center field.

■ The 16th hole at Cypress Point, in California, called by many the most famous hole in the world—as well as the most beautiful, the most photographed, and the most difficult par three.

■ Heartbreak Hill, between miles 16 and 18 of the Boston Marathon route.

■ Center ice at the Montreal Forum.

■ The Carlisle Indian Industrial School fields, where Jim Thorpe played as a collegian.

■ Ebbets Field, where the Brooklyn Dodgers played (and where the Jackie Robinson Apartments stand today).

■ Centre Court, Wimbledon.

■ The Bonneville Salt Flats, Utah, site of so many world land speed records.

■ The English Channel, the most famous test for the endurance swimmer.

■ The Green Monster at Fenway Park.

■ The starting line at the Indianapolis Motor Speedway.

■ The Champs Elysées in Paris, the final section of the world's most prestigious bicycle race, the Tour de France.

■ Berlin's Olympic Stadium, site of Jesse Owens's four gold medal-winning performances.

■ Center court, Madison Square Garden.

■ The Elysian Fields, in Hoboken, New Jersey, where the first baseball game was played.

■ Maracaña, in Rio de Janeiřo, the biggest soccer stadium in the world and the 1950 site of perhaps the most famous World Cup match of all, the final between Brazil and Uruguay.

■ The home stretch at Churchill Downs, in Louisville, Kentucky.

■ Olympia, at the northwestern tip of Peloponmesus, site of the original Olympic Games.

■ The Thames River, where the Henley Regatta is held.

■ Rome, site of the Circus Maximus and the Colosseum— the ancient meccas, respectively, of chariot racing and gladiator fights.

■ The Royal and Ancient Club, St. Andrews (also called the "Old Course" or the "Old Lady"), Kingdom of Fife, Scotland, simply the most famous 18 holes in the world.

■ The Holmenkollen in Norway, site of the oldest and most prestigious ski jumping event in the world.

■ The waters off Newport, Rhode Island, site of so many America's Cup races.

■ YMCAs in Massachusetts—the one in Springfield, where James Naismith invented basketball in 1891, and the one in Holyoke, where William G. Morgan invented volleyball in 1895.

■ The Bislett track in Oslo, Norway, legendary for great distance performances.

5
NAMES

THE MOST APPROPRIATELY NAMED FIGURES IN SPORTS

Some athletes spend their careers trying to live down their unfortunate names—reserve NBA center Frank Brickowski, major league pitcher Bob Walk, pro golfer Bobby Cruickshank come to mind. Others may live up to their names, literally. Stephanie Hightower became a champion American hurdler, Andy Payne triumphed in the 1928 "Bunion Derby," a 3,422-mile coast-to-coast footrace, James Lightbody won the 1904 Olympic 1,500m race. And if the planets line up just so, as they seemed to on January 26, 1960, anything is possible. On that date, a West Virginia high school basketball player scored 135 points in a single game. His name was Danny Heater, his hometown Burnsville.

Here are some athletes whose names seem aptly to have anticipated their pursuits, talents, or circumstances.

◼ Largest Agbejemisin, 6'7", 225-pound center for the Wagner College basketball team

◼ Syd Thrift, former general manager for the Pittsburgh Pirates and New York Yankees

◼ Ernie Shavers, bald boxer

◼ Marjorie Gestring, springboard diving gold medalist, 1936 Olympics

◼ Jeff Float, Olympic swimmer

- Willie Thrower, NFL quarterback

- Jack Crouch, major league catcher, 1930s

- Steve Axman, football coach of the Northern Arizona University Lumberjacks

- Mike Quick and Mac Speedie, NFL wide receivers

- Johnny High, one of 11 Phoenix Suns players involved in the biggest drug bust in professional sports history, in 1987

- Steve Stonebreaker, NFL linebacker, 1962–68, and his son, Michael, Notre Dame linebacker; Jim Youngblood, linebacker, and Jack Youngblood, defensive end, both NFL

- Ban Johnson, American League president, 1901–27, who suspended, among others, John McGraw in 1902 for umpire-baiting, Ty Cobb in 1912 for going into the stands to attack a heckler, Boston Red Sox pitcher Carl Mays in 1919 for leaving his team for two weeks, and Babe Ruth twice in 1922 for umpire-baiting

- Johnny Podres, pitcher for the San Diego Padres (in 1969, his final year as a player), and Ken Houston, defensive back for the Houston Oilers, 1967–72

- Margaret Court, tennis champion

- Lake Speed, auto racer

- Upset, the horse that beat Man O' War in the 1919 Sanford Memorial Stakes at Saratoga Springs, the only loss of Man O' War's career

- Joe Don Looney, 1960s NFL fullback and renowned as one of football's biggest flakes

121

AT LEAST 14 OTHER BOXERS NAMED MUHAMMAD OR ALI

After heavyweight champion Cassius Clay changed his name in 1964, in accordance with his new faith, many other black athletes followed suit, boxers especially.

■ Abdullah Muhammad (original name: Lee Holloman, heavyweight, Dallas)

■ Kato Ali (Tony Curry, junior lightweight, Philadelphia)

■ Abdul Haleem Muhammad (Edward Riley, middleweight, East Orange, New Jersey)

■ Ali Salaam (Henry Hank, Jr., junior middleweight, Gary, Indiana)

■ Dwight Muhammad Qawi (Dwight Braxton, light heavyweight and cruiserweight, Philadelphia)

■ Ali Karim Muhammad (Dwayne Thompson, welterweight, Chicago)

■ Hassan Ali (Herman Ingram, bantamweight, Newark)

■ Matthew Saad Muhammad (Matt Franklin, light heavyweight, Philadelphia)

■ Ferra Khan Ali (Ron Merriweather, junior lightweight, Newark)

■ Asmar Reheem Muhammad (Walter Cowans, Jr., welterweight, Milwaukee)

■ Eddie Mustafa Muhammad (Eddie Gregory, light heavyweight, Brooklyn)

■ Terrance Alli (Terrence Halley, junior lightweight, Guyana and Brooklyn)

■ Fred Muhammad (Fred Grogan, heavyweight, Denver)

■ Akbar Ali Muhammed (Charles Buckner, middleweight, Chicago).

Four more that we'd like to mention:
■ General Ali (middleweight, Philadelphia)

■ Slim Ali (light heavyweight, Washington, D.C.)

■ Ali Allen (heavyweight, Patterson, New Jersey)

■ Ali Jr. (bantamweight, Philippines)

One from Rivington, New Jersey:
■ Furgan Ali (light heavyweight)

Honorable mention:
■ Understanding Allah (William Greenshaw, light heavyweight, Brooklyn)

Mention honorable:
■ Sugar Brown (Bilal Ali, middleweight, Newark)

Don't ask us:
■ Abdur Rahim Muhammad (The Great Muhammad, middleweight, Brooklyn)

We have no idea what to do with, but we thought you should be aware of him:
■ Alhamza "U.F.O." (Maurice Veabro Boykin, welterwe Chicago)

ARE YOU SURE WE HAVEN'T MET BEFORE? THEN WHY DOES YOUR NAME SOUND SO FAMILIAR?

■ Craig James, New England Patriot running back, and Jim Craig, 1980 U.S. Olympic hockey goalie

■ John Thomas, 1960s high jump world record holder, and Tommy John, eternal pitcher

■ John Salley, Detroit Piston center-forward, and Sally John, wife of Tommy John

■ Samoa Samoa, former Washington State University quarterback, and Samoa Samoa (see above)

■ Johnny Jackson, San Francisco 49er defensive back, and Jack Johnson, first black heavyweight boxing champion

■ sailboarding, another name for windsurfing, and boardsailing, another name for windsurfing

■ Kenny Williams, Detroit Tiger outfielder, and Bill Kenney, Kansas City Chief quarterback

■ Jimy Williams, former Toronto Blue Jay manager, and Bill James, author of countless *Bill James Baseball Abstracts*

CLEVER NHL NICKNAMES

Of all the major sports—of *all* sports, perhaps—hockey has left us the most impoverished legacy of nicknames. This may be confirmed simply by noting the sobriquet of the sport's best player: Gretzky "The Great." On other occasions, he is referred to colorfully as "Gretz."

A small sampling of other evocative hockey nicknames:

Willie "Hubie" Huber
Doug "Hicksy" Hicks
Bob "Boydie" Boyd
Bob "Bournie" Bourne
Jim "Schony" Schoenfeld
Frank "Sully" Sullivan
Jim "Watty" Watson
Paul "Woodsy" Woods
Wally "Hergie" Hergesheimer
Ellard "Obie" O'Brien
Pat "Pricey" Price
Stephen "Wochy" Wojciechowski
Phil "Espo" Esposito
John "Fergie" Ferguson
   (and Lorne "Fergie" Ferguson)
Craig "Rammer" Ramsay
Dave "Lummer" Lumley
Pete "Stemmer" Stemkowski
Rod "Zainer" Zaine
Pete "Drisk" Driscoll
Rick "Duds" Dudley
Mark "Pav" Pavelich
Jim "Pep" Peplinski
Mark "Mess" Messier
Jerry "Topper" Toppazzini
   (and Zellio "Topper" Toppazzini)

THE OFFSPRING OF UNIMAGINATIVE PARENTS

Hockey is not alone in its uninspired nicknaming. From 1929 to 1932, the NFL included one franchise known as the Stapleton Stapes, and in the 1960s, the dominant triumvirate of golfers Arnold Palmer, Jack Nicklaus, and Gary Player was known—brace yourself—as "The Big Three." The award for colorlessness, however, clearly goes to the Canadian Football League. Currently, there are all of eight teams in the league, including the Ottawa Rough Riders and the Saskatchewan Roughriders. Apparently, the space makes a difference.

Let's just say that the parents of not a few world-class athletes were simply tired the day that they named their offspring, and leave it there.

■ Billy Williams, Chicago Cub slugger and outfielder

■ Pete Peeters, NHL goalie

■ John Johnson, 12-year NBA forward

■ Bob Robertson, Pittsburgh Pirate first baseman

■ Eddie Edwards, 1988 British Olympic ski jumper and folk hero

■ Tony Anthony, Detroit heavyweight

■ Tommy Thompson, Boston Brave outfielder, 1930s

■ Don O'Donoghue, NHL right wing

■ Willie Wilson, Kansas City Royal outfielder

■ Anthony Toney, Philadelphia Eagle running back

■ University of Illinois Illini (the "Fighting" middle name does not absolve them)

And a double honor to Hall of Fame pitcher Robin Roberts, who spent most of his career with the Philadelphia Phillies.

Some athletes are blessed with a name, look, background, or talent that inspires a unique nickname. There's Virgil "Fire" Trucks, for example, and Emil "Hill Billy" Bildilli; lanky George "The Stork" Theodore and home appliance–like William "The Refrigerator" Perry; quarterback Jack "The Throwin' Samoan" Thompson and Swedish world heavyweight champion Ingemar Johannson, whose right hand was known as "Thor's Hammer"; shot-blocking Marvin "The Human Eraser" Webster and sure-handed infielder Bob "Death to Flying Things" Ferguson.

Others are not so lucky. Failing certain obvious distinctions, they quickly become characterized by their most generic feature. A bespectacled player becomes "Spec," a southpaw "Lefty" (there have been over 150 of them in baseball's first hundred years), a tall player "Stretch," a redhead "Red," a towhead or gray-hair "Whitey," a Fitzsimmons "Fitzy." Here are some other names that, given one or two basic circumstances, will almost certainly be applied.

A boxer—or any athlete, for that matter—with a Ray somewhere in his name will become "Sugar." (See boxers "Sugar" Ray Robinson, "Sugar" Ray Leonard, "Sugar" Ray Seales, basketball player Michael "Sugar" Ray Richardson, etc.)

An athlete from the Netherlands or of real or perceived Dutch extraction, regardless of his jumping ability, will be called "The Flying Dutchman." (See tennis player Tom "The Flying Dutchman" Okker, soccer great Johann "The Flying Dutchman" Cruyff, baseball legend Honus "The Flying Dutchman" Wagner, who was actually German but thought to be Dutch, etc.)

A team executive, especially a general manager, named

Jack will be called "Trader," whether he makes many trades or not. (See San Diego Padres GM "Trader" Jack McKeon, Detroit Pistons GM "Trader" Jack McCloskey, etc.)

A baseball player named Durham will be called "Bull." (See Leon "Bull" Durham, Louis "Bull" Durham, Donald "Bull" Durham, Ed "Bull" Durham, etc.)

A Native American will be called Chief. (See major leaguers John "Chief" Meyers, Charles "Chief" Bender, Moses "Chief" Yellowhorse, Allie "Big Chief" or "Superchief" Reynolds, etc.)

A baseball team located in Milwaukee will adopt a name having to do with beer. (See the 1891 American Association Milwaukee Brewers, the 1901 American League Milwaukee Brewers, the present-day American League Milwaukee Brewers, etc.)

A Joe who is fast and strong will evoke thoughts of smoke. (See hard-throwing pitcher "Smoky" Joe Wood, Negro League fastballer "Smoky" Joe Williams, hard-punching heavyweight "Smokin'" Joe Frazier, etc.)

A player named Brown, especially an outside shooter in basketball or a deep threat wide receiver in football, will be called "Downtown." (See basketball gunner "Downtown" Freddie Brown, speedy Cincinnati Bengal "Downtown" Eddie Brown, outfielder "Downtown" Ollie Brown, etc.)

An athlete of Italian extraction will at some point be known as "The Italian Stallion." (See running back Franco "The Italian Stallion" Harris, Alabama running back Johnny "The Italian Stallion" Musso, fictional boxer Rocky "The Italian Stallion" Balboa, etc.)

128

SHARED NAMES I

Both members in each of the following pairs of sports figures answer to the same name. If one chooses to see it, the similarity between them extends beyond that.

■ Roger Craig, San Francisco 49er running back, and
Roger Craig, San Francisco Giant manager.

■ Steve Ontiveros, mediocre pitcher in the 1980s, and
Steve Ontiveros, mediocre third baseman in the 1970s

■ Mike Marshall, Los Angeles Dodger in the 1980s and
Mike Marshall, Los Angeles Dodger in the 1970s

■ Keith Jackson, burly NFL tight end, and
Keith Jackson, burly ABC commentator

■ Charles Smith, NBA forward and former Big East star, and
Charles Smith NBA guard and former Big East star

■ Robert T. ("Bobby") Jones, golfing immortal, and
Robert T. Jones, golf course architect immortal

■ Glenn Davis, Army's "Mr. Outside," and
Glenn Davis, Houston Astros' "Mr. Inside"

■ John Thompson, basketball Hall of Famer from the 1920s, and
John Thompson, Georgetown coach and future basketball Hall of Famer

■ Tim Brown, great 1980s and 1990s Los Angeles Raiders kickoff returner, and
Tim Brown, great 1960s Philadelphia Eagles kickoff returner

■ Bob Miller, 6'1" left-handed pitcher for the 1962 New York Mets, and
Bob Miller, 6'1" right-handed pitcher for the 1962 New York Mets

SHARED NAMES II

We weren't finished.

■ Mike Tyson, world heavyweight champion, and
Mike Tyson, St. Louis Cardinal reserve infielder in the 1970s

■ Bill Russell, basketball great, and
Bill Russell, baseball so-so

■ Eddie Murray, Los Angeles Dodger belter, and
Eddie Murray, Detroit Lion booter

■ Chris Evert, tennis great, and
Chris Evert, thoroughbred great named after the tennis great

■ John Lloyd, Negro League baseball star, and
John Lloyd, former Mr. Chris Evert

■ Pascual Perez, 1950s flyweight champion, and
Pascual Perez, turnoff-missing pitcher

■ John Henry Johnson, journeyman pitcher in the 1970s and 1980s, and
John Henry Johnson, Pro Football Hall of Fame fullback
(and John Henry, Hall of Fame horse)

130

- Bob Gibson, great pitcher for the St. Louis Cardinals, and
  Bob Gibson, lousy pitcher for the Milwaukee Brewers

- Dick Stockton, tennis player, and
  Dick Stockton, NBA voice

- Joe Morgan, superstar second baseman for the Cincinnati Reds, and
  Joe Morgan, manager of the Boston Red Sox

- Mike Reid, golfer, and
  Mike Reid, defensive tackle for the Cincinnati Bengals

- Larry Brown, Washington Redskin running back, and
  Larry Brown, San Antonio Spur basketball coach, and
  Larry Brown, Pittsburgh Steeler tight end

- Joe Morris, New York Giant running back, and
  Joe Morris, second-place horse in the 1910 Kentucky Derby

- Jimmy "The Greek" Snyder, betting expert, and
  Jimmy "Not the Greek" Snyder, former Seattle Mariner manager

- Jim Thorpe, all-around superstar, and
  Jim Thorpe, golfer

- Fernando Valenzuela, Los Angeles Dodger pitcher, and
  Fernando Valenzuela, 1990s jockey

- Joe DiMaggio, baseball immortal, and
  Joe DiMaggio, *Sports Illustrated* contributing photographer

- John Madden, football commentator and former coach, and
  John Madden, breeder of five Kentucky Derby winners

THE 20 BEST NAMES IN SPORTS

Everyone who writes about sports, especially baseball, eventually gets around to compiling a list of their favorite sports names. While we're not everyone, this book does, after all, purport to be the ultimate collection of sports lists, so here goes our small contribution. This list contains a curiously large number of major league pitchers, a fraternity that has contributed a disproportionate number of colorful names to the world. But then we dedicate our list to Van Lingle Mungo, the Brooklyn Dodger and New York Giant pitcher who has graced more lists of this variety—and even inspired the 1970 song, "Van Lingle Mungo," a chronicle of memorable names—than any other athlete living or dead.

- Maurice Archdeacon, 1920s Chicago White Sox outfielder

- André Champagne, NHL left wing, 1962–63

- Cletus Elwood "Boots" Poffenberger, 1930s pitcher

- Ossee Schreckengost, turn-of-the-century catcher

- Edward Wineapple, 1920s pitcher

- Calvin Coolidge Julius Caesar Tuskahoma "Buster" McLish, pitcher, 1944–64

- Fatima Whitbread, British javelin Olympian

- Morris Titanic, NHL left wing, mid-1970s

- Fair Hooker, Cleveland Browns receiver

- James Bluejacket, 1910s pitcher

- Climax, Saskatchewan, the hometown of 1970s NHL defenseman Gord Kluzak

■ Vitautris Casimirus Tamulis, pitcher in the 1930s and 1940s

■ Onix Concepcion, 1980s shortstop

■ Thane Gash, Cleveland Brown safety

■ Vida Blue, Oakland Athletic and San Francisco Giant pitcher, 1970s and 1980s

■ Heinie Manush, Hall of Fame outfielder, 1923–1939

■ Harthorne Wingo, New York Knick forward, 1972–76

■ Coy Bacon, NFL defensive lineman in the 1960s and 1970s

■ And, finally, the 1976 Olympic rowing tandem that won the silver medal in the pair-oared shell without coxswain, Calvin Coffey and Michael Staines.

THE BRIEFEST NAMES IN SPORTS

Brevity is the soul of wit, not to mention Mike Witt, the economically named New York Yankee pitcher. Here are some other athletes who are best appreciated by PA announcers and those who sew names on the backs of uniforms.

WILLIE PEP	world featherweight boxing champion
HENK VINK	Dutch motorcycle champion
J. TORCHIO (just J.)	University of California football player, 1980–83

ZENON M (just M)	Cal Poly-Pomona basketball player, 1986–87
RON CEY	Los Angeles Dodger and Chicago Cub third baseman
RAY GUY	Oakland Raider punter
HAP DAY	NHL defenseman and coach, Toronto Maple Leafs
ED OTT	Catcher for the Pittsburgh Pirates and California Angels, 1974–81
HU NA	Chinese tennis player
PELÉ	Brazilian soccer immortal
ZEV	1923 Kentucky Derby and Belmont winner
I	Argentina-born colt in 1930

THE MOST OFFBEAT AND IRREVERENT NICKNAMES

■ Pepe Munoz of Mexico, 200m breaststroke champion at the 1968 Olmpics, was called "Tibio" (lukewarm) because his father was from Aguascalientes (hot waters) and his mother was from Rio Frio (cold river).

■ A Philadelphia Phillie and Pittsburgh Pirate pitcher in the 1930s and 1940s, Hugh "Losing Pitcher" Mulcahy, had a career won-lost record of 45-89. In his four full seasons, he twice led the National League in losses.

■ Journeyman infielder Larry Cox was called Larry—but not because that was his name. He was nicknamed "Larry" for the character in the Three Stooges.

■ The defunct Southern Hockey League had a team in Georgia called the Macon Whoopees.

■ Boxer Peter Crawley, who held the bareknuckles prize ring crown for only seven days in 1827, was nicknamed "Young Rump Steak."

■ John "Superbrat" McEnroe was given this nickname by the British press for his legendary complaining during his Wimbledon matches and elsewhere. In 1981, McEnroe became the only Wimbledon champion to be denied membership to the All-England Club (though he was accepted to the club when he won again in 1983).

■ In the mixed doubles draw of several tennis tournaments in the 1920s, tennis champion Suzanne Lenglen of France partnered a "Mr. G"—King Gustav V of Sweden.

■ The end who played opposite Don Hutson, the brilliant Alabama flanker, was known simply as "the other end." Hutson's silent partner eventually came out of the shadows to coach football at Kentucky and Alabama, where Paul "Bear" Bryant grew into his better-remembered nickname.

■ Pearce "What's the Use" Chiles had a brief major league career at the turn of the century.

■ Several major leaguers have labored under disparaging, less-than-masculine tags, including Charles "The Old Wom-

135

an in the Red Cap" Pabor, Grayson "Grandmother" Pearce, William "Mary" Calhoun, and Frank "Flossie" Oberlin.

MUSICAL SPORTS FIGURES

There is a high correspondence between names in the sports and music world. We have taken note of this because that's just the kind of thing that we take note of.

■ JIM MORRISON, journeyman infielder and Doors lead singer

■ STEVE HOWE, former Los Angeles Dodger pitcher and Yes lead guitarist

■ BOB WELCH, Oakland Athletic pitcher and former Fleetwood Mac member

■ JOE JACKSON, shoeless baseball legend and British singer

■ MICHAEL JACKSON, Georgetown University basketball guard, Seattle Seahawk linebacker, and single-gloved megastar

■ DARRYL/DARYL HALL, University of Washington defensive back and Hall and Oates co-namesake

■ JOHN OATES, journeyman catcher and Hall and Oates co-namesake

■ JOHNNY RAY, All-Star second baseman and 1950s rock star

■ MUDDY WATERS, Michigan State University football coach, 1980–82, and blues legend

- **DAVE STEWART,** Oakland Athletic pitcher and Eurythmics star

- **JAMES BROWN,** CBS basketball announcer and jailbird soul singer

- **BOB WEIR,** British hammer-throw Olympian and Grateful Dead guitarist

- **ALBERT KING,** basketball player and blues legend

- **BOBBY BROWN,** American League president and soul star

- **DAVE CLARK,** Chicago Cub outfielder and Beatles imitator

- **KENNY ROGERS,** Texas Ranger pitcher and pop-country star

HUMAN TYPOS

Baseball fans thought they had misheard, in 1981, that the Atlanta Braves had broken in a rookie outfielder named Brett Butler. *Rhett* Butler, it must have been a takeoff on Rhett Butler, one of Atlanta's favorite sons, Clark Gable from *Gone With the Wind,* and it was not a particularly funny takeoff, at that. Well, Butler—Brett, that is—has since moved on to Cleveland and then San Francisco, effectively clearing up that confusion, but the names in each of the following pairs of sports figures look enough alike, without being identical, that if you came across one or the other while reading the sports pages— late at night, after an especially trying day—you might believe you'd encountered a typo. Is this a legitimate basis

137

on which to build a list? Frankly, no, but we will not let that stop us.

Robby Thompson, San Francisco Giant player, 1980s, and
Bobby Thompson, New York Giant player, 1950s

Owen Davidson, 1960s tennis star from Australia, and
Sven Davidson, 1950s tennis star from Sweden

Ralph Simpson, ABA star, 1970s, and
Ralph Sampson, NBA star, 1980s

Toni Seelos, great Austrian slalomer in the 1930s, and
Toni Sailer, great Austrian slalomer in the 1950s

Chris McMullin, who made a record 29 of 29 free throws for Dixie College in the NJCAA national finals in 1982, and
Chris Mullin, Golden State Warrior star and a career 88-percent free-throw shooter through 1988–89

Cot Deal, mediocre pitcher, 1947–54, and
Coot Veal, mediocre shortstop, 1958–63

Johnny "Lam" Jones, University of Texas running back and wide receiver, 1976–79, and
Johnny "Ham" Jones, University of Texas running back, 1976–78, and
A. J. "Jam" Jones, University of Texas running back, 1978–81

Gerry Cooney, great white hope, 1980s, and
Gerrie Coetzee, great white hope, 1980s

Paul McNamee, Australian tennis player and doubles partner of Peter McNamara, and
Peter McNamara, Australian tennis player and doubles partner of Paul McNamee

New York Mets, baseball team, and
New York Jets, football team, and

New York Nets, relocated basketball team, and
New York Sets, defunct World Team Tennis team

Hank Sauer, underappreciated National Leaguer of the
    1940s and 1950s, and
Hank Bauer, underappreciated American Leaguer of the
    1940s and 1950s

Shirley "Cha Cha" Muldowney, drag-racer, and
Clarence "Choo Choo" Coleman, former New York Met
    catcher, and
Juan "Chi Chi" Rodriguez, Seniors Tour golfer

Donald Trump, a driving force behind the United States
    Football League, and
Donald Crump, commissioner, Canadian Football League

...AND SOME MORE STRIKING
NAME TANDEMS

Babe Pinelli, major league player and umpire, and
Babe Parilli, University of Kentucky and NFL quarterback

Francis Ouimet, U.S. Open golf champion, and
François Ouimet, NHL defenseman, mid-1970s

Alibi Ike, Ring Lardner's excuse-making baseball player,
    and
Abebe Bikila, two-time Olympic marathon champion from
    Ethiopia

Kyle Macy, University of Kentucky and NBA guard, and
Kyle Mackey, New York Jets backup quarterback

Hal Smith, major league catcher, 1955–64, and
Tal Smith, former Houston Astro GM, and
Al Smith, major league utility man, 1953–64

Mel Purcell, pro tennis player, 1980s, and
Mel Parnell, Boston Red Sox pitcher, 1947–56

Joan Benoit, 1984 Olympic marathon champion, and
Joe Benoit, NHL right wing, 1940s

Q, X, AND Z

A brief celebration of athletes whose names begin
with any one of our three most neglected letters.

Q

■ New Zealander Dick Quax, former 5,000m world record holder

■ Donald Quarrie, Olympic sprinter from Jamaica

■ Adrian Karl Quist, Australian tennis player

■ Anne Quast, U.S. Amateur golf champion in 1958, 1961, and 1963

X

There has yet to be a player in the major leagues
whose last name started with an X, though minor league
infielder Joe Xavier made it to the Triple-A level of the
Milwaukee Brewer organization in 1989.

■ Xu Haifeng, free pistol gold medalist in 1984 and the
first Chinese athlete to win an Olympic medal

■ Thomas Xenakis, second in rope climbing, 1896 Olympics

■ Dana X. Bible, football coach at the Universities of Nebraska and Texas, 1930s and 1940s

■ Chen Xiaoxia, fourth in platform diving at the 1984 Olympics

■ Xavier "The X Man" McDaniel, Seattle Supersonic forward

Z

■ Tony Zale, middleweight champion, 1940–48

■ Robert Carl Zuppke, football coach, University of Illinois, 1913–41

■ Zachary Zorn, world record holder in the 100m freestyle swim, 1968

■ Zola Budd, world-class distance runner

■ Golfers Fuzzy Zoeller and Kermit Zarley

■ Pirmin Zurbriggen, World Cup and Olympic skier

■ Zelmo "Big Z" Beaty, NBA and ABA star

■ Max Zaslofsky, 1950s basketball great

■ Max, Tony, Joaquin, Luis and Alan Zendejas, NFL placekickers

■ Emil Zatopek, four-time gold medalist distance runner from Czechoslovakia

■ Carlos Zarate, boxer, who knocked out Alfonso Zamora in the fourth round of a 1977 bantamweight bout known as "The Battle of the Z's."

THE MOST REVERENT NICKNAMES

■ On the New York City playgrounds, Knick guard Earl Monroe was known as "Black Jesus."

■ Hall of Fame goaltender Frankie Brimsek, who had 10 shutouts as a Boston Bruin rookie in 1938–39, was called "Mr. Zero."

■ For 17 years (1914–30) before the baseball team from Brooklyn was known as the Dodgers, they were called the Robins in honor of their manager, Wilbert Robinson.

■ Finland's Matti Jarvinen, who defined his event by breaking the javelin record 10 times between 1930 and 1936, was called "Mr. Javelin."

■ First baseman Frank Chance, the final putout in the immortalized Tinker-to-Evers-to-Chance double play combination, became the Chicago Cub manager in 1905 and led them to three pennants in his first three full years, and a fourth one in 1910. He was called "Peerless Leader" by his troops. This was later shortened to "P. L. Chance."

■ Steve Zungul, Major Indoor Soccer League star, was tabbed "The Lord of All Indoors."

■ Louis Sockalexis, a member of the Penobscot Indian tribe, played well for the 1897 Cleveland Spiders until he reportedly fell from a second-story window during a Fourth of July drinking bout and hurt his ankle. Two years after his death in 1913, Cleveland held a contest for a new team name. Fans chose to call the team the "Indians" in Sockalexis's honor.

■ The Cleveland team that baseball legend Napoleon Lajoie played for and managed in the early 20th century was known as the "Naps."

■ The Hundred-Guinea Cup, the prize awarded in 1851 to the winner of an international yachting regatta around the Isle of Wight, was won by the schooner, *America,* sent over by the New York Yacht Club. The owners of *America* deeded the trophy to the NYYC, who renamed it Americas Cup. The top prize in yachting has been called that ever since, and only once has a non-American boat claimed the trophy.

■ The nickname of umpire Doug Harvey, who joined the National League in 1962, is "God."

OFFENSIVE NICKNAMES

There have been some unwittingly offensive team names in sports—the Vancouver Canucks in hockey, the New York Yankees in baseball, if you so choose. And there have been some names that were disparaging—the West German media, for example, called countryman and swimming champion Michael Gross "The American" because of his disdain for the press—but stopped short of turning truly offensive.

The following nicknames are offensive.

■ Sam Langford, a black boxer in the first part of the 20th century, was called the "Boston Tar Baby." Harlond Clift, a white baseball player, was called "Darkie" because Harlond sounded like "Harlem." Babe Ruth, who often barnstormed against Negro League clubs, was sometimes called "Nigger Lips" by major leaguers (all of whom were white).

■ Boxer Johnny Dundee, born in Italy, was known as "The Scotch Wop."

■ Abe Attell, featherweight champion in the early 20th century, was called "The Little Hebrew."

■ In the 1940s, the Southern Association had a team called the Atlanta Crackers.

■ The Boston Bruin line of Milt Schmidt, Bobby Bauer, and Woody Dumart was known as "The Kraut Line."

■ Ivan Wilfred Johnson, New York Ranger defenseman in the 1920s and 1930s, was nicknamed "Ching-A-Ling Chinaman." Cheap homers—ones hit over a short fence—used to be known as "Chinese homers."

SOX

Chicago White Sox, American League
Chicago Black Sox, 1919 version of the White Sox
Baltimore Black Sox, Negro League
Boston Red Sox, American League
Utica Blue Sox, Class A New York–Penn League
Fort Myers Sun Sox, Senior Professional Baseball Association
Paterson Silk Sox, semi-professional, northern New Jersey, early 20th century
Toledo Glass Sox, American Association, 1950s
Reno Silver Sox, Class A California League
Colorado Springs Sky Sox, Class AAA Pacific Coast League
Winter Haven Super Sox, Senior Professional Baseball Association
Scranton Red Soxx, Atlantic Collegiate League

Honorable mention:
Presbyterian (South Carolina) Blue Hose

THE HARDEST NAMES TO PRONOUNCE OR SPELL

You say potayto, I say "potahto." Seattle Mariners manager Jim Lefebvre says "La-Feever," journeyman outfielder Joe Lefebvre says "La-Fay." Names that are hard to spell or pronounce are botched so routinely that their owners would be wise to come up with some mutually satisfactory shorthand, like Duke University basketball coach Mike Krzyzewski (pronounced shuh-SHEF-sky), who is known simply as "Coach K," and New York Jets running back Nuu Faaola, which is a considerable improvement over his given name, Sinatausilinuu Faaola.

■ Bill Mlkvy (MILK-vee), 1949–52 Temple University basketball player, nicknamed "The Owl Without a Vowel."

■ Bobby Czyz (CHAZ), boxer.

■ Bob Ctvrtlik (stuh-VERT-lick), U.S. Olympic volleyball player.

■ Jackie Ickx, auto race champion, and Eddy Merckx, five-time Tour de France winner, both Belgian.

■ Carl Yastrzemski (yuh-STREM-ski), Boston Red Sox Hall of Famer.

■ Nantclwyd Hall, Wales, the birthplace of tennis.

■ Slobodan Zivojinovic and Zeljko Franulovic, Yugoslavian tennis players.

■ John and Stan Smrke, brief NHL left wings.

■ Juli Veee (note the third "e"), MISL soccer star.

145

■ Awaawaanoa Place in Honolulu, once-address of New York Mets pitcher Sid Fernandez.

■ Heikki Riihiranta, Finnish left wing.

■ Nnenna Lynch, Villanova University distance runner.

■ Napoleon Lajoie (lah-ZHWAH), baseball Hall of Famer.

■ Andy Papathanassiou, Stanford University offensive lineman.

■ Alex Wojciechowicz, Hall of Fame football player.

■ Giorgio Chinaglia (kee-NAHL-yuh), soccer star.

■ Jiri Crha, Czech goaltender, NHL.

■ Doug Gwosdz (GOOSH), journeyman catcher, nicknamed "Eyechart."

7 GOOD ATHLETES NAMED FOR BETTER ATHLETES

■ Willie Mays Aikens, who played in the major leagues for eight years, was born on October 14, 1954, 12 days after Willie Mays helped the New York Giants sweep the Cleveland Indians in the World Series.

■ Rogers Hornsby McKee pitched for the Philadelphia Phillies in 1943 and 1944. The year before McKee made it to the big leagues, his namesake was elected to the Baseball Hall of Fame.

■ Kareema Williams, from Southeast High School in Wichita, Kansas, was a basketball Parade All-America in

1986. Kareem Abdul-Jabbar was a Parade All-America, too, in 1964, as well as the NBA's all-time leading scorer.

■ Charles "Chuck" Klein Stobbs compiled a 107-130 record as a pitcher over 15 major league seasons. Chuck Klein was a Triple Crown–winning outfielder, and began his career with the most productive first few years of anyone in the history of the game.

■ Jack Dempsey Cassini appeared in eight major league games and had no at-bats. He weighed 175 pounds, 17 pounds fewer than his namesake, the heavyweight champion of the world from 1919 to 1926.

■ Larry Doby Johnson was born in Cleveland in 1950, when Larry Doby was a star for the Indians. Johnson debuted as a catcher for the Indians in 1972, played briefly for the Montreal Expos, and then for three games with the Chicago White Sox in 1978, where his manager was Larry Doby.

■ Elston Howard Turner, who played in the NBA from 1981–89, was born in 1959, the only year that Turner's namesake, New York Yankees catcher Elston Howard, did not play in the World Series in his first 10 years in the majors.

AND 1 GOOD ATHLETE NAMED FOR A LESS GOOD ATHLETE

■ Chuck Connors Person, basketball star for Auburn and the Indiana Pacers, was named for Chuck Connors, who had a brief and unillustrious career with both baseball's Brooklyn Dodgers and Chicago Cubs, *and* basketball's

Boston Celtics. Connors went on to greater fame as the star of the television series "The Rifleman."

30 LEGENDARY NICKNAMES

Most skilled athletes are christened with a nickname early on, in recognition of their talents or personality. Occasionally, an athlete of such rare stature comes along that several nicknames attach themselves to him or her; Babe Ruth and Muhammad Ali would rank at the top of this select group. Besides "Babe," George Herman Ruth was known at times as "Bambino," "The Sultan of Swat," "The Caliph of Clout," "The King of Clout," "Jidge," "Slambino," and "The Wizard of Whack," to name a very few. Not only do we also know Ali by his former name, Cassius Marcellus Clay, Jr., but as "The Greatest," "The Louisville Lip," and "The Mouth," as well. Basketball legend Jerry West was both "Mr. Clutch" and "Zeke from Cabin Creek."

Some nicknames, by themselves, are great—Darryl "Chocolate Thunder" Dawkins, for instance. Others have greatness thrust upon them: the athlete is brilliant enough and so associated with his or her nickname that it is hard to think of one without the other. As a nickname, "The Big O" is just all right, but because it belongs to Oscar Robertson, we remember it.

The following is a collection of the most vividly remembered nicknames in sport. If you take umbrage at the omission of certain obvious names, you are invited to write your own book of sports lists.

THE GEORGIA PEACH   —Ty Cobb

BROADWAY JOE   —Joe Namath

THE GALLOPING GHOST—Harold "Red" Grange

THE MANASSA MAULER	—Jack Dempsey
THE ROCKET	—Maurice Richard, Rod Laver
AIR	—Michael Jordan
DR. J	—Julius Erving
THE BIG TRAIN	—Walter Johnson
LITTLE MO	—Maureen Connolly
SWEETNESS	—Walter Payton
MR. OCTOBER	—Reggie Jackson
THE STILT	—Wilt Chamberlain
THE MAN	—Stan Musial
CASEY	—Charles Dillon Stengel
TOO TALL	—Ed Jones
CRAZY LEGS	—Elroy Hirsch
YOGI	—Lawrence Peter Berra
SHOE	—Willie Shoemaker
SHOELESS JOE	—Joe Jackson
THE GOLDEN JET	—Bobby Hull
THE GOLDEN BEAR	—Jack Nicklaus
THE YANKEE CLIPPER	—Joe DiMaggio
CHARLIE HUSTLE	—Pete Rose
PISTOL	—Pete Maravich
PEE WEE	—Harold Reese

CATFISH	—James Augustus Hunter
THE FLYING FINN	—Paavo Nurmi
SAY HEY	—Willie Mays
THE BROWN BOMBER	—Joe Louis
MAGIC	—Earvin Johnson, Jr.

6
POLITICS

KEEP YOUR MOUTH SHUT AND NOBODY GETS HURT: 5 EXAMPLES OF HOW MANAGEMENT FEELS ABOUT THE RIGHTS OF ITS EMPLOYEES

■ One day after speaking out on behalf of the NFL players' union in 1987, All-Pro tackle Brian Holloway was traded from the New England Patriots to the Los Angeles Raiders.

■ Pauline Betz Addie, Wimbledon champion in 1946, was suspended in 1947 for her public support of a women's professional tennis tour.

■ When Toronto Maple Leaf Jimmy Thomson and Detroit Red Wing Ted Lindsay tried to organize an NHL players union in the 1950s, they were traded immediately to the perennially cellar-dwelling Chicago Black Hawks.

■ In February 1989, the National Labor Relations Board ruled that former Seattle Seahawks wide receiver Sam McCullum had been illegally discharged just before the start of the 1982 season because of his activities as the team's player union representative. The Seahawks were ordered to give McCullum back pay with interest, as well as a job "substantially equivalent" to the one that he lost.

■ Reportedly, when Green Bay Packer All-Pro center Jim Ringo brought an agent with him to see coach Vince Lombardi and help to negotiate Ringo's 1964 contract, Lombardi, who viewed agents unfavorably, retreated to his office to make a phone call, and re-emerged to tell Ringo that he had just been traded to the Philadelphia Eagles.

SAY IT AIN'T SO: 9 BRUTAL TRUTHS ABOUT ATHLETES AND COMPETITION

Mark Twain once said that it was preferable to keep one's mouth shut and give the appearance of being stupid rather than to open it up and remove all doubt.

The sentiment might be paraphrased for athletes who give the appearance of being jaded, callous, mercenary, or lacking in humanity, and often all four qualities at once. Are they or aren't they? Maybe it's better that we not know for sure.

Sometimes we find out anyway.

▣ The Pittsburgh Pirates called off Willie Stargell Hall of Fame Day in 1988 because Stargell reportedly wanted more money and gifts than they had offered.

▣ Before Joe Theismann's junior year at Notre Dame, the school's sports information director suggested that the quarterback change the pronunciation of Theismann— "THEEZ-man"—to "THIGHS-man," to rhyme with Heisman, as in Trophy. Theismann did, but ended up second in the voting for the award in 1970 to Stanford's Jim Plunkett.

▣ Ho-Jun Li of North Korea, Olympic gold medalist in the small-bore rifle competition in 1972, explained his success: "I thought I was shooting at my enemies. Our Prime Minister, Kim-Il Sung, told us prior to our departure to shoot as if we were fighting our enemies. And that's exactly what I did." Li later said that he was misquoted.

▣ Bill Johnson, after winning the Olympic downhill gold

medal in 1984, was asked what the victory meant to him: "Millions. We're talking millions."

■ In 1986, New York Giants linebacker Lawrence Taylor said that he liked to inflict "kill shots" on players—hits that were so hard that "the snot comes from [the victim's] nose and he starts quivering on the ground."

■ John L. Sullivan, the great heavyweight champion, refused to fight Peter Jackson, a black Australian and leading challenger, because he was "a member of the colored race."

■ In *Visions of Eight*, a documentary about the 1972 Munich Olympics—the Games marred by the terrorist killings of 11 Israelis—a British marathoner was asked, "How does the slaughter of the Israelis affect you?" "It postpones my race for a day," he answered.

■ Middle-distance runner Ben Jipcho reflected on his poor times—only one sub-four minute mile in 27 tries—in his first two years on the pro track circuit: "I am a professional. I run for money, not for times. I realize people like to see Ben Jipcho run sub-four minute miles, and Ben Jipcho enjoys running sub-four minute miles more than anything else in the world—except counting money."

■ Heavyweight Mike Tyson's philosophy of boxing: "I always try to catch [opponents] right on the tip of the nose, because I try to push the bone right into the brain."

BREAKING THE COLOR BARRIER

1884: Fleet Walker became the first black major league baseball player.

1904: Charles Follis, with the Shelby (Ohio) Athletic Club, became the first black professional football player.

1904: George Poage was one of the first two blacks to compete in the Olympics, in the 400m competition, and also became the first black runner to win an Olympic medal, taking third place in the 400m hurdles.

1908: Jack Johnson became the first black heavyweight boxing champion.

1908: John Taylor became the first black to win an Olympic gold medal, in the 4x400m relay.

1922: Fritz Pollard, player-coach for the Milwaukee Badgers (and later for the Hammond Pros in 1923–25), became the NFL's first black head coach, preceding Art Shell by 67 years.

1924: Long-jumper De Hart Hubbard became the first black to win an individual Olympic gold medal.

1947: In one of the most significant events in sports, the white walls of baseball began to crumble when Montreal Royal Jackie Robinson was called up to the parent club, the Brooklyn Dodgers, to become the first black baseball player in the modern era. Later that year, the Dodgers called up Dan Bankhead, the first black pitcher, and the Cleveland Indians called up Larry Doby, the first black American Leaguer.

1948: High-jumper Alice Coachman became the first black woman to win an Olympic gold medal.

1949: Jackie Robinson became the first black MVP in the major leagues.

1949: George Taliaferro, a University of Indiana backfield star, became the first black player drafted by an NFL team when the Chicago Bears picked him in the 13th round.

1950: Chuck Cooper of Duquesne became the first black

player drafted by the NBA when the Boston Celtics picked him in the second round.

1950: Earl Lloyd of the Washington Capitals became the first black player in the NBA, October 31, 1950, in Rochester, against the Royals.

1950: Althea Gibson became the first black tennis player accepted to compete in the U.S. Championships at Forest Hills.

1953: Willie Thrower became the first black NFL quarterback.

1955: Jim Tucker and Earl Lloyd became the first blacks to play on an NBA championship team, the 1954–55 Syracuse Nationals.

1955: Jockey Isaac Murphy was part of the inaugural group elected to the National Horse Racing Hall of Fame. Murphy, one of the great riders in American history, was the first jockey—black or white—to ride three Derby winners. (At the turn of the century, most jockeys were black, and black jockeys won 15 of the first 28 Derbies. The last black jockey to ride in the Derby was Jess Conley, in 1911.)

1956: Althea Gibson became the first black tennis player to win a major title, the French Open.

1957: Gibson became the first black player to win Wimbledon and the U.S. Championships.

1957–58: Willie O'Ree became the first black hockey player to play in the NHL, in a two-game stint for the Boston Bruins. He played for them for most of the 1960–61 season.

1959: Pumpsie Green became the first black member of the Boston Red Sox. The Red Sox were the last major league team to integrate.

1961: John McLendon became the first black to coach a professional modern-era team, the Cleveland Pipers of the American Basketball League.

155

1961: Ernie Davis of Syracuse became the first black Heisman Trophy winner.

1963: Arthur Ashe became the first black tennis player to compete on the U.S. Davis Cup team.

1963: Elston Howard became the American League's first black MVP (by this time, the National League already had 11 black MVPs.)

1966: Bill Russell became the first black NBA head coach, for the Boston Celtics.

1966: Basketball head coach John McLendon became the first black to coach at a predominantly white college, Cleveland State.

1966: Emmett Ashford became the first black umpire, for the American League. In 1973, Art Williams became the National League's first black umpire.

1968: Jim Hines won the first all-black final in Olympic history, in the 100m.

1969: John McLendon became the first black head coach in the ABA for the Denver Nuggets.

1971: Bill White became the first black baseball announcer when he joined the New York Yankees broadcast team.

1975: Lee Elder became the first black to play in the Masters golf tournament.

1975: Frank Robinson became the first black major league manager, for the Cleveland Indians.

1975: Willie Wood became the first black head coach of a modern-era professional football team, the Philadelphia Bell of the World Football League. In 1980, he became the first black head coach in the Canadian Football League, for the Toronto Argonauts.

1975: Al Attles's Golden State Warriors defeated K. C. Jones's Washington Bullets in the NBA Finals, the first championship matchup of black head coaches in professional sports.

1979: Lee Elder became the first black golfer to take part in the Ryder Cup competition.

1984: John Thompson of Georgetown University became the first black to coach an NCAA basketball champion.

1986: George Branham III became the first black bowler to win a PBA title, the Brunswick Memorial World Open in Glendale Heights, Illinois.

1986: Debi Thomas became the first black U.S. singles figure skating champion, and the first black world women's figure skating champion.

1989: Bill White became the first black to head a major professional sports league in America when he was hired as National League president.

1989: Bertram Lee became the first black majority owner of a major professional team, the Denver Nuggets.

10 UGLY SCENES FROM SPORTS HISTORY

■ In 1972, Boston Marathon officials dragged the first woman entrant, Kathy Switzer, off the course to prevent her from finishing the race.

■ Near the end of the 1954–55 NHL season, Montreal Canadiens star Maurice Richard was involved in an on-ice altercation that culminated in his hitting a linesman over the head with his stick. When the league suspended Richard for the last week of the regular season and the entire playoffs, protests erupted in Montreal and a riot ensued. There was looting in the city, a fire was set off, and millions of dollars of damage was reported.

■ In the 1933 Kentucky Derby, the jockey on Head Play, Herb Fisher, twice grabbed for the saddlecloth of Broker's Tip jockey Don Meade. Meade shoved Fisher's hand away. After the finish, Fisher slashed Meade with his whip and they later got into a fistfight. Each jockey was suspended for 30 days, but the penalty did not include stakes races.

■ In a basketball game between Minnesota and Ohio State on January 25, 1972, a brawl broke out at Williams Arena in Minneapolis with 36 seconds left and Ohio State leading 50-44. Dave Winfield, a Gopher forward, was in the center of the fight. One source called it "an ugly, cowardly display of violence." After the brawl, Minnesota's Corky Taylor and Ron Behagen were suspended for the rest of the season.

■ South Korean boxer Byun Jong-il's loss by decision in a 119-pound boxing match at the 1988 Seoul Olympics set off a huge brawl in which the referee was attacked and chairs were flung into the ring. Reportedly among the perpetrators were several Korean members of the Olympic security force.

■ Jimmy Connors was penalized a point, then a game, and then the match, and eventually fined $20,000 and suspended for 10 weeks, for his protest of a call in the fifth set of a semifinal match with Ivan Lendl at the Lipton Tournament in Boca Raton, Florida, on February 21, 1986. Connors ranted, stormed the umpire's chair, and finally sat down and refused to play.

■ A hockey fight between the Minnesota North Stars and

the Boston Bruins on February 26, 1981, resulted in 81 penalties totaling 392 minutes, and 12 ejections.

◼ Cincinnati Red Pete Rose and New York Met Bud Harrelson brawled during Game 3 of the 1973 National League playoffs, a fight set off by Rose's hard slide into second base. When Rose went out to left field in the bottom of the inning, fans threw garbage at him, and Cincinnati manager Sparky Anderson pulled the Reds from the field. They did not return until a Mets' contingent headed by manager Yogi Berra and outfielder Willie Mays went out to left field and pleaded with the fans to settle down.

◼ There have been numerous stomach-turning injuries in sports, including those in which bones have been visibly and explicitly broken. The nation watched as Joe Theismann's leg broke in a Monday Night Football game in 1985, and saw Cincinnati Bengal Tim Krumrie break his leg in Super Bowl XXIII. The ankle of Los Angeles Dodger Tommy Davis was so badly broken in a second-base slide against the San Francisco Giants in 1965 that some of the Giant infielders became physically ill at the sight.

◼ Monique Ellis and Bobbi Jo Lister—the respective wives of Seattle Supersonics players Dale Ellis and Alton Lister—got into a March 1988 fistfight 10 minutes after Seattle had beaten the Los Angeles Lakers, 114-110, at the Seattle Center Coliseum. The fight, which erupted when a woman claiming to be Monique Ellis's sister kicked and punched Mrs. Lister, interrupted Seattle coach Bernie Bickerstaff's press conference 50 yards away. The two players' wives apparently had been at odds since Alton Lister had signed a four-year, $4.2 million contract in the off-season while Dale Ellis had been unable to renegotiate the final year of a contract that was paying him $325,000 annually.

IT'S ENOUGH TO MAKE US SICK:
A COMPARISON BETWEEN YESTERYEAR'S BASEBALL SUPERSTARS AND TODAY'S JOURNEYMEN

The total payroll for the first all-professional baseball club, the Cincinnati Red Stockings of 1869, was $9,300. In 1936, 67 years later, the average annual baseball salary was $4,500. In 1989, 53 years after that, the average salary was nearly $500,000.

This lists the 1989 salaries earned by various current baseball players, and a selected year's salary of various stars of the past. (Note that salaries jumped significantly in 1990.)

First Baseman

Nick Esasky: $570,000

Lou Gehrig, 1927: $8,000
Bill Terry, 1931: $23,000

Second Baseman

Ron Oester: $650,000

Jackie Robinson, 1952: $40,000

Third Baseman

Rance Mulliniks: $650,000

Pie Traynor, 1932: $14,000

Shortstop

Scott Fletcher: $1,200,000

Honus Wagner, 1908: $5,000
Phil Rizzuto, 1950: $50,000

160

Outfield

Candy Maldonado:
$900,000

Larry Sheets: $660,000

Darnell Coles: $460,000

Terry Puhl: $950,000

Mike Davis: $987,500

Babe Ruth, 1927:
$70,0000

Mickey Mantle, 1965:
$100,000

Willie Mays, 1965:
$105,000

Ted Williams, 1951:
$100,000

Ty Cobb, 1908: $4,500

Joe DiMaggio, 1941:
$37,500

Catcher

Rich Gedman:
$1,150,000

Bo Diaz: $900,000

Roy Campanella,
1957: $45,000

Pitcher

Richard Dotson:
$900,000

Steve Trout: $1,090,000

Don Carman: $575,000

Jim Clancy: $1,150,000

Bob Gibson, 1969:
$125,000

Bob Feller, 1940: $27,500

Cy Young, 1901: $3,000

Rollie Fingers, 1974:
$65,000

THE 1980s: THE AGE OF ENLIGHTENMENT CONTINUES

Eight ambassadors for world harmony share their views:

■ Los Angeles Dodgers General Manager Al Campanis in April 1987, speaking on an episode of ABC's "Nightline" that commemorated the 40th anniversary of Jackie Robinson's breaking the baseball color barrier: "I truly believe that [blacks] may not have some of the necessities to be, let's say, a field manager or perhaps a general manager. . . . Why are black men or black people not good swimmers? Because they don't have the buoyancy." Soon after making these comments, Campanis lost his job.

■ Pitcher Bob Knepper, with the Houston Astros in 1988, on the pursuit by minor league umpire Pam Postema to win a major league job: "This is not an occupation a woman should be in. In God's society, woman was created in a role of submission to the husband. It's not that woman is inferior but I don't believe women should be in a leadership role." Knepper also said, "NOW [National Organization of Women] is such a blowhard organization. They are a bunch of lesbians."

■ Track athlete Joaquim Cruz, on Florence Griffith Joyner and Jackie Joyner-Kersee at the 1988 Olympics: "Florence, in 1984, you could see an extremely feminine person. But today she looks more like a man than a woman, and Joyner herself, she looks like a gorilla."

■ John McEnroe, at the 1983 Forest Hills Tournament of Champions, after being hit in the side by a ball struck by his Czech opponent, Tomas Smid: "You'll be sorry the day you hit me, you fucking Communist asshole."

■ University of Indiana basketball coach Bobby Knight, responding to a question from NBC newscaster Connie Chung on how he handled stress, in 1988: "I think if rape is inevitable, relax and enjoy it."

■ Detroit Piston Dennis Rodman, after his team had been beaten by the Boston Celtics in the seventh game of the 1987 Eastern Conference finals: "Larry Bird is overrated in a lot of areas . . . way overrated. Why does he get so much publicity? Because he's white. You never hear about a black player being the greatest."

■ Jimmy "The Greek" Snyder, asked on the occasion of

Martin Luther King's birthday in 1988 about the progress that blacks had made in American society: "If they take over coaching like everybody wants them to, there's not going to be anything left for white people. All the players are black. The only thing that the whites control are the coaching jobs." Snyder lost his job as football analyst for CBS Sports.

◪ Washington Redskins running back John Riggins to Supreme Court Justice Sandra Day O'Connor at the Washington Press Club's annual Salute to Congress, in 1985: "Loosen up, baby. You're too tight." Riggins had just asked O'Connor when she would pose for a pinup poster.

9 FAMOUS STRIKES AND BOYCOTTS

◪ In 1977, Chicago Black Hawks star Bobby Hull sat out one game to protest hockey violence.

◪ At the 1956 Melbourne Olympics, Egypt, Iraq, and Lebanon boycotted to protest Israel's takeover of the Suez Canal.
   In a separate political act that year, Holland, Spain, and Switzerland boycotted to protest the Soviet invasion of Hungary.

◪ In 1973, Yugoslav tennis player Nikki Pilic refused to play for his country's Davis Cup team and was banned by the International Lawn Tennis Federation. The players boycotted in support of Pilic, and the Association of Tennis Players (ATP) demanded that Wimbledon accept Pilic. Wimbledon refused, and all but 3 of the 82 ATP players boycotted, including 13 of the 16 seeded players at Wimbledon. The three exceptions were Romanian Ilie Nastase, Englishman Roger Taylor, and Australian Ray Keldie. Czech Jan Kodes won the tournament.

◪ On January 14, 1989, Georgetown University basketball

coach John Thompson walked off the court before a game with Boston College to protest Proposition 42, which prevents freshmen who do not meet entrance standards from receiving their scholarships. Thompson claimed that the proposition was racially biased.

■ In a 1976 boycott, African nations, led by Tanzania, protested the inclusion in the Olympics of New Zealand, whose rugby team had made a tour of South Africa. Iraq and Guyana also boycotted.

■ In 1980, President Jimmy Carter led a boycott, which also included West Germany and Japan, of the Moscow Olympics, to protest the Soviet invasion of Afghanistan.

■ In 1984, the Soviet Union returned the favor and led many Communist countries in a boycott of the Los Angeles Olympics.

■ At the 1912 Olympics, in one of the more petulant boycotts of all time, the Italian Fencing Federation proposed lengthening the épée blade to 94 centimeters. When the proposal was rejected, the Italians refused to participate.

5 DISTASTEFUL EPISODES IN WHICH POLITICS INFECTED SPORTS

Politics play too large a role in professional sports, as well as supposedly amateur ones, namely the Olympics. To list all of the occasions in which nationalism, greed, and generally ugly behavior have affected the outcome of a contest, or who got to play in it, or where it should be played, requires a book in itself. The 1972 Olympic massacre of 11 Israeli athletes, baseball's tacit "whites only" rule for decades, point shaving, boxers taking dives, Olympic boycotts, biased judging and officiating—the list of people manipulating sport for political and monetary gains is endless.

Others have used the field of play as a forum for making more egalitarian-minded points, but they have abused sport nonetheless.

We offer just a sampling of invasions, from warfare to television, into the purity of sports.

■ At the 1956 Olympic Games, Hungary and the Soviet Union faced each other in water polo a month after Soviet troops had invaded Hungary. The "Blood in the Water" match was punctuated by brawls and was finally stopped by the referee with Hungary leading 4-0.

■ The "Futbol War" in 1969 between El Salvador and Honduras was sparked by soccer matches that fueled existing tensions. It was also known as the Soccer War, the One-Hundred Hour War, and the Football War. The two countries met in a World Cup qualifying round in June of 1969. Honduras won the first leg on June 8. El Salvador won the second leg on June 15, necessitating a decisive third game. Both games had set off fierce rioting. In Honduras, Salvadoran residents were attacked, and hundreds of thousands of migrants fled across the border. Reprisals were made against Hondurans in El Salvador. Diplomatic relations were cut off. On June 24, El Salvador declared a state of siege. That day, El Salvador defeated Honduras 3-2 in a neutral Mexico City site. Fighting intensified. On July 3, a Honduran plane was reported to have attacked Salvadoran border troops. On July 14, Salvador forces invaded Honduras. Honduras bombed San Salvador and Acajuta. On July 18, a cease-fire was made.

The death toll was estimated at 2,000.

■ Emily Davison, a suffragette who was frustrated by the English Parliament's refusal to grant women the right to vote, brought attention to the cause in 1913 by running onto the famed Epsom Downs track during the Derby Stakes, Britain's premier race, and into the path of the leading horse, owned by King George V. To the horror of the crowd, Davison was trampled and killed.

■ American tennis star Bill Tilden was suspended and ruled ineligible to play in the 1928 Davis Cup, but the French Federation Cup, wanting a full house at their new Roland Garros Stadium, petitioned the president. Eventually the American ambassador in Paris was instructed to usurp the power of the U.S. Davis Cup captain and reinstate Tilden.

■ Because of commitments to advertisers, NBC cut away from the November 17, 1968 New York Jets–Oakland Raiders football game with minutes remaining and the Jets leading, 32-29, to begin its presentation of the movie *Heidi.* Oakland scored two touchdowns in the game's thrilling final 42 seconds to win, 43-32, and set off a barrage of complaints from viewers who had been denied the exciting finish. The contest would forever come to be known as "The Heidi Game."

A HAPPIER MARRIAGE OF SPORTS AND POLITICS: 6 MOMENTS IN WHICH LIFE'S HARSHER REALITIES WERE SOFTENED BY THE SPIRIT OF COMPETITION

■ In 1967, a cease-fire was declared during the Biafran War so that soccer great Pelé could visit both sides of the front.

■ The father of tennis champion Fred Perry was a Labour member of Parliament and was afraid to leave the House to watch his son at Wimbledon because his party was governing in a minority situation. Arthur Steel-Maitland, leader of the opposition, arranged what is termed "live pairs" for the senior Perry. A member of the opposition who would have been voting against the government in a debate would agree to stay away until the return of his pair—namely, Perry, off watching his son.

■ Harold Connolly, American hammer thrower, and Olga Fikotová, Czech discus thrower, met during the 1956 Olympics and corresponded by mail after she returned to Prague, and he to Boston. Connolly visited Prague and asked the Czech government for permission to bring her to the United States to marry her. The government refused, but the U.S. State Department intervened and permission was granted. Connolly and Fikotová were married, with Czech marathoner Emil Zatopek as the best man. In 1960, both Mr. and Mrs. Connolly competed for the U.S. team.

■ The political and cultural isolation that the U.S.S.R. underwent for 30 years following the October Revolution was broken first in 1946 by the reaffiliation of the country's soccer federation with the Federation Internationale de Football Association.

■ With Jesse Owens one foul away from being disqualified in the long jump at the 1936 Berlin Olympics, Luz Long, his German competitor and main rival, introduced himself and gave Owens a tip: Make a mark several inches before the takeoff board and jump from there. Owens did that and qualified easily. Owens went on to win (not surpassing Long until his next-to-last jump) and was congratulated first by Long, who won the silver medal, in full view of Adolf Hitler. Owens wrote, "You can melt down all the medals and cups I have, and they wouldn't be a plating on the 24-carat friendship I felt for Luz Long at that moment."

■ The first American to visit China after it was reopened to the West in 1971 was table tennis champion Leah "Ping" Neuberger.

AND 1 MOMENT IN WHICH THE PREDOMINANCE OF SPORTS OR POLITICS IS HARD TO DETERMINE

■ While American light-heavyweight Mike McTigue was winning the world title over Battling Siki in a 20-round victory inside a Dublin arena on St. Patrick's Day, 1923, the Sinn Fein insurrection, in which Irish rebels were using gunfire on the British, was going on outside.

17 OF THE MOST NOTORIOUS DISQUALIFICATIONS AND SUSPENSIONS

■ Lee Calhoun was suspended for the 1958 track season for receiving gifts on a TV game show called "Bride and Groom." (He came back in 1960 to win his second Olympic gold medal in the 110m hurdles, leading a fourth consecutive United States sweep in the event.)

■ Richard Higham is the only baseball umpire expelled from the game for life, for dishonesty. He had informed gamblers on how to bet on games that he was umping, and was banished from the National League on June 24, 1882.

■ In the 1940 U.S. Open at Canterbury, Ohio, two golfing threesomes were disqualified for teeing off 28 minutes early for their final round, in an attempt to beat an impending storm. One of the disqualified golfers, Ed "Porky" Oliver, shot a 71 for a 287 total, the same as champion Lawson Little and Gene Sarazen (whom Little beat in a playoff).

■ On June 8, 1920, Cincinnati Reds outfielder Edd Roush

was ejected from the game for taking a nap in the outfield during a break in play.

■ In 1936, Germany's Toni Merkens won the 1,000m cycling sprint gold medal despite interfering with the second-place cyclist. Instead of being disqualified, Merkens was fined 100 marks.

■ Heavyweight champion Muhammad Ali was suspended from March 23, 1967, through September 25, 1970, for evading the draft.

■ Tennis player Ilie Nastase was banned for a year from representing Romania in Davis Cup play after an outburst in a 1977 match with Britain.

■ At the 1924 Paris Olympics, a demonstration broke out when French middleweight boxer Roger Brousse was disqualified for biting his opponent in their quarterfinal bout.

■ In the 1980 Olympic 20,000m walk finals, 7 of the 34 walkers were disqualified for illegal technique.

■ Golfer Severiano Ballesteros was disqualified from the 1980 U.S. Open for being late for his starting tee time on the second day.

■ Jimmy Connors won three legs of the tennis Grand Slam in 1974—all but the French, from which he had been banned because he had signed a contract with World Team Tennis.

■ The NCAA levied the "death penalty" on SMU's football team on February 25, 1987, for violating NCAA rules, including making payments of approximately $61,000 to players.

■ In 1972, swimmer Rick DeMont had his Olympic gold medal for the 400m freestyle taken away because he had taken asthma medication, Marex, that contained ephedrine, a banned drug. DeMont had been taking the medicine since he was four years old, and the American team physicians had neglected to check what was in Marex.

DeMont became the first American since Jim Thorpe to be forced to return his gold medal.

■ At the Mexico City Olympics in October of 1968, Tommie Smith and John Carlos gave the Black Power salute on the 200m victory stand during the playing of the American National Anthem. They were barefoot, wore black gloves, and bowed their heads. They said that the clenched fists represented black strength and unity, the bare feet were reminders of black poverty, and the bowed heads showed that expressions of freedom in the National Anthem did not apply to blacks. The United States Olympic Committee suspended both men and ordered them to leave the Olympic village.

■ Rocky Graziano had his boxing license revoked because he did not report an attempted bribe to throw a fight with Reuben Shank in 1948. (The fight did not come off because Graziano had injured his back while training. Graziano said that he treated all bribe attempts with disdain and saw no need to report them.)

■ Lee Trevino was disqualified from the 1981 PGA for not signing his card.

■ The Parrot, the Pittsburgh Pirate mascot, was suspended for a game for throwing a Nerf ball at umpire Fred Brocklander.

OBSCENELY OVERPAID ATHLETES

We're not quite finished with our gripes about the compensation of athletes. Most fans are fed up by the money paid to overdeveloped boys who happen to have mastered skills that, last we looked, do little for world peace or hunger. Tales of overpaid superstars and, worse, supremely overpaid lesser athletes seem each day to take up more space in the sports pages. Not to belabor the idea, we will pluck out just a few instances that disgust us.

Hockey: Derek Sanderson was signed to a $2.5 million contract by the Philadelphia Blazers of the WHA in 1972. By midseason, they paid him a large sum not to play for them.

Football: Steve Young signed a $40 million contract, to be paid out over 43 years, with the Los Angeles Express of the USFL. Through the 1989 NFL season, Young was the backup quarterback for the San Francisco 49ers.

Baseball: Bill Caudill collected a record $3.3 million buyout after he was cut by the Toronto Blue Jays in the spring of 1987. The former record was $2.7 million paid to Len Barker by the Atlanta Braves in 1986. George Foster, waived in 1986 by the New York Mets, received $2 million, and Damaso Garcia, released by the Atlanta Braves in 1988, got $1.7 million.

Golf: For a hole-in-one he made at a 1987 tournament, Dan Pooley received $1 million—more than he had earned during his whole PGA career, and 10 times more than that earned by the winner of the tournament.

Boxing: On June 27, 1988, Mike Tyson made at least $21 million for knocking out Michael Spinks in 91 seconds. Michael Spinks made at least $13.5 million for being knocked out by Mike Tyson in 91 seconds.

7

TEAMS AND RIVALRIES

WITH FRIENDS LIKE THAT...

To succeed in sports, it is imperative that you be able to distinguish friends from foes, teammates from opponents. Presumably, friends and teammates are the ones that rally and help and support you.

Then again, it can be a mistake to presume.

■ At the 1988 Olympics, Americans Calvin Smith and Lee McNeill made an illegal baton exchange on the third leg of the first-round heat of the 4x100m relay. The heavily favored defending champion U.S. team was disqualified, thus denying teammate Carl Lewis a shot at repeating his four gold medal–winning performance in 1984, an unprecedented duplication that he had dreamed of achieving.

■ Toronto Blue Jays outfielder George Bell was named the dirtiest player in baseball in a poll in the *Toronto Globe*.

■ On February 2, 1962, pole vaulter John Uelses cleared a world record 16'1¼". As track officials moved to verify the height of the bar, fans congratulating Uelses accidentally knocked over the vault supports, thus negating the jump.

■ The night before Cleveland Indians catcher Ray Fosse was injured badly when he was bowled over at home plate by Cincinnati Red Pete Rose in the 1970 All-Star game in Cincinnati, Fosse was a dinner guest at Rose's home.

■ In 1989, two Buffalo Bill coaches beat each other up after watching a videotape of the previous week's game. When they were Los Angeles Dodger teammates, Don Sutton and Steve Garvey wrestled—not playfully—in the locker room.

■ In the 1976 Olympic 200m race, Hasely Crawford suffered a cramp after 50 meters and was listed as not finishing. However, a track fan pointed out that Crawford had never left his lane until he jogged past the finish line, giving him a time of 1:19.60.

■ In 1977, Texas Rangers second baseman Lenny Randle was suspended for 30 days, lost $13,000 in salary during the suspension, and was fined $10,000 after assaulting Rangers manager Frank Lucchesi and putting him in the hospital for five days.

■ Countrymen Kenneth McArthur and Christian Gitsham of South Africa were leading the Olympic marathon in 1912 when they came to a water stand two miles from the stadium. McArthur said that he would wait for Gitsham to take a drink, but he kept on running, opening a lead that Gitsham could not overcome.

■ Byron Nelson's caddie accidentally kicked his golf ball, leading to a penalty stroke that helped cost Nelson the 1946 U.S. Open.

Honorable mention 1:
■ The manager of the 1943 American League All-Stars, New York Yankees skipper Joe McCarthy, did not use any of the six Yankees who were on hand for the game.

Honorable mention 1A:
■ Although referees and officials should not be counted on as either friends or teammates, athletes have a right to count on them at least to pay attention. In the 1932 Olympic Games, France's Jules Noël had apparently made a winning discus throw on his fourth attempt but none of the officials saw where the throw landed because at the time they were all watching the pole vault. Noël was given

an extra throw but could not duplicate his effort and did not earn a medal.

BIG AND LITTLE

Some nicknames are as much a testament to an athlete's affiliation to a better-known teammate or sibling or just contemporary, as they are to the prowess of the athlete himself. The following is a list of athlete pairs who have, for better or worse, forged at least a part of their place in history with each other.

■ Major leaguers Jeff Pfeffer and his brother, Big Jeff Pfeffer

■ Hall of Famers Paul "Big Poison" Waner and Lloyd "Little Poison" Waner

■ Hockey Hall of Famers Maurice "The Rocket" Richard and his brother, Henri "The Pocket Rocket" Richard

■ New York Islanders Duane "Dog" Sutter and his younger brother, Brent "Pup" Sutter

■ Olympic swimming contemporaries Johnny "Tarzan" Weismuller and Australian Andrew "Boy" Charlton

■ William "The Refrigerator" Perry, 325-pound Chicago Bear, and Gerald "The Ice Cube" NcNeil, 140-pound Cleveland Brown

■ Cincinnati Reds starting catcher Ernie "The Big Slug" Lombardi and his backup, Willard "The Little Slug" Hershberger

■ Hall of Fame left wing Frank "Big M" Mahovlich and his brother, center Pete "Little M" Mahovlich

■ Fierce tennis rivals Helen "Helen the First" Wills and Helen "The Other Helen" Jacobs

14 SETS OF THE MOST EVENLY MATCHED COMPETITORS

When going head-to-head or simply when compared to each other, the following pairs of teams or individuals were—for one brief moment, maybe for years—exquisitely well-matched.

■ In Game 1 of the opening round of the 1936 Stanley Cup playoffs, the Detroit Red Wings beat the Montreal Maroons, 1-0, in six overtimes, the longest game in Cup history.

■ The football teams of Fordham University and the University of Pittsburgh played to scoreless ties in 1935, 1936, and 1937.

■ Through 1988, the Boston Celtics' home playoff record was 165-54. Through 1988, the Los Angeles Lakers' home playoff record was 164-54.

■ Through nine innings on May 2, 1917, the Chicago Cubs' Jim "Hippo" Vaughn and the Cincinnati Reds' Fred Toney pitched the only double no-hitter in major league history. (Vaughn eventually gave up two hits and a run in the 10th inning.)

■ Cary Middlecoff and Lloyd Mangrum played the longest sudden death in history, at the 1949 Motor City Open.

After 11 holes, they were declared co-winners by mutual agreement.

■ In match-play competition at the 1932 PGA, Johnny Golden finally beat Walter Hagen on the 43rd hole.

■ In the 1975 Surrey Grass Court Championships in Surbiton, England, Anthony Fawcett and Keith Glass played one game of 37 deuces and 80 points. The game lasted 31 minutes.

■ In a 1969 girls' high school basketball game in Tennessee, Chattanooga East Ridge defeated Ooltewah 38-37 in 16 overtimes.

■ The most fumbles in an NFL game is 14. When they set the record in 1940, the Chicago Bears mishandled the ball seven times, and the Cleveland Browns did, too.

■ In a match in Lyons, France, tennis stars Jaroslav Drobny and Budge Patty finally called it a draw at 21-19, 8-10, 21-21.

■ Leon Cadore of Brooklyn and Joe Oeschger of Boston both pitched all 26 innings—the longest stints ever by a pitcher in a single game—before their May 1, 1920 game was called for darkness, with the score tied 1-1.

■ Jimmy Barry and Casper Leon, bantamweights, fought to a draw twice in world title fights, in May and December of 1898.

■ Abe Attell and Owen Moran, featherweights, drew in their two world title fights in January and September of 1908.

■ For a salary arbitration hearing in 1987, the Atlanta Braves and pitcher David Palmer both submitted a figure of $750,000.

AND 1 SET OF THE MOST EVENLY MATCHED COMPATRIOTS

■ Ethel Catherwood, 1928 high jump gold medalist, married Harold Osborn, 1924 high jump gold medalist.

I'VE GOT YOUR NUMBER: ATHLETES AND TEAMS AND THEIR FAVORITE PATSIES

pat sy (pat'se) n., pl. -sies. *Slang*. A person who is cheated, victimized, or made the butt of a joke. [Origin unknown.]

In sports, a patsy is the player or team that you most love to face because you have so much success against him or them—for a season, a few years, a career. There's just something about them that makes you thrive—you match up well perhaps, or you love their home field, or maybe you just plain have them psyched out. A patsy does not have to be a bad player or team; in fact, your mediocre and lousy opponents might give you a lot of trouble while a very good opponent is your patsy.

In each of the following cases, the patsy was no slouch.

■ Larry Jaster vs. the Los Angeles Dodgers, 1966: St. Louis Cardinals pitcher Jaster faced the National League champion Dodgers five times, and shut them out each time. He gave up 24 hits, all singles, in 45 innings, and had a 0.00 ERA. Against the rest of the league that year, Jaster was 6-5 with a 4.66 ERA. (His final totals were 11-5, 3.26 ERA.)

■ Steve Foley vs. Dan Fouts, career: Denver Broncos defensive back Foley made 44 interceptions in his career, 13 off of San Diego Chargers quarterback Fouts.

■ The Montreal Canadiens vs. the Boston Bruins, this century: 25 times these two teams have met in the Stanley Cup playoffs, and the Bruins have lost 21 times, including 18 straight from 1946–87.

■ Neale Fraser vs. Alex Olmedo, 1959: That year, Australian tennis star Fraser swept the U.S. Championship singles, doubles, and mixed doubles titles. In all three finals, Olmedo was on the other side of the net.

■ The Boston Celtics vs. the Los Angeles Lakers, 1960s: The Lakers reached the NBA Finals six times in the decade, each time losing to the Celtics.

■ Hub Pruett vs. Babe Ruth, 1922–24: During those years, Ruth batted .315, .393, and .378, and hit 35, 41, and 46 home runs, respectively, but he was .190 in 30 at-bats with one home run against the St. Louis Browns lefty reliever Pruett. Pruett, who threw a screwball, struck Ruth out 15 times, including 10 of the first 11 times he faced him. Pruett's lifetime mark was 29-48, with a 4.63 ERA. After Pruett retired, he became a doctor and thanked Ruth for putting him through medical school because, Pruett claimed, his success against Ruth was the main reason that he was kept in baseball.

■ Vince Coleman vs. the New York Mets catching staff, his career through 1989: The St. Louis Cardinals outfielder had never been thrown out attempting to steal a base by a Met catcher. Coleman is 53-for-53 and counting.

■ Rich Gossage vs. Rickey Henderson, career, and Roger Clemens vs. Cory Snyder, start of career: Henderson struck out eight of the first nine times he faced Gossage in the American League, and then again in the 1984 All-Star game. Snyder struck out the first nine times he faced Clemens.

■ Bob Neyland–coached Tennessee vs. Bear Bryant–coached Kentucky, and Notre Dame vs. Bear Bryant–coached Alabama, career: Against the Volunteers, Bryant's Wildcats were 0-5-2; against the Fighting Irish, Bryant's Crimson Tide was 0-4.

■ Billy Williams vs. Steve Blass, September 5, 1969: The Chicago Cub outfielder had his way with the Pittsburgh Pirate pitcher, collecting two doubles and two home runs. What makes this game remarkable is that while Blass was Williams's patsy on that day, the rest of the Cubs were *Blass's* patsy: he gave up only four hits, all of them collected by Williams. Blass won the game.

■ Any bowl opponent vs. a Bo Schembechler–coached team: Schembechler's Michigan Wolverines were 5-12 in bowl games from 1970–90.

■ The Chicago Cubs vs. Don Sutton, early in his career: The Los Angeles Dodger pitcher lost the first 13 times he faced the Cubs.

■ Ned Yost vs. Tommy John, and Tommy Hutton vs. Tom Seaver, careers: Yost, a .212 career hitter, hit .833 (10-for-12, with two home runs) off of John; Hutton, a .248 hitter, hit .700 against future Hall of Famer Seaver.

■ Rod Laver vs. Arthur Ashe, 1960–74: Over that span, the American lost 18 straight matches to the Australian.

■ Harry Coveleski vs. the New York Giants, 1908, and Frank Lary vs. the New York Yankees, 1960s: Philadelphia Phillies pitcher Coveleski earned the nickname of "The Giant Killer" by beating them three times in the final week of the season, to kill the Giants' pennant hopes; Detroit Tigers pitcher Lary was known as "The Yankee Killer."

■ The New York Yankees vs. the Brooklyn Dodgers, 1940s and 1950s: From 1941 to 1956, the two teams met in seven

World Series, several of which are considered classics, but the Dodgers managed only one championship, in 1955.

■ Henry Tillman vs. Mike Tyson, as amateurs: Tillman twice defeated the future heavyweight champion to qualify for the Olympic team in 1984, when he won the heavyweight gold medal.

9 OF THE FRIENDLIEST RIVALRIES

■ In the 1936 Olympic pole vault competition, Japanese Shuhei Nishida and Sueo Oe finished tied for second. They refused to vault off for placing and instead decided by drawing lots that Nishida would be second and Oe third. When they got home, they had their medals cut in half and fused back together so that each had a medal of half silver and half bronze.

■ Australian tennis stars Roy Emerson and Fred Stolle cooked each other breakfast at their Putney flat before playing in Wimbledon finals in 1964 and 1965.

■ Jackie Fields and Joe Salas, best friends growing up in Los Angeles, fought for the 1924 Olympic featherweight gold. Fields won and then went to his locker room and cried.

■ After his second run in the 1984 Olympic slalom, Phil Mahre immediately got on the walkie-talkie with advice for Steve, his twin brother and the only person left who could deprive him of his gold medal. Phil won the gold and Steve took the silver.

■ In 1987, Chris Evert won *La Trophée de la Femme* at the Pierre Barthes Club in Cap d'Agde. She thought the Cartier-designed silver leopard and gold ball that she had received was something Martina Navratilova would like, so she gave it to her. It was valued at 20,000 pounds.

■ In 1979, defending U.S. Amateur champion John Cook talked Mark O'Meara into playing in the tournament and put him up at his condominium. O'Meara beat Cook in the finals.

■ Rafer Johnson and C. K. Yang together attended UCLA and helped each other train for the 1960 decathlon. After the 1,500m, the final event of the competition, the two men fell against each other for support. Johnson edged Yang for the gold.

■ The 1984 featherweight weightlifting medal ceremony marked the first time a platform was shared by athletes from China (gold medalist Chen Weiqiang) and Taiwan (bronze medalist Wen-Yee Tsai). They shook hands and praised each other.

■ In 1973, Secretariat beat Riva Ridge, his stablemate at Meadow Stable, in the initial running of the Marlboro Cup. The horses were ridden on different occasions by jockey Ron Turcotte. Riva Ridge won the Kentucky Derby in 1972, and Secretariat won it a year later.

THE MOST DOMINANT TANDEMS IN SPORTS

The following pairs of teammates or opponents (individuals, teams, or countries) dominated their sports or specialties to an outlandish extent.

■ Between 1937 and 1973, Australia and the United States won the Davis Cup every year except for 1940–45, when there was no competition. No other country even made it to the finals from 1938 until 1960.

■ The University of Pennsylvania and Princeton University won 17 straight Ivy League basketball titles between them until Brown broke their hold in 1986.

■ Either Bill Russell or Wilt Chamberlain led the NBA in rebounding for 16 out of 17 years, from 1957–73.

■ Between 1966 and 1979, Larry Mahan or Tom Ferguson was PRCA all-around rodeo world champion every year but 1971–72.

■ Between them, Jimmy Connors and John McEnroe won all seven U.S. Open men's tennis singles titles from 1978 through 1984.

■ Philadelphia Eagle Russ Craft had four interceptions and his teammate Joe Sutton three, as they combined for seven interceptions in one September 24, 1950 game against Chicago Cardinals quarterback Jim Hardy.

■ For every year from 1971 to 1980 but one, either Jack Nicklaus or Tom Watson was the PGA Tour's leading money-winner.

■ The Los Angeles Lakers and Boston Celtics accounted for 8 of the 10 NBA titles in the 1980s. One of those two teams was runnerup five times.

■ From 1960 to 1976, only one Australian Championship women's singles final did not include Margaret Court or Evonne Goolagong or both.

■ In 1961, New York Yankees Roger Maris, with 61, and Mickey Mantle, with 54, combined for 115 home runs.

■ In 1910, Philadelphia Athletics pitchers Jack Coombs (31-9, 1.30 ERA, 35 complete games) and Chief Bender (23-5, 1.58 ERA, 25 complete games) formed a devastating 1-2 starting punch, with a combined record of 54-14. (Just

182

six years later, on the same Philadelphia A's team, pitchers Jack Nabors, at 1-20, and Tom Sheehan, 1-16, combined for a 2-36 record between them, an equally devastating 1-2 punch in reverse.)

■ On February 22, 1981, Quebec Nordique teammates and brothers Peter and Anton Stasny combined for 16 points in a single NHL game. Peter scored four goals and recorded four assists while Anton scored three times and had five assists.

■ Reggie and Laurie Doherty dominated Wimbledon in the 1890s and early 1900s. Reggie won four singles titles in a row; after a one year break, Laurie won five in a row. Together, they won the doubles title 8 times in 10 years.

■ A Soviet or Japanese gymnast has won the men's all-around title in every Olympics since 1952. The U.S. men's team's win in 1984 was the only time the Soviets or Japanese did not win the team competition over the same span.

5 THREE-HEADED MONSTERS

And sometimes there are *three* forces that are head and shoulders above the competition.

■ From 1941–42 to 1959–60, the Stanley Cup was won by only the Montreal Canadiens (eight times), the Toronto Maple Leafs (six times), and the Detroit Red Wings (five times).

■ From 1924–52, no competitor from a country other than Norway, Finland, or Sweden finished in the top eight in 15-km Olympic Nordic skiing, and only one outsider finished in the top eight in the 50km. In 1952, those three countries earned the first 17 places in the 15km race.

■ James Braid, John Henry Taylor, and Harry Vardon, British golfing greats from the 1890s through the 1920s, were born within 13 months of one another and became known as "The Great Triumvirate." For the 21 years from 1894 to 1914, Vardon won the British Open six times, Taylor and Braid five each.

■ From 1966–88, the Sportswriter of the Year (voted for by the National Sportscasters and Sportswriters Association and selected national media) was awarded only to the Associated Press's Will Grimsley (four times), *Sports Illustrated*'s Frank Deford (six times), and *The Los Angeles Times*'s Jim Murray (13 times).

■ From 1975 through 1989, the 500cc world motorcycle champion rode either a Suzuki, Honda, or Yamaha.

TAKE THAT!
9 EXERCISES IN SPORTS ONE-UPMANSHIP AND REVENGE

In the first game of a September 21, 1934 doubleheader, St. Louis Cardinals ace Dizzy Dean three-hit the Brooklyn Dodgers. In the second game, Paul Dean, Dizzy's brother, no-hit Brooklyn. Apparently, Dizzy later claimed that had he only known his brother was going to pitch a no-hitter, he would have pitched one, too. For Dizzy, the gauntlet had been dropped after his day's work was done. In the following cases, however, a standard was set and then someone else came along to match it, or top it.

■ Only three times in NFL history have consecutive kickoffs been returned for touchdowns. It happened last on

December 20, 1987, when Sylvester Stamps of the Atlanta Falcons ran back a kickoff 97 yards for a score. San Francisco 49er Joe Cribbs returned the ensuing kickoff for a 92-yard touchdown.

■ On December 19, 1987, Boston Bruin Ken Linseman scored a goal at 19:50 of the 3rd period. St. Louis Blue Doug Gilmour scored two seconds later, at 19:52, the quickest response in NHL history.

■ In 1976, the U.S.S.R., Czechoslovakia, and Hungary angered Federation Cup officials by withdrawing from the tennis competition to protest the Cup's inclusion of South Africa. The following year, the Federation Cup board banned all three protesting countries from competition for protesting the previous year.

■ Jim Maloney and Don Wilson pitched back-to-back no-hitters—Maloney for the Cincinnati Reds against the Houston Astros on April 30, 1969, Wilson the following day for the Astros over the Reds. It was only the second time this had happened in major league history. In 1968, Gaylord Perry pitched one on September 17 for the San Francisco Giants over the St. Louis Cardinals, and Cardinals pitcher Ray Washburn returned the favor the next day by no-hitting the Giants.

■ About baseball, Yogi Berra once said, "Ninety percent of this game is half-mental." Philadelphia Phillies manager Danny Ozark took him a step further by once saying, in earnest, "Half this game is ninety-percent mental."

■ On Mother's Day, 1939, the parents of Cleveland Indian Bob Feller traveled from Iowa to see their son pitch in Chicago against the White Sox. At one point, a foul ball hit by Chicago batter Marv Owen struck Feller's mother, broke her glasses, and opened a cut, for which she later needed stitches. Feller asked for time and went into the stands to see how his mother was, then returned to strike Owen out. Feller won the game.

■ In destroying the rest of the field at the 1912 Olympics,

Jim Thorpe may have done himself more harm than good: one of the competitors whom Thorpe overwhelmed in the pentathlon and decathlon was Avery Brundage, who finished sixth in the former competition and could not even finish the latter. Brundage later became president of the International Olympic Committee (1952–72) and was empowered to return to Thorpe the two Olympic medals that had been taken from him decades before, following charges that Thorpe had played semipro baseball and thus forfeited his amateur standing. A year after Brundage took office, Thorpe died, unredeemed. Not until 1982, a decade after Brundage had left the IOC presidency, was Thorpe's name restored to the record book. In 1983, Thorpe's children were finally presented with his gold medals.

■ For the 1965–66 season, San Francisco Warrior's center Wilt Chamberlain signed a contract for $100,000. His great rival, Boston Celtics center Bill Russell, then had his own contract negotiated so that he would be paid $100,001.

10 MEMORABLE NICKNAMES OF TEAMS...

Bronx Bombers	(New York Yankees)
Monsters of the Midway	(Chicago Bears)
Big Red Machine	(1970s Cincinnati Reds)
Broad Street Bullies	(1970s Philadelphia Flyers)
Flying Frenchmen	(Montreal Canadiens)
Gashouse Gang	(1930s St. Louis Cardinals)

Phi Slamma Jamma	(1982–84 University of Houston basketball)
Four Musketeers	(1920s French tennis stars René Lacoste, Henri Cochet, Jean Borotra, and Jacques Brugnon)
Whiz Kids	(1950 Philadelphia Phillies; early 1940s University of Illinois basketball)
Doctors of Dunk	(1980s University of Louisville basketball)

...AND 10 PARTS OF TEAMS...

Punch Line	(1940s Montreal Canadien line of Maurice Richard, Toe Blake, and Elmer Lach)
Purple People Eaters	(1960s and 1970s Minnesota Viking front four, including Jim Marshall, Carl Eller, Alan Page, and Gary Larsen, and later, Doug Sutherland)
Twin Towers	(Houston Rockets center-forwards Ralph Sampson and Akeem Olajuwon)

187

$100,000 Infield	(The 1911 Philadelphia Athletic infield—Stuffy McInnis, 1B; Eddie Collins, 2B; Jack Barry, SS; Home Run Baker, 3B)
$1,000,000 Infield	(The 1948 Philadelphia Athletic infield—Ferris Fain, 1B; Pete Suder, 2B; Eddie Joost, SS; Hank Majeski, 3B)
Steel Curtain	(1970s Pittsburgh Steeler front four, including "Mean" Joe Greene, Ernie Holmes, L. C. Greenwood, and Dwight White)
Fearsome Foursome	(1960s Los Angeles Ram front four, including Deacon Jones, Lamar Lundy, Roosevelt Grier, and Merlin Olsen)
Long Island Power Company	(1970s–80s New York Islander line of Bryan Trottier, Mike Bossy, and Clark Gillies)
Legends 1 and 1A	(1970s New York Knick backcourt of Walt Frazier and Earl Monroe)
Mr. Inside and Mr. Outside	(1940s Army backfield of Doc Blanchard and Glenn Davis)

...AND 10 FAN CLUSTERS

Arnie's Army	(Arnold Palmer fans)
Lee's Fleas	(Lee Trevino fans)
Franco's Italian Army	(Pittsburgh Steeler Franco Harris fans)
Cheese Heads	(Milwaukee Brewer fans)
Dawg Pound	(Cleveland Brown fans)
Jack's Pack	(Jack Nicklaus fans)
K Corner	(New York Met Dwight Gooden fans)
Coneheads	(New York Met David Cone fans)
Rambis Youth	(scrappy rebounder Kurt Rambis's horn-rimmed fans)
Bleacher Bums	(Chicago Cub fans)

AN EMBARRASSMENT OF RICHES

Some regions or schools or teams or conferences are so superior that they almost seem to be competing among themselves. After New York Giant Willie Mays won the 1954 National League MVP Award over their beloved Duke Snider, Brooklyn Dodger fans said that Mays might be the best centerfielder in the game, but he was only the third best in New York (behind New York Yankee Mickey Mantle, as well).

Internal, comradely competition may help to produce for some team, or league, a statistical cornucopia.

■ The 1928 New York Yankees had the top three RBI men in their league: Lou Gehrig and Babe Ruth were tied for the lead, with teammate Bob Meusel third. In 1932, the Philadelphia Phillies repeated the feat in the National League as Don Hurst, Chuck Klein, and Pinky Whitney ran 1-2-3.

■ In 1985, the Big East basketball conference provided three of the Final Four teams—St. John's, Georgetown, and eventual national champion Villanova.

■ After the 1972 college bowl games were played, the final national rankings for the 1971 season listed Nebraska first, Oklahoma second, and Colorado third—all Big Eight schools. Nebraska had gone undefeated; Oklahoma had lost once, to Nebraska; and Colorado had lost twice, to Nebraska and Oklahoma.

■ The 1965 Michigan State University football team set a record by placing seven men on All-America squads. They placed five more in 1966, for a two-year total of 12, another record.

■ The state of Oklahoma has an unusual number of fast and run-happy baseball players. Five of the top six places for most stolen bases in a high school season are held by five different Oklahoma schools.

■ In 1959, Johnny Unitas's main targets—Ray Berry, Lennie Moore, and Jim Mutschuller—were 1, 2, and 4 among NFL receivers.

■ In 1986, New York Mets pitchers Bob Ojeda, Dwight

Gooden, Sid Fernandez, and Ron Darling were ranked 1, 2, 3, and 4 in National League winning percentage.

■ The Edmonton Oilers had the first (Wayne Gretzky), second (Jari Kurri), and fourth (Mark Messier) top scorers in the NHL for the 1986–87 season.

JUST A FEW OF THE MOST FRUSTRATED ATHLETES AND TEAMS OF ALL TIME

■ Hungarian fighter Laszlo Papp won the Olympic middleweight boxing gold medal in 1948 and the light middleweight golds in 1952 and 1956, became the first boxer from a Communist country to turn professional, won the European title, and was prevented by the Hungarian government from fighting for the world title.

He retired undefeated.

■ There are many tales of undefeated and ultimately untested teams:

The University of Kentucky basketball team finished at 25-0 in 1954 and was ranked #1 in the country but declined an invitation to the NCAA tournament because three stars, all graduate students—Cliff Hagan, Frank Ramsey, and Lou Tsiropolos—would not have been allowed to play in the tournament. The team voted 9-0 to play in the tournament without them but coach Adolph Rupp overruled the team.

In college football, Colgate's 1932 team gained fame for being "unbeaten, untied, unscored upon, and uninvited." The Rose Bowl bypassed the Red Raiders for twice-tied University of Pittsburgh, which lost to the University of Southern California.

■ Bill Sharman, who would star for the Boston Celtics and later coach the Los Angeles Lakers to an NBA championship, was also a major leaguer, if briefly. He was called up by the Brooklyn Dodgers at the end of the 1951 season and was sitting on the bench during a September 27 game against the Boston Braves when umpire Frank Dascoli ejected the Dodger battery of Preacher Roe and Roy Campanella, as well as the whole Brooklyn bench, after a disputed play at home. Sharman did not get to see any action during the pennant stretch and earned the distinction of having been ejected from a major league game without having played in one.

■ In 1953, Ben Hogan was prevented from an attempt to win the modern golfing Grand Slam because the PGA tournament was held simultaneously with the British Open. That year, Hogan won the U.S. Open, the Masters, and the British Open.

14 OF THE MOST UTTERLY DOMINANT TEAMS AND COUNTRIES IN SPORTS HISTORY

■ In 1909, Yale's football team not only went undefeated, untied, and unscored upon, but did not allow an opponent inside the 25-yard line. In 1888, Yale outscored their 13 opponents 698-0, a record that still stands. From 1876–1900, Yale football was 231-10-11.

■ The New York Yankees are without question the most renowned team in baseball history, and probably in all of sports, mostly because they were overwhelmingly good. From 1927–62, the team won 19 World Series in 36 years, including five in a row from 1949–53 and four in a row from 1936–39; they lost in the World Series just four times during that 36-year period. In the 16-year span from 1949 to 1964, the Yankees won 14 pennants. From 1954–63, the American League MVP was a Yankee eight times. The 1939 Yankees outscored their opponents by 411 runs, the largest differential in the modern era.

◼ Canada's hockey team was so dominant that it received one of the ultimate compliments in sport: in the 1928 Olympic competition, Canada was simply advanced straight to the final round while the other 10 nations were divided into three pools, the winner of each joining Canada in the finals. On the way to winning their third hockey gold in a row, Canada held the opposition to no goals while averaging 13 a game.

◼ U.S. sailors kept the America's Cup for 132 years, the most sustained domination in any sport, until Australia won it in 1983. The United States recovered the Cup in 1987.

◼ From 1969 through 1988, Taiwan won the Little League World Series 13 times in 20 years. They captured the title in 1969-'71-'72-'73-'74-'77-'78-'79-'80-'81-'86-'87-'88.

◼ The University of North Carolina women's soccer team won the first NCAA women's soccer championship in 1982, and then every one through the decade except for 1986 (when they lost in the title game).

◼ India's men's field hockey team won the Olympic gold from 1928, in its first attempt, until 1960, when Pakistan beat them, 1-0, in the finals at Rome. Before that loss, India won 30 straight matches and outscored its opponents 196-8. In three matches against the United States, India won by a combined 47-1 score. India came back to win the gold in 1964.

◼ The Soviet Union women's gymnastics team won eight consecutive gold medals in team combined exercises from 1952, when that nation, as the Soviet Union, first showed up at the Olympics, until 1984, when they boycotted. They won it again in 1988.

◼ Since the first modern Olympic Games in 1896, the

United States has performed extraordinarily well. Some of the many Olympic events in which the United States has dominated include:

The 4x100m men's relay, which it has won 13 out of 17 times, losing only by disqualification (1912, 1960, and 1988) and boycott (1980);

The long jump, which it has won 18 of 21 times;

The pole vault, which it won in 16 straight Olympics, from 1896 to 1968;

The eight-oared crew race, which it won 8 of the first 10 times it was held, from 1900–56;

Men's swimming, winning 12 of 13 events in 1976;

Men's sprints, winning 14 of 21 100m golds, and 14 of 20 200m golds.

■ The Finns have produced many of the world's greatest distance runners. From 1912 to 1936, only twice would the Olympic 5,000m and 10,000m not be won by a Finn.

■ Since 1890, Johns Hopkins University's lacrosse team has won or co-won 42 NCAA championships.

■ In the last 100 years, there have been 43 heavyweight world champions. Of those, 36 have been Americans.

■ Anchored by Joan Joyce, the greatest woman softball player ever, the Raybestos Brakettes from Stratford, Connecticut, won the national women's major fast pitch championship 14 times from 1966 to 1983.

■ Since 1948, no woman from outside of Eastern Europe has held the world shot-put record.

8
SEX AND DEATH

KILLED IN THE LINE OF DUTY

Some sports are more obviously dangerous than others—boxing, auto racing, football, to name three—and the number of athletes who have lost their lives competing in these sports is substantial. Since 1884, there have been approximately 500 ring deaths, seven in world title fights. Dozens of drivers have been killed during warm-ups, qualifying runs, and actual races; the worst accident in auto-racing history took place at Le Mans in 1955, when driver Pierre Levegh's car spun out of control and careened into the stands, killing himself and 86 others, and seriously injuring 108 people, mostly spectators. President Theodore Roosevelt tried to ban college football, without success, when 18 players died and 73 more were seriously hurt in the year 1905 alone. (At Roosevelt's urging, the flying wedge was outlawed, a neutral zone between opposing lines was instituted, and the legalization of the forward pass soon followed, in 1906.)

But along with these three sports, less violent sports, too, have claimed lives. The following is a list of some of those who unwittingly participated in their final sporting event.

■ Richard Wertheim, 60, the center service linesman in the 1983 U.S. Open boy's final, was killed when, stationed behind the baseline, he was hit in the groin by a ball off the racket of Stefan Edberg. Wertheim toppled backward in his chair and fractured his skull against the ground. His family sued the United States Tennis Association for negligence but lost.

■ Bill Masterton, 29, a Minnesota North Star rookie, died on January 15, 1968, from a massive internal brain injury sustained in a game with the Oakland Seals two days earlier. Masterton had fallen over backward after being checked, and hit his head on the ice. He is the only known pro hockey death in the modern era.

■ In 1920, Cleveland Indian Ray Chapman became the only baseball player killed during a major league game. While at bat at the Polo Grounds, Chapman was hit in the head by New York Yankees pitcher Carl Mays. Chapman took two steps toward first, collapsed, and never regained consciousness.

■ Phil Klusman, 43, a sportswriter for the *Bakersfield Californian*, was killed by an errant hammer throw during a practice round of an NCAA Division II track and field meet at Cal State–Los Angeles, on May 23, 1986.

■ Soviet diver Sergei Shalibashvili died of a massive cerebral hemorrhage after hitting his head on the edge of the platform while attempting a reverse three-somersault tuck at the World University Games in Edmonton, in July of 1983.

■ Fourteen-year-old baseball fan Alan Fish died of a head injury four days after being struck by a foul ball hit off the bat of Manny Mota at Dodger Stadium, May 16, 1970. The boy's parents sued the Dodgers for negligence but the jury absolved the team of blame.

■ By 1928, 6 of the first 15 Indianapolis 500 winners had died while racing—Dario Resta, Howdy Wilcox, Gaston Chevrolet, Jimmy Murphy, Joe Boyer, and Frank Lockhart. The 1929 winner, Ray Keech, was killed two weeks later on a midwestern dirt track.

■ The first athlete to die in the Olympics was Portuguese marathoner Francisco Lazaro, 21, who collapsed from sunstroke and heart trouble near the end of the 1912 race in Stockholm. He died the next day.

■ In the 1960 Olympic road race, Danish cyclist Knut Jensen became the second person to die in the Olympics. He collapsed from sunstroke and fractured his skull. It was later discovered that he had taken Ronicol, a blood circulation stimulant, before the race.

■ Vladimir Smirnov of the Soviet Union, Olympic gold medalist in the foil in 1980, died when the foil of his opponent in the 1982 world championships in Rome, Matthias Behr of West Germany, snapped and pierced Smirnov's mask, penetrated his eyeball, and entered his brain. Smirnov died nine days later.

■ On April 30, 1981, photographer Michael Zia of the *Tigard Valley Times* (Oregon) was taking pictures of the mechanical rabbit at Multnomah Kennel Club dog-racing track in Fairview, Oregon, and did not see the approaching rabbit's motor, which struck him in the face and severed his arm. He never regained consciousness after the accident. His arm was reattached and then reamputated when it became infected. Zia died on May 11 of a massive pulmonary hemorrhage.

■ The 1987 world champion bull rider Lane Frost, 25, was gored and trampled by a bull on July 30, 1989, at the Cheyenne Frontiers Day Rodeo. In the past 19 years, there have been an estimated 11 rodeo deaths.

■ Switzerland's Felix Endrich, 1953 world champion in the two-man bobsled, died less than a week after his victory while running a four-man sled down the same course at Garmisch-Partenkirchen. He crashed into a tree and was killed instantly.

■ Kazimierz "Kay" Skrzypeski, British luger, was killed during a trial run on the Olympic course two weeks before the 1964 Innsbruck Games.

■ Chuck Hughes, Detroit Lion wide receiver, collapsed and died on the field during a game against the Chicago Bears, on October 24, 1971. His heart attack was the result of a blood clot, caused by an injury that he sustained during the game.

■ The thoroughbred Swale collapsed and died of a heart attack after a 10-minute workout at Belmont Park on June 17, 1984. Swale had won the Kentucky Derby in May and the Belmont in June.

■ At least 130 motorcyclists have been killed in the 80-year history of the Isle of Man Tourist Trophy.

■ In 1902, in a cavalry endurance race from Brussels to Ostend, 16 of 29 horses died.

■ Three drivers died in the 22-day, 7,979-mile Paris-to-Dakar rally in 1988, as did three spectators. Three others died in a fire started accidentally by a support team. The rally began in Versailles and crossed over the Sahara Desert.

■ Russell Mockridge, cycling double gold medalist in 1952, was hit by a bus and killed while competing in the 1958 Tour of Gippsland race in Melbourne.

■ Prominent boxers who have killed in the ring include Sugar Ray Robinson, Ezzard Charles, Primo Carnera, and Ray "Boom Boom" Mancini. Boxer Frankie Campbell, brother of baseball star Dolf Camilli, was killed by Max Baer in 1930.

REPELLENT SEX CRIMES INVOLVING AMERICA'S TEAM: YOUR DALLAS COWBOYS

■ Rafael Septien, while the placekicker for the Cowboys, was indicted on January 22, 1987, in the sexual assault of a

10-year-old friend of his roommate's daughter. Septien pleaded not guilty. On April 8, 1987, he offered a plea of guilty to a charge of indecency with a child, and was sentenced to 10 years' deferred probation and a $2,000 fine.

■ On November 30, 1970, Cowboys wide receiver Lance Rentzel was charged with indecent exposure and released on bail. According to charges made by the district attorney, Rentzel had exposed himself to a 10-year-old girl on November 19 in North Dallas. He pleaded guilty and was given five years' probation provided that he receive psychiatric and medical treatment. He had pleaded guilty to a similar charge four years before.

■ Retired football star Thomas "Hollywood" Henderson, who had spent most of his career as a linebacker with the Cowboys, was sentenced on June 11, 1984, to four years and eight months in prison for sexually assaulting two teenage girls and then offering them a $10,000 bribe not to testify against him. The charges Henderson faced stemmed from his assault of a 17-year-old quadriplegic and her 15-year-old friend in November of 1983.

SIMILARLY REPELLENT SEX CRIMES INVOLVING AMERICA'S PUTATIVE EMBODIMENT OF EVIL: THE OAKLAND RAIDERS/LOS ANGELES

ATHLETES INVOLVED IN MURDER

▣ In 1907, Vere Thomas St. Leger Gould, Wimbledon finalist in 1879, was convicted of murdering a Danish widow whose dismembered body he attempted to freight in two luggage trunks from France to England. He died on Devil's Island in 1909.

▣ On January 19, 1900, at a farm near North Brookfield, Massachusetts, Marty Bergen, catcher for Boston's National League team, axed his wife and children to death. He then killed himself.

▣ Auto racer LeeRoy Yarbrough, the top driver on the 1969 stock-car circuit, died December 8, 1984, having spent his last four years in mental institutions because he had tried to strangle his 65-year-old mother in 1980. The judge had ruled then that Yarbrough was not guilty of attempted murder because, at the time of the incident, Yarbrough did not have the capacity to tell right from wrong.

▣ In 1980, six years after retiring from football, former Kansas City Chiefs tackle Jim Tyrer shot his wife to death, and then himself, at their Kansas City home.

▣ British featherweight Owen Swift killed men in two separate bouts, in 1834 and 1838. For the first killing, of Anthony Noon, Swift served six months in prison; for the second killing, of Brighton Bill, Swift was acquitted. He retired from fighting after the acquittal.

▣ On October 15, 1910, on the ranch of middleweight champion Stanley Ketchel, a jealous farmhand named Walter A. Dipley interrupted Ketchel's breakfast and killed him in an argument over Ketchel's girlfriend.

▣ Brian Spencer, an NHL player from 1969 to 1979, was indicted on December 12, 1987, for murder and kidnapping. He stood trial in the fall of 1987 in Palm Beach County, Florida, and was eventually acquitted. In June of 1988, Spencer was himself murdered in Riviera Beach, Florida, when a man walked up to the truck in which Spencer was a passenger and demanded money. The man then shot Spencer, 39, in the chest.

■ In June 1929, Dr. James H. Snook, a gold medalist for the 1920 U.S. Olympic military revolver team, was arrested for first-degree murder in the killing of Theora Hix, his 25-year-old mistress. Snook confessed that he had used a hammer to beat Hix after violent sex. Snook died in the electric chair.

WOMEN COMPETING WITH, AND AGAINST, MEN

■ In 1988, Winning Colors became the third filly to win the Kentucky Derby. Genuine Risk won it in 1980 and Favored Regret won in 1915.

■ Jackie Mitchell struck out Babe Ruth and Lou Gehrig in an exhibition baseball game in 1931. Babe Didrickson toured briefly as the only female member of the House of David baseball team, and pitched an inning against the Philadelphia Athletics in an exhibition game.

■ Driver Janet Guthrie was the first woman to qualify for and compete in the Indianapolis 500. In May of 1976, she competed in the qualifying round but failed to win a place in the actual race when she had to withdraw her car with mechanical problems. In 1977, she competed but had to quit after 27 laps because her car again failed. She finished the race in 1978, completing 190 laps and finishing ninth.

■ Jimmy Connors is the only great male tennis player coached by a woman—his mother, Gloria. Billie Jean King was the first woman to coach a co-ed sports team, the Philadelphia Freedom of World Team Tennis, in 1974.

▨ Lynnette Woodard became the first female member of the Harlem Globetrotters, in October 1985. Nancy Lieberman competed for the Springfield Fame of the United States Basketball League on June 10, 1986, the first woman in a men's pro league.

▨ Edna Jameson, director of the Cleveland Indians ticket office in 1948, became the first woman to receive a World Series share.

▨ In 1954, Marguerite Norris, president of the NHL Detroit Red Wings, was presented with the Stanley Cup. She became the first woman to have her name engraved on the Cup. Sonie Scurfield, co-owner of the Calgary Flames, became the second, in 1989.

▨ Los Angeles Rams owner Georgia Frontiere is the only woman who owns an NFL team.

▨ Women compete head-to-head with men in all equestrian competitions and classes. In 1972, Lisolett Linsenhoff of West Germany became the first female individual equestrian gold medalist. Women and men also began to compete with each other in Olympic shooting competitions in 1968, though some of the events are segregated by sex. In 1976, American Margaret Murdock won a silver medal in the small-bore rifle, three positions competition, becoming the first woman to win an Olympic shooting medal.

▨ LPGA pro Cathy Sherk, winner of the women's U.S., Canadian, and world amateur championships, qualified in the summer of 1989 for the men's $100,000 Times-BIC Ontario Open. The only women to have appeared in a PGA-sanctioned event before that were Kathy Whitworth and Mickey Wright, who teamed to play in the 1985 Legends Classics on the PGA Seniors Tour.

■ Eleanor Engel signed to play minor league baseball with the Harrisburg (Pennsylvania) Senators of the Inter-State League in June 1952. National Association president George Trautman, backed by major league commissioner Ford Frick, voided the signing. Engle appeared in uniform but never played.

■ The majority of the fastest English Channel swims have been accomplished by women.

■ Diana Crump was the first female jockey to ride against males, at Hialeah on February 7, 1969, and later became the first woman jockey to ride in the Kentucky Derby. Barbara Jo Rubin was the first woman jockey in the United States to win a pari-mutuel race, on February 22, 1969, at the Charles Town (West Virginia) racetrack.

■ Julie Krone is considered the greatest woman jockey in history. She is the first ever to win five races in one day at a New York track, first to win a riding title at a major track, and first to ride in the Breeder's Cup, finishing fourth in 1988. In her career, she has ridden to more than 1,000 victories, for over $25 million in purses.

■ Amanda Clement was the first woman umpire in organized baseball. Starting in 1903, she umped six years in the Dakotas, Nebraska, Iowa, and Minnesota.

■ Eva Shain became the first woman judge for a heavyweight title fight on September 29, 1977, for a bout between Muhammad Ali and Earnie Shavers.

■ From 1985–88, Carol White coached the Georgia Tech football team's placekickers.

■ Libby Riddles won the Iditarod dogsled race in 1984. Susan Butcher won it in 1986, 1987, 1988, and 1990. In 1990, Butcher set a course record.

THE MOST NOTABLE SUICIDES IN SPORTS

■ Shingo Furuya, managing director of Japan's Hanshin Tigers, jumped from his eighth-floor hotel window and killed himself because he was despondent over negotiations with one of the team's star players—American Randy Bass—and because Hanshin was in sixth place in a six-team league. After learning of Furuya's suicide, Hanshin decided to go ahead with its game against the Yomiuri Giants, and interim manager Minoru Murayama announced that in memory of Furuya, Hanshin wanted to win at any cost. Hanshin lost, 1-0.

■ Catcher Willard Hershberger is the only major league player in this century to commit suicide during the season. In 1940, he was Ernie Lombardi's backup on the Cincinnati Reds, which would go on to win the pennant that year. On August 3, the day after Hershberger, 29, played poorly in the second game of a doubleheader in Boston—he went hitless in five at-bats—he cut his throat over the bathtub in his hotel room.

■ Peter Gregg, the all-time leading winner of the International Motor Sports Association GT Championship, committed suicide in December 1980, at age 40. Earlier that year, on June 10, while Gregg was trying to qualify for the 24 hours of Le Mans, he suffered a concussion and double vision, and was forced to miss half of the 14 IMSA GT events on the 1980 schedule. A friend of Gregg's said that the driver had been despondent over not being able to race.

■ Colonel M. Lewis Clark, the man who founded the Kentucky Derby and built Churchill Downs, committed suicide on April 22, 1899. He shot himself in the head with a pistol, primarily because of his failing health.

■ Larry Bethea, Dallas Cowboy defensive lineman, killed himself in 1987 after suffering drug and financial problems. The suicide occurred hours after Bethea was named as a suspect in two armed robberies.

■ In 1971, Bruce Gardner, a former pitching phenom for the powerhouse University of Southern California baseball team, killed himself on the mound at USC.

■ National League President Harry Pulliam shot himself during the 1909 season. During the previous season, he had let stand umpire Hank O'Day's ruling on Fred Merkle's notorious boner (which helped cost the New York Giants the pennant), a decision for which Pulliam was much abused.

■ Takeichi Nishi, 1932 Olympic gold medal winner for equestrian jumping, died in a mass Japanese suicide in World War II.

■ Jake Powell, one of the outfielders with whom the New York Yankees tried to replace Babe Ruth in the 1930s, shot himself in the head at a Washington, D.C. police station in November of 1948 after being picked up for writing bad checks. Powell had been suspended from baseball for 10 days in 1938 when he said in a radio interview that he was a "cop" who liked "beating up niggers and then throwing them in jail."

■ Kokichi Tsuburaya, who became a national hero in Japan after finishing third in the 1964 Olympic marathon in Tokyo, was ordered to begin training immediately for the 1968 Olympics. In 1967, he suffered two injuries and spent three months in the hospital. When he started running again, he realized that he would never approach his prior form. On January 9, 1968, Tsuburaya killed himself by using a razor blade to cut his right carotid artery. He left a note that said simply, "Cannot run anymore."

■ Richard Johnson, basketball star for Long Beach State, shot himself with a .38-caliber revolver in June 1978, shortly after being passed up in the NBA draft. In his suicide note he admitted to a drug problem.

■ Win Mercer, a turn-of-the-century pitcher and infielder, died in a San Francisco hotel room in 1903. According to a newspaper account, "Mercer... had attached a hose to a gas jet, gone to bed with the end of the hose in his mouth and the bed clothing pulled over his head." Mercer had been hired to manage the American League Detroit team the following year. He had become depressed when treatment failed to cure a pulmonary ailment.

■ Of the 70 known major leaguers who have committed suicide, none was a left-handed pitcher.

NEW YORK GIANTS WHO HAVE BEEN DIAGNOSED WITH CANCER SINCE THE TEAM MOVED TO NEW JERSEY IN 1976

■ Dan Lloyd, linebacker —malignant lymphoma, 1980

■ Doug Kotar, running back —brain tumor, 1983

■ John Tuggle, running back —blood vessel cancer, 1986

■ Karl Nelson, tackle —Hodgkin's disease, 1987

9 INDIVIDUAL SPORTS FIGURES KILLED IN AIR CRASHES

■ March 31, 1931: Notre Dame football coach Knute Rockne, age 43, in Kansas.

■ October 27, 1949: Marcel Cerdan, age 33, former world

middleweight champion, en route to fight Jake LaMotta for the title.

■ February 13, 1964: Ken Hubbs, Chicago Cub second baseman, in a crash in Utah. He had been named the National League Rookie of the Year in 1962.

■ July 24, 1966: Golfer Tony Lema, shortly after winning the British Open. He was 32.

■ August 31, 1969: Rocky Marciano, who retired as unbeaten heavyweight champion, in a private plane near Des Moines. He was 46.

■ December 31, 1972: Roberto Clemente, future baseball Hall of Famer, en route to Managua, Nicaragua, to aid earthquake victims.

■ March 3, 1974: John Cooper, 1964 silver medalist in the 400m hurdles, age 33. He was one of 346 people killed in a Turkish Airlines crash over France.

■ June 24, 1975: New York Nets forward Wendell Ladner, age 26. The identity of his burned body was partially confirmed by the 1974 ABA championship ring on his finger.

■ August 2, 1979: Thurman Munson, New York Yankee catcher, in Canton, Ohio. He was 32.

9 TEAMS KILLED IN AIR CRASHES

■ May 4, 1949: Torino, the Italian soccer champion, returning home after a game in Lisbon. The plane crashed into the Superga Basilica near Turin. The entire team, including reserves, coaches, and trainers, was killed.

■ February 6, 1958: English soccer champion Manchester United, returning home from a European Cup match in

Belgrade. The plane crashed at Munich airport, killing eight players, the manager, trainer, a secretary, and eight journalists.

■ October 29, 1960: The Cal Poly-San Luis Obispo football team, near Toledo, Ohio. Sixteen team members were killed.

■ February 15, 1961: The U.S. figure skating team, near Berg, Belgium, 18 team members were killed.

■ April 3, 1961: Green Cross, a first-division Chilean soccer team, returning to Santiago from a game in Osorno. The plane crashed into the side of Las Lastimas Mountains, killing all passengers.

■ September 26, 1969: The Bolivian soccer team, called "The Strongest," returning home to La Paz from an out-of-town game. The plane crashed in the Andes. The entire team of 19 players and all club officials died.

■ November 14, 1970: The Marshall University football team, when their chartered plane crashed in Kenova, West Virginia, forty-three players and coaches died.

■ December 13, 1977: The University of Evansville (Indiana) basketball team, soon after taking off in dense fog. Twelve team members and head coach Bobby Watson perished.

■ March 14, 1980. The U.S. amateur boxing team, near Warsaw. Twenty-two team members were killed.

HOMOSEXUALITY IN SPORTS

It is hard to tell how extensive a role homosexuality plays in professional athletics because to this day discussion of its presence, especially in men's sports, remains taboo. A man who succeeds on the field is viewed as having greater sexual—heterosexual—powers and confidence. Statements to the contrary are unwelcome among the jock fraternity.

■ Dave Kopay, NFL running back from 1964–72 for the San Francisco 49ers, Detroit Lions, Washington Redskins, New Orleans Saints, and Green Bay Packers, was the first professional athlete to admit his homosexuality openly. He discussed it in his book, *The David Kopay Story*.

■ Jerry Smith, tight end for the Washington Redskins from 1965–77, talked anonymously about his homosexuality in a *Washington Star* article in the early 1970s, and had a brief affair with Dave Kopay when they were teammates. Smith died of an AIDS–related disease on October 15, 1986, possibly the first professional athlete in America to do so.

■ Baron von Cramm, the great and gentlemanly German tennis player who opposed the Nazi regime, was summoned home from Davis Cup play in 1937 and imprisoned by the Gestapo for alleged homosexual offenses.

■ In 1981, Marilyn Barnett, the former lover of tennis player Billie Jean King, sued King unsuccessfully for palimony.

■ Glenn Burke, a .237 lifetime hitter for the Los Angeles Dodgers and Oakland Athletics from 1976–79, is the only major leaguer known to admit publicly to his homosexuality.

■ American tennis great Bill Tilden, a homosexual, was jailed twice on indecency charges.

■ Dave Pallone, the former National League umpire (1979–88)—best remembered for being bumped in an argument by Cincinnati Reds manager Pete Rose, which led to a controversial month-long suspension for Rose—felt that he was fired because he was gay. He said, "Leading a double life for a decade was not easy. Obviously, I could never be myself. I'd be introduced in a gay bar, for instance, and the inevitable question was, 'What do you do for a living?' For years, I would lie."

■ After Pam Parsons resigned in 1981 as women's basketball coach at the University of South Carolina for what she said were personal reasons, a local newspaper reported that Parsons had been driven from her job by an allegation by the mother of one of the players that Parsons had had a lesbian relationship with a player and had made sexual advances toward another. *Sports Illustrated* printed similar accusations. Parsons sued *SI* for libel and lost. Federal charges were in turn filed against her and Tina Buck, one of Parsons' former players, for lying at the trial when they said that they had not patronized a lesbian bar in Salt Lake City. Parsons and Buck both pleaded guilty.

19 OF THE STRANGEST AILMENTS, FREAKIEST INJURIES, AND WEIRDEST DEATHS

■ St. Louis Cardinal Vince Coleman was knocked out of the remainder of postseason play in 1985 when the tarpaulin-spreading device at Busch Stadium ran over his left leg during a workout before Game 4 of the National League playoffs.

■ Eddie Machen, once a top heavyweight contender, fell to his death while sleepwalking in his San Francisco apartment.

■ James Mitchel, a top American competitor in the now-defunct stone throw competition, was forced out of his event in the 1906 Interim Olympics in Athens because he had dislocated his shoulder when the ship he took to Europe hit a wave.

■ On January 1, 1977, former major league pitcher Danny Frisella was killed near Phoenix in a dune-buggy accident.

■ Six weeks before the 1956 Olympics, Czech Emil Zatopek suffered a hernia while training with his wife on his shoulders. He still finished sixth in the marathon.

■ Spectacular Bid lost the 1979 Belmont—and the Triple Crown—because he stepped on a safety pin that he had picked off of his leg bandage. It penetrated his front left hoof.

■ Lyle Kurtenbach, a 41-year-old spectator, was killed by a flying tire at the 1987 Indianapolis 500.

■ Detroit Tigers second baseman Lou Whitaker hurt his knee while dancing at a wedding.

■ Christine Truman was out of tennis for most of 1962 after she put her foot through a rotten floorboard on a tennis court in Jamaica.

■ In 1983, Jack Newton, a 33-year-old Australian golfer, lost his right arm when he accidentally walked into the spinning propeller of a small airplane.

■ On November 29, 1900, 13 fans died while watching the California–Stanford football game when the Pacific Glass Works factory roof they were viewing from collapsed and they fell into vats of molten glass.

■ Before a game with the Detroit Tigers on April 12, 1978, Texas Rangers relief pitcher Rogelio Moret stood trance-like for at least 45 minutes in the locker room, holding a shower shoe in his extended hand. After he was given five sedative injections, he was taken to a local neuropsychiatric hospital. The team physician called it "a definite catatonic state."

■ San Francisco Giant Dave Dravecky broke his arm while delivering a pitch in a 1989 game. His arm had already been weakened by surgery to remove a malignant tumor.

■ In July 1883, Matthew Webb, the first person to swim the English Channel, died attempting to swim the violent Whirlpool Rapids below Niagara Falls.

■ New York Mets pitcher Bob Ojeda was lost for the 1988 National League playoffs when he almost sliced off his left middle finger while gardening with an electric hedge clipper.

■ On July 17, 1914, New York Giants outfielder Red Murray was struck by lightning while running the bases. He was not seriously injured.

■ A bird dropping hit Boyd Gittins in the eye and dislodged his contact lens before he reached the first hurdle at the 1968 Olympic semi trials, forcing him to pull out of the race. (He later won a runoff to qualify for the trials, where he earned a spot on the Olympic team.)

■ A year after his best season, Pittsburgh Pirates pitcher Steve Blass inexplicably lost his control. In 1972, when he was 19-8, he walked 84 batters in 249⅔ innings. In 1973, he walked 84 in 88⅔ innings. By 1974, Blass was out of baseball.

■ At the 1984 Los Angeles Olympics, several American cyclists, including Steve Hegg, gold medalist in the 4,000m individual pursuit, "blood boosted"—a technique in which some of one's blood is extracted, frozen, and then re-injected just before competition to increase hemoglobin level and endurance. However, some cyclists did not have time to freeze their own blood and instead injected themselves with other people's blood. Two of the racers became ill.

SEXISM IN SPORTS

■ The International Olympic Committee refused to add the women's 3,000m run for the 1980 Moscow Olympics because the distance was "deemed a little too strenuous for women." In the 1928 Olympic 800-yard run, several women collapsed, inciting IOC president Compte de Baillet-Latour to try and rid the Games of all women's track competition. Women's running events of longer than 200 meters were eliminated until 1960, when the 800m was reinstated. In 1972, the 1,500m was added. In 1984, the 3,000m and marathon were added.

■ In August 1890, W. S. Franklin announced the formation of a women's professional baseball league. He required that players be under 21 years old, good-looking, and have a good figure.

■ In the 1920 Olympics, American figure skater Theresa Weld was cautioned by the judges for making jumps considered unsuitable for a lady. Previously, it had been considered "unfeminine behavior" to jump altogether.

■ Women were not allowed on center court for the Italian championship tennis finals until the late 1960s.

■ In early bobsled races, two of the five riders had to be women, but could not drive or work the brakes.

■ In 1936, Avery Brundage, while president of the U.S. Olympic Committee, said, "I am fed up to the ears with women as track and field competitors...her charms sink to something less than zero. As swimmers and divers, girls are [as] beautiful and adroit as they are ineffective and unpleasing on the track." In 1952, Brundage became president of the International Olympic Committee.

- Before 1916, women were not allowed to attend boxing matches.

- The Women's AAA in Britain did not allow women to compete in long-distance road races until 1975.

- The 1900 Paris Olympic field was made up of 1,308 men competitors and 11 women.

- In 776 B.C., ancient Greeks banned women as competitors and spectators from the Olympic Games. Any married woman caught near the stadium was hurled from a cliff.

13 ATHLETES WHO DIED FROM WAR

- Germany's Alfred Flatow, Olympic gold medalist in the parallel bars in 1896, was exterminated in a German concentration camp in 1945.

- A year after winning the 400m at the 1920 Olympics, Great Britain's Eric Liddell (of *Chariots of Fire* fame) joined his father in China to do missionary work. He died of a brain tumor in a Japanese internment camp in China during World War II.

- Freddie Tait, the British Amateur golf champion in 1896 and 1898, died in the Boer War.

- German Luz Long, 1936 Olympic silver medalist and great friend to American track star Jesse Owens, was killed in the Battle of St. Pietro, July 14, 1943.

- Ron Zinn, sixth in the Olympic 20,000m walk in 1964, was killed in Vietnam less than nine months later, at age 26.

- Laurie Doherty, Wimbledon champion from 1902–06, died serving for the Air Ministry during World War I.

- Norwegian-born American ski jumper Torger Tokle, who broke 24 records in his career, was killed while fighting with the U.S. Army in Italy in 1945.

- Endre Kabos, Hungarian Olympic gold medalist in the saber in 1936, was killed when the Budapest Margaret Bridge blew up in World War II.

- Hall of Fame pitcher Christy Mathewson died of tuberculosis in 1925, presumably from poison gassing that he had suffered in France in World War I.

- Jean Bouin of France and George Hutson of Great Britain, the silver and bronze medalists respectively in the 1912 Olympic 5,000m race, were both killed in action in 1914.

- Anthony Wilding, four-time Wimbledon winner (1910–13) from New Zealand, was killed in action at Neuve Chapelle, France, in 1915, at age 31.

- Attila Petschauer, Hungarian gold medalist in the Olympic team saber competitions in 1928 and 1932, was tortured to death in 1943 while fighting in the Ukraine.

9

OFF THE FIELD, AND EXTRA-CURRICULAR ACTIVITY

THE HALF DOZEN MOST LEGITIMATE EXCUSES IN SPORTS HISTORY FOR NOT PERFORMING WELL—OR AT ALL

■ Susan Butcher, four-time winner of the Iditarod dogsled race, did not finish in 1985. She and her dog team were trampled by moose.

■ Gladiators were being prepared to fight in 79 A.D., in Pompeii, but never participated. Mt. Vesuvius erupted and lava buried the city and everyone in it. Four gladiators were found shackled in chains in one room, and in another, 17 more who had tried to take refuge from the volcano.

■ The Wichita State University football team went 0-9 in 1960. Soon after the season started, a plane crash killed 14 players, the coach, and the athletic director. The team was reinforced with freshmen for the remainder of the season.

■ The NHL's New York Americans suspended operations in 1942 and eventually disbanded in 1945 because they had lost most of their players to World War II.

■ Pelle Lindbergh, Philadelphia Flyer goalie, was voted to the NHL All-Star team in 1986 but did not play because he was killed in an auto accident in November 1985. He became the first dead man voted to an all-star team.

■ New York Yankees first baseman Lou Gehrig hit just .143 in limited time in 1939. At the time, he was suffering from amyotrophic lateral sclerosis, the disease that would soon kill him (and later bear his name).

THE HALF DOZEN WORST EXCUSES IN SPORTS HISTORY FOR NOT PERFORMING WELL—OR AT ALL

■ Outfielder Claudell Washington, after being traded in 1978 from the Texas Rangers to the Chicago White Sox, failed to report for four days. "I overslept," he explained.

■ Ted Tinling designed a special dress for Betty Hilton, a top British player, in 1948. She wore the dress and lost badly to American Louise Brough in a Wightman Cup match. Hilton's defeat was blamed on her self-consciousness over the color of her dress.

■ In the 1987 U.S. Open, John McEnroe blamed his boorish on-court behavior on temporary insanity, brought about by the tension of his wife expecting their second child.

■ The same excuse was used after a Japanese baseball game in September 1982 between the Taiyo Whales and the Hanshin Tigers in Yokohama, in which two Tiger coaches brutally beat up an umpire on national television. The coaches pleaded temporary insanity and were suspended for the rest of the season.

■ Fullerton State football coach Gene Murphy said that one of his players claimed that he was late because he had "pulled his wrist while running."

■ After he missed a basketball practice, New York Net Sly Williams called the team's office and attempted to pass himself off as his brother. "Sly has some personal problems," Williams said. "There's been a slight death in the family."

217

THE WORST EXCUSE FOR NOT ALLOWING SOMEONE TO PERFORM

■ John Kelly (father of Princess Grace of Monaco), who would go on to win three Olympic rowing gold medals, was refused entry to the 1920 Diamond Sculls at Henley, England, because, as a bricklayer, he had had an unfair advantage in developing bigger muscles than his gentlemen-competitors.

NO EXCUSE, PERIOD

■ On July 21, 1970, San Diego Padres manager Preston Gomez removed pitcher Clay Kirby in the ninth inning of a game against the New York Mets, even though Kirby was pitching a no-hitter. The relief pitcher not only lost the no-hitter but the game, as well.

LOS ANGELES DODGERS IN 1960s TV SIT-COMS

One reason so many professional athletes include southern California on their wish list of trade destinations is the weather. Another is the generally comfortable lifestyle. Another is the beach. The main reason, of course, is that with Hollywood nearby, you greatly increase your chance of making a cameo appearance in a movie or TV show.

Immortality may be achieved in many ways. For Dodger righthander Don Drysdale, that may mean pitching a record 58 consecutive scoreless innings, as he did in 1968. With television syndication, however—not to mention the fact that Orel Hershiser has now broken Drysdale's once seemingly untouchable record—it's more likely that Drysdale will achieve immortality because of his guest appearance the following year in "The Flying Nun."

■ Jim Lefebvre, infielder, on "Batman," 1966, ABC. "Batman's Anniversary: A Riddling Controversy": A two-episode show to celebrate Batman's anniversary with the Gotham Police Department. The Riddler wants to legalize crime; Lefebvre plays a henchman.

■ Sandy Koufax, pitcher, on "Dennis the Menace," 1962, CBS. "Dennis and the Dodger": Mr. Quigley offers to coach the boys' baseball team to keep the kids and their families as customers.

■ Lefebvre and Al Ferrara, outfielder, on "Gilligan's Island," 1966, CBS. "High Man on the Totem Pole": Gilligan, the "headhunter," finds a head on a totem pole with a striking resemblance to himself. Lefebvre and Ferrara play savages.

■ Maury Wills, shortstop, on "Get Smart," 1969, NBC. "The Apes of Rath": K.A.O.S. transforms an ape into a human being so that he can act as their agent, but when a bell rings, he reverts back to ape form and wreaks havoc.

■ Larry Sherry and Stan Williams, pitchers, on "The Tom Ewell Show," 1961, CBS. "Out of Left Field": A real estate deal grows out of an accidental meeting between Tom and the two Dodgers.

■ Vin Scully, announcer, on "Karen," 1964, NBC. "Beethoven or Baseball": Confusion reigns when Karen makes three dates for Saturday night.

■ Scully and Don Drysdale, pitcher, on "The Joey Bishop Show," 1964, CBS. "Joey and the Dodgers": Joey is stranded without guests when the Dodger game goes into extra innings.

■ Willie Davis, outfielder, and Drysdale on "The Flying Nun," 1969, ABC. "The Big Game": Sister Bertrille (Sally Field) enjoys a moral victory in spite of her baseball team's loss by a score of 43-1.

■ Drysdale on "Leave It To Beaver," 1962, ABC. "The Long Distance Call": Beaver and his friends make a long distance call to Drysdale.

■ Drysdale on "Our Man Higgins," 1963, ABC. "Who's on First?": Higgins invites Drysdale to make an appearance at the Little League season opener.

■ Drysdale on "The Donna Reed Show," 1962, ABC. "The Man in the Mask": Jeff is chosen to umpire a girl's baseball game and gets tips from Drysdale.

■ Drysdale on "The Donna Reed Show" again in 1962. "All Those Dreams": Jeff and his family take a trip to Chicago and he decides to interview Drysdale.

6 THINGS WITH WINGS OR TAILS THAT MADE AN IMPACT

■ A dog named Pickles found the World Cup soccer trophy that had been stolen in England in 1966 prior to the competition. Pickles found the cup wrapped in a newspaper, buried in a garden.

■ Golfer Lloyd Mangrum's chances of winning the 1950 U.S. Open disappeared when he was penalized two strokes for lifting his ball to brush off a bug during an 18-hole playoff with Ben Hogan and George Fazio. Mangrum, who trailed Hogan by a stroke at the time of the incident on the 16th green, lost by four strokes.

■ With the score tied 14-14 in the 1985 Orange Bowl, the University of Oklahoma was penalized 15 yards for unsportsmanlike conduct when its horse-drawn wagon, the "Sooner Schooner," rode onto the field to celebrate an apparent 22-yard field goal during the third quarter. In fact, the field goal had been nullified by an illegal-procedure call. The two penalties moved the ball back 20 yards, where a 42-yard field goal attempt was blocked. Oklahoma went on to lose 28-17 to the University of Washington, costing them a shot at the national title.

■ Just before an Oakland Athletics–Kansas City Royals game in June 1986, A's slugger Dave Kingman, who neither liked, nor was liked by, the press, had a live rat delivered to the press box to sportswriter Susan Fornoff of *The Sacramento Bee*.

■ At Toronto's Exhibition Stadium on August 4, 1983, New York Yankees outfielder Dave Winfield accidently killed a sea gull with a between-innings throw toward the bullpen. Winfield was met by several plainclothes policemen after the game and taken to a Toronto station house, where he was charged with cruelty to animals. He posted the $500 bond, and a day later the charges were dropped.

■ A Sudanese soccer match between Betuan and Al Kubra in the early 1970s was interrupted in the 62nd minute by lions on the field.

A DOZEN GOLF TOURNAMENTS THAT ARE, OR WERE, NAMED FOR SHOW-BUSINESS PEOPLE

■ The Jamie Farr Toledo Classic (LPGA Tour)

- The Bob Hope Chrysler Classic (PGA Tour)

- The Gatlin Brothers Southwest Classic (Seniors Tour)

- The Nabisco Dinah Shore (LPGA)

- The former Ed McMahon Quad Cities Open is now the Hardee's Golf Classic (PGA)

- The former Andy Williams San Diego Open is now the Shearson-Lehman-Hutton Open (PGA)

- The former Sammy Davis, Jr. Greater Hartford Open is now the Canon Greater Hartford Open (PGA)

- The former Glen Campbell Los Angeles Open is now the Nissan–Los Angeles Open (PGA)

- The former Bing Crosby National Pro-Am is now the AT&T Pebble Beach National Pro-Am (PGA)

- The former Jackie Gleason Inverarry Classic is now the Honda Classic (PGA)

- The former Dean Martin Tucson Open is now the Northern Telecom Open (PGA)

- The former Danny Thomas Memphis Classic is now the Federal Express St. Jude Classic (PGA)

3 VERY STUPID QUESTIONS...

- To Raiders quarterback Jim Plunkett at the Super Bowl: "Jim, is it your father that's blind and your mother that's dead, or your mother that's blind and your father that's dead?"

■ To New York Yankees pitcher Don Larsen, after his perfect game in the 1956 World Series:
   "Is it the best game you've ever pitched?"

■ To Washington Redskin Doug Williams at the Super Bowl:
   "How long have you been a black quarterback?"

...AND 6 VERY SNAPPY ANSWERS

■ Boxer Bruce Woodcock, after being knocked out by Tami Mauriello, was asked which punch bothered him the most:
   "The last one."

■ Washington Redskins running back Duane Thomas, asked how it felt to play in the Super Bowl, the ultimate football game:
   "If it's the ultimate game, how come they're playing it again next year?"

■ On the 18th hole, in the second round of the 1961 Los Angeles Open, Arnold Palmer's game fell apart. He was asked how he could have shot a 12:
   "I missed my putt for an 11."

■ *New York Daily News* sportswriter Jenny Kellner, when confronted in the New York Jets' locker room in 1981 by an unclothed Mark Gastineau, who asked her expansively, "What do you think of this?"
   "It looks like a penis, only smaller," she answered.

■ Babe Ruth, when told that president Herbert Hoover earned less than the $80,000 that Ruth was demanding in 1930:

"I had a better year than he did."

■ Washington Redskins quarterback Sammy Baugh, when asked if the 73-0 rout that his team had just suffered in the 1940 NFL title game against the Chicago Bears would have turned out differently, had Redskin Charlie Malone not dropped a wide-open pass in the end zone in the first quarter:

"Yeah, it would have been 73-7."

THE WORLD'S MOST FAMOUS LINEUP

The comedy team of Bud Abbott and Lou Costello first performed their signature routine, "Who's on First?," on the "Kate Smith Show" on radio in the early 1940s, then later in the 1945 movie, *The Naughty Nineties*, and many times in between and after.

Here is the lineup from the routine, around the horn:

Pitcher—Tomorrow

Catcher—Today

First Baseman—Who

Second Baseman—What

Third Baseman—I Don't Know

Shortstop—I Don't Give a Darn
    (or sometimes "I Don't Care")

Left fielder—Why

Center fielder—Because

The name of the right fielder is not referred to in the routine.

THE MOST MEMORABLE
TRADES IN SPORTS

■ In 1948, the Brooklyn Dodgers wanted Ernie Harwell, announcer for the Atlanta Crackers of the Southern Association, to be their broadcaster. Earl Mann, owner of the Crackers, needed a catcher. The Dodgers sent Cliff Dapper, who was catching for their Triple-A Montreal Royals team, to Atlanta for Harwell.

■ In 1972, New York Yankees pitchers Mike Kekich and Fritz Peterson traded wives and families—or, viewed another way, Susanne Kekich and Marilyn Peterson traded husbands and families. Mrs. Kekich moved in with Fritz, but Marilyn Peterson eventually decided not to live with Mike.

■ On September 2, 1988, Mel Turpin of the Utah Jazz became the first NBA player traded to another country when he was sent to Zaragoza of Spain for José Ortiz.

■ In 1986, in the Trade of the Kevins, the New York Mets traded Kevin Mitchell, Kevin Armstrong, Kevin Brown, Shawn Abner, and Stan Jefferson to the San Diego Padres for Kevin McReynolds, Gene Walter, and Adam Ging.

■ On July 14, 1972, NFL owner Carroll Rosenbloom traded his Baltimore Colts to Robert Irsay for the Los Angeles Rams.

In 1978, Irv Levin, owner of the Boston Celtics, gave his NBA franchise to Buffalo Braves owner Hank Iba, and in return received the Braves franchise, which he then moved to San Diego, where they became the Clippers.

■ In January of 1983, Tom Martin of the Western Hockey League's Seattle Breakers was traded to Victoria for a team bus. "I didn't think that much about it at the time," said Martin. "But it was a real nice bus."

■ In the middle of the 1960 season, the fourth-place Cleveland Indians traded their manager, Joe Gordon, to the sixth-place Detroit Tigers for *their* manager, Jimmy Dykes.

■ Quarterback Jacky Lee was leased by the Denver Broncos from the Houston Oilers during the 1964 and 1965 seasons. The Broncos needed help after a 2-11-1 season in 1963, and made a deal in which they sent Bud McFadin, a first-round draft choice, and cash to the Oilers for Lee for two seasons. In 1966, the lease expired and Lee was returned to Houston.

■ On March 15, 1978, the San Francisco Giants traded seven players and $390,000 for Oakland Athletics pitcher Vida Blue.

In 1959, Los Angeles Rams General Manager Pete Rozelle sent seven players and two draft choices to the Chicago Cardinals for star running back Ollie Matson. In 1952, the Rams dealt 11 players for Les Richter.

On October 12, 1989, the Dallas Cowboys traded running back Herschel Walker to the Minnesota Vikings for up to 12 players: Vikings Jesse Solomon, David Howard, Ike Holt, Darrin Nelson, and Alex Stewart; a 1992 #1 draft choice; and six conditional draft choices spread over three years.

226

◪ New York Yankees fan Sal Durante retrieved Roger Maris's 61st home run ball and traded it in for $5,000 and two trips to the West Coast.

◪ Dale Holman was playing for Syracuse against Richmond on June 30, 1986, when the game was suspended. Before the game was resumed, Holman was released and signed with the Braves organization. Holman was called up to the Richmond club and played in the continuation of the Syracuse game, this time for Richmond. He had a single and double for Richmond to go with the double and two RBIs he'd had for Syracuse.

◪ On November 5, 1976, the Pittsburgh Pirates traded catcher Manny Sanguillen and $100,000 for Oakland Athletics manager Chuck Tanner.

On June 18, 1987, the New York Rangers General Manager Phil Esposito traded their 1988 first-round draft choice and $100,000 to the Quebec Nordiques for Quebec coach Michel Bergeron.

◪ Rocky Colavito, the 1959 American League home run co-champion, was traded for Harvey Kuenn, the 1959 American League batting champion, after the 1959 season.

◪ In February of 1921, the Cincinnati Reds traded outfielder Ed "Greasy" Neale and Jimmy Ring to the Philadelphia Phillies for Eppa Rixey. Neale later coached in the NFL and was elected to the Pro Football Hall of Fame, while Rixey was later elected to the Baseball Hall of Fame. Ring was also thrown into a 1926 trade of Hall of Famers Frank Frisch for Rogers Hornsby.

◪ Dickie Noles was traded from the Chicago Cubs to the Detroit Tigers late in the 1987 season for a player to be named later. At the end of the season, Noles was designated as the player to be named later.

◪ The Gold Coast Suns of the new Senior Professional
227

Baseball Association acquired the rights to pitcher Luis Tiant for 500 teddy bears.

■ Max Flack and Cliff Heathcote played against each other in the first game of a May 30, 1922 doubleheader between the St. Louis Cardinals and the Chicago Cubs, then were traded for each other and played on the other side in the second game.

■ Between March 1955 and June 1961, the New York Yankees and Kansas City Athletics made 17 trades involving 64 players.

■ Wayne Nordhagen and Dick Davis were traded for each other twice in the same week. On June 15, 1982, the Toronto Blue Jays traded Nordhagen to the Philadelphia Phillies for Davis. That same day, Philadelphia traded Nordhagen to the Pittsburgh Pirates for Bill Robinson. Days later, the Pirates traded Nordhagen to Toronto for Davis.

COCKY AND GOOD:
THE MOST FAMOUS BOASTS

■ In one of the most renowned moments of confidence in sports, quarterback Joe Namath, in a speech to the Miami Touchdown Club three days before the 1969 Super Bowl, predicted that his New York Jets would upset the Baltimore Colts, who were favored to win by 17 points. "I guarantee it," he said. The final score was Jets 16, Colts 7.

■ In 1932, on the Monday after Stanford's varsity lost to

USC for the first time ever, Stanford's freshman football team vowed never to lose to USC during their playing days. They became known as "The Vow Boys" and lived up to their promise, beating the Trojans in 1933, 1934, and 1935.

■ Before the 1984 Olympic men's downhill competition in Sarajevo, American skier Bill Johnson said, "I don't even know why everyone else is here. They should hand [the gold medal] to me . . . this course was designed for me, and everyone else can fight for second place." Johnson won the gold.

■ It was just before his 1964 fight with Sonny Liston that Cassius Clay first said "I am the greatest," using a line that he borrowed from wrestler Gorgeous George. Liston did not come out for the seventh round, and for more than a decade, Clay—later Muhammad Ali—lived up to his self-titled superlative.

■ Before teeing off, golfing great Walter Hagen would often ask, "Well, who's going to be second?"

■ Lloyd Honeyghan bet $5,000 on himself at 5-1 odds in his welterweight title fight with Donald Curry in September of 1986. Honeyghan won the fight.

■ Bobby Riggs bet on himself to sweep the men's singles, men's doubles, and mixed doubles at Wimbledon in 1939, and did just that.

■ On the night that the Los Angeles Lakers won the NBA title in 1987, coach Pat Riley said that his team would become the first to repeat as champions since the Boston Celtics had accomplished the feat 20 years earlier. "I'm going to guarantee everyone we're going to repeat," Riley said. The Lakers repeated.

10 EXAMPLES OF LANGUAGE ABUSE BY PEOPLE NOT NAMED CASEY STENGEL OR YOGI BERRA

New York favorite sons Casey Stengel and Yogi Berra both gained as much affection and popularity for the way they expressed themselves—at once comically confounding and bracingly clear—as they did for the way they played, coached, and managed the game of baseball. Their malapropisms have been well documented elsewhere, but there is room in the sports world for others to rise to the verbal heights that Casey and Yogi did routinely.

◼ While announcing the "Game of the Week," broadcaster and former St. Louis Cardinals pitching great Dizzy Dean referred to courage as "testicle fortitude."

◼ Chicago Cubs announcer Jack Brickhouse once said an unaccompanied singer had performed the National Anthem "Acapulco."

◼ Phil Heck, University of California linebacker in the mid-1970s, once said of Golden Bears quarterback Joe Roth, "I'd give my right arm to be in his shoes."

◼ Heck's teammate, University of California linebacker Pete Citta, speaking of a knee injury suffered by Heck, said, "You could tell his knees were in the back of his mind."

◼ San Francisco Giant broadcaster and former major leaguer Ron Fairly once said, "Last night, I neglected to mention something that bears repeating."

◼ Before going up against New York Mets ace Dwight Gooden in a 1989 preseason game, New York Yankees first baseman Don Mattingly said, "His reputation preceded him before he got here."

■ New York Mets announcer Ralph Kiner once segued into a commercial by saying, "We'll be back after this word from Manufacturers Hangover."

■ San Diego Padres announcer Jerry Coleman, renowned for his unintentionally twisted imagery, said that on a wild pitch, baserunner Keith Hernandez had taken off "with the crack of the ball."

■ During the 1989 NFL season, San Francisco 49ers offensive tackle Bubba Paris asserted that the defending champions would not get complacent by "resting on our morals."

■ In 1982, Texas Rangers outfielder Mickey Rivers said, "Ain't no sense in worrying about things you got control over, 'cause if you got control over them, ain't no sense in worrying. And there ain't no sense worrying about things you got no control over, 'cause if you got no control over them, ain't no sense worrying."

HOW TEETH AND DENTISTRY
HAVE IMPACTED ON THE SPORTS WORLD

■ In 1895, in the first professional football game, John Brailler, a future dentist from Latrobe, Pennsylvania, was paid $10 to play quarterback for Latrobe against rival Jeannette (Pennsylvania) and helped his team to win, 12-0.

■ When ex–heavyweight boxing champion Leon Spinks was mugged on January 16, 1982, they not only took his money and the jewelry he was wearing, but also removed his two gold front teeth.

■ Edward Flynn, Olympic welterweight gold medalist in 1932, became a dentist in New Orleans.

■ On July 14, 1925, world flyweight champion Pancho Villa, age 23, died of blood poisoning, the result of an infected tooth.

■ At the turn of the century, Coburn Haskell, a Cleveland dentist, invented a dimpled ball that was made of elastic thread and wound under tension around a rubber core. It would be, the precursor of the modern golf ball.

■ Peter George, who won the Olympic middleweight weightlifting gold medal in 1952, became a dentist in the U.S. Army.

■ Mark Spitz had planned on becoming a dentist after retiring from competitive swimming. He won seven gold medals at the 1972 Olympic Games and never got around to dental school.

■ LSU football star Billy Cannon, winner of the 1959 Heisman Trophy, became a Baton Rouge orthodontist. He was later sentenced to five years in prison and fined $10,000 for counterfeiting.

■ When heavyweight champion Jack Johnson returned to his dressing room on October 16, 1909 after pummeling Stanley Ketchel in a 12th-round knockout to retain the heavyweight title, he found two of Ketchel's teeth lodged in his glove.

EXAMPLES OF RELIGION'S PLACE IN SPORTS

Many athletes have declined to compete on certain days for religious reasons. One of the most celebrated instances was of Los Angeles Dodgers pitcher Sandy Koufax, who would have started Game 1 of the 1965 World Series but did not because it took place on Yom Kippur.

Eric Liddell, whose life was chronicled in the movie, *Chariots of Fire*, withdrew from the 100m and the 4 × 100m relay at the 1924 Olympics because the heats or final were run on Sunday. He spent the Sunday of the 100m heats delivering a sermon at a Scottish church in Paris. (He finished third in the 200m and won the gold in the 400m.)

At the 1900 Olympic Games, the following Americans refused to participate in their events because they were held on Sunday: William Remington and Walter Carroll in the high jump final, John Cregan and Alex Grant in the 1500m, and Dixon Boardman, Harry Lee, and William Moloney in the 400 final.

Tennis player Dorothy Round also refused to play on Sunday in the U.S. and French championships.

■ Pittsburgh became the last major league city to allow Sunday baseball, on April 29, 1934.

■ At the 1900 Olympics, Meyer Prinstein was prohibited by his coach from taking part in the long jump final on Sunday—even though Prinstein was Jewish. He won the silver medal on the strength of his jump from the qualifying round.

■ El Sayed Nosseir, an Egyptian and an Olympic gold medalist weightlifter in 1928, would raise his arms and face to the sky before each lift and call out for Allah's assistance.

■ In 1980, at the age of 27, Dave Meyers quit the NBA's Milwaukee Bucks to spend more time at his activities as a Jehovah's Witness.

■ Boxer Max Baer was not Jewish despite wearing a Star of David on his trunks. Before each at-bat, hitting star Wade Boggs, who is also not Jewish, draws a חי (the Hebrew word "chai," which means life) in the dirt with his bat.

■ Dust Commander was blessed by Archbishop Emanuel Milingo of Zambia at Keeneland before the running of the Blue Grass Stakes, which Dust Commander won. He later won the 1970 Kentucky Derby in an upset.

■ Orel Hershiser knelt on the mound to say a prayer after winning the 1988 World Series. He has also sung hymns to himself to relax while pitching.

■ Elzbieta Krzesinska read the New Testament between jumps at the 1956 Melbourne Olympics. She won the long jump gold medal.

■ In September 1974, the New York Stars WFL game against the Detroit Wheels at Downing Stadium on Randall's Island, New York, was moved from a Wednesday to a Tuesday because of Yom Kippur.

■ Willie Davis, Los Angeles Dodger outfielder in the 1960s, was a practicing Buddhist.

THE BRONX ZOO

New York Yankee player and manager Billy Martin was known not just for his pinstriped heart but for his fury—on the field, in the dugout, even far away from the field or the dugout. The controversies that followed him were well-chronicled by the New York press during his five stints as Yankee skipper.

Billy Martin's lawyer has a nice house.

■ Chicago Cubs pitcher Jim Brewer sued Martin in 1960 after Martin broke Brewer's jaw in a brawl. Brewer was awarded $10,000 by a circuit court jury in Chicago.

■ In 1983, Umpire Dale Ford sued Martin in Federal Court in Philadelphia. Martin had called Ford a "stone liar" after Ford ejected him from a game in Chicago.

■ In 1957, Martin and Yankee teammates Mickey Mantle, Yogi Berra, Hank Bauer, and Johnny Kucks brawled at New York's Copacabana club. Martin was fined $1,000 and soon after was traded to the Kansas City Athletics.

■ Umpire Terry Cooney went to a Toronto court in 1981 to formally charge Martin, then the Oakland Athletic manager, with common assault, after a game in which Cooney had ejected Martin for questioning strike and ball calls, and Martin had responded by bumping Cooney, kicking dirt on his shoes, and throwing dirt at his back. Cooney dropped the charges after Martin dropped an appeal of his one-week suspension and $1,000 fine, and also apologized.

■ In addition to innumerable brawls on the baseball field, Martin was involved in several extracurricular altercations. In 1978, he fought a Nevada sportswriter; in 1979, a Minnesota marshmallow salesman; and in 1983, 1985, and 1988, hotel bar patrons in California, Baltimore, and Arlington (Texas), respectively. We believe there were others.

■ One day after Martin died, the Internal Revenue Service filed three liens against his estate to collect $86,137 in back taxes.

15 PROMINENT EX-CHEERLEADERS

Dwight Eisenhower
Patty Hearst
Joyce Brothers
Donna Rice

James Stewart
Ann-Margret
Lily Tomlin
Carly Simon
Jane Pauley
Raquel Welch
Marcee Gross
Dinah Shore
Cybill Shepherd
Dyan Cannon
Gerald Ford

ATHLETES WHO MADE AN IMPACT ON THE WORLD OUTSIDE OF SPORTS

■ Byron "Whizzer" White, who led the NCAA and later the NFL in rushing, became a United States Supreme Court Justice.

■ Gino Marchetti, Hall of Fame defensive end for the Baltimore Colts in the 1950s and 1960s, started Gino's, the national fast-food chain.

■ Olympic 400m hurdler Edward H. White became Astronaut Lieutenant Colonel White and a member of the Gemini 4 crew.

■ Thomas Sopwith, who challenged unsuccessfully for the America's Cup in 1934 and 1937 with his yachts *Endeavour* and *Endeavour II*, started an aviation firm that produced World War I military aircraft such as the Triplane and the famous Sopwith Camel, which downed 1,294 enemy aircraft.

■ 1932 Olympic swimming gold medalist Clarence "Buster" Crabbe gained great recognition playing Tarzan, Flash Gordon, and Buck Rogers in the movies. Three other

Olympic medalists also played Tarzan—swimmer Johnny Weissmuller, the most renowned portrayer; shotputter Bruce Bennett (whose real name was Herman Brix); and marathoner Glenn Morris.

■ Billy Sunday played major league baseball for eight years (1883–90) and was the first outfielder to execute an unassisted double play before he went on to become America's most famous evangelist in the early 20th century.

■ Alfred Gilbert, gold medalist in the pole vault in 1908, invented the Erector Set.

■ Major league catcher Moe Berg became a spy and helped to discover the whereabouts of German nuclear physicist Werner Heisenberg during World War II.

■ Many athletes have acted in movies, usually forgettable roles in forgettable films. A few, however, have appeared in film classics: Adhemar Ferreira da Silva, the Brazilian triple jump world record holder in the 1950s, appeared in *Black Orpheus* in 1958; Giuseppe Gentile of Italy, the 1968 Olympic triple jump bronze medalist, acted opposite Maria Callas in *Medea;* and boxer Eddie Mustafa Muhammad played a boxer in Martin Scorcese's 1980 film, *Raging Bull.* Victor McLaglen, the opponent in 1909 for heavyweight champion Jack Johnson's first title defense, would later win an Academy Award for his performance in *The Informer.*

■ In 1917, Rutgers end Paul Robeson became the second black All-America in football (Fritz Pollard was the first), then went on to a renowned concert career as a bass-baritone and became a political activist, as well.

■ Philip Baker, 1920 Olympic silver medalist in the 1,500m who later changed his name to Philip Noel-Baker, was a member of the British Parliament for 36 years. He won the 1959 Nobel Peace Prize for his work toward disarmament.

■ Bobby Avila, the Cleveland Indian who won the 1954

American League batting title, later became mayor of Vera Cruz, Mexico.

■ Benjamin Spock, a member of Yale's Olympic gold medal eight-oared crew in 1924, wrote one of the world's all-time best-selling books, *Baby and Child Care*, and ran for president in 1972 as a People's Party candidate.

5 UNUSUAL CRIMES FOR WHICH ATHLETES HAVE BEEN CONVICTED

Athletes have served time in prison for crimes such as drug dealing and smuggling (National League MVP Orlando Cepeda, Miami Dolphins running back Mercury Morris); armed robbery (Detroit Tigers base stealer Ron LeFlore, boxer Rubin "Hurricane" Carter), and racketeering (Denny McLain, baseball's last 30-game winner). Others have been on the wrong side of the law, and some have served time, for more unusual transgressions.

■ Jack Johnson, the first black heavyweight boxing champion, was convicted in 1912 of violating the Mann Act (White Slave Act). He was charged with "transporting" a white woman for "immoral" purposes. He fled to Europe to avoid imprisonment.

■ In 1973, Jerry Priddy, American League infielder from 1941–53, was found guilty of attempted extortion. He threatened to blow up the steamship *Island Princess* if he did not get $250,000.

■ Dino Ciccarelli of the Minnesota North Stars was sentenced to one day in jail and fined $1,000 for his on-ice attack of Toronto Maple Leaf defenseman Luke Richardson, on August 24, 1988. Ciccarelli was the first NHL player to go to jail for attacking another player.

■ Armin Hary of Germany, gold medalist in the 1960 Olympic 100m, was convicted in 1981 of diverting Roman Catholic Church funds for personal investment.

■ Latu Vaeno, a New Zealand rugby player, was jailed for six months for biting off the ear of an opponent on December 5, 1985.

10
EXTREMES

THE SHORTEST-LIVED GLORY

Perhaps the only thing more thrilling in sports than achieving a great victory or personal goal is the enjoyment of that moment, basking in it, sharing it with family and friends and fans. For some athletes, unfortunately, that pleasure is not long-lived. And others may not realize that the first or second time that they get to experience such a joyous athletic moment is also the last.

■ In the 1980 Olympic pentathlon, Soviet Olga Rukavishnikova finished second in the final event, the 800m, to set a world record—for 4/10 of a second. When her countrymate, Nadezhda Tkachenko, who had been leading the competition after four events, finished in third place, right behind Rukavishnikova, she established a new world record.

■ In the 1972 season finale against the Kansas City Chiefs, Atlanta Falcons running back Dave Hampton reached the 1,000-yard mark for the season. The game was stopped briefly to award him the ball. A few plays later, Hampton was thrown for a six-yard loss. He carried the ball one final time, for a one-yard gain, and finished the season with 995 yards.

■ Two hours after what was probably the biggest win of his tennis career—a semifinal victory over Frenchman Yannick Noah at the 1989 Lipton International Players Championships at Key Biscayne, Florida—Austrian Thomas Muster was hit by a car and suffered knee ligament damage while heading for a restaurant in downtown Miami.

▣ In what would be his only major league game, 21-year-old Ray Jansen went 4-5 for the 1910 St. Louis Browns, giving him a lifetime .800 average. More than 20 brief major leaguers have a lifetime average of 1.000. While most had one hit in their one at-bat, John Paciorek went 3-for-3, drew a pair of walks, and scored four times for the Houston Colts in the final game of the 1963 season. The next season, Paciorek started in the minor leagues, then had a back operation, and never got to play again in the big leagues.

▣ Bill Barilko scored the winning overtime goal in the fifth and final game of the 1951 Stanley Cup finals to help the Toronto Maple Leafs beat the Montreal Canadiens, then died that summer in a plane crash.

▣ The only run batted in of Philadelphia Phillie Howie Bedell's 1968 season broke the record 58 consecutive-innings scoreless streak of Los Angeles Dodgers pitcher Don Drysdale. It was also the third and last RBI that Bedell had in his career.

▣ Richard Sanders, bantamweight wrestling silver medalist in 1972, died at 23 in a car accident seven weeks after the Olympics.
    Odon Tersztyanszky of Hungary, gold medalist in the saber in 1928, died in a car accident outside Budapest 10 months later.
    Ivo van Damme, silver medalist in the 800m in 1976, died in a car crash on December 29 of that year, at age 22.

▣ Tony Tucker held the heavyweight boxing title for 64 days (May 3–August 2, 1987), the shortest reign for any heavyweight in history. Tony Canzoneri held the light-welterweight title for 33 days (May 21–June 23, 1933), the shortest reign of any boxing champion.

▣ On March 12, 1956, in an NBA game against the St. Louis Hawks, Syracuse National Dick Farley fouled out after playing only five minutes.

■ New York Yankees infielder Brian Doyle, with only 52 previous major league at-bats, hit .438 (7-for-16) in the 1978 World Series. He would have only 147 more at-bats in his major league career.

■ Jack Givens scored 41 points to help Kentucky beat Duke for the 1978 NCAA basketball title. He played two seasons in the NBA, and averaged 6.7 points a game for his career.

■ Detroit Tigers pitcher Floyd Giebell's third major league victory beat the Cleveland Indians and future Hall of Famer Bob Feller, 2-0, and helped the 1940 Tigers clinch the pennant. Giebell would not win another major league game.

In his pitching debut on April 14, 1967, at Yankee Stadium, Billy Rohr of the Boston Red Sox came within one out of a no-hitter. He lost that but still won the game, beating Whitey Ford 3-0. Rohr won just two more games in his major league career.

■ In the first significant tournament Lee Mackey, Jr., ever competed in, he shocked the golf world by shooting a 33-31-64 at the 1950 U.S. Open to break by one stroke Jimmy McHale's 1947 record for a round at the Open, and took the lead by three strokes. The next day, with a flock of fans in tow, Mackey bogeyed the second hole, double-bogeyed the fourth, bogeyed the fifth, and shot a second-day 81, good enough for a 22nd-place tie. He shot 75-77 over the last 36 holes and won $100 for tying for 25th place.

SHORT-LIVED IGNOMINY

■ In 1969, their first season, the Seattle Pilots baseball

team went 64-98 and finished in last place. It was also their last season because the franchise moved to Milwaukee.

25 BAD THINGS ABOUT SPORTS

1. John 3:16
2. The Wave (a special citation is awarded to Chicago Cub fans who, according to the team's publicist, have never done the Wave at Wrigley Field)
3. The insistence on giving every big fight its own name, such as "The Thrilla in Manila," "The War on the Shore," "The Preacher and the Puncher," etc.
4. Everything on ESPN except basketball, football, baseball, and SportsCenter
5. Time of possession statistics
6. The NHL playoff system
7. The Norris Division
8. Singers who perform the national anthem as if it's a career move
9. Witless banners using the initials of the network covering the game
10. North-South games
11. East-West games
12. All college bowl games except the Big Four
13. The Pro Bowl
14. Skins matches in golf
15. Exhibition matches in tennis
16. Leroy Neiman (See also *Bad Things About Art*)
17. The Heisman Trophy media derby
18. Presidential calls to winning locker rooms (after the World Series, the Super Bowl, the NBA Finals)
19. Don King and Bob Arum
20. The constant "Hi, Mom's" and fingers indicating "We're #1"
21. Another John Madden commercial
22. Relentless corporate sponsorship of bowl games, "Plays

of the Week" segments, scoreboard updates, errors, hits, strikes, balls, etc.
23. Any and all boxing commissions
24. Kareem Abdul-Jabbar's farewell tour
25. TV timeouts

...AND 25 MORE BAD THINGS ABOUT SPORTS

1. George Steinbrenner
2. Charles Barkley "Fat Man" promotional night at the Philadelphia Spectrum
3. Golfers dressing in the classic knickers style
4. Golfwear period
5. ABC's "Battle of the Superstars"
6. Los Angeles fans leaving in the seventh inning of Dodger games, and the middle of the fourth quarter of Laker and Ram games (and the middle of the third period of King games)
7. Endless TV shots of Jack Nicholson and Dyan Cannon cheering for the Lakers
8. Most team mascots
9. T-shirts under basketball jerseys
10. Coaches' highlight shows
11. The floor of Off-Track Betting outlets
12. Dancing in the end zone
13. Goggles in basketball
14. The NFL TV replay rule
15. The old Vancouver Canucks uniforms
16. Baseball players charging money for autographs
17. Joe Paterno's speech at the 1988 Republican National Convention
18. Dumping Gatorade on winning coaches
19. Any Thanksgiving event involving the Detroit Lions
20. Any non-Thanksgiving event involving the Detroit Lions

21. Fans who think that a camera trained upon them is a cue to act like an idiot
22. Athletes who unretire
23. Long, drawn-out cheers for any player whose name sounds remotely like "Lou"
24. Announcers who invariably follow such cheers by saying, "No, they're not booing. They're saying 'Cooooop'"
25. George Steinbrenner, again

BOYS AMONG MEN, GIRLS AMONG WOMEN: THE MOST PRECOCIOUS ATHLETES OF ALL TIME

■ Montreal Canadiens goalie Ken Dryden won the Conn Smythe Trophy as the 1971 Stanley Cup playoff MVP. The next season, he won the Calder Trophy for Rookie of the Year. Dryden had played in few enough regular season games the previous year to still be considered a rookie in 1971–72.

■ When Mats Wilander won the French Open in 1982 at age 17, becoming at the time the youngest winner ever of a Grand Slam men's singles title, he achieved a rare distinction: he had won the French boy's and men's titles in consecutive years.

■ When swimmer Alex Baumann was having trouble producing a urine sample after his 400m individual medley victory in the 1984 Olympics, officials gave him a beer. In the middle of his third beer, they found out that he was under-aged and gave him a soft drink instead.

In 1980, after scoring 42 points playing center against the Philadelphia 76ers and becoming, at age 20, the youngest player to win the NBA playoff MVP Award, Magic Johnson celebrated with his Los Angeles Laker teammates in the winning locker room, but was still legally too young to drink the champagne.

■ On July 19, 1952, 12-year-old Joe Relford, the batboy for Fitzgerald in the Georgia State League, appeared in a minor league game. Relford was used as a pinch hitter with Fitzgerald losing 13-0 and the crowd chanting, "Put in the batboy." He grounded out sharply to third. He stayed in the game to play center field and made a putout.

■ The youngest major leaguer ever was Joe Nuxhall. In 1944, at age 15, he pitched two-thirds of an inning for the Cincinnati Reds, allowing two hits, five walks, and five runs.

■ Kathy Horvath is the only player ever to win all four junior tennis age groups (the U.S. Girls Clay Courts) in consecutive years.

■ In the 1964-65 season, Dave DeBusschere became the youngest player-coach in the NBA when, at 24, he both coached and played power forward for the Detroit Pistons.

■ In 1924, Bucky Harris, 27, took over as manager for the Washington Senators and led them to two pennants and a World Series title in his first two years. Lou Boudreau, at 24, became the Cleveland Indians manager after the 1941 season. Roger Peckinpaugh managed the 1914 New York Yankees for 17 games at the age of 23.

■ Mike Tyson became the youngest heavyweight champion ever when, at 20, he knocked out Trevor Berbick in November of 1986. Floyd Patterson was 21 when he beat Archie Moore for the title in 1956.

■ Wilfred Benitez, then 17, became the youngest boxer to win a world title, defeating Antonio Cervantes in a 15-round decision for the junior welterweight title, on March 6, 1976.

■ Seve Ballesteros won the 1980 Masters at age 23. Gene

Sarazen won the 1922 PGA at age 20. Tom Morris, Jr. won the 1868 British Open at age 17.

■ In a 1963 game, the Houston Colts used an all-rookie lineup and lost 10-3 to the New York Mets.

■ Gertrude Ederle of the United States is the youngest world record holder. She was 12 when she set the record for the women's 880-yard freestyle swim (13 minutes, 19 seconds) on August 17, 1919.

■ At age 19, Dwight Gooden became the youngest major leaguer to appear in an All-Star Game. Al Kaline (20) was the youngest to win a batting title, and Vida Blue (22) the youngest to win an MVP Award.

■ The youngest person to participate in a world title event was an anonymous French boy, who was coxswain for the Netherlands' gold medal–winning rowing pair at the 1900 Olympics. It is known that he was not more than 10 and perhaps as young as 7. He replaced the regular coxswain, who was deemed too heavy.

■ Bob Mathias, at 17, was the youngest male track and field Olympic gold medalist ever when he won the 1948 decathlon.

■ Bill Willoughby was the youngest NBA player ever, debuting in 1975 at age 18 for the Atlanta Hawks. Darryl Dawkins also began at 18, while Moses Malone began his pro career at age 19, with Utah of the ABA.

■ Twenty-two-year-old Gary Kasparov became the youngest world champion in chess history when he defeated 34-year-old Anatoly Karpov for the title in 1985.

■ At eight, Joy Foster represented Jamaica in the 1958 West Indian Championships in table tennis.

■ In 1988, 11-year-old Thomas Gregory of England swam the English Channel.

■ The youngest individual Olympic gold medalist is American Marjorie Gestring, who was 13 when she won the springboard diving title at the 1936 Berlin Games.

■ In 1975, Houston McTear, 18 years old and a high school junior, equaled the world record in the 100-yard dash (9.0 seconds).

MEN AMONG BOYS, WOMEN AMONG GIRLS: THE MOST EXPERIENCED ATHLETES OF ALL TIME

■ Hoyt Wilhelm was the first player still active in the major leagues while eligible for a pension.

■ Gerhard Weidner of West Germany is the oldest world record breaker. He was 41 when he set a 20-mile walk record on May 25, 1974.

■ The oldest jockey to win the Kentucky Derby is Willie Shoemaker. He was 54 when he rode Ferdinand, who was trained by 73-year-old Charlie Whittingham, to the 1986 Derby win.

■ Amos Alonzo Stagg coached the College of the Pacific football team at age 84, then assisted Amos Alonzo Stagg, Jr., his son, at Susquehanna University until he was 90. He retired from coaching at 98.

■ Archie Moore, at 48, was the oldest boxer to hold a world title, the light heavyweight crown. Jersey Joe Walcott, at 37, became the oldest man to win the heavyweight title when he won a 15-round decision over Ezzard Charles in 1952.

■ Darrell Evans is the oldest home run champion, hitting 40 for the Detroit Tigers in 1985 at the age of 38.

■ The oldest Olympic gold medalist is Oscar G. Swahn, who, at 64, was part of the 1912 Olympic team running deer shooting competition. He won a silver medal in shooting at the 1920 Games, at age 72.

■ In 1967, the Toronto Maple Leafs, with an average age of 31, became the oldest lineup ever to win the Stanley Cup.

■ In 1976, Minnie Minoso played in three major league games for the Chicago White Sox at age 53, and became the oldest player to get a hit. He pinch-hit twice in 1980, at age 57, going 0-for-2.

It is surmised that Satchel Paige was 59 when he pitched in a 1965 game. He hurled three scoreless innings for the Kansas City Athletics, giving up one hit and striking out one.

■ Hale Irwin is the oldest golfer to win the U.S. Open, at 45, in 1990.

■ Cy Young (41) is the oldest to throw a no-hitter, Warren Spahn (42) to win 20 games, and Honus Wagner (37) to win a batting title.

■ Gardner Mulloy is the oldest man to win a Wimbledon final. At age 43, he won the 1957 men's doubles title with Budge Patty. The oldest woman to win at Wimbledon is Margaret Osborne du Pont, who was 44 when she and Neale Fraser captured the 1962 mixed doubles crown.

■ Masao Takemoto, a member of Japan's Olympic team in 1960 at age 40, is the oldest gymnastics gold medalist in history.

■ In 1980, Hub Kittle became, at 63, the oldest man to appear in an organized baseball game when he started for Springfield, the AAA farm team for the St. Louis Cardinals, against Iowa in an American Association game. Kittle retired the side in order in the first inning and threw one pitch in the second inning before leaving the game.

◼ Sam Snead is the oldest winner of a PGA tourney—the 1965 Greater Greensboro Open—at 52 years, 10 months, and became, in 1974, the oldest to make the cut at the Masters, at 61. He tied for third in the PGA championship in 1974 at age 62.

◼ Gordie Howe played 25 years in the NHL, six more in the WHA, then returned to the NHL in 1979–80 for one more year. As a 51-year-old grandfather, he made the all-star team.

◼ Clifford Batt, 68, of Australia swam the English Channel in 1987.

◼ Luke Appling, at age 75, hit a home run off of Warren Spahn in the 1981 Cracker Jack's Old-Timers Game at RFK Stadium, in Washington, D.C. Dubbed "Home Run" Appling, he was suddenly in hot demand on the banquet circuit.

◼ In 1984, the horse John Henry, nine years old, won the Turf Classic at Belmont and the Arlington Million.

◼ Former Yale All-America guard William "Pudge" Heffelfinger played in an organized football game at age 66.

◼ Joe Sweeney, 71, was a member of the Salem (Massachusetts) State College tennis varsity.

25 GOOD THINGS ABOUT SPORTS

1. The revoking of the balk-set rule in the 1989 book of *Official Baseball Rules*

2. Nike ads
3. Super slow-mo
4. Slam dunk contests
5. Always saving Joe DiMaggio to be introduced last at baseball oldtimers' games
6. Rotisserie leagues
7. Michael Jordan's "love of the game" contract clause
8. Home run-hitting contests
9. The penalty shot in hockey
10. Bob Uecker
11. Swimsuit issues
12. Touchdown bombs
13. Magic vs. Larry
14. Tailgate parties
15. Sudden-death overtime in hockey
16. Sudden-death overtime in football
17. Wayne Gretzky stickhandling
18. Dwight Gooden pitching
19. Doubleheaders
20. Florence Griffith Joyner running
21. Plays of the Week
22. Plays of the Month
23. Plays of the Year
24. Sugar Ray Leonard dancing
25. Wrigley Field fans who throw opponents' home run balls back, with disdain

ENOUGH IS ENOUGH ALREADY: COMMENTS, CONTESTS, AND IDEAS THAT SHOW SERIOUS SIGNS OF GETTING CARRIED AWAY

Englishman Henry Higgins, a toreador in Spain, once said, "I would rather be gored in the Madrid ring than fail." To paraphrase Alexander Woollcott: Not on our carpet, Hank.

Some more examples of excess:

■ The seventh hole at the Sano Course at the Satsuki Golf Club in Japan is the longest in the world. It is par seven, 909 yards long.

■ On December 29, 1989, at the funeral Mass for New York Yankee player and manager Billy Martin, Bishop Edwin Broderick said, "We gather here this morning not to celebrate Billy's way of life, but to pray that his is a safe slide into home plate. We pray as he negotiates his lifelong contract with St. Peter that Billy would agree to play it out on the bench, in the bullpen, even in the locker room until the divine umpire, the inventor of instant replay, decides that Billy really is in shape for the eternal World Series. . ."

■ There have been four different AFLs (American Football League) in professional football history, the first one in 1926.
     The name "New York Yankees" was used for four pro football teams in five leagues from 1926–49. If that wasn't enough, there was also a New York Yanks in the NFL in the 1950–51 seasons.

■ After Australia won the America's Cup sailing competition for the first time ever in 1983, Australian broadcaster Rob Mundel called it "the race . . . of the millennium."

■ In the 1912 Olympic middleweight Greco–Roman semifinal, Russia's Martin Klein and Finland's Alfred Asikainen wrestled outdoors for 11 hours, stopping every half hour for a refreshment break. Klein won by a pin but was too tired to compete in the final.

■ There have been six major league players named William Moore.

■ After he died, the heart of Pierre de Coubertin, the founder of the modern Olympics, was removed and placed in a monument in a sacred grove in Olympia, Greece.

■ Cleveland Municipal Stadium used to be 435 feet down each foul line. The distance from home plate to dead center field in New York's old Polo Grounds was 483 feet.

■ The Miami Dolphins and the Los Angeles Raiders are the only NFL teams to have helmets painted on their helmets.

■ French tennis great Suzanne Lenglen often entered the court wearing a fur coat, no matter how warm the weather.

■ Canadian Diana Gordon-Lennox, downhill and slalom skier at the 1936 Olympics, wore a monocle while competing.

■ English cyclist Tommy Simpson, who collapsed from fatigue and drugs in the 1967 Tour de France, said "Put me back on my bike" just before he died.

■ The longest professional baseball game—a 1981 International League contest in which the Pawtucket Red Sox beat the Rochester Red Wings, 3-2, in 33 innings—took eight hours and 25 minutes of actual playing time but 66 days from start to finish, because the game was suspended before completion.

■ In February 1990, heavyweight contender Evander Holyfield turned down a three-fight, $40-million deal because he thought he could be "leaving money on the table." (A $50-million deal, Holyfield said, "could tempt" him.)

DAVIDS AMONG GOLIATHS

■ Robert James Fitzsimmons is the lightest heavyweight champion, 167 pounds, in history. He defeated James Corbett, March 17, 1897. The shortest heavyweight champ was Tommy Burns, at 5'7". He beat Marvin Hart on February 23, 1906.

■ At 6'5", Charles Barkley is the shortest rebound champion in NBA history (1986–87).

■ Walter Payton, 5'10", holds the NFL record for most number of carries, 3,692, and rushing yards, 16,193.

■ Barney Sedran, 5'4", starred at CCNY from 1909–11, and played on 10 pro basketball championship teams in 15 years.

■ Wee Willie Keeler was 5'4½" and Hack Wilson was 5'6". Both are in the Baseball Hall of Fame. Harry Chappas, 5'3", played shortstop for the Chicago White Sox from 1978–80.

■ Although bareknuckles champion Tom Johnson was six inches shorter and 70 pounds lighter than Isaac Perrins, his opponent and challenger, he beat Perrins in one hour and 15 minutes, on October 22, 1789.

■ Tyrone Bogues is the shortest NBA player ever, at 5'3½". Spud Webb, 5'7", won the NBA All-Star Slam Dunk competition in 1986.

■ Scott Hamilton was 5'2½" and 108 pounds when he won the men's figure skating gold at the 1984 Winter Olympics.

■ In an Olympic judo match in 1976, 5'6½", 259-pound Sumio Endo of Japan beat 7'0", 350-pound Jong-Gil Pak of North Korea.

■ Five-foot, eight-inch 135-pound Michael Chang won the 1989 French Open.

■ Golfer Fred McLeod, winner of the 1908 U.S. Open, weighed 108 pounds.

■ Young Zulu Kid, an American flyweight fighter, was

4'11". Jimmy Wilde, a flyweight world champion, weighed 96 pounds.

■ St. Louis Brown Eddie Gaedel, who walked in his only major league at-bat, stood 3'7" and weighed 65 pounds.

■ In 1980, Liechtenstein's Hanni Wenzel won the slalom and giant slalom gold medals and the downhill silver, and her brother, Andreas, won the giant slalom silver. The Wenzels' four medals converted to one medal for every 6,250 people in the country.

ATTA BOY!:
THE GREATEST DEBUTS AND STARTS

On April 25, 1933, New York Yankees rookie Russ Van Atta, in his first start, hurled a five-hit shutout over the pennant-bound Washington Senators in Griffith Stadium, went 4-for-4 at the plate, scored three runs, knocked in one, and the Yanks won, 16-0.

Here are the best examples of athletes and teams who started things—their careers, a season, a game—in spectacular fashion.

■ On October 30, 1943, Toronto Maple Leaf Gus Bodnar scored a goal against the New York Rangers 15 seconds into the first period of his first NHL game.

■ On September 14, 1951, Bob Nieman of the St. Louis Browns became the only player to homer in his first *two* major league at-bats.

Gary Gaetti, Bert Campaneris, and Chuck Tanner, among others, all hit the first major league pitch they ever saw for home runs.

With his first big league swing, San Francisco Giants

first baseman Will Clark hit a homer off of all-time strike-out king Nolan Ryan.

■ Bennie Oosterbaan, assistant football coach at the University of Michigan, became the head coach in 1948, won all nine games and the national title, the first and only man to do that in his first year as head coach.

Forty-one years later, Steve Fisher replaced Bill Frieder as head coach of Michigan's basketball team as the NCAA tournament started, and led them to their first-ever national championship. He is the only coach known to have won a national title before he had won a regular season game.

■ Jockey Steve Cauthen won the Kentucky Derby in his first attempt, riding Affirmed in 1978.

■ In Nancy Lopez's first full season on the LPGA tour, she won nine tournaments, including a record five in a row.

■ Minnesota Vikings quarterback Fran Tarkenton threw four touchdown passes in his first NFL game, a 1961 victory over the Chicago Bears.

■ On May 6, 1953, St. Louis Brown Alva Lee "Bobo" Holloman, became the only major leaguer in the modern era to throw a no-hitter in his first start (he had pitched in relief four times before that).

■ Pittsburgh Steelers running back Franco Harris's famous "Immaculate Reception" in 1972 was made in the first playoff game of his career.

■ In the first game of the 1951 season, Los Angeles Rams quarterback Norm Van Brocklin threw for an NFL record 554 yards against the New York Yankees football team at the Los Angeles Coliseum.

■ At age 16, Aaron Krickstein won the first tournament he entered as a professional, the Israel Tennis Center Classic.

■ Dick "Night Train" Lane set the NFL record for most interceptions in a season, 14, when he was a rookie.

■ Marvell Wynne, Tony Gwynn, and Jack Clark hit back-to-back-to-back home runs on Opening Day, 1989, for the San Diego Padres. It was the first time that feat was achieved on the first day of the season.

■ Wilt Chamberlain, in 1959–60, and Wes Unseld, in 1968–69, are the only two players to be named NBA MVP's in their rookie years.

Fred Lynn, Boston Red Sox rookie outfielder in 1975, is the only baseball player to win a major league MVP Award in his first year.

■ The Atlanta Braves won their first 13 games in 1982. The Milwaukee Brewers won their first 13 games of the 1987 season.

■ In his first college game, LSU wide receiver Carlos Carson caught five passes, all for touchdowns.

■ On May 21, 1952, the Brooklyn Dodgers scored 15 runs in the first inning against the Cincinnati Reds.

■ Toe Blake coached the Montreal Canadiens to the Stanley Cup in his first five years as coach, from 1955–56 to 1959–60.

■ In 1940, Cleveland Indians pitcher Bob Feller became the only pitcher to throw an Opening Day no-hitter.

■ Cecil Travis got five hits in his first major league game.

■ In 1977, Ted Cox got six hits in his first six official at-bats for the Boston Red Sox.

■ Walter Johnson pitched seven Opening Day shutouts.

■ The Dallas Cowboys had an Opening Day win streak of 17 years, from 1965 to 1981.

■ In his first NHL game on February 14, 1977, Philadelphia Flyer Al Hill scored five points.

■ On April 12, 1962, Pete Richert struck out the first six major league batters he ever faced.

Dave "Boo" Ferris began his pitching career with 22 consecutive scoreless innings.

■ Tony Lema won the British Open in his first try, in 1964.

■ In 1961–62, New York Yankees manager Ralph Houk became the first man to lead his team to World Series victories in his first two years at the helm. In 1963, he again won the pennant.

■ In his first five full seasons in the majors, Chuck Klein won four home run titles.

■ In his rookie year in the NHL, Wayne Gretzky led the league in scoring and assists, won the Hart Trophy as league MVP, and the Lady Byng Trophy for gentlemanly play and effectiveness.

■ Baltimore Colts kicker Jim O'Brien was a rookie when he made a field goal with five seconds left to beat the Dallas Cowboys in Super Bowl V.

■ Jack Nicklaus won the U.S. Open in his first year on the tour, and added the Masters and PGA after less than two years as a pro.

■ In his freshman year, University of Louisville center Pervis Ellison won the 1988 Final Four MVP Award.

■ New York Giants picher Rube Marquard won his first 19 decisions in the 1912 season.

■ Hank Aaron hit his 714th home run, tying him with Babe Ruth, with his first swing of the 1974 season.

■ From 1937 to 1949, the New York Yankees did not lose

a World Series Game 1. They won nine in a row during that stretch.

■ In 1934, Chicago Bear Beattie Feathers became the first NFL back ever to gain 1,000 yards, and he did it in his rookie year.

■ Joe Jackson hit .408 in his first full season, with the 1911 Cleveland Indians.

■ In 1973, Ben Crenshaw won his first tournament as a member of the PGA. Robert Gamez repeated that feat to win the Tucson Open in January of 1990.

■ Michigan State placekicker Rolf Mojsiejenko's first field goal attempt in college, against Illinois in 1982, was a successful 61-yarder.

7 OPENINGS NOT TO WRITE HOME ABOUT

■ In his NHL debut on January 10, 1980, Boston Bruins goalie Jim Stewart gave up three goals in the first four minutes, and two more goals before the first period ended. He was yanked with the score 5-2, sent to the minors, and never played in the NHL again.

■ Kevin Cogan, starting from the front row at the 1982 Indianapolis 500, initiated a pile-up during the 80 mph pace lap that knocked Mario Andretti, Roger Mears, Dale Whittington, and himself out of the race before it had even begun.

■ Brazil's Maria de Amorin served 17 double faults in a row at the start of her first match at Wimbledon in 1957. She lost to Mrs. L. Thung of Holland, 3-6, 6-4, 1-6.

■ On July 11, 1974, in the World Football League's first nationally televised game, between the Jacksonville Sharks and the New York Stars, the lights at the Gator Bowl went out at halftime, delaying the start of the second half for 10 minutes.

■ In his major league debut on May 18, 1912, Aloysius J. Travers gave up 14 runs and 26 hits. It was his only game.

■ The Baltimore Orioles began the 1988 season by losing 21 games in a row, a major league record for the start of a season.

■ On February 4, 1987, the Sacramento Kings went 9:06 before scoring a point against the Los Angeles Lakers at the Forum. At the time, the score was 29-0. In the quarter, the Kings were outscored 40-4 and went 0-18 from the field. They did not make a field goal until the second quarter, on their 22nd attempt.

IMPRESSIVE EXAMPLES OF VERSATILITY

The following athletes have shown a rare ability to perform a variety of skills, or a singular skill in different ways, or in different places.

The point is, they're all versatile.

■ Dave Kingman played for four teams in 1977, one in each division: the New York Mets, the San Diego Padres, the New York Yankees, and the California Angels.

■ Al Oerter won four consecutive Olympic discus gold medals, each on a different continent.

■ As a quarterback, Washington Redskin Sammy Baugh

holds the NFL record for highest average gain per pass in a game (24 passes for 446 yards, average gain per pass of 18.58 yards, on October 31, 1948, against Boston). As a punter, Baugh holds the NFL record for highest yard-per-punt average in a season (35 punts for 1,799 yards, a 51.4-yard-per-punt average, in 1940). As a defensive back, he co-holds the record for most interceptions in a game, four, against Detroit, November 14, 1943.

■ John Wooden was elected to the Basketball Hall of Fame as a player in 1960, and then rehonored as a coach in 1972.

■ Bob Fitzsimmons is the only boxer in history to have held the heavyweight, light-heavyweight, and middleweight titles at different times during his career. Georges Carpentier fought in every weight division from featherweight to heavyweight. Ted "Kid" Lewis of England fought successfully in all divisions from bantamweight to heavyweight.

■ Veikko Hakulinen of Finland won three gold medals, each in a different event (50km Nordic skiing, 30km race, and 4×10km relay), each in a different Olympics (1952, 1956, 1960).

■ Ex–New York Jet Joe Klecko made the Pro Bowl at three different positions. Denver Bronco Karl Mecklenburg has played seven different positions.

■ Rusty Staub is the only man to play at least 500 games with four different teams (the Houston Astros, the Montreal Expos, the New York Mets, and the Detroit Tigers).

■ When he was at the University of Minnesota in the late 1920s, Bronko Nagurski was named All-America at both fullback and defensive tackle in the same season.

■ Wilt Chamberlain is the only person to lead the NBA, at various times, in scoring, rebounding, and assists in a season.

■ In 1978, Cleveland Indian Andre Thornton hit for the

cycle (single, double, triple, home run), with each hit coming off of a different pitcher.

■ San Francisco 49ers running back Roger Craig is the only player in NFL history to gain more than 1,000 yards each rushing and receiving in a single year.

■ Rick Barry won scoring titles in the NCAA, the ABA, and the NBA.

■ Weeb Ewbank is the only coach to lead an NFL and an AFL team to the pro football title—the 1958 and 1959 Baltimore Colts and the 1969 New York Jets.

■ Switch hitters Garry Templeton and Willie Wilson are the only two players to get 100 or more hits from both sides of the plate in a season.
　　On April 30, 1979, Gary Pellant of the Carolina League Alexandria Mariners became the first professional baseball player to hit a home run from opposite sides of the plate in the same inning.

■ Bert Campaneris and Cesar Tovar are the only two major leaguers to play every position (except DH) on the field in a single game.

■ Hank Greenberg, Stan Musial, and Robin Yount are the only major leaguers to win MVP Awards at different positions.

■ Jimmy Connors won the U.S. Open tennis title on three different surfaces. He won on grass in 1974, on clay in 1976, and on hardcourt in 1978, 1982, and 1983. Billie Jean King is the only woman to win U.S. singles titles on all four surfaces: grass, clay, carpet, and hard.

■ Carl Westergren won three Greco–Roman Olympic golds, each in a different division.

■ The 1965 Los Angeles Dodgers had an all-switch-hitting infield of Wes Parker, Jim Lefebvre, Maury Wills, and Jim Gilliam.

■ In one 1989 game against the New Jersey Devils, Pittsburgh Penguin Mario Lemieux scored a goal short-handed, on a penalty shot, on a power play, at even strength, and into an empty net.

8 REALLY IMPRESSIVE EXAMPLES OF VERSATILITY

■ Transsexual Rene Richards is the only tennis player to compete in both the men's and women's draw in the U.S. Championships: as Richard Raskind in 1960, she lost 6-0, 6-1, 6-1 in the first round to Neale Fraser; as Richards in 1977, she lost 6-1, 6-4 in the first round to Virginia Wade.

■ Martina Navratilova is the only player to play on winning Federation Cup teams for two different nations—Czechoslovakia in 1975, and the United States in 1982 and 1986.

■ Karoly Takacs, a member in 1938 of Hungary's world championship pistol shooting team, had his right hand—his shooting hand—severely damaged by a grenade. Takacs switched to his left hand and won the gold medal 10 years later, in 1948.

■ Stan Kasten is president of both the Atlanta (baseball) Braves and the Atlanta (basketball) Hawks.

■ Hank Gowdy is the only major leaguer to have served both in World War I and World War II.

■ In the 1940s, the Bluegrass All-Stars barnstormed throughout the Southeast, performing their music at the ballpark and then taking on the local baseball team.

■ In 1978, Texas Rangers pitcher George "Doc" Medich administered CPR to a 61-year-old fan who had suffered a heart attack. Medich was involved in a similar incident as a Pittsburgh Pirate in 1976.

■ Dora Ratjen, fourth in the 1936 Olympic high jump, was discovered to be a hermaphrodite and banned from competition in 1938.

9 OF THE MOST MEMORABLE DAYS IN SPORTS HISTORY

When Atlanta Braves slugger Bob Horner hit four home runs in a 1986 game against the Chicago Cubs, becoming only the 11th major leaguer to do so, he said after the game, "I had a good week today." It's a line that's often dusted off when an athlete (or team) has that rare kind of day—when everything is so well-synched that he performs better than ever before, maybe even seeming to exceed his capabilities, a day when records fall, often by the bushel, a day when heroic pictures are burned into the mind's eye; in short, the kind of day that, years later, at least 100,000 people claim to have been on hand for.

■ *July 23, 1952:* Brazil's Adhemar Ferreira da Silva broke his own triple jump world record four times in six attempts in the Olympic finals.

■ *May 25, 1935:* At the Big Ten championships at Ann Arbor, Michigan, Jesse Owens broke five world records and equaled a sixth in 45 minutes. At 3:15 P.M., he won the 100-yard dash in 9.4 seconds to tie the world record; at 3:25, he long-jumped—his only attempt of the day—26'8¼" for a world record that would stand for 25 years; at 3:45, he ran the 220-yard dash in 20.3 seconds for a world record and was also credited with the world record in the

200m; at 4:00 P.M., he ran the 220-yard low hurdles in 22.6 seconds, the first time anyone had broken 23 seconds. He was also given credit for the world record in the 200m hurdles.

■ *October 25, 1974:* John Bunch of Elkins (Arizona) High School rushed for 608 yards against Winslow High School.

■ *April 26, 1905:* It was not hard to choose the defensive star of the game as Chicago Cubs centerfielder Jack McCarthy started three double plays, a feat no other outfielder has ever accomplished, and each runner he shot down represented the tying run. The Cubs beat the Pittsburgh Pirates, 2-1.

■ *April 20, 1912:* The Boston Red Sox played the first game ever at Fenway Park, and the Detroit Tigers played the first game ever at Tiger Stadium. (Both home teams won.)

■ *November 8, 1980:* Passing records across America fell like autumn leaves. Portland State's Neil Lomax threw for eight touchdowns, including a record seven in the first quarter, in a 105-0 win over Delaware State. Illinois' Dave Wilson threw for a Big Ten record 621 yards and six TDs against Ohio State; Purdue's Mark Herrmann also surpassed the old record on that day with 439 yards against Iowa; Duke's Ben Bennett passed for an Atlantic Coast Conference record 469 yards against Wake Forest; and Washington's Tom Flick set an NCAA record by completing 16 of 17 passes (94.1 percent) against Arizona. (BYU's Jim McMahon could only manage 464 yards that day against North Texas State.)

■ *October 16, 1976:* In College Station, Texas, Texas A&M placekicker Tony Franklin made three field goals against Baylor, by no means an extraordinary day for a kicker, but one was a 64-yarder and another a 65-yarder. That's not all, though: 300 miles away, in a game against East Texas State, Ove Johannson of Abilene Christian University kicked a 69-yard field goal, the longest in the history of football.

■ *April 12, 1985:* Marty Burke of Huffman (Alabama) High School hit three grand slams against Woodlawn High School.

■ *July 4, 1932:* Babe Didrickson entered the women's AAU championships (which also served as the Olympic trials) as a one-woman team. She took part in 8 of the 10 events and won 6 of them, setting world records in the 80m hurdles, the javelin, and the high jump. She also won the shot put, long jump, and baseball throw, and was fourth in the discus. She won the team title with 30 points, earning 8 points more than the 22-woman group from the University of Illinois.

11
THE GAME AND THE PLAYERS

THE MOST NOTABLE DELAYS, POSTPONEMENTS, AND CANCELLATIONS

■ The first Wimbledon final in 1877 was delayed a day so that fans could watch the Eton vs. Harrow cricket match, which always took place on the second Saturday in July.

■ On September 15, 1946, the second game of a Chicago Cubs–Brooklyn Dodgers doubleheader was postponed when gnats descended on Ebbets Field in the sixth inning. The sun was shining and fans waved white scorecards to shoo the insects, creating a hazard to the players' vision. The Dodgers 2-0 lead was good enough for a win, since five innings had been completed.

■ The WHA's Philadelphia Blazers, who played in a refurbished convention hall, could not play their first game because no one knew how to make ice. It cracked whenever skated upon.

The two games of the 1927 Stanley Cup finals that went into overtime were both eventually called because of rough ice.

■ From 1917–18, the Indianapolis 500 was suspended for the war. The Speedway's brick track became a landing strip and the garages were used as hangars for army planes.

■ A 1963 Minnesota Twins–Washington Senators game in Washington was called off because of a civil rights march.

■ The U.S. Amateur golf championship was postponed a week in 1901 because of the death of President McKinley.

■ On June 15, 1976, a baseball game at the Houston Astrodome was rained out when the city was flooded with up to 10 inches of water. The Astros and the Pittsburgh Pirates made it to the Dome, but fans, umpires, and stadium personnel did not.

■ A flu epidemic caused the cancellation of the remainder of the 1919 Stanley Cup series between the Seattle Metropolitans and the Montreal Canadiens, with the series tied 2-2-1.

■ The Billy Conn–Bob Pastor heavyweight fight, scheduled for May 11, 1942, was postponed when Conn broke his left hand in a fight with his father-in-law, Jimmy Smith, at an Irish post-christening party.

■ On May 20, 1960, a Chicago Cubs–Milwaukee Braves game was called because of fog at Milwaukee County Stadium. Umpire Frank Dascoli took three crew members into the outfield and had Frank Thomas of the Cubs hit a fungo. When none of the umpires nor any of the three Cub outfielders could see the ball, Dascoli wiped out the game, which was tied 0-0 in the fifth inning.

■ On January 28, 1961, a basketball game between West Hazelton (Pennsylvania) High School and McAdoo was rained out with West Hazelton leading, 31-29, because an open window caused condensation on the floor of the heated gym.

■ In November 1989, officials at Northeastern canceled their final football game of the season at James Madison in Virginia after blood tests showed that 21 of their players had not developed antibodies to the measles virus.

■ Many games have been forfeited because of rowdy fans, including the final game ever played in Washington, in 1971, before the Senators left for Texas, as fans stormed the field for souvenirs. The Rangers were the recipients of a forfeit win from the Indians in 1974 on the evening of Cleveland's promotional disaster, Ten Cent Beer Night.

■ The 1989 World Series between the Oakland Athletics and the San Francisco Giants was delayed for 10 days because of the Bay Area's worst earthquake since 1906.

■ The University of California had its entire 1889 football schedule rained out.

11 SPORTS FIGURES WHO EARNED THEIR PAYCHECKS

On June 25, 1976, Texas Rangers shortstop Toby Harrah established a standard for inactivity. He played an entire doubleheader without handling a single chance, a major league record. Most likely, Harrah would have preferred to have some balls hit his way, get into the flow, enjoy himself.

The following athletes and teams did not have this problem.

■ On May 27, 1984, Manuela Maleeva beat Virginia Ruzici in the Italian Open quarterfinals—a match that took three days to complete because of rain—then beat Carling Bassett in the semifinals and Chris Evert in the finals.

■ Oakland Athletics relief pitcher Darold Knowles appeared in all seven games of the 1973 World Series.

■ On November 1, 1924, Forest Peters, a freshman for Montana State's football team, kicked 17 field goals in 22 attempts.

■ Jim Galvin, pitcher for the 1878 Buffalo Bisons of the International Association, gave the most impressive display of pitching stamina in a season in baseball history. Of 116 league and non-league games, he pitched in 101, of which 96 were complete games. His record was 72-25-3, with 17 shutouts. He started and finished the first 23 games that the team played and pitched at least 895 innings.

■ Boxer Johnny Greb had 44 fights in 1914.

■ In the 1968–69 season, Walt Bellamy played in 88 regular season NBA games, six more than the scheduled 82. Bellamy was traded from the New York Knicks to the Detroit Pistons in midseason.

■ When running back Red Grange first signed with the Chicago Bears in 1925, they tried to capitalize immediately on his fame by playing 16 games in a little over a month.

■ Los Angeles Dodger Mike Marshall is the only pitcher in baseball's modern era to appear in 100 games in a season—106 games in 1974.

■ Welterweight champion Henry Armstrong accepted five welterweight title defenses between October 9 and 30, 1939. He won them all.

■ In a 1925 victory over the University of California, Stanford's All-America running back Ernie Nevers ran the ball on all but three of his team's offensive plays.

■ In June 1989, announcer Vin Scully called 45 innings of baseball in 29 hours: a 10-inning NBC daytime "Game of the Week" in St. Louis on June 3, the Los Angeles Dodgers' 22-inning marathon that night in Houston, and a 13-inning Dodgers–Astros game the next day.

WORTH THE PRICE OF ADMISSION: THE MOST FUN AND EXCITING TEAMS AND EVENTS

The styles of some teams and athletes are methodical, deliberate, yawn-inspiring. Then there are others that, win or lose, are styled somehow to perpetually engage us. A team may be naturally thrilling (in which case, you can be sure, they will come to be called "The Cardiac Kids"), or spectacularly inept, or too strange or brilliant or comical for us to know what it is. Athletes and teams that most of us would like to have seen, or see—at least once, anyway— might include the laughable 1962 New York Mets; "Air Coryell"—the San Diego Chargers under pass-happy coach Don Coryell in the late 1970s and 1980s; the brilliant and explosive John McEnroe; colorful golfers Lee Trevino and Chi Chi Rodriguez, to name a few.

Some games or matches are like that, too. They may or may not pit the best against the best but they are intensely competitive, or they somehow feel big, historic.

Whatever qualities they possess, dull isn't one of them.

■ The 1930 Philadelphia Phillies had eight .300 hitters; an astonishing team batting average of .315; a team ERA of 6.71, a major league record for ineptitude; and a defense that made 239 errors. They were also a last-place team, 40 games out of first.

■ The first official American ski race was conducted in 1854 in Sierra County, California. The race was a straight downhill, with no turns, on 15-foot skis.

■ The 1957 University of North Carolina Tar Heels won the NCAA title by winning two consecutive triple-overtime games—74-70 over Michigan State, and then 54-53 over Kansas and Wilt Chamberlain.

■ In the 1964 Stanley Cup finals between the Toronto

Maple Leafs and the Detroit Red Wings, the winning goal in each of the first three games was scored in the final minute of play, and five of the first six games were decided by one goal.

■ The men's 1973 Wimbledon doubles and 1975 U.S. Open doubles crowns were won by perhaps the most volatile pairing in tennis history—Ilie Nastase and Jimmy Connors.

■ The scores of the Holiday Bowl in 1979, 1980, and 1981 were, respectively, 38-37, 46-45, and 38-36. BYU was involved in all three games.

■ In 1934, in one of the most famous moments in All-Star history, New York Giants pitcher Carl Hubbell struck out the following five future Hall of Famers in a row: Babe Ruth, Lou Gehrig, Jimmie Foxx, Al Simmons, and Joe Cronin.

■ The two greatest underdogs and fan favorites at the 1988 Calgary Olympics were the Jamaican bobsled team and English ski jumper Eddie "The Eagle" Edwards. Edwards finished dead last in his competition, while the Jamaicans crashed on their third heat and skipped the fourth and final heat.

■ Each of the five games in the 1951 Stanley Cup finals was tied at the end of regulation. The Toronto Maple Leafs defeated the Montreal Canadiens, four sudden-death victories to one.

■ In the closest finish in Grand Prix racing, Brazilian Ayrton Senna beat Englishman Nigel Mansell in the 1986 Spanish Grand Prix by 0.014 seconds—1:48:47.735 to 1:48:47.749.

■ At the 1979 U.S. Open, John Lloyd beat Paul McNamee 5-7, 6-7, 7-5, 7-6, 7-6.

■ From 1982 through the end of the decade, the NCAA basketball title games were decided by the following point margins: 1, 2, 9, 2, 3, 1, 4, and 1 (in overtime).

■ One of the rules of luge, a dangerous sport to begin with, requires that one of four runs must be negotiated at night.

■ The 1981–82 Denver Nuggets are the only NBA team ever to go an entire season scoring 100 points or more in every game. They are also the only team to go an entire season allowing 100 points or more in every game.

EXERCISES IN FUTILITY

■ Wilt Chamberlain holds the record for the most free throws attempted in one game, 10, without making one. He also holds the record for the second-most number of free throws attempted, nine, without making one.

■ On two occasions, NBA player Howie Dallmar took 15 shots from the field and made none. In one 1978 NBA final game against the Washington Bullets, Seattle Supersonic Dennis Johnson went 0-for-14 from the field.

■ Through 1989, four managers had lost every World Series game they had ever managed: Donie Bush with the 1927 Pittsburgh Pirates, Gabby Hartnett with the 1938 Chicago Cubs, Eddie Sawyer with the 1950 Philadelphia Phillies, and Roger Craig with the 1989 San Francisco Giants.

■ Bobby Wallace spent the most years as an active major leaguer, 25, without playing on a pennant winner. Buddy

Bell retired after playing 2,405 games and never appearing in postseason play. In more than a quarter century of managing, Gene Mauch never won a pennant.

■ In 1961, Puerto Rican jockey Juan Vinales retired at age 28, after making 360 career mounts and winning no races.

■ In the 1968 World Series, St. Louis Cardinals shortstop Dal Maxvill went 0-for-22.

■ The 1953–54 NBA Baltimore Bullets had a road record of 0-20.

■ Terry Felton, who pitched for the Minnesota Twins from 1979–82, finished his career with a record of 0-16.

■ New York Mets pitcher Randy Tate was 0-for-41 at the plate in 1975, his only season. Chicago Cubs pitcher Bob Buhl went 0-for-70 for the 1962 season.

■ Fred Merkle went to the World Series five times in eight years with three teams, and lost each time.

■ Carlton Fisk is 0-9 in All-Star games in which he played. Fisk was also named to the 1974 All-Star team but did not play because of an injury. The American League lost that game, too.

■ Through 1989, the Seattle Mariners had not had a winning season in the history of their franchise.

■ Philadelphia Eagles owner Bert Bell founded the NFL draft in 1936 but could not sign any of the nine picks his club made that first year.

■ In a doubleheader on July 2, 1933, the St. Louis Cardinals were shut out 1-0 in 18 innings in the first game, and 1-0 in regulation in the second game.

IF YOU SHUT IT OFF:
5 GAMES, 2 MATCHES, 1 FIGHT,
1 SERIES, AND 1 SEASON YOU MIGHT
HAVE WALKED OUT ON, AND
PROBABLY SHOULDN'T HAVE

Some games are dull from beginning to end, some exciting from beginning to end, some start off with a rush and dissipate from there.

Variations on each of these aside, the fourth and last possibility is the kind of game most dreaded by the fan who invariably walks out in the seventh inning, if not before: a contest that one side dominates at the outset, but that eventually turns into a thriller, or goes to overtime, or yields a record-setting performance. It is almost as if one or more of the players had not shown up at the beginning and then, almost inexplicably, bounces to life.

This list is dedicated to all of those Los Angeles Dodger fans who, to beat the traffic, left before the end of Game 1 of the 1988 World Series. If they timed it right, they made it home just as the late news was showing the replay of Kirk Gibson hitting one of the most famous World Series home runs of all time.

■ On November 18, 1972, the Milwaukee Bucks were leading the New York Knicks comfortably, 86-68, at Madison Square Garden with 5½ minutes to play... but the Bucks did not score another point in the game, while the Knicks scored 19, to win 87-86.

■ France's Laurent Dauthuille was ahead on the scorecards of all three judges in the last round of his world middleweight title fight with Jake LaMotta on September 13, 1950... until there were 13 seconds remaining in the fight, when LaMotta knocked Dauthuille out.

■ On April 17, 1976, the Philadelphia Phillies were being

humiliated 13-2 by the Chicago Cubs on a windy day at Wrigley Field... when the Phillies came back to win 18-16 in 10 innings, largely on the strength of four Mike Schmidt home runs.

■ In the second quarter of a 1974 game, Notre Dame was romping over the University of Southern California at the Rose Bowl, 24-0... but Trojan running back Anthony Davis woke up and scored four touchdowns, USC totaled 55 points in the next 17 minutes, and the *Trojans* romped, 55-24.

■ John McEnroe beat Bjorn Borg handily in the first set of the 1980 Wimbledon final, 6-1... but those who shut it off there to play Sunday-morning doubles at the club missed a Borg victory that eventually went five sets and included a fourth-set tiebreaker, won 18-16 by McEnroe, that is considered by many the most exciting game in tennis history.

■ The Chicago Bears were beating the punchless New York Giants 13-3 entering the fourth quarter of their 1934 NFL title game... but behind 27 fourth-quarter points, the Giants won going away, 30-13.

■ In the 1987 Federation Cup finals, Chris Evert and Pam Shriver were on their way to a slaughter over Steffi Graf and Claudia Kohde, 6-1, 4-0... until the German team awoke. Graf and Kohde went on to win 1-6, 7-5, 6-4.

■ On November 10, 1984, the University of Miami, at home in the Orange Bowl, was stunning Maryland 31-0 at the half and imagining the avalanche of scoring that might occur... and it did, as Maryland scored six second-half touchdowns to squeak out a thrilling road upset, 42-40.

■ In the 1942 Stanley Cup finals, the Toronto Maple

Leafs were down three games to zero to the Detroit Red Wings, who were probably starting to think about their victory parade . . . until Toronto proceeded to win the last four games of the series to become the only major professional team to have accomplished such a comeback in a championship final.

■ The 1914 Boston Braves were in last place on July 19 . . . and gained 21½ games on the New York Giants to win the National League pennant. Dubbed the "Miracle Braves," the charmed team went on to sweep the World Series—the first sweep in Series history—over a heavily favored Philadelphia Athletic team that featured five future Hall of Famers.

CONTESTS WE'RE GLAD THAT WE MISSED, OR WISH WE HAD: THE MOST UNEXCITING OCCASIONS, TEAMS, AND ATHLETES

Why are we fans? Because we enjoy the fun and excitement of a competition that pits talented athletes against one another, or an athlete showing mastery against some objective standard. Not every competition, however, is engaging; perhaps the opponents are too well matched, or mismatched, or simply intent on slowing down the flow of a contest to a virtual standstill to gain an edge.

This is one reason why remote control was invented.

■ In the 1964 Olympics, sprint cyclists Giovanni Pettenella of Italy and Pierre Trentin of France, each waiting for the other one to start first so that he could follow and "draft" —force the lead cyclist into fighting the wind for the trailing cyclist—stood still on their bicycles for 21 minutes, 57 seconds.

■ In an 1881 football contest between Yale and Princeton

that came to be known as "The Block Game," Princeton held the football for the entire first half without trying to score, and Yale did the same thing in the second half. The 60 minutes of inactivity inspired a rule change that required the offensive team to try moving the ball at least five yards in three tries ("downs") or relinquish the ball.

◼ In the Olympic free pistol competition, shooters are allotted 2½ hours to fire 60 shots.

◼ Dean Smith's maddening, if successful, use of the four-corner stall with his University of North Carolina Tar Heels in the 1970s helped lead to the institution of the shot clock in college basketball.

◼ First baseman Mike Hargrove was nicknamed "The Human Rain Delay" because it took him so long to get set in the batter's box. His soulmate in basketball, Milwaukee Buck Ricky Pierce, had one of his free throws voided by referee Jack Madden for delay of game, on April 5, 1988. Madden claimed that Pierce, a notoriously slow foul shooter, had violated the 10-second rule before taking his second shot.

◼ In a boy's basketball game on March 7, 1941, Las Animas (Colorado) High School defeated La Junta, 2-0, in overtime.

◼ The average margin of victory in the seven previous Super Bowls (counting back from XXIV) is 27 points.

◼ In their first heavyweight bout in 1871, neither Joe Coburn nor Jem Mace landed a punch.

◼ For most fans, the Los Angeles Rams of the 1970s meant a deliberate—that is, boring—style of play: very little passing, and not very much running around end, either. They were so boring, in fact, that coach Chuck Knox resigned under pressure despite winning five divisional titles in five years. "I'd rather have a team with an even record with exciting games than one that goes to the playoff and then loses," said Rams owner Carroll Rosenbloom in 1978.

WHAT THEY PLAY FOR:
10 TROPHIES AND ARTIFACTS
FOUGHT OVER IN
COLLEGE FOOTBALL RIVALRIES

Minnesota–Michigan — The Little Brown Jug

California–Stanford — The Axe

Texas–Oklahoma — The Cowboy Hat

Notre Dame–Michigan
State — The Megaphone

Florida–Miami (Florida) — The Seminole War Canoe

Clemson–South Carolina — The Tea Cup

Princeton–Rutgers — The Rusty Old Cannon

Wichita–Wichita State — The Dog Collar

Idaho–Montana — The Wooden Beer Stein

Susquehanna–Lycoming — Amos Alonzo Stagg's
Bronze Felt Halt

THE MOST MEMORABLE TIES

Victory brings joy, defeat, despair. A tie? A tie, it's said, is like kissing your sister. Yet, while many ties may be psychologically indigestible, the following deadlocks had at least something noteworthy to recommend them.

■ Yevgeny Grishin of the U.S.S.R. tied for the 1,500m speedskating gold in 1956. In 1960, he skated in the same event and again tied for the gold.

■ In the inaugural London Marathon in 1981, American Dick Beardsley and Norwegian Inge Simonsen held hands to cross the finish line in a tie.

■ In the 1944 Carter Handicap at Aqueduct, thoroughbreds Bossuet, Brownie, and Wait a Bit crossed the finish line together, in a triple dead heat.

■ In the 100m freestyle at the 1984 Olympics, Americans Nancy Hogshead and Carrie Steinseifer finished in a dead heat, earning the first double gold medals in Olympic swimming history.

■ Unbeaten Michigan State and unbeaten Notre Dame played to a 10-10 tie in 1966. The game's finish has become one of the most famous in college football history as the Irish ran out the clock to preserve the tie and their top ranking. Notre Dame is still criticized to this day for making little, if any, attempt to risk winning the game.

■ The National Football League has not seen a scoreless tie since a 0-0 contest on November 7, 1943 between the New York Giants and the Detroit Lions.

■ Martin Sheridan and Ralph Rose of the United States finished in a dead heat in the 1904 Olympic discus competition, each of them throwing exactly 128′ 10½″. In the "throw-off," they were each awarded three throws. Sheridan won by over seven feet.

■ Five times in the National League and twice in the American League have two teams tied for first place at the end of the regular season. Remarkably, the Dodgers—first in Brooklyn, then in Los Angeles—have been involved in all five National League ties, losing four and winning one. The Boston Red Sox have been involved in both American League playoffs, and have lost both.

In 1980, the Houston Astros and Los Angeles finished at 92-70 atop the National League West. Houston won a one-game playoff.

In 1978, the New York Yankees and Red Sox finished at 99-63 in the American League East. The Yankees won a one-game playoff at Fenway Park.

In 1962, Los Angeles and the San Francisco Giants finished at 101-61. The Giants won the National League pennant by taking the best-of-three playoff, two games to one.

In 1959, Los Angeles and the Milwaukee Braves finished at 86-68. The Dodgers won the National League pennant by sweeping the playoff, two games to none.

In 1951, the New York Giants and Brooklyn Dodgers finished at 96-58. The Giants won the playoff, two games to one, and took the National League pennant.

In 1948, the Cleveland Indians and the Red Sox were tied at 96-58 atop the American League. Cleveland won a one-game playoff at Fenway Park.

In 1946, the St. Louis Cardinals and Brooklyn finished tied at 96-58. St. Louis won the best-of-three-game playoff, two games to none, for the National League pennant.

■ Of their 76 regular season games in the 1969–70 season, the Philadelphia Flyers played in an NHL record 24 ties.

■ In the 11th game of the 1960 AFL season, the Buffalo Bills were beating the Denver Broncos 38-7 late in the third quarter and managed to settle for a tie.

■ The Brooklyn Dodgers and the Cincinnati Reds played in the longest scoreless tie in baseball, 19 innings at Ebbets Field, on September 11, 1946.

BRIDESMAIDS

Some of the more habitual second-place finishers and runners-up:

■ Stirling Moss never won the world driving champion-

281

ship, coming in second from 1955–58 and third from 1959–61.

■ The St. Louis Blues made the Stanley Cup finals in 1968, 1969, and 1970, and got swept each year.

■ Both the Minnesota Vikings and the Denver Broncos have lost in each of their first four Super Bowl appearances.

■ Philadelphia Warriors great Hal Greer made the All-NBA second team seven times. He never made the first team.

■ Gottfried von Cramm was Wimbledon runner-up three years in a row, from 1935–37.
　　Ken Rosewall was 0-for-4 in Wimbledon singles finals.

■ American swimmer Shirley Babashoff won six Olympic silver medals (plus two golds, both in relays).

■ Brian Orser won the Olympic men's figure skating silver medal in 1984 and again in 1988.

■ Guy Lewis made five trips to the Final Four and never won an NCAA crown. He lost in 1967, 1968, 1982, 1983, and 1984, each time to the eventual national champion.

■ American Jack Davis was credited with the same time as the champion in the 110m hurdles in both 1952 and 1956—on each occasion, setting an Olympic record—but was edged out for the gold both times. (Before 1972, times were measured in tenths of seconds and so a runner-up who was anywhere from one hundredth to nine hundredths of a second behind the winner might show an identical clocking.)

■ Alydar came in second to Affirmed in each of the three Triple Crown races in 1978.

■ For four years in a row, 1969–72, American figure skater

Julie Holmes took second place to Janet Lynn at the U.S. championships.

■ In 1984, golfer Greg Norman tied with Fuzzy Zoeller at the U.S. Open. In an 18-hole playoff, Norman lost by eight strokes. In the 1986 Masters, Norman bogeyed the final hole and finished one stroke behind Jack Nicklaus. At the 1986 U.S. Open, Norman led going into the final round but fell all the way to twelfth (Ray Floyd won). At the 1986 PGA, Norman finished second to Bob Tway, after leading by four strokes with nine holes to play. At the 1987 Masters, Norman finished in a four-way tie in regulation and lost to Larry Mize in the playoff. At the 1989 Masters, Norman bogeyed the final hole to miss the playoff. At the 1989 British Open, Norman lost in a three-way playoff with Wayne Grady and winner Mark Calcavecchia.

THE DANDIEST STREAKS IN SPORTS

Included among the most famous streaks in sports would have to be Joe DiMaggio's 56-game hitting streak in 1941; UCLA's string of 88 wins and seven consecutive NCAA basketball titles; in tennis, Martina Navratilova's 74 consecutive singles wins in 1984 and Bjorn Borg's five Wimbledons, from 1976 to 1980; Edwin Moses's 107-race unbeaten streak in the 400m hurdles that spanned 11 years and 22 countries; the Boston Celtics eight consecutive NBA titles (1959–66); and the run of five straight championships accomplished by the New York Yankees in baseball (1949–53), and the Montreal Canadiens in hockey (1956–60).

Here are some of the other memorable streaks by teams and individuals.

■ Boxer Lamar Clark holds the record for most consecutive knockouts, 44, from 1958–60. The most consecutive first-round knockouts is 18, by One-Round Hogan, in 1910.

■ Chick Hearn had broadcast 2,245 consecutive Los Angeles Laker games through the 1988–89 season.

■ Relief pitcher Paul Linblad went from 1966 to 1974—385 games—without making an error.

■ Green Bay Packers quarterback Bart Starr threw 294 consecutive passes without an interception during the 1964 and 1965 seasons.

■ For six years—from August 1973 to May 1979—Chris Evert did not lose a singles match on clay. She had won 125 consecutive matches when Tracy Austin finally ended the streak by beating her in the 1979 Italian Open semifinals.

■ The University of Oklahoma won 47 straight football games from 1953–57, and from 1946–59 had a 74-game win streak in the Big Eight.
    The longest unbeaten streak in college football is 63 games, by the University of Washington, from 1907–17 (they won 59 and tied 4).

■ Pitcher Jim Barr of the San Francisco Giants retired a record 41 consecutive batters in 1972.

■ Illinois defensive back Al Brosky intercepted at least one pass in 15 consecutive games in the early 1950s.

■ In the 1945 Stanley Cup finals, Toronto Maple Leafs goalie Frank McCool had three consecutive shutouts and went 192 minutes without allowing a goal.

■ In the 1922 season, the Pittsburgh Pirates enjoyed a five-game stretch in which every hitter in the lineup—including pitchers, pinch hitters, and other replacement players—got at least one hit.

■ Scott Palmer made a hole-in-one in each of four consecutive rounds from October 9–12, 1983, at Balboa Park, San Diego.

■ Kareem Abdul-Jabbar scored in double figures in 787 consecutive games. The streak started on December 4, 1977, and was stopped exactly 10 years later, on December 4, 1987.

■ In 1957, Ted Williams reached base 16 consecutive times: he had four homers, two singles, nine walks, and was hit by a pitch.

■ On January 5, 1971, the Harlem Globetrotters lost to the New Jersey Reds, 100-99, breaking their consecutive-games winning streak at 2,495.

■ The Buffalo Germans, a barnstorming basketball team at the turn of the century, won 111 straight games.

■ The Philadelphia Flyers once went an NHL record 35 games without a loss, from October 14, 1979 through January 6, 1980. During that period, they won 25 games and tied 10.
    In 1982, the New York Islanders won a record 15 consecutive games.

■ Annemarie Moser-Proll won 11 consecutive World Cup downhill races from December 1972 to January 1974.

■ In 1967, Wilt Chamberlain made a record 35 field goals in a row.

■ During the 1980–81 season, Calvin Murphy sank a record 78 free throws in a row.

■ In the 1940s, Byron Nelson was "in the money" in 113 consecutive tournaments. In 1945, he played 19 consecutive rounds under 70.

■ The U.S. women's tennis team won the Wightman Cup 21 times in a row from 1931 to 1957. (There was a six-year break for World War II.)

■ Between 1948 and 1954, Emil Zatopek won 38 consecutive races at 10,000m.

■ East German backstroker Roland Matthes was undefeated for seven years until American John Naber beat him in 1974.

■ Roberto Clemente hit safely in all 14 World Series games in which he played—7 games in 1960, and 7 more in 1971.

■ Woody Stephens was the trainer for five consecutive Belmont winners, 1982–86.

■ From 1947 to 1949, the Toronto Maple Leafs won nine straight games in the Stanley Cup finals.

■ In 1932, the New York Yankees won their 12th consecutive World Series game.

■ In 1974, Los Angeles Dodgers pitcher Mike Marshall appeared in 13 consecutive games.

■ In the 1971–72 season, the Los Angeles Lakers won a record 33 games in a row.

■ New York Giants pitcher Carl Hubbell won 24 games in a row in 1936–37.

■ Walter Alston signed 23 consecutive one-year contracts to manage the Brooklyn, and then Los Angeles, Dodgers before he retired in 1976.

■ From 1979 to 1983, Dave Jennings punted 623 times without having one blocked.

■ When right-handed Ivan Lendl won the U.S. Open in 1985, he broke a streak of lefty men's singles winners at the Open that began in 1974 with Jimmy Connors. (Oddly, besides Martina Navratilova, Bertha L. Townsend is the only other left-hander to win the women's U.S. draw, and she did it back in 1888 and 1889.)

◼ In 1925, Brooklyn Robin Milt Stock got four hits in each of four consecutive games.

◼ The Cleveland Browns went 21 seasons, 1950–71, without being shut out.

◼ In May of 1938, Bob Seeds of the International League's Newark Bears hit a home run in four successive innings.

◼ Since 1900, only twice has a major league team scored at least one run in every frame of a nine-inning game—the New York Giants on June 1, 1923, and the St. Louis Cardinals on September 13, 1964.

◼ From 1981 into the next decade, every Super Bowl featured at least one starting quarterback whose first name started with a "J": Jim Plunkett (1981), Joe Montana (1982), Joe Theismann (1983), Joe Theismann and Jim Plunkett (1984), Joe Montana (1985), Jim McMahon (1986), John Elway (1987), John Elway (1988), Joe Montana (1989), and Joe Montana and John Elway (1990).

◼ Chris Evert won at least one Grand Slam singles title a year for 13 years, from 1974 to 1986.

◼ Jack Nicklaus and Arnold Palmer each won at least one tournament for a record 17 consecutive years.

◼ Johnny Unitas threw for at least one touchdown in 47 consecutive games, from 1956–60.

THE PUREST RULES IN BASEBALL

Purity may be found in every sport, with the obvious exceptions—professional wrestling, tractor pulls, dwarf throwing, a few others. Generally, there are the players and the field, perhaps there is a ball, maybe a stick of sorts, always an objective. Simple. Some games and their practitioners succeed more than others in remaining true to the ideal; among America's popular sports, golf has probably comported itself the most admirably. But there is purity elsewhere. There is purity in Wimbledon, where there are still no stadium lights, and the tournament always begins at 2 P.M. There is purity in fall Saturdays in the Ivy League, where football games are still played primarily for the fun they engender, not the revenue they produce. And there is purity in the Cleveland Browns' uniforms, which eschew fancy color schemes, and in their simple helmets, the only ones in the NFL without emblems.

No sport, though, is more conscious of its tradition than baseball. We come close to being overwhelmed by the skyrocketing salaries, the Multiplex Domes, the exploding scoreboards, yes, but then we still have Cracker Jack and seventh-inning stretches, Topps baseball cards and the sign behind home plate that says NO PEPPER GAMES, and there are still 108 double stitches in a regulation baseball. And, most important, there is still the game itself, infinitely varied but infinitely simple, too. Home, first, second, third, home again. In a hundred years, the playing field has changed little, and why not? Sportswriter Red Smith said, "Ninety feet between bases is perhaps as close as man has ever gotten to perfection."

From the book of *Official Baseball Rules* (1989), here are some other elegances.

■ Rule 1.01: "Baseball is a game between two teams of nine players each..."

■ Rule 1.10a: "The bat shall be a smooth *round* stick..."

■ Rule 4.02: "The players of the home team shall take their defensive positions, the first batter of the visiting team shall take his position in the batter's box, the umpire shall call 'Play' and the game shall start."

■ Rule 5.03: "The pitcher shall deliver the pitch to the

batter who may elect to strike the ball, or who may not offer at it, as he chooses."

■ From Rule 9.05 (General Instructions to Umpires): "It is better to consult the rules and hold up the game ten minutes to decide a knotty problem than to have a game thrown out on protest and replayed."

■ Rule 10.05.b: "A base hit shall be scored...when a batter reaches first base safely on a fair ball hit with such force, or so slowly, that any fielder attempting to make a play with it has no opportunity to do so."

■ And these definitions from Rule 2.00:

"A DOUBLE PLAY is a play by the defense in which two offensive players are put out as a result of continuous action, providing there is no error between putouts."

"The BATTERY is the pitcher and catcher."

"A FLY BALL is a batted ball that goes high in the air in flight...A LINE DRIVE is a batted ball that goes sharp and direct from the bat to a fielder without touching the ground...A GROUND BALL is a batted ball that rolls or bounces close to the ground."

"A DOUBLE-HEADER is two regularly scheduled... games, played in immediate succession."

"The BATTER'S BOX is the area within which the batter shall stand during his time at bat."

"An OUTFIELDER is a fielder who occupies a position in...the area of the playing field most distant from home base."

"A THROW is the act of propelling the ball with the hand and arm to a given objective..."

"A WILD PITCH is one so high, so low, or so wide of

the plate that it cannot be handled with ordinary effort by the catcher."

" 'SAFE' is a declaration by the umpire that a runner is entitled to the base for which he was trying."

6TH MEN, PINCH HITTERS AND ROLE PLAYERS: THE MOST NOTABLE SUBSTITUTES

■ Red Auerbach believed that the Boston Celtics could demoralize their opponents if their first substitution strengthened rather than weakened the team on the floor. Building on this philosophy, the Celtics developed some of the best "bench players" in all of sports, including the NBA's first great sixth man, Frank Ramsey. Other Celtics who made a great impact but often did not start included John Havlicek, Don Nelson, Paul Silas, and early in his career, Kevin McHale, who twice won the NBA's Sixth Man Award. Among the league's other teams, notable sixth men include Cazzie Russell, Irv Torgoff, Michael Cooper, Roy Tarpley, and Dennis Rodman.

■ Jesse Owens replaced Marty Glickman on the U.S. 4×100m relay team at the 1936 Berlin Olympics, and Ralph Metcalfe replaced Sam Stoller. Glickman and Stoller were the only two Jews on the U.S. track team and the only two members who did not compete.

■ In the bottom of the sixth inning of Game 6 of the 1947 World Series, Brooklyn Dodger Al Gionfriddo replaced Eddie Miksis defensively in the outfield. With two outs in the inning, Gionfriddo made one of the most famous catches in World Series history, robbing New York Yankee Joe DiMaggio of a three-run home run that would have tied the game.

■ In the 1922 Walker Cup competition, Bernard Darwin, covering the match for *The London Times*, was called to replace Robert Harris, the British team captain, who had become ill. Darwin, twice a semifinalist in the British Amateur (and the grandson of Charles Darwin), won his single.

■ Minnesota Viking Bob Berry made it to three Super Bowls—as backup quarterback to Fran Tarkenton—and did not get to play in any of them.

■ On September 28, 1960, in one of the most memorable replacements in baseball history, Boston Red Sox Carroll Hardy took over in Fenway Park's left field for Ted Williams in the ninth inning of Williams's last game. In the eighth inning, Williams had hit a home run in what would be the final at-bat of his career.

■ The Texas A&M "12th Man" kickoff team is made up of regular students at the school who try out during the first week in August.

■ There have been numerous tandems of great pitchers working with preferred catchers who were not the first-string. In 1930, Brooklyn Dodgers backup catcher Hank DeBerry caught 35 games, all when Dazzy Vance pitched. The battery had played together in the minor leagues, came up together to the majors, and DeBerry had caught Vance's 1925 no-hitter.

In 1976, Philadelphia Phillie Tim McCarver was Steve Carlton's personal backstop, catching 32 of his 35 starts, though Bob Boone was the team's starting catcher. "When Steve and I die," McCarver said, "we are going to be buried in the same cemetery, sixty feet, six inches apart."

Detroit Tigers second-stringer Bruce Kimm caught all 29 of Mark Fidrych's starts in 1976.

■ San Diego Chargers running back Hank Bauer played almost exclusively in goal-line situations during the 1979 season. He carried the ball 22 times all year and scored eight touchdowns.

■ From the middle of the 1939 season through 1942, Chicago White Sox great Ted Lyons, in the twilight of his career, pitched almost exclusively on Sundays.

.500

One of the worst things you can say about a professional sports team is, "They're a .500 club." (Theoretically, "They're a .400 club," is a worse thing to say but no one ever says that.) Considering that every game results in one win and one loss (or two ties); that at each season's end, the cumulative winning percentage of all teams in any league is .500; and that there should be roughly, and often exactly, as many teams worse than a .500 club as there are teams that are better, the comment should not be treated as the condemnation that it is. Someone's got to be at .500, and it's a lot better than being a cellar dweller.

None of that matters; pointing out anyone's .500-ness is still not a nice thing to do.

Some of the more exquisite examples:

■ During the 1979–80 season, San Antonio Spurs coach Doug Moe was replaced with the basketball team's record at 33-33. Bob Bass took over and the team went 8-8 the rest of the way.

■ The 1967 Pittsburgh Pirates were 42-42 under manager Harry Walker and 39-39 under Danny Murtaugh.

■ As Brooklyn Dodger manager, Walter Alston was 7-7 in two World Series. The team then moved west. Alston's record managing the Los Angeles Dodgers in World Series games was 13-13.

■ Rube Marquard pitched for 18 seasons. Of those, eight were winning seasons, eight were losing, and two were exactly .500.

■ The 1907 Detroit Tigers pitcher George Mullin won exactly 20 games—but he lost exactly 20 games, as well.

■ In 1985, the Cleveland Browns won the AFC Central title with an 8-8 record. They were the only team in the division to reach .500.

■ The Minnesota Twins of 1972–73, the San Diego Padres of 1982–83, and the Montreal Expos of 1988–89 are the only major league teams to play .500 ball in consecutive seasons.

ONE DOZEN THINGS
IN PROFESSIONAL SPORTS THAT
YOU COULD PROBABLY DO
WITHOUT EMBARRASSING YOURSELF

1. Coach first base
2. Shoot free throws as well as former ABA and NBA
   player Kim Hughes (40-percent career foul shooter)
3. Sink a two-foot putt (with no break)
4. Intentionally walk a batter
5. Hold for a point-after attempt
6. Roll a frame or two in a professional bowler's tournament
7. Umpire the left-field or right-field lines at the All-Star
   Game
8. Sit out a two-minute penalty
9. Make a soccer throw-in
10. Drive in the back row on the pace lap
11. Make the proper club selection
12. Net-judge in tennis

TANKING:
9 NOTED EXAMPLES OF NOT
GIVING IT YOUR ALL

"Tanking"—willfully putting out a half-hearted effort—is a delicate subject in sports. It suggests athletes on the take or who don't care, coaches and general managers conniving for a higher draft pick, the 1919 Black Sox. Nonetheless, tanking has been known, admittedly or not, to happen.

◼ With the University of Florida leading Miami 45-8, the entire Gator defense fell to the ground, letting Hurricane quarterback John Hornibrook run in uncontested for a touchdown so that Florida quarterback John Reaves could have another shot at breaking Jim Plunkett's career passing record. Florida got the ball back with 1:06 to go and Reaves set the record. Miami coach Fran Curci called it "the worst thing I have ever seen in football."

◼ Speaking before a Senate subcommittee on June 14, 1960, middleweight Jake LaMotta confessed to throwing a fight against Billy Fox in 1947.

◼ Pancho Gonzalez, who had lost 24-22 in the first set of his first-round Wimbledon match in 1969 with 26-year-old Charlie Pasarell, was booed when he seemed to give up in the second set and lose it, 6-1, because he was disgusted that the match was not being suspended for failing light. When the match continued the next day, however, the 41-year-old Gonzalez took the next three sets, 16-14, 6-3, and 11-9, saving seven match points in the last set of what became the longest match ever played at Wimbledon.

◼ On November 30, 1983, with the Portland Trail Blazers nearing a club scoring record of 150 points, Denver Nuggets coach Doug Moe, fed up with his team's defense, called time-out with 1:12 left in the game and told his players,

"Let them have it. You understand what I'm saying, don't you?" The Nuggets let the Blazers score five uncontested lay-ups in the closing minute for a 156-116 win. Moe was fined $5,000 and suspended for two games.

■ Ingemar Johansson of Sweden was disqualified in the super heavyweight final at the 1952 Olympics for not making sufficient effort against American H. Edwards Sanders. Johansson did not throw a single punch. He was denied his silver medal because of the disqualification. (It was finally awarded to him in 1982.)

■ In a 1960 Greco–Roman lightweight wrestling competition, Russian Avtandil Koridze needed a fall to qualify for the gold medal match with a Yugoslavian wrestler. In his bout with Bulgarian Dimitro Stoyanov, Koridze said something to Stoyanov with one minute left in the bout, then threw him to the ground and pinned him. Yugoslavia protested, and Stoyanov was disqualified. Koridze was not punished and went on to win the gold.

■ On April 2, 1987, in a close game between the Houston Rockets and the Phoenix Suns, starting forward Ralph Sampson did not play the fourth quarter, center Akeem Olajuwon sat out the final 8:31, and forward Rod McCray played only 4:43 of the period. Even when Houston got within 96-94 with 6:42 to play, coach Bill Fitch did not substitute. Sampson, Olajuwon, and McCray were seen laughing on the bench. Dallas Mavericks coach Dick Motta, who was watching the game, suggested that the Rockets were "messing around" in order to set up a favorable playoff schedule, which meant avoiding the Los Angeles Lakers as long as possible. Motta was suspended for one game and his team was fined $5,000 for his comments.

■ On the night in 1982 that the Oakland Athletics' Rickey Henderson was trying to break Lou Brock's single-season steal record, manager Billy Martin ordered Fred Stanley to get picked off of second base to open a steal opportunity for Henderson.

■ On the final day of the 1976 baseball regular season,

Kansas City Royal George Brett, who was virtually tied for the lead in the American League batting title race with teammate Hal McRae, hit what seemed to be a routine fly ball. However, Minnesota Twins outfielder Steve Brye suddenly stopped and the ball bounced over his head for an inside-the-park home run. McRae, the next batter, grounded out and ended up at .3321, with Brett at .3333. McRae, who is black, accused Twins manager Gene Mauch, who is white, of ordering Brye, who is white, to let the ball hit by Brett, who is white, fall safely. Mauch denied the charge. "I would protect the integrity of the game at all costs," Mauch said.

IRONMEN

Here are some of the most durable men in sports, and their consecutive-games playing streaks:

Football:
> 282—Jim Marshall, Cleveland Browns (1960), Minnesota Vikings (1961–79)

Basketball:
> 906—Randy Smith, NBA: Buffalo Braves, San Diego Clippers, Cleveland Cavaliers, New York Knicks, San Diego Clippers, Atlanta Hawks (February 18, 1972–March 13, 1983; the streak ended when he was given his release)
> 1,041—Ron Boone, ABA-NBA

Hockey:
> 962—Doug Jarvis, Montreal Canadiens, Washington Capitals, Hartford Whalers (October 8, 1975–April 5, 1987; including every game for the first twelve years of his career)

Major League Baseball:
  2,130—Lou Gehrig, New York Yankees (June 1, 1925–April 30, 1939; the last game of the streak was the last game of his career)

Japanese Baseball:
  2,215—Sachio Kinugasa, Hiroshima Toyo Carp (October 19, 1970–October 22, 1987)

And some of the most durable *and* loyal men in sports—the sampling of following athletes and coaches who have had the longest continuous reigns, in years, with one team:

Football:
  Coaching:
    29, Tom Landry, Dallas Cowboys, 1960–88
    29, Curly Lambeau, Green Bay Packers, 1921–49
    23, Steve Owen, New York Giants, 1931–53

Baseball:
  Playing:
    23, Brooks Robinson, Baltimore Orioles, 1955–77
    23, Carl Yastrzemski, Boston Red Sox, 1961–83
    22, Cap Anson, Chicago Cubs, 1876–97
    22, Stan Musial, St. Louis Cardinals, 1941–63 (except 1945, when he was in military service)
    22, Mel Ott, New York Giants, 1926–47
    22, Al Kaline, Detroit Tigers, 1953–74
  Managing:
    50, Connie Mack, Philadelphia Athletics, 1901–50

Basketball:
  Playing (NBA):
    16, John Havlicek, Boston Celtics, 1962–78
  Coaching (college):
    42, Ed Diddle, Western Kentucky, 1923–64
    42, Ray Meyer, DePaul, 1943–84
    41, Adolph Rupp, Kentucky, 1931–72 (the team was on probation for one year)

◾ *Boxing and Wrestling:* Heavyweight champion Muhammad Ali fought Japanese wrestler Antonio Inoki in Tokyo, in 1976. The 15-rounder—in which Inoki spent most of the time lying on the mat, kicking up at Ali—was called a draw.

◾ *(Basketball,) Track, and Horse Racing:* In 1986, New York Knick Kenny Walker defeated a pacer named Pugwash by a nose in a 1/16th-mile match race at Monticello Raceway. Walker's time was 10.4 seconds, a world record for a human versus a horse.

◾ *(Football,) Track, and Horse Racing:* The record that Walker broke had been set by former New York Giants defensive back Beasley Reece, who had defeated a horse named Super Chris.

◾ *Tennis and Ice Skating:* In 1953, tennis stars Gardner Mulloy and Bobby Riggs played a charity exhibition on skates.

◾ *Roller Derby, Tag Motorcycling, Team Handball, and Criminal Assault:* The 1975 James Caan movie *Rollerball* featured a futuristic and violent international sport in which players, propelled around a track by motorcycles, would attempt to throw a metal ball into a goal that was defended by large men wearing metal-studded gloves. Jonathan E., Caan's character, was the top scorer for the Houston team.

◾ *Basketball and Tennis:* University of Florida's 7'2" center Dwayne Schintzius was suspended for the first four games of the 1989–90 season for hitting a Florida student named Paul Sullivan over the head with a tennis racket.

Honorable mention: The New Zealand syndicate that

challenged the San Diego Yacht Club to race for America's Cup in 1988 believed that the Americans engaged unfairly in hybrid yachting when New Zealand's 133-foot monohull was routed by the SDYC's 60-foot catamaran.

THE MOST NOTABLE FALLS IN SPORTS

■ American runner Mary Decker has been involved in several falls:

In 1974, at a U.S.A.–U.S.S.R. meet in Moscow, Decker was shoved off the track by Sarmite Shtula in the 4×800m relay. Decker threw her relay baton at Shtula, picked it up, finished the race, and again threw her baton at Shtula.

At the 1983 Millrose Games in New York, Decker shoved Puerto Rican runner Angelita Lind to the ground when she failed to move aside and let Decker pass.

In her most famous fall, in the 1984 Olympic 1,500m race, Decker tripped, fell, and screamed at South African Zola Budd, who also fell. Budd was initially disqualified for the incident, but after watching videotapes, a jury voted unanimously to reinstate her.

■ American speedskater Dan Jansen fell going around the first turn of the 1988 Winter Olympic 500m race, just a few hours after learning of the death of his sister, Jane. Four days later, in the 1,000m, Jansen was on a gold medal-pace when he fell on a straightaway two-thirds of the way through the race.

■ In the men's Olympic slalom in 1952, skier Antoin Miliordos of Greece fell 18 times and was so disgusted that he sat down and crossed the finish line backward.

■ In the fourth and clinching game of the 1970 Stanley Cup finals, Boston Bruins star defenseman Bobby Orr flew through the air, lunged, and fell as he scored the overtime goal against the St. Louis Blues, to give the Bruins their first Stanley Cup in 29 years. The image of Orr sprawled on the ice has become one of the most enduring in hockey history.

■ At the 1972 Munich Olympics, American miler Jim Ryun tried to squeeze between two runners in the opening heat of the 1,500m when he tripped and fell. He got to his feet but did not qualify. It turned out to be his last amateur race.

■ Cuban sprinter Silvio Leonard seriously injured his leg at the 1975 Pan-Am games in Mexico City when he pulled a muscle as he crossed the finish line, was unable to stop, and fell into a 10-foot moat that surrounded the track.

■ Heavyweight champion Jack Johnson was believed by some to have taken a fall in his outdoor title fight against Jess Willard in Havana, Cuba, on April 5, 1915. In one of the most famous photographs in boxing history, Johnson is seen on the canvas, shielding his eyes from the sun as the referee counts the champion out in the 26th round.

■ Finn Lasse Viren fell during the 12th lap of the Olympic 10,000m in 1972, got up, and still won—and set a world record in the process.

AND ONE NOTABLE FALL THAT NEVER HAPPENED

■ On November 19, 1978, the John McVay–coached New York Giants led the Philadelphia Eagles 17-12 with 31 seconds to go and possession of the ball. Instead of falling down, Giants quarterback Joe Pisarcik attempted to hand off to fullback Larry Csonka, but the ball bounced off of Pisarcik's hands and Eagles defensive back Herm Edwards picked up the loose ball and ran for the winning touchdown, thus setting off perhaps the darkest moment in the history of the Giants franchise.

13 HERALDED UPSETS

If games were played on paper, there would be no upsets. The deeper, more talented team would win and that would be that. But since games are usually played on grass and turf and clay and hardwood, the outcome occasionally differs from the expected.

Any list of notable upsets would probably include the New York Mets' win over the Baltimore Orioles in the 1969 World Series, the American hockey team's semifinal victory over the Soviets at the 1980 Olympics, and Truman over Dewey, 1948. We have included here some of the other most heralded upsets of all time.

■ James L. Corbett beat John L. Sullivan in the first heavyweight fight under Marquis of Queensberry rules, September 7, 1892. Corbett, outweighed by 34 pounds—178 to 212—knocked out Sullivan in the 21st round.

■ Arthur Ashe beat Jimmy Connors in the 1975 Wimbledon finals by playing a tactical match designed to slow down the pace of the game and upset Connors's rhythm. The year before, Connors had won the Wimbledon and U.S. Open finals, losing a total of just eight games in six sets.

■ In Brazil in 1950, in what has been called "the greatest upset in the history of international competition," the United States defeated England 1-0 in World Cup play. The American goal was scored by a Haitian immigrant from New York named Joe Gaetjens, who was carried around the field on the shoulders of Brazilian fans.

301

■ Native Dancer's only loss was to Dark Star in the 1953 Kentucky Derby, in one of horse-racing's biggest upsets ever.

Dragon Blood, ridden by Lester Piggot, started at 10,000-to-1 odds in the Primio Naviglio at Milan on June 1, 1967, and won.

■ The Kirkland (Washington) Little League team shocked Taiwan, the perennial champions, in 1982.

■ Unknown American Billy Mills won the 10,000m Olympic gold medal in 1964. Mills, who was 7/16 Sioux Indian, ran 46 seconds faster than his previous best.

■ In 1921, the Centre (Kentucky) College Prayin' Colonels football team beat Harvard 6-0 at Cambridge, and used only five substitutes (plus the starters) to do it. The loss was the Crimson's first intersectional defeat in 40 years.

■ In 1938, the Chicago Black Hawks, with eight Americans on their squad, surprised the Toronto Maple Leafs and won the Stanley Cup.

■ In 1984, 17-year-old Australian Jon Sieben pulled off one of the biggest upsets in Olympic swimming history, when he out-touched West German star Michael Gross in the 200m butterfly, Gross's best event. Sieben set a world record (1:57.04) and bettered his previous personal best by more than four seconds.

■ In Tokyo on February 10, 1990, James "Buster" Douglas shocked the sporting world and won the world heavyweight belt when he became the first man to knock out Mike Tyson. Odds for the fight, considered by most to be a Tyson tune-up for his bout with #1-ranked challenger Evander Holyfield, were not even posted by many Las Vegas bookmakers.

■ In 1899, Sewanee (Tennessee) College won 12 straight football games, including five games in six days. Among their opponents were teams from much larger Tennessee, Georgia, Georgia Tech, Texas, Tulane, Louisiana State, Mississippi, and Auburn. Of the 12 schools, only Auburn even scored on the tiny college.

■ On December 23, 1982, Ralph Sampson and his #1-ranked, undefeated Virginia Cavaliers were beaten 77-72 by Chaminade, an NAIA school in Hawaii that had a student body of 850 and a basketball program that was just seven years old.

RUNNING AWAY WITH IT:
A FEW OF THE MOST MEMORABLE
ROUTS OF ALL TIME

■ On April 22, 1939, skier Toni Matt finished the Inferno, a course that begins atop New England's highest mountain, in 6 minutes, 21.4 seconds. He finished *one minute* ahead of Dick Durrance, the runnerup. It is the largest winning margin in the history of modern American skiing.

At the 1956 Cortina Winter Olympics, Toni Sailer, the first skier to sweep the Alpine events, won the giant slalom competition by more than six seconds, and the downhill by 3.5 seconds.

■ The Kansas City Royals beat the St. Louis Cardinals 11-0 in Game 7 of the 1985 World Series.

■ The New York Rangers lost to the Detroit Red Wings 15-0, the most lopsided score in NHL history, on January 23, 1944.

■ Bobby Locke won the 1948 Chicago Victory National Championship by 16 strokes, the largest winning margin in PGA Tour history.

In the U.S. Open, Bobby Jones won the 36-hole playoff with Al Espinosa by 23 strokes, 141 to 164.

■ The largest margin of victory in an NBA game is 63 points: in 1972, the Los Angeles Lakers beat the Golden State Warriors, 162-99.

■ Secretariat won the 1973 Belmont on June 9 by 31 lengths.

On the same track on September 4, 1920, Man O' War won the Lawrence Realizations Stakes by 100 lengths, or more than a quarter of a mile, over the only other entrant, Hoodwink.

■ On its way to the 1980 Olympic women's basketball gold, the Soviet Union won their games by an average of 45 points. (The United States did not compete because of the boycott.)

■ In the 1953 Wimbledon doubles semifinals, Shirley Fry and Doris Hart won by a 6-0, 6-0 score. In the final, they again won 6-0, 6-0.

■ In the first Rose Bowl in 1902, Michigan beat Stanford, 49-0. The worst Super Bowl drubbing ever was the San Francisco 49ers' 55-10 pasting of the Denver Broncos in 1990.

12
FAMILY

LESSER-KNOWN SIBLINGS

All of these "lesser" brothers and sisters were at least competent athletes. Some rose to the top of their sport, hung around for the cup of coffee, then moved on to another profession; others were quite talented and forged respectable sports careers. But their athletic accomplishments in each case were overshadowed publicly by those of their more famous siblings.

That's how they got to be lesser-known.

■ Sam Wright played in the major leagues for three years and hit .109. His two brothers, Harry and George, are in the Baseball Hall of Fame.

■ Jeanne Evert, Chris's sister, played on the women's tennis tour briefly in the late 1970s.

■ Mack Robinson, Jackie's older brother, was second to Jesse Owens in the 1936 Olympic 200m.

■ Adeline Gehrig, sister of Lou, competed in the 1924 Olympics as a fencer. She was American women's foil champion from 1920 to 1923.

■ Henry Mathewson appeared in the major leagues in two seasons, compiling a record of 0-1. His brother, Christy, won 373 games, which ties him for the third-highest total in major league history.

■ Eddie Payton, brother of Walter, was a running back and kick returner for four NFL teams in five years.

■ Yo-Yo Davalillo, brother of 16-year veteran Vic, played in 19 games for the 1953 Washington Senators.

■ Nelson Munsey, older brother of Chuck Muncie, was a defensive back for the Baltimore Colts from 1972–77, and for the Minnesota Vikings in 1978. Chuck not only outshined Nelson on the field but changed the spelling of the family name.

■ George Dickey hit .204 in six seasons. His brother, Bill, one of the greatest catchers of all time, is in the Baseball Hall of Fame.

■ Carol Lewis, sister of Carl, was an Olympian in the long jump in 1984 but did not win a medal.

■ Joey LaMotta, brother of middleweight champion Jake, was also a professional boxer.

■ Joe and Johnny Evers combined to play in 1,784 major league games—1 for Joe and 1,783 for Johnny. Tommie and Hank Aaron hold the record for home runs by brothers with 768—13 for Tommie and 755 for Hank. The stolen base record for brothers is held by the Wagner boys: 4 for Albert "Butts" Wagner, and 722 for Honus.

■ Marlene Floyd, sister of Raymond Floyd, is a member of the LPGA tour. Janet LePera, sister of Donna Caponi, has played on the LPGA tour. Bobby Wadkins, Lanny's brother, also plays on the PGA tour.

■ Former San Francisco Giants reliever Randy Moffitt is the brother of tennis great Billie Jean King.

■ Bubba Wyche, Sam's brother, was a quarterback for the WFL Detroit Wheels in 1974, the same year that Sam was quarterback for Detroit's other professional football team, the NFL Lions.

■ Faye Throneberry, brother of Marv, had an eight-year major league career and a lifetime average of .236, one point lower than Marv's.

■ Darren Flutie, Doug's brother, was a wide receiver for Boston College.

■ Pat McEnroe, John's brother, was ranked 356th in the world in singles after the 1989 season.

■ Ozzie Canseco, José's twin brother, is an outfielder in the Oakland Athletics farm system. Gordon Hershiser, Orel's brother, is a pitcher in the Los Angeles Dodgers minor leagues.

■ Phil and Orrin Olsen, brothers of Hall of Famer Merlin, both played in the NFL. Phil was a defensive lineman for the Los Angeles Rams from 1971–74, teaming with Merlin. Orrin was a center for the Kansas City Chiefs in 1976.

■ Buddy Baer, younger brother of heavyweight champion Max, twice lost to Joe Louis in heavyweight title fights.

■ Dave Dryden, Ken's brother, was also a professional goaltender and both lost 57 NHL games in their career. Dave, however, won just 48 NHL games while Ken won 258.

WINNING IS THICKER THAN BLOOD OR MARRIAGE

There are many instances of athletic family members and spouses helping and sharing—hockey-playing brothers on the same line looking to feed each other the puck: fathers and sons who have worked together to win Olympic gold in yachting; Bob Kersee rooting for and coaching his wife, long-jumper and heptathlete Jackie Joyner-Kersee. The emotions stirred up by family loyalty push some past sensible behavior, as was the case when Minna Wilson climbed into a boxing ring in Southampton, England, in the summer of 1989, and with one of her shoes began to batter the head of boxer Steve McCarthy, who himself had been administering a third-round battering to Wilson's son, former British light heavyweight champion Tony Wilson. We may condemn Mrs. Wilson for her methods but not her show of fealty.

Fealty is not something that many in the following list will ever be accused of.

■ In 1987, Pittsburgh Steelers President Dan Rooney fired his brother, Art Rooney, Jr., vice president of player personnel, who had been with the organization for 26 years.

■ In the early 1970s, Clark Graebner, the World Team Tennis player-coach of the Cleveland Nets and recently separated from his wife, Carole, also a member of the Nets, traded her to the Pittsburgh Triangles.

■ In December of 1968, Los Angeles Dodgers General Manager Al Campanis traded his son, Jim, to the Kansas City Athletics for two minor leaguers.

■ John Laupheimer, a senior USGA administrator, assessed British Curtis Cup member Mary Everard a penalty stroke because her caddie had cleaned off a ball—an infringement of Rule 23.2—that Everard had marked and lifted at the request of her playing companion. Laupheimer and Everard had been married earlier that year.

■ Paul Brown, so revered that his team, the Cleveland Browns, was named for him, was fired as head coach and general manager on January 9, 1963, by owner Art Modell.

■ Washington Senators owner Clark Griffith sold his nephew, Sherry Robertson, to the Philadelphia Athletics in May

1952 for an undisclosed sum of money. Robertson was the brother of Calvin Griffith, the Senators' vice president and Clark's adopted son.

■ On June 28, 1989, San Diego Padres General Manager Jack McKeon traded his son-in-law, Greg Booker, to the Minnesota Twins for Freddie Toliver.

IT'S MY BALL, SO I'LL MAKE THE RULES: 6 EXAMPLES OF FAVORITISM AND NEPOTISM IN SPORTS

On the other hand, there have been occasions in sports where competitive judgment has been sacrificed to help out a friend or relative, or to give privileged treatment to someone who perhaps didn't earn it by athletic prowess.

A few examples:

■ Haiti's Olympic track teams in 1972 and 1976 consistently finished last with awful times. The country's despot, "Baby Doc" Duvalier, peopled the teams with friends and trusted soldiers, regardless of their athletic abilities.

■ Earle Mack played five games spread out over three seasons for the Philadelphia Athletics, managed and owned by his father, Connie. Earle's career statistics were two hits in 16 at-bats for a .125 average.

■ William Marcy "Boss" Tweed, the kingpin of Tammany Hall, placed almost all of the members of the New York Mutuals, a semipro baseball team from 1860–71, on the New York City payroll as clerks and street sweepers. Tweed was also president of the Mutuals.

■ In 60 A.D., the Roman Emperor Nero instituted an

Olympic Games in his honor and entered a musical event specially created for him, which he won.

■ The Duke of York, who was the second son of King George V and Queen Mary and who later became King George VI, played in the men's doubles draw at Wimbledon in 1926. He and Sir Louis Grieg, later the chairman of the All-England Club, were beaten in the first round.

■ The California Angels players retired #26 in honor of the contributions made to the team by Gene Autry. It should be mentioned that Gene Autry is the owner of the California Angels.

Note: There is no doubt that San Francisco 49ers quarterback Steve Young has earned his place in the NFL on merit, after a spectacular career at Brigham Young University. However, while his acceptance to BYU was certainly of great benefit to the school (and Young's professional career), it cannot have been a surprise for him since his great-great-great-grandfather is Brigham Young.

ATHLETIC MOTHERS AND MOTHERS-TO-BE

■ In a 1969 race six days before she gave birth, jockey Mary Bacon rode a mount that was a mare in foal. "The four of us finished last," Bacon said after the race.

■ Fanny Blankers-Koen, the great Dutch track and field star and mother of two, practiced with her baby carriage next to the track. At the 1948 London Olympics, she won all four women's track events—the 100m, 200m, 80m hurdles, and the 4×100m relay. (She did not enter the long jump, though she held the world record.) She was called "the Flying Housewife."

■ When Evonne Goolagong beat Chris Evert in 1980 to win Wimbledon, she became the first mother to win the singles title since Dorothea Lambert Chambers in 1914.

■ At the world shooting championships in 1970, Margaret Murdock won the standing small-bore rifle event while four months pregnant. In 1952, Juno Irwin was 3½ months pregnant with her second child when she won the Olympic bronze in platform diving.

■ Of the 20 Russian women medal winners at the 1956 Olympic, 10 of them were pregnant.

■ The U.S.S.R.'s Tatyana Kazankina had her first child in 1978, two years after winning the Olympic 1,500m race. In 1980, she defended her title. In 1982, she had another child, and in 1984, she set world records in the 2,000m and 3,000m.

American sprinter Evelyn Ashford had a daughter in May, 1985 and the following year was ranked #1 in the world in the 100m.

Ingrid Kristiansen ran the fastest marathon of her career five months after having a son.

■ Nancy Lopez had a daughter in 1983 and two years later won LPGA Player of the Year honors. She had another daughter in 1986 and two years later was again named Player of the Year.

GIVING BIRTH TO SPORTS

Historians like to determine the lineage of things: George Washington was the Father of his Country, Necessity is the Mother of Invention. The need to determine who, in spirit, gave birth to what is apparently rampant among historians of sport, too.

◼ Senda Berenson Abbot, a coach who helped popularize her sport and was later inducted into its Hall of Fame, has been called "The Mother of Women's Basketball."

◼ Dr. James Dwight, a former player, referee, and president of the USTA, has been called "The Father of American Tennis"; Mary Ewing Outerbridge, who, while vacationing in Bermuda, saw British officers playing a racket game and had equipment sent to her Staten Island home, is "The Mother of American Tennis"; and Hazel H. Wightman, a top American player in the first half of the century and the donator of the Wightman Cup, is "The Queen Mother of Tennis."

◼ Duke Kahanamoku, who played a major role in introducing his sport to the world, is "The Father of Modern Surfing."

◼ Baron Pierre de Coubertin, who helped rekindle an idea dead for 1,500 years, is known as "The Father of the Modern Olympics."

◼ Jack Broughton, who, among his other achievements, helped to devise "mufflers" (gloves) to minimize the risk of facial damage, is known as "The Father of British Boxing" or, simply, "The Father of Boxing," while Jacob Hyer, who fought in the first American championship bout, was called "The Father of the American Ring."

◼ Hugo Meisl, a coach and innovator, is known as "The Father of Austrian soccer."

◼ Fred C. Waghorne, who popularized the technique of tossing the hockey puck between opposing players, has been called "The Father of the Face-Off."

◼ Dr. Elisha Warfield, an early-19th-century horse breeder, was called "The Father of the Kentucky Turf."

■ Harry Wright, who organized the Cincinnati Red Stock-ings, baseball's first professional team, was often called "The Father of the Game."

■ Konnie Savickus is known as "The Father of Lithuanian Basketball."

■ Friedrich Ludwig Jahn (1778–1852) is called "The Fa-ther of German gymnastics."

■ Dr. Kenneth Cooper is called "The Father of Aerobics."

THE BEST SPORTS PEDIGREES

What happens when parents want their kids to go into the family business and the family business happens to be big-time sports? It's a lot easier for the kids to disappoint, for one: so few succeed at that level, and your last name doesn't count for much when you're trying to hit a 95-mile-an-hour fastball.

On the other hand, the offspring of great athletes do have the benefit of good genes. Here are some notable lineages in sports.

■ Ramanathan Krishnan was India's #1 men's tennis player in the 1960s. His son, Ramesh, was their #1 player in the 1980s.

■ Auto racing is famous for its familial heritages. There are three generations of Pettys—Lee, Richard, and Kyle—and the father-son teams of Al Unsers (Sr. and Jr.), Mario and Michael Andretti, and Bobby and Davey Allison.

■ Ron Retton, the father of Olympic gold medal gymnast Mary Lou Retton, was co-captain with Jerry West of the University of West Virginia basketball team that lost in the

1959 NCAA finals. Retton was also a shortstop in the New York Yankees farm system until 1963.

■ Golfer Catherine Lacoste, daughter of tennis legend René, won the U.S. Women's Open in 1967, becoming the only amateur to do so. Catherine also won the U.S. and British amateur titles. Lacoste's mother, Thion de la Chaume, won the French women's golf title six times and the British title once, the first Frenchwoman to do so.

■ All thoroughbred horses in the world today are descended from at least one of three stallions: Darley Arabian, Byerly Turk, and Godolphin Barb. Fifty-two of the first 61 Kentucky Derby winners carried the blood of Lexington, who was regarded as the most successful stallion ever. In 20 years of stud duty at Woodburn Farm, Lexington topped the sire list 16 times, including 14 years in a row. Lexington sired more than 600 colts and fillies, 260 of them winners.

■ Golfer Clay Heafner played for the American Ryder Cup team in 1949 and 1951. His son, Vance, played for the 1977 American Walker Cup team. Both were unbeaten.

■ Jack Nicklaus, Jr. won the 1985 North and South Amateur and played in the 1986 British Amateur before turning professional.

■ Through 1989, Leo Nicholson and his son, Dean, had been the only men's basketball coaches since 1929 at Central Washington University in Ellensburg, Washington. Leo coached from 1929–64; Dean took over in 1965.

■ Hungarian Imre Nemeth, Olympic gold medalist in the hammer throw in 1948, fathered Miklos Nemeth, gold medalist in the javelin in 1976.

■ Norway's Peder Lunde won an Olympic yachting gold medal in 1960. His father and mother, Peder and Vibeke, had won silvers in 1952; his grandfather, Eugen, had won a gold in 1924.

■ Peter Press Maravich—"Pistol Pete"—played basketball at LSU for his father, Press.

■ Einer Ulrich was a Danish Davis Cup star for 15 years, from 1924–38. His sons, Torben and Jorgen, were mainstays of the Danish Davis Cup for 25 years, Torben from 1948, Jorgen from 1958.

■ Tom Hyer, America's first heavyweight champ, was the son of Jacob Hyer, the first American to fight professionally in public.

■ Erna Bogen, the daughter of 1912 Olympic team saber silver medalist Albert Bogen, was bronze medalist in the 1932 women's foil. Erna married seven-time fencing gold medalist Aladar Gerevich. Their son, Pal, won two bronze medals in the team saber in 1972 and 1980.

■ Harry Caray is the broadcasting voice of the Chicago Cubs. His son, Skip, is the voice of the Atlanta Braves and Atlanta Hawks, and Skip's son, Chip, is the voice of the NBA Orlando Magic.

6 HAPPY FAMILIES

To make the moment special, an athlete wants to share his or her individual achievement with family and turn it into a group achievement. For certain families, that's literally what it is.

■ On August 21, 1975, Paul and Rick Reuschel of the Chicago Cubs became the only brothers to combine for a major league shutout.

■ In 1979, sisters Arta, Sherri, Denean, and Mattina Howard set a national high school record in the mile relay

(3:44.89) while running for San Gorgonio High School in San Bernardino, California.

■ At the 1981 Indianapolis 500, Bill Mears, working in the pits for his son, saved Rick's life by putting out a fire on his suit.

■ In 1943, left wing Doug Bentley set an NHL record with five points in a single period. His brother, Max, helped him, recording four assists.

■ The Swedish Olympic team that won the cycling team time trial silver medal in 1968 was made up of four brothers: Erik, Gosta, Sture, and Tomas Pettersson. All four later changed their last name to Faglum, which was the name of their home village.

■ Larry Yount, who pitched one game for the Houston Astros in 1971, is the agent for his brother, two-time American League MVP Robin Yount.

OEDIPAL TRIUMPHS
AND FAMILIES THAT COMPETE
AGAINST EACH OTHER

■ The only home run of Joe Niekro's batting career came on May 29, 1976, off his brother, Phil.

■ In 1906, Alex Smith defeated his brother Willie for the U.S. Open golf title. In 1910, Alex again won the title, this time in a playoff over his brother Macdonald.

■ Fifty-year-old Bobby Allison held off his son, Davey, to win the 1988 Daytona 500.

Al Unser, Sr., edged his son, Al, Jr., 151 points to 150, to win the CART-PPG championships in 1985.

316

■ In 1973, Madame and Mademoiselle Becquet—mother and daughter—ran against each other in the French 800m national championships.

■ In a classic transfer of power from one generation to the next, "Young" Tom Morris succeeded his father, "Old" Tom Morris, as British Open champion in 1868. In 1869, Young and Old Tom finished 1-2.
   In the 1903 British Open, Tom Vardon finished second to his brother, Harry.

■ In his major league debut on May 31, 1979, Detroit Tiger Pat Underwood pitched 8⅓ innings of three-hit ball and beat his brother, Toronto Blue Jays pitcher Tom Underwood, 1-0.

■ German sporting-goods giant Adidas was started by Horst Dassler. Their major antagonist and rival, Puma, was started by Rudolf Dassler, his brother.

■ Twins Sylviane and Patricia Puntous of Montreal finished 1-2 in the 1983 and 1984 Ironman women's triathlons.

■ Matty and Felipe Alou are the only brothers to finish 1-2 in a batting title race, in the National League in 1966.

■ In 1906, the Honorable Denys Scott defeated the Honorable Osmund Scott, his brother, in the final of the Italian Open Amateur golf championship.

■ With four games remaining in the 1985 season, Wade Phillips took over coaching the New Orleans Saints after his father, Bum, resigned.

■ In the middle of the 1989–90 NHL season, Washington Capitals coach Bryan Murray was fired and replaced by his brother, Terry.

■ In 1884, in the first Wimbledon women's final, Maud Watson beat her sister Lillian in three sets.

William Renswhaw beat his brother Ernest in the 1882, 1883, and 1889 Wimbledon finals.

■ Oedipal Jam: For one of his dunks in the 1986 Slam Dunk competition, New York Knicks guard Gerald Wilkins planned to play out his own genteel variation on the Oedipal myth by soaring over his mother, seated in a chair in the three-second lane. (Ultimately, Wilkins decided against elements of the jam and merely leapt over an empty chair—perhaps an even more compelling metaphor.)

■ Surrogate Oedipal success: In 1921, Harry Heilmann won the batting title, outhitting his manager, Ty Cobb, by five points.

Honorable mention: On April 29, 1931, catcher Rick Ferrell of the St. Louis Browns *almost* broke up a no-hitter being pitched by his brother, Cleveland Indian Wes Ferrell. On a ball that Rick hit into the hole, the Cleveland shortstop made a tough play but his throw pulled the first baseman off the bag. It was ruled an error, a call that would later be questioned.

15 FAMOUS ATHLETIC MARRIAGES

World-class athletes are so used to being in the public eye that they often feel most comfortable with other high-profile people. Such commingling has produced celebrated marriages: baseball's Leo Durocher and actress Laraine Day, tennis player Gottfried von Cramm and Woolworth heiress Barbara Hutton, jockey Robyn Smith and Fred Astaire, John McEnroe and actress Tatum O'Neal, and perhaps most famous of all, Joe DiMaggio and Marilyn Monroe. Both parties breathe the same rarified air. In a famous exchange, Monroe, after spending part of her honeymoon performing for troops in Korea, said to her new husband, "Joe, Joe, you never heard such applause." "Yes, I did," DiMaggio said simply.

But just sharing fame does not guarantee an understanding of the particular demands that the athlete faces. Perhaps the best partner for an athlete can only be another athlete. Many couples have tested the idea. When Jackie Jensen, All-America football player and 1958 American League Most Valuable Player, married Zoe Ann Olsen, 1948 Olympic springboard diving silver medalist, they became known as "the sports world's most famous sweethearts." Leslie Godfree and Kathleen "Kitty" McKane Godfree were compatible enough to become, in 1926, the only married couple ever to win the Wimbledon mixed doubles championship.

The following is a list of a few of the most famous unions of athletes, some of whom would seem supremely well matched.

■ Soviet Valery Borzov, once the "fastest man in the world" (gold medalist in the Olympic 100m and 200m in 1972)/
Lyudmila Tourischeva, winner of eight Olympic and four gold medals in gymnastics

■ Nancy Lopez, LPGA star/
Ray Knight, 1986 World Series MVP

■ East German swimmer Roland Matthes, winner of eight Olympic and four gold medals/
East German swimmer Kornelia Ender, winner of eight Olympic and four gold medals

■ Chris Evert, tennis great/
John Lloyd, tennis okay

■ Chris Evert, tennis great/
Andy Mill, skiing okay
(Chris Evert, tennis great, was also once engaged to Jimmy Connors, tennis great.)

■ Mary Decker, track great/
Ron Tabb, marathon good

- Mary Decker, track great/
  Richard Slaney, discus okay

- Don Drysdale, Hall of Fame pitcher/
  Ann Meyers, UCLA All-America and 1976 Olympic basketball player

- Florence Griffith Joyner, 1988 Olympic sprints gold medalist/
  Al Joyner, 1984 Olympic triple jump gold medalist

- Jackie Joyner-Kersee, Olympic heptathlon and long jump champion/
  Bob Kersee, coach of Jackie Joyner-Kersee

- Emil Zatopek, Czech distance star and winner of four Olympic distance gold medals/
  Dana Zatopkova, 1952 Czech Olympic javelin gold medalist
  (On the same day that Zatopkova won the javelin title with an Olympic record throw, Zatopek won the 5,000m, on the way to an unprecedented sweep of the 5,000m, 10,000m, and the marathon. The two Czechs were also born on the same day, September 9, 1922.)

- Carol Heiss, 1960 women's figure skating Olympic gold medalist/
  Hayes Jenkins, 1956 men's figure skating Olympic gold medalist

- Carling Bassett, highly ranked singles player/
  Robert Seguso, highly ranked doubles player

- Sandra Farmer, 1989 World Cup Champion in the 400m hurdles/
  David Patrick, 1989 World Cup champion in the 400m hurdles

- Irina Rodnina, 1976 and 1980 Olympic figure skating pairs gold medalist/
  Aleksandr Zaitsev, her partner
  (Rodnina also won a gold in 1972 with Aleksei Ulanov,

who married Lyudmila Smirnova, who won the pairs silver in 1972 with a different partner.)

MORE ATHLETIC SIBLINGS

■ The greatest number of brothers to play in the major leagues is five, the Delahanty boys, who played from 1888 to 1915: Ed, the best of them, an outfielder; Frank, an outfielder; Jim, an infielder; Joe, an outfielder; and Tom, an infielder.

Four O'Neill brothers—Steve, Jim, Jack, and Mike—played in the majors, from 1901–28.

■ John and Tracy Austin won the 1980 Wimbledon mixed doubles, the first brother-sister combination to do so.

■ Placekicker Mike Duvic is the University of Dayton's all-time leading scorer in football. His brother John, also a kicker, is Northwestern's all-time leading scorer.

■ Boog Powell and Carl Taylor, his stepbrother who played in the majors for six years with Pittsburgh and St. Louis, both had career averages of .266.

■ From September 22–26, 1975, brothers Gaylord and Jim Perry had identical major league won-lost totals—215-174.

■ Bunny Austin was the first male player to appear at Wimbledon in tennis shorts. His sister, Joan Lycett, was the first woman to play on Centre Court without stockings.

■ William Dod won an archery gold medal in 1908 and his sister Lottie, a tennis star, won an archery silver medal in the national round competition at the same Games. They are the first brother-sister Olympic medalists.

■ Scott Cornwell of Parkton Hereford won the Maryland state high school cross-country title in 1970. His brother Greg won it in 1971. Their brother David won it in 1972, 1973, and 1974. And *their* brother John won it in 1977.

■ All three major league Alou brothers—Felipe, Matty, and Jesus—played together in the same outfield for the San Francisco Giants, in a game on September 15, 1963.

■ Lucious, Lee Roy, and Dewey Selmon were each All-America football players at the University of Oklahoma.

■ Brothers Joey, Keith, Ross, and Jim Browner all played in the NFL.

■ Six Turnesa brothers played pro golf. Among them, Jim won the 1952 PGA; Willie won the U.S. Amateur in 1938 and 1948; and Joe was runner-up to Walter Hagen at the 1927 PGA.

■ During the 1980s, six Sutter brothers played in the NHL.

■ There were five boxing brothers known as "The Fighting Zivics," the best of whom, Fritzie Zivic, was a world welterweight titleholder in 1944–45.

■ Brothers Paul and Lloyd Waner are both in the Hall of Fame.

■ Cheryl Miller, basketball star for the University of Southern California, is the sister of Reggie Miller, star guard for the Indiana Pacers, and of Darrell, a catcher for the California Angels.

■ Soviet wrestlers Sergei and Anatoly Beloglazov, twin brothers, won gold medals in the bantamweight and flyweight divisions, respectively, at the 1980 Olympics.

Twins Ed and Lou Banach were both wrestling gold medalists in 1984.

◧ Hayes Jenkins won the men's figure skating gold in 1956, and younger brother David won it in 1960.

◧ Lionel Hebert won the PGA in 1957, and his brother Jay won the title in 1960.

◧ Joe Corbett, younger brother of heavyweight champion James J. Corbett, was 24-8 in 1897 for Baltimore of the National League.

◧ Brothers Vijay, Anand, and Ashok Amritraj of India all played on the professional men's tennis tour.

◧ Clete and Ken Boyer are the only brothers to hit home runs in the same World Series, and they did it in the same game. In Game 7 of the 1964 Series, Ken hit one for the St. Louis Cardinals and Clete hit one for the New York Yankees.

◧ Brothers Mike and Jerry Quarry both lost on the same card on one June 1972 night in Las Vegas.

◧ The Mullen boys—Calgary Flame Joey and New York Ranger Brian—grew up playing roller hockey in Hell's Kitchen in New York City.

◧ Nancy and Cliff Richey were both highly ranked tennis players in the 1960s.

◧ Frank McGuire coached the 1957 University of North Carolina Tar Heels to the NCAA title. His brother, Al, won the 1977 NCAA title with Marquette.

◧ Dixie and Harry Walker both won major league batting titles.

◧ Golfers T. C. and T. M. Chen of Taiwan are brothers. Tze-Chung won the Los Angeles Open in February 1987 in a playoff with Ben Crenshaw. Tze-Ming is a leading player on the Asian-Japanese tour.

◧ Golfers Jerry Pate and Bruce Lietzke are brothers-in-law.

■ Bob and Ken Forsch are the only brothers to pitch no-hitters.

■ Don and Bruce Curry are the only brothers to hold boxing world titles simultaneously, reigning together from May 20, 1983 to January 29, 1984. Don was welterweight champion and Bruce light-welterweight champion.

■ Leon and Michael Spinks held the heavyweight world title at different times.

13
HISTORY

DÉJÀ VU:
17 OF THE MOST HAUNTING CASES

So many athletes play so many games so many days of the year that it should not seem unusual for circumstances to repeat themselves. Some repetitions, however, are particularly powerful in the way that they recall previous events.

■ In 1936, Jesse Owens was one foul away from elimination in the Olympic long jump when competitor Luz Long offered him a helpful tip: Play it safe by making a mark several inches before the takeoff board. Owens made a successful jump and would go on to win the gold medal, with Long taking the silver. In 1968, Bob Beamon was one foul away from elimination when competitor Ralph Boston offered the same tip to Beamon that Long had offered Owens. Beamon would go on to win the gold medal, with Boston taking the bronze.

■ In the 1973 National League playoffs between the New York Mets and the Cincinnati Reds, Bud Harrelson and Pete Rose got into a bench-clearing fight at second base. Several years later, Harrelson's son, Buddy Jr., and Rose's son, Pete Jr., got into a fight near the Phillies batting cage in Philadelphia, where their fathers were teammates.

■ After a 1925 game, Philadelphia Athletics infielder Jimmy Dykes was asked why he hadn't slid into second base. "I couldn't," he said. "I carry my cigars in my back pocket and I was afraid I'd break them." In 1982, Montreal Expo

Tim Raines avoided feet-first slides because he kept his cocaine vial in his back pocket and was afraid that he would break it.

■ Harry Agganis, Boston University quarterback star from 1949–52, signed with the Boston Red Sox and played first base for them in 1954. In 1955, he died of a massive pulmonary embolism. Tony Gastall, a Boston University quarterback star (1953–54) after Agganis, signed with the Baltimore Orioles in 1955. In 1956, he died when the plane he was piloting crashed into Chesapeake Bay.

■ Movie star Paul Newman was kicked off of the Kenyon College JV football team for brawling. Movie star Robert Redford was kicked off of the University of Colorado baseball team for drinking and missing practice.

■ In the 1960 Wimbledon quarterfinals, Earl Buchholz held match point five times against Neale Fraser but eventually retired because of muscle cramps. In the U.S. Championship semifinals later that year, Buchholz had match point three times against Rod Laver and again had to default because of cramps.

■ In 1936, Jersey Joe Walcott knocked out Phil Johnson in three rounds in Philadelphia. Fourteen years later, Walcott knocked out Harold Johnson, Phil's son, in three rounds in Philadelphia.

■ In 1960, in front of a partisan American crowd in Squaw Valley, California, Bill Christian and his teammates upset the Soviet Union in the semifinals and went on to win America's first Olympic hockey gold medal. In 1980, in front of a partisan American crowd in Lake Placid, New York, Dave Christian, Bill's son, and his teammates upset the Soviet Union in the semifinals and went on to win America's second Olympic hockey gold medal.

■ In 1907, Detroit Tiger Charlie "Boss" Schmidt popped up to make the last out of the World Series against the Cubs. The next year, Schmidt grounded into the last out of the 1908 Series, also against the Cubs.

■ In 1981, the New York Islanders eliminated the New York Rangers from the Stanley Cup playoffs and made it to the finals. In 1982, the Islanders eliminated the Rangers and eventually made the finals. In 1983, the Islanders eliminated the Rangers and eventually made the finals. In 1984, the Islanders eliminated the Rangers and eventually made the finals.

■ Los Angeles Dodgers pitcher Don Drysdale's record scoreless-innings streak in 1968 continued at one point only after an umpire invoked an infrequently used rule to decree that an opposing batter had not tried to get out of the way of a pitch by Drysdale that had hit the batter with the bases loaded. Twenty years later, in 1988, Dodgers pitcher Orel Hershiser's scoreless-innings streak, which broke Drysdale's, continued at one point only after an umpire invoked an infrequently used rule to call a double play rather than a force out, stating that an opposing runner going from first to second had slid outside the base-path. The call ended the inning and negated the run that had crossed the plate. Both calls were made against the San Francisco Giants.

■ In 1920, world heavyweight champion Jack Dempsey and his manager, Jack Kearns, were indicted on charges of conspiracy to avoid the draft during World War I. They were found not guilty. In 1967, heavyweight champion Muhammad Ali was sentenced to five years in jail for refusal to join the army during the Vietnam War. The sentence was overturned in 1970.

■ On August 23, 1952, Bob Elliott of the New York Giants was ejected by umpire Augie Donatelli for complaining and kicking dirt over a called strike two. Bobby Hofman finished the at-bat by being called out on strikes and was also ejected by Donatelli.

■ Korean Olympic boxer Dong-Kih Choh, disqualified in his 1964 semifinal for holding his head too low, sat in the middle of the ring and refused to leave for 51 minutes. South Korean boxer Byun Jong-il, loser of a disputed decision in a 119-pound bout in the 1988 Olympics, sat in a corner of the ring and refused to leave for 67 minutes.

◪ In 1923, Detroit Tigers pitcher Herman Pillette went 14-19 to lead the American League in losses. Twenty-eight years later, in 1951, St. Louis Browns pitcher Duane Pillette, Herman's son, went 6-14 to lead the American League in losses.

◪ In a game against the Houston Astros on July 21, 1975, New York Met Felix Millan had four singles. After each hit, Joe Torre, the next batter, hit into a double play, wiping Millan out.

◪ On January 29, 1989, Chris Dudley of the Cleveland Cavaliers went to the foul line to shoot two free throws. He missed his first shot and then again, but on the second miss, Washington Bullet Darrell Walker was called for a lane violation. Dudley missed again, but Dave Feitl of the Bullets committed a lane violation. Dudley missed again, but Feitl again committed a lane violation. Dudley then missed for the fifth straight time.

WHAT IF...?

History—sports and world—and various cherished records might be a little different but for a wrinkle here or there.

What if...

◪ Cuban dictator Fidel Castro, who had gotten a tryout with the old Washington Senators on September 27, 1947, had been called back?

◪ CBS/ABC sportscaster Brent Musburger had flourished in his 1959 job as a Midwest League umpire?

■ World War II had not interrupted Chicago Cubs owner Phil Wrigley from installing lights at Wrigley Field in 1942? (For the war effort, he donated the lights that he had bought to a shipyard.)

■ Pearl Harbor had not interfered with the vote on whether the St. Louis Browns could move to Los Angeles in 1941?

■ Eulace Peacock, who had beaten Jesse Owens in the 100m and the long jump at the 1935 AAU championships, had not been kept out of the 1936 Olympics by a hamstring injury?

■ School custodian Pop Stebbins *had* found "two boxes about 18 inches square"—precisely what James Naismith had asked him to bring, for the new game he was inventing—rather than some old peach baskets? (Presumably, the NBA would today stand for National Boxball Association.)

■ New York Yankees owner George Steinbrenner, when an assistant football coach at Northwestern and Purdue, had loved and been good at it?

■ Football legend Red Grange had remained discouraged by the stiff competition at the University of Illinois, which made him walk off the team as a freshman? Basketball superstar Michael Jordan had become discouraged when he did not make his high school varsity as a sophomore?

■ Mickey Mantle had not been turned down for military service because of a knee injury? Ted Williams, Bob Feller, Joe DiMaggio, and Stan Musial *had* been turned down for military service?

■ Jack Crawford had won just one more set in the 1933 U.S. Championship final, and thus the Grand Slam, to become the first player to do it? (Who but real tennis aficionados knows his name now?)

■ Cuban Teofilo Stevenson, who won the super heavyweight gold medal at the 1972, 1976, and 1980 Olympics and was considered to be in Muhammad Ali's class, had turned professional?

■ The coin flip between the 12th Earl of Derby—who conceived of a one-mile run for three-year-olds at Epsom Downs in England and who would become the namesake of a famous American horse race—and Sir Charles Bunbury, over whether to call the Epsom race the Derby Stakes or the Bunbury Stakes, had gone the other way? (Then perhaps the major event on the American racing calendar today would be known as the Kentucky Bunbury.)

THE MOST FAMOUS QUOTATIONS IN SPORTS HISTORY

The sounds we associate with sports are varied—the static of a crackly but trusted radio, the knock of wood against ball or the bounce of rubber on parquet, the music of the game, the noise of the fans, the often-annoying organist, the catch phrases we associate with different sports—"Play ball!"; "Gentlemen, start your engines"; "On your mark . . ."; "Let the games begin." Our ears prick up at the occasional offering from the public address announcer—"That was *goaltending*"; "Ladies and gentlemen, now pitching for the Baltimore Orioles . . ."—and it all makes a sort of symphony.

The avid fan remembers, too, the words of often unintentional poets about the game, lines that resonate for their simplicity, their passion, their wisdom. It does not matter that most of us never actually heard these words spoken; the words have often enough appeared in print or been quoted that we hear them in the mind's ear.

■ "Float like a butterfly, sting like a bee."
—Cassius Clay's strategy for his 1964 fight with Sonny

Liston. The line was probably coined by Clay's corner man, Drew "Bundini" Brown.

■ "When the one Great Scorer comes to write against your name—He marks—not that you won or lost—but how you played the game."
—Grantland Rice.

■ "It ain't over till the fat lady sings."
—Washington Bullets coach Dick Motta's rallying cry with his team down two games to one to the Seattle Supersonics in the 1978 NBA finals. He was right: the Bullets won the series in seven games.

■ "Let's play two."
—Ernie Banks.

■ *"No más."*
—Roberto Duran to Sugar Ray Leonard in the eighth round of their second welterweight title fight, 1980.

■ "You are the pits of the world!"
—John McEnroe to Wimbledon chair umpire Edward James, in McEnroe's first-round match in 1981 against Tom Gullikson.

■ "We wuz robbed."
—Manager Joe Jacobs after his fighter, Max Schmeling, lost his heavyweight championship to Jack Sharkey in a 15-round decision in New York, June 1932.

■ "I shoulda stood in bed."
—Again, fight manager Jacobs, after leaving his sickbed to attend a 1934 World Series game and betting on the wrong team.

■ "Win one for the Gipper."
—Knute Rockne's admonition to the Notre Dame team at halftime of a scoreless Army–Notre Dame game in 1928. According to legend, Notre Dame quarterback George Gipp, dying of a viral throat infection, had told Rockne to save the inspirational ploy for just the right moment.

There is some dispute about whether the deathbed scene ever really took place.

■ "There goes Ted Williams, the greatest hitter who ever lived."
—What Ted Williams—according to his autobiography, *My Turn at Bat*—wanted people to say about him when he walked by.

■ "Four-four-four."
—Moses Malone, predicting three consecutive NBA playoff series sweeps for the Philadelphia 76ers in 1983. They missed a triple sweep by one game, losing the fourth game of the Eastern Conference finals to the Milwaukee Bucks.

■ "He can run but he can't hide."
—Joe Louis's warning before beating Billy Conn in their heavyweight title fight.

■ "Nice guys finish last."
—Brooklyn Dodgers manager Leo Durocher, talking to some writers before a game with the last-place New York Giants, gestured toward the Giants and said, "Take a look at them. All nice guys. They'll finish last. Nice guys. Finish last."

■ "Gentlemen, you are about to play football for Yale against Harvard. Never in your lives will you ever do anything so important."
—Yale's football coach Tad Jones to his players before "The Game."

■ HARVARD BEATS YALE, 29-29.
—Headline in *The Harvard Crimson* the day after undefeated and previously untied Harvard scored 16 points in the last minute of their 1968 game to deadlock the undefeated and previously untied Bulldogs.

■ "Whoever wants to know the heart and mind of America had better learn baseball."
—Jacques Barzun, *God's Country and Mine*, 1954.

■ "Don't look back. Something might be gaining on you."

—The sixth and final of "Satchel Paige's Rules for Staying Young," first published in *Collier's* magazine.

- "Hit 'em where they ain't."
—Wee Willie Keeler's advice for hitting success
Keeler was a lifetime .345 hitter.

- "The bigger they are, the harder they fall."
—Heavyweight Bob Fitzsimmons about Jim Jeffries, who outweighed him by 53 pounds, before their 1899 title fight. Jeffries knocked out Fitzsimmons in the 11th round.

- "Good field, no hit."
—Report filed by scout Mike Gonzalez about a minor league prospect.

- "I'm the straw that stirs the drink."
—Reggie Jackson, shortly after being signed as a free agent by the New York Yankees.

- "I lost it in the sun."
—Brooklyn Dodgers pitcher Billy Loes, on missing a ground ball in the 1952 World Series.

- THIS IS NEXT YEAR
—Headline in the *New York Daily News*, after the Dodgers won their only world championship in Brooklyn, in 1955.

- "Thanks, King."
—Jim Thorpe to Sweden's King Gustav V, who presented a bust of himself to Thorpe for winning the 1912 Stockholm Olympic pentathlon.

- "I ain't got no quarrel with them Viet Cong."
—Muhammad Ali's explanation for his decision not to report for the draft in 1966.

- "Just win, baby."
—Oakland Raider owner and general manager Al Davis. The appeal has become the team's motto.

■ "These are the saddest of possible words: 'Tinker-to-Evers-to-Chance.'"
—From "Baseball's Sad Lexicon," by newspaperman and poet Franklin P. Adams. The poem was first published in *The New York Evening Mail*, July 1910.

■ "Say it ain't so, Joe."
—A small boy to "Shoeless" Joe Jackson, as Jackson emerged from the courtroom after testifying in the grand jury investigation of the 1919 Chicago Black Sox. Jackson denied to his death that such a plea was ever made.

10 NON-IMMORTALS WHO HAD A NOSE FOR HISTORICAL OCCASIONS

Some athletes who are not great have a knack for being on hand for more than their share of great moments. Perhaps it is fate, perhaps it is their only way of getting into the record books, perhaps it is something to make a list of.

■ Bobby Thomson, who hit possibly the most famous home run in baseball history, was replaced by a young outfielder named Willie Mays on the New York Giants. Thomson was traded to the Milwaukee Braves, where he was replaced by a young outfielder named Hank Aaron.

■ John Mohardt blocked for George Gipp (of "Win one for the Gipper" fame) when he was a running back at Notre Dame, blocked for Red Grange when he was with the NFL Chicago Bears, and pinch-ran for Ty Cobb when he was with the Detroit Tigers.

■ When he was with the Oakland Raiders in 1976, placekicker Fred Steinfort replaced George Blanda, the NFL's all-time leading scorer. When Steinfort was traded to Denver in 1980, he replaced Jim Turner, the NFL's then-second all-time leading scorer.

■ Bert Campaneris has appeared in 11 no-hitters, the most in major league history.

Cesar Tovar has broken up the most no-hitters in history, ruining five games between 1967 and 1975.

■ Major league second baseman Davey Johnson is a trivia buff's dream: he batted behind both Hank Aaron, the all-time home run king in America, and Sadaharu Oh, the all-time home run king in Japan; he is the last man to get a hit off of Sandy Koufax; and he made the final out of the 1969 World Series against the underdog New York Mets (whom he would later manage).

■ Harvey Kuenn was the final batter in two of Sandy Koufax's four career no-hitters, in 1963 and 1965.

■ On May 6, 1925, Paul "Pee Wee" Wanninger replaced shortstop Everett Scott to break Scott's then-record 1,307 consecutive-games playing streak. Almost four weeks later, Wanninger would give way to pinch hitter Lou Gehrig in the first game of the consecutive-games streak that would break Scott's record.

■ Cesar Geronimo was the 3,000th strikeout victim of both Bob Gibson and Nolan Ryan.

■ Tracy Stallard was a pivotal victim in two of the most famous baseball moments of the 1960s. He gave up Roger Maris's 61st home run on the last day of the 1961 season and he was the losing pitcher in Jim Bunning's perfect game on Father's Day, 1964.

AND 1 IMMORTAL WHO HAD A NOSE FOR HISTORICAL OCCASIONS

■ Washington Senators pitching great Walter Johnson yielded his first hit ever, in his losing debut on August 2, 1907, to Ty Cobb. Johnson's final appearance in baseball—as a pinch hitter, in 1927—was somewhat obscured because it was the same game in which Babe Ruth hit his 60th home run.

"THE GAME OF THE CENTURY"

In any century, presumably, there can be only one "Game of the Century"—*if* one—in any sport. However, those who would most likely apply the label—sports promoters—are not known to be the most judicious bunch, and they have trotted out the phrase more times than fans would care to hear. Boxing promoters especially are notorious for their overzealous billing of virtually every fight as one for the ages.

From all of those games and matches and fights deemed to be *the* sporting event of the century, a few stand out. Some were billed "The Game of the Century" beforehand and failed to live up to the title; others made no pretense to the title and in retrospect, because of the fierceness of the competition and the exciting finish, have come to be regarded as such.

■ The first Muhammad Ali–Joe Frazier bout in 1971 was dubbed "The Fight of the Century." Frazier won a 15-round decision in New York.

■ The 1958 sudden-death NFL title game between the Baltimore Colts and the New York Giants has been called pro football's "Game of the Century." The Colts won, 23-17.

■ The 1935 matchup between unbeatens Notre Dame and Ohio State has been called "The Game of the Century." Notre Dame won 18-13 on a last-seconds touchdown pass from Bill Shakespeare to Wayne Miller.

■ Notre Dame was involved in at least one other monumental game with a Big Ten opponent. The 10-10 tie between Notre Dame and Michigan State in 1966, which determined the national championship, has been called college football's "Game of the Century."

■ When Lew Alcindor's UCLA Bruins took on Elvin Hayes's Houston Cougars at the Astrodome on January 20, 1968, it was called college basketball's "Game of the Century." Houston won by two points, 71-69, as Hayes outscored Alcindor, 39-15 (Alcindor was recovering from an eye injury suffered the previous week).

■ In 1926, in the only meeting of their careers, tennis great Suzanne Lenglen defeated Helen Wills in what was proclaimed "The Match of the Century."
    The Billie Jean King–Bobby Riggs showdown in 1973 was billed as "The Tennis Match of the Century."

■ The three contests in the 1940s between Tony Zale and Rocky Graziano have been called the "greatest series of fights in boxing history."

■ The 1937 Davis Cup match between American Don Budge and German Gottfried von Cramm was voted "The Greatest Match Ever." Budge won in five sets, after being down 2-5 in the final set.

■ The 1921 fight between Jack Dempsey and European champion Georges Carpentier was proclaimed "The Battle of the Century." Dempsey won in a fourth-round knockout.

■ "The Mile of the Century" was contested in 1935 at

337

Princeton, where New Zealand's Jack Lovelock defeated Glenn Cunningham.

The next supposed "Mile of the Century" took place in 1954 in Vancouver, British Columbia, where England's Roger Bannister ran 3:58.8 to beat world record holder John Landy of Australia, who ran 3:59.6.

14 WHO FOLLOWED IN THE STEPS OF LEGENDS

■ Steve Patterson: After Lew Alcindor graduated from UCLA, Patterson took over at center and, in his junior and senior years, averaged 12.5 and 12.9 points, respectively, and helped the Bruins to win national championships in 1970 and 1971.

■ Leroy Kelly: A 1,000-yards-in-a-season rusher, Kelly was Jim Brown's successor as running back for the Cleveland Browns.

■ Bill Terry: The great New York Giant first baseman replaced the man who had managed the Giants for 31 years, John McGraw. Terry led the team to three pennants and one world championship in 10 years.

■ Heartley "Hunk" Anderson: After Knute Rockne was killed in a plane crash, Anderson succeeded him as football coach at Notre Dame, compiling a 16-9-2 record from 1931–33.

■ Manny Sanguillen/Richie Zisk: Sanguillen, a catcher, started in right field for the Pittsburgh Pirates on Opening Day in 1973, the first game after Roberto Clemente's death, but that year the position was patrolled mostly by Zisk, who batted .324 with 10 home runs and 54 RBIs.

◨ Ray Perkins: A former player under Alabama coach Paul "Bear" Bryant, Perkins succeeded the outgoing coach after the 1982 season.

◨ Phil Bengston: As Vince Lombardi's replacement as coach of the Green Bay Packers, Bengston compiled a 20-21-1 record from 1968–70.

◨ Garry Maddox: In 1972, Maddox hit .266 as the San Francisco Giant centerfielder after Willie Mays was traded to the New York Mets. Maddox hit .319 and .284 in the next two years before he was traded in 1975 to the Philadelphia Phillies.

◨ Gene Bartow: In the first two years after John Wooden retired, Bartow compiled a 52-9 record as the UCLA basketball coach, from 1975–76.

◨ Doug DeCinces: Taking over the hot corner from Brooks Robinson, the Baltimore Orioles new first-string third baseman hit .234 in 1976.

◨ Joe B. Hall: Successor to Adolph Rupp as basketball coach at the University of Kentucky, Hall compiled a 297-100 record from 1973–85 and won the national championship in 1978.

◨ Jim Gilliam: The Brooklyn Dodger pushed Jackie Robinson out of his second-base job in 1953, hitting .278 and leading the league in triples.

◨ Joe Nolan: In 1981, Nolan replaced Johnny Bench as the Cincinnati Reds' regular catcher and hit .309.

◨ Terry Miller: When O. J. Simpson was traded in 1978, Miller replaced him in the Buffalo Bills backfield and rushed for 1,060 yards that season.

12 IMMORTALIZED ATHLETES

Many athletes have been turned into legends not so much because of their talents and accomplishments—though those are obvious components with great athletes—but because of the lore surrounding their lives. Perhaps the most mythologized athlete of this century has been Joseph Jefferson "Shoeless Joe" Jackson, who has helped to inspire an astonishing outpouring of creativity: songs ("Shoeless Joe from Hannibal, Mo." from the musical *Damn Yankees*), books (W. P. Kinsella's *Shoeless Joe;* Eliot Asinof's *Eight Men Out*), and much more. Jackson was a brilliantly talented baseball player and, as a member of the 1919 Black Sox, a tragic figure—an immortal-in-waiting if there ever was one.

The following athletes—some great, some downright obscure—have become part of our mythology in a way that far exceeds what they ever or never did on the field of play.

■ Either Dan Casey or his brother Dennis, major leaguers in the 1880s, are the reputed models for Ernest Lawrence Thayer's poem "Casey at the Bat."

■ Yugoslav ski jumper Vinko Bogataj has been immortalized by the opening segment of ABC's "Wide World of Sports." His vicious wipeout off a ski jump at the 1970 World Ski Flying Championships in Oberstdorf, West Germany, has come to embody the "agony of defeat."

■ Ed Smith, a New York University football player who played briefly in the NFL, posed for the Downtown Athletic Club Trophy—later renamed the Heisman Trophy—that was sculpted by Frank Eliscu.

■ Eddie Waitkus, a career .285 hitter and one of the 1950 Philadelphia Phillie "Whiz Kids," was partially the model for Roy Hobbs in Bernard Malamud's novel *The Natural*.

Waitkus was mysteriously shot by Ruth Steinhagen, an obsessed fan, who told him, "For two years you have been bothering me and now you are going to die." Waitkus did not die but healed enough to be named Comeback Player of the Year and lead the Phillies to the pennant. In the novel, Hobbs is mysteriously shot by an obsessed fan but returns to lead the fictional New York Knights into pennant contention.

■ Chuck Wepner, a New Jersey club fighter nicknamed "The Bayonne Bleeder," was Sylvester Stallone's inspiration for *Rocky*. Wepner got his big chance when he fought heavyweight champion Muhammad Ali on March 24, 1975, in Cleveland. As Rocky would, Wepner, 32-9-2 at the time, earned a moral victory by going the distance—or almost—with the champ: Wepner was knocked out with 19 seconds left in the 15th round of the fight that Ali called the toughest of his career.

■ Harold Sakata, the 1948 Olympic silver medalist in light-heavyweight weightlifting, earned cult status by portraying "Oddjob" in the James Bond movie *Goldfinger*.

■ Terry Schroeder, a U.S. Olympic water polo player, modeled for the nude Olympic statue in front of the Los Angeles Coliseum.

■ Brian Dowling, quarterback for Yale in the late 1960s (and later in the NFL), is the inspiration for the football-helmeted "B.D." in Garry Trudeau's comic strip "Doonesbury." As a starting quarterback, Dowling, whose career at Yale overlapped Trudeau's, compiled a 16-1-1 record in his junior and senior years.

■ The model for the graceful silhouetted player that appears on the NBA official logo—emblazoned on every NBA uniform—is Hall of Fame guard Jerry West.

■ René Lacoste, one of the "Four Musketeers"—the four great Frenchmen who, along with Bill Tilden, dominated tennis in the 1920s and early 1930s—gained much greater fame when he founded a clothing company and chose as its logo an alligator—which symbolized his own tenacious determination as a player to hang on and devour opponents. His shirts have come to be known, simply, as "Lacostes."

■ The life of Annie Oakley (1860–1926), one of the greatest shooters of all time (she consistently scored 100-for-100 in trapshooting), was the basis for the popular Irving Berlin musical *Annie Get Your Gun*.

■ Mario Mendoza, a journeyman infielder with Seattle, Pittsburgh, and Texas from 1974–82, was a lifetime .215 hitter and finished five seasons batting under .200. To hit below the "Mendoza Line" has come to mean having a sub-.200 batting average.

DEBUNKING 11 SPORTS MYTHS

Stories about athletes, who are so often viewed in heroic terms, achieve a grandeur, a mythic quality, without much nudging. Sometimes the stories are actually true; other times they just make for good stories. Every now and then, it's important to clean out the locker and set the record straight. What follows is a list of myths, and the truths behind them.

■ There is an asterisk affixed to Roger Maris's home run record:

For eight years, there were, in fact, separate records kept for 154- and 162-game seasons. In 1969, however, the Special Baseball Rules Committee determined that baseball would have one set of records and that "no asterisk or official sign shall be used to indicate the number of games scheduled."

■ Tinker-to-Evers-to-Chance formed a great double-play combination:

These three Chicago Cubs were immortalized by the Franklin P. Adams poem, "Baseball's Sad Lexicon," but during their time together from 1906 to 1909, they actually completed only 54 double plays—fewer than 14 DPs, on average, a year.

■ Wilt Chamberlain was routinely outplayed throughout his career by Bill Russell:

While Russell's Boston Celtics won 85 games and lost only 57 against Wilt's teams, in those 142 contests Chamberlain averaged 28.7 points and an identical 28.7 rebounds to Russell's 14.5 points and 23.7 rebounds.

■ "The Four Horsemen" of Notre Dame, 1922–24, were swift, strong, and big:

While the Four Horsemen—Harry Stuhldreher, Jim Crowley, Don Miller, and Elmer Layden—were swift and strong, the four backs averaged just 165 pounds.

■ Having sex too soon before a competition will harm one's athletic performance:

Bob Beamon claimed that the only time he had sex right before a long jump competition was on the eve of his world record–shattering jump at the 1968 Olympics.

To enhance training, Eastern European nations have secluded male athletes with their wives the night before an important competition, in the belief that sexual activity dissipates nervous tension. Sexual activity *after* a competition is considered potentially harmful, because the athlete is depleted.

■ Harold Abrahams, the sprinter whose athletic and collegiate exploits were portrayed in the film *Chariots of Fire*, raced around the courtyard of Trinity College in Cambridge, and his victory in the 100m was redemption for his failure in the 200m:

Lord Burghley ran around the courtyard, and the 100m preceded the 200m.

■ Enos "Country" Slaughter scored all the way from first on a single in Game 7 of the 1946 World Series:

Slaughter *did* score from first base on the hit, but the batter, Harry Walker, was credited with a double on the play.

■ Dorando Pietri, the marathoner who stumbled and staggered in the waning moments of the 1908 Olympic marathon, was a flash-in-the-pan:

Although Pietri, from Italy, is most famous for a marathon that he had trouble completing, he regularly beat Johnny Hayes, the American who defeated him in the Olympics, in a series of races held during the American marathon craze at the beginning of the century. In one 1909 race at Madison Square Garden, Pietri lapped Hayes five times.

■ "The Seven Blocks of Granite" was the name inspired by Vince Lombardi and his six defensive linemates on the Fordham football powerhouse of the late 1930s:

They were indeed called that—but the name was a retread, having been applied to the Fordham defensive line in 1930, six years before Lombardi starred for them.

■ New York Giant Dusty Rhodes was a great career pinch hitter:

While Rhodes had one remarkable year—1954—and several clutch performances, including key pinch hits in the first three games of that year's World Series, his career pinch-hitting average is .212.

■ Vince Lombardi originally said, "Winning isn't everything, it's the only thing":

The line was first uttered by Henry R. "Red" Sanders, head coach at Vanderbilt and UCLA, in 1940. John Wayne repeated it in the 1953 movie *Trouble Along the Way*. On April 8, 1962, in a speech in Milwaukee, Lombardi said, "Winning isn't everything; trying to win is."

THE MOST COMPELLING
FIRSTS IN SPORTS

Records, they say too frequently, were made to be you-know-what, and most great athletes who do something better than anyone has ever done it before usually get to see someone else come along and do it a little bit better. But those who were *first* to do something: they can live in peace that their place in history, however small, is untouchable.

We've compiled a few of the most compelling "firsts" in sports.

■ The first NCAA school to have a women's athletic team placed on probation for recruiting violations:
   Northeast Louisiana University (basketball), 1986.

■ The first winning Super Bowl coach to wear headphones on the sidelines:
   Bill Walsh, San Francisco 49ers, Super Bowl XVI, 1982.

■ The first Little Leaguer to play in the major leagues:
   Joey Jay, 1961.

■ The first *Sports Illustrated* cover subject:
   Eddie Mathews, Milwaukee Braves, 1954.

■ The first to score a Super Bowl touchdown:
   Max McGee of the Green Bay Packers, 1967.

■ The first American woman known to dunk a basketball in official competition:
   Georgeann Wells of West Virginia University, December 21, 1983, in a game against the University of Charleston.

■ The first to swim 100 meters in under a minute:
   Johnny Weissmuller, July 9, 1922.

■ The first sprinter to break 10 seconds in the 100m:
   Jim Hines, 9.9 seconds, at the 1968 AAU Championships.

■ The first woman to run the marathon in under three hours:
   Adrienne Beames of Australia, August 31, 1971 (2:46.30).

■ The first marathoner to average under five minutes per mile:
   Derek Clayton of Australia, December 3, 1967 (2:09:36.4).

■ The first lunar athlete:
   Alan Shepard, Jr., February 6, 1971. As Apollo 14 commander, he hit a six-iron shot on the moon.

■ The first high school student to break the four-minute mile:
   Jim Ryun, 3:58.3, in 1965 for Wichita East High School.

■ The first ex-athlete to become a broadcaster:
   Jack Graney, former leftfielder for the Cleveland Indians, in 1932.

■ The first President to throw out the first ball of the season:
   William Howard Taft, April 14, 1910, in Washington, for a game against Philadelphia.

■ The first All-America football team selected by Walter Camp:
   January 7, 1899, published in *Collier's Weekly*.

■ The first baseball team to draw one million fans in a year:
   The Chicago Cubs, in 1927.

■ The first year that the New York Yankees won a World Series:
   1923.

■ The first NBA player to reach 20,000 career points:
   Bob Pettit, 1964.

■ The first major league game played at night:
   May 24, 1935 at Crosley Field in Cincinnati.

■ The first time the result of an Olympic final was changed after viewing film of the event:
   1932, the 110-yard hurdles. Donald Finley was originally listed as fourth but moved to third, ahead of Jack Keller, and awarded the bronze medal.

■ The first player to win the tennis Grand Slam:
   Don Budge, 1938.

■ The first woman to win the tennis Grand Slam:
   Maureen "Mo" Connolly, 1953.

■ The first major leaguer to hit a home run:
   Ross Barnes, 1876.

■ The first lefty to win a golf major:
   Bob Charles, the 1963 British Open.

■ The first Latin player elected to Cooperstown:
   Roberto Clemente, 1973.

■ The first black player elected to Cooperstown:
   Jackie Robinson, 1962.

■ The first thoroughbred to reach $1 million in career earnings:
   Citation.

■ The first golfer to reach $1 million in career earnings:
   Jack Nicklaus, 1970, after taking second place in the Bing Crosby Pro-Am.

■ The first woman golfer to reach $1 million in career earnings:

Kathy Whitworth, 1981, after taking third place in the U.S. Women's Open.

■ The first track and field Olympian disqualified for taking drugs:
Danuta Rosani, discus thrower from Poland, 1976, for steroids.

■ The first designated hitter:
Ron Blomberg, New York Yankees, April 6, 1973.

■ The first race of the modern Olympics:
Opening heat of the 100m dash, 1896 (won by Francis Lane of Princeton in 12⅕ seconds).

■ The first college team to have two 200-yard rushers in the same game:
Tulsa, on November 2, 1985, with Gordon Brown (214 yards) and Steve Gage (206 yards) in a 42-26 win over Wichita State.

■ The first Jewish player in the major leagues:
Lipman Pike, 1876.

■ The first soccer-style kicker in pro football:
Cornell's Pete Gogolak, who signed a contract with the Buffalo Bills in 1964.

■ The first pitcher to throw a curveball:
Candy Cummings, 1867.

■ The first baseball player to reach 3,000 career hits:
Cap Anson, 1897.

■ The first Indianapolis 500 winner to average more than 100 miles per hour:
Peter DePaolo, 101.27 mph in 1925, in a Duesenberg Special.

■ The first million-dollar gate for a fight:
1921, Georges Carpentier vs. Jack Dempsey.

■ The first paid football coach with faculty status:
Amos Alonzo Stagg, at the University of Chicago, 1892.

■ The first woman play-by-play announcer for a network NFL game:
Gayle Sierens, December 27, 1987, for NBC, the Seattle Seahawks at the Kansas City Chiefs.

■ The first woman to be named Athlete of the Year by *Sports Illustrated:*
Billie Jean King, 1972.

AND JUST A FEW BEST LASTS

It's a much more fleeting endeavor to say who did something last than who did something first, since with many records it is obviously just a matter of time before someone else comes along to become the new *last* person to do something. As of this writing, for example, we know that Bob Horner is the last to hit four home runs in one game (in 1986), George Foster the last to hit 50 home runs in one season (52, in 1977), Affirmed the last horse to win the Triple Crown (in 1978), and Cincinnati Red Tom Browning the last pitcher to throw a perfect game (in 1988). Any or all of these distinctions could be outdated within a year, and most likely at least one will fall before the century lets out.

So we will just offer a very few lasts, some of which may change soon, some of which will not.

■ The last active Brooklyn Dodger to play in the majors:
Bob Aspromonte, 1971, New York Mets.

■ The last bareknuckles heavyweight title fight:

July 8, 1889. John L. Sullivan knocked out Jake Kilrain in the seventh round.

■ The last legal spitball pitcher:
   Burleigh Grimes, 1934.

■ The last player who did not wear a glove on the field:
   Jerry Denny, Louisville, 1894.

■ The last baseball team to start the season with a scheduled doubleheader:
   The Chicago White Sox against the Oakland Athletics, 1971. (Oakland had already played a game.)

■ The last ABA champions:
   The New York Nets, 1976.

■ The last National Leaguer to hit .400:
   Bill Terry, .401 in 1930.

■ The last National Leaguer to win baseball's Triple Crown:
   Joe Medwick, 1937.

■ The last golfer to win the Grand Slam:
   Bobby Jones, 1930 (then, the Slam was the Open and Amateur championships in the United States and Britain).

■ The last to start both ends of a doubleheader:
   Wilbur Wood, on July 20, 1973.

■ The last year with no managerial changes in the major leagues:
   1942.

IT'S APPROPRIATE

The history of sport is filled with stories of the unforeseeable. A great man fails miserably in the clutch. Or maybe a lesser man accomplishes something spectacular. Who would have guessed, for example, that Don Larsen, the pitcher with one of the worst season winning percentages ever for anyone with more than 20 decisions (3-21, in 1954) would become, two years later, the only man in history to pitch a perfect World Series game?

But sometimes things that should happen *do* happen. If you didn't know the following facts, you might well have guessed them. It's appropriate, for instance . . .

▨ that the first home run in Yankee Stadium should be hit by Babe Ruth. He did it on April 18, 1923, in the first game ever played at "The House That Ruth Built." Ruth hit a three-run homer in the third inning and the Yankees won, 4-1, over the Boston Red Sox.

▨ that the player to receive the first official warning in Wimbledon history should be John McEnroe. He got it in the 1980 semifinals against Jimmy Connors (a contest in which McEnroe saved seven match points to win).

▨ that the first NFL game played in a Scandinavian country should include the Minnesota Vikings. They hosted the Chicago Bears in Gothenburg, Sweden, in a preseason game in 1988.

▨ that the date on which New Orleans should officially be named the site of a new NFL franchise was All Saints Day, November 1, 1966.

▨ that the first official car speed record—91.370 mph, set in January of 1904—should be recorded by Henry Ford.

■ that the Los Angeles Lakers' NBA record 33-game winning streak in 1971–72 should be stopped, on January 9, 1972, by the Milwaukee Bucks and Lew Alcindor—later to become Kareem Abdul-Jabbar, the centerpiece of the Laker dynasty of the 1980s.

■ that the first career NFL reception by Don Hutson, the league's all-time leader in touchdown receptions until Steve Largent broke the record in 1989, should go for an 83-yard touchdown.

■ that the first notable title won by Bjorn Borg, who captured dozens of championships but who is best remembered for winning five consecutive Wimbledons, should be the boys' singles at Wimbledon, in 1972.

9 POSSIBLY OVERLOOKED MOMENTS THAT SIGNALED A MAJOR CHANGE IN SPORTS

Certain moments in the history of sport prefigured a change that might well have been anticipated. In 1947, for instance, when Jackie Robinson became the first black in the major leagues' modern era, it was clear that the character of the game would forever be altered. In 1972, President Richard Nixon signed Title IX, part of the Higher Education Act—legislation that barred sex bias in athletics and other activities at colleges receiving federal assistance—which led to a considerable expansion in women's athletics.

Other moments have caused changes that were equally or almost as significant, but the profundity of the moment was not necessarily gauged at the time.

■ In September of 1972, the U.S.S.R. surprised the world by compiling a competitive 3-4-1 record in their series with Canada, after everyone had expected Canada

352

to sweep. Not long after the series, NHL scouts began to scour Europe for players, and the league began to adapt to the more open, passing-intensive European style of play.

■ The 24-second clock was used for the first time in an NBA game on October 30, 1954, when the Rochester Royals defeated the Boston Celtics, 98–95. The clock radically transformed pro basketball into the fast-paced, high-scoring game that it has become.

■ On October 27, 1906, the first forward pass in a professional football game was completed. George "Peggy" Parratt of Massillon, Ohio threw it, and Dan "Bullet" Riley caught it, in a victory over the combined Benwood-Moundsville team. Football's connection to rugby would grow increasingly remote as the forward pass was exploited as an offensive weapon.

■ In 1970, Billie Jean King, along with Rosie Casals, led a boycott of the Pacific South West Championships, where the men's prize money was 10 times greater than the women's. Helped by *World Tennis* magazine publisher Gladys Heldman, they formed the Women's Pro Tour, sponsored by Virginia Slims, which would grow to its current immense success.

■ In the 1966 NCAA finals, Texas Western, with five black starters, beat Adolph Rupp's University of Kentucky team, with five white starters, an event called "'Brown vs. the Board of Education' of college basketball." The notion of black "quotas" ended and helped to change the complexion—figuratively and literally—of the game.

■ No soccer competition was included at the 1932 Los Angeles Olympics, an absence that helped to stifle the progress of the game in America. The popularity of amateur soccer in the United States had been growing during that era and the showcasing of world-class soccer on American soil, at the L.A. Games, would have given the sport needed credibility.

■ To raise money in 1877 for a "pony-roller" for

croquet, a club in England held a tennis tournament, which proved a success. The All-England Croquet Club would hold the competition again and the Wimbledon tournament grew into the most famous and prestigious tennis competition in the world.

■ Due to snow, the 1932 NFL title game was played indoors at Chicago Stadium. Because of the 80-yard field, the game rules were modified and were so successful that they would lead to permanent rule changes concerning hashmark positioning, having goalposts at the goal line, and permitting passes from anywhere behind the line of scrimmage.

■ East German swimmers wore skintight, semi-see-through Lycra suits at the 1973 swimming world championships, in Belgrade, Yugoslavia, an occasion that coincided with the beginning of East Germany's domination of women's swimming. They had not won a single event at the 1972 Olympics; in 1976, they took 11 of 13 gold medals. "Belgrade suits" soon became standard.

7 VERY GOOD ATHLETES
WE'LL REMEMBER PRIMARILY
FOR THEIR MISFORTUNES

■ Brooklyn Dodgers pitcher Ralph Branca, for the home run he gave up to New York Giant Bobby Thomson in 1951, "the shot heard 'round the world." Branca pitched for 12 years and had a .564 winning percentage.

■ Brian Piccolo, the subject of the movie *Brian's Song*, for dying young of cancer. Piccolo won the NCAA rushing title in 1964 for Wake Forest and played for four years with the Chicago Bears.

▣ New York Yankee Wally Pipp, for giving way one summer day to a rookie first baseman named Lou Gehrig, who proceeded not to miss a game for the next 13 years. Pipp was a 15-year veteran who twice won the American League home run title.

▣ Quarterback Art Schlichter, for the gambling addiction that helped to shorten his stay in the NFL. Schlichter had enjoyed an illustrious career at Ohio State.

▣ Los Angeles Laker Kermit Washington, for delivering a December 1978 punch to Houston Rocket Rudy Tomjanovich that caused massive facial injuries requiring several operations. Washington was not only a top NBA power forward for nine years but, ironically, considered around the league as one of the kindest men in the game.

▣ California center Roy "Wrong Way" Riegels, for running the wrong way with a fumble that set up the decisive score for Georgia Tech in the 1929 Rose Bowl. Riegels was an All-America and a team co-captain the following year.

▣ Brooklyn Dodgers catcher Mickey Owen, for the third strike that he dropped against the New York Yankees in Game 4 of the World Series in 1941. Earlier that season, Owen had set a National League record for most consecutive errorless chances in a season by a catcher.

14
GREATS

IF YOU THINK THEY'RE GOOD,
YOU SHOULD SEE THE THIRD-STRING:
THE GREATEST PLAN B'S IN SPORTS

■ In 1960, the U.S. reserve swim team set the world record in a 400m freestyle relay qualifying round.

■ Boxer Buster Mathis injured his hand and could not compete in the 1964 Olympics. The man he beat at the Olympic Trials, Joe Frazier, took his place and won the super heavyweight gold medal.

■ In 1928, New York Rangers coach Lester Patrick, age 44, was pressed into duty as goalie because of an injury to Lorne Chabot. Patrick won a 2-1 overtime game in the Stanley Cup finals, which the Rangers won, three games to two.

■ In the 1984 Olympics, West German swimmer Thomas Fahrner set an Olympic record in the 400m freestyle in the consolation race.

■ Norwegian Birger Ruud went to the 1948 Olympics as ski jumping coach but decided to compete in place of a less experienced team member. Ruud won the silver medal.

■ Ten days before the 1918 Kentucky Derby, Exterminator was purchased as a workhorse to extend Sun Briar in workouts. When Sun Briar did not train well, Exterminator started in his place and won the Derby against 30-1 odds. Iron Liege replaced the 1957 Derby favorite General Duke, who had become lame, and won.

■ Soviet gymnast Olga Korbut, the darling of the 1972 Olympics, qualified for the Games only as an alternate but got to compete after a teammate was injured.

MODELS OF PERFECTION

Perfection in anything outside of nature is rare. But some examples in sports do come to mind: the 1972 Miami Dolphins, who recorded the only perfect—unbeaten and untied—season in NFL history; Rocky Marciano, the only heavyweight champion to go through his whole professional career without a loss, recording a spotless 49-0 record; Nadia Comaneci, the first gymnast to earn a 10 at the Olympics, in 1976; Don Larsen's perfect game in 1956, the only one in World Series history; in golf, the hole-in-one.

Here are some other examples of individual contests (or parts of them), seasons, and, in that uncommon instance, careers that were devoid of blemish in one way or another.

■ Jayne Torvill and Chrisopher Dean of Great Britain were awarded the maximum number of points possible when they received perfect 6s from all nine judges for artistic presentation in the World Ice Dance Championships at Helsinki, on March 12, 1983, and again at Ottawa, in March of 1984. They hold the record for receiving the most 6s in a career, and the most in one competition.

■ In the 1924 Olympic rapid-fire pistol competition, 8 of the 55 competitors had perfect scores, and all eight were again perfect in the second-round shoot-off. After five rounds, American Henry Bailey and Swede Wilhelf Carlberg were left, each having hit 48 targets in a row. They were perfect in the sixth shoot-off, as well, and Bailey was perfect in the seventh despite a stuck cartridge. Carlberg then missed two, and Bailey won the gold.

◼ The 1957 NCAA basketball champions, the University of North Carolina, were 32-0. The 1976 Indiana University basketball team won the national title, and also sported a 32-0 record.

◼ As of 1986, the only known "golden set"—in which one player wins every point in the set—in tennis's open era was recorded by Bill Scanlon in a first-round win over Marcos Hocevar, at the WCT Gold Coast Cup at Delray Beach, Florida.

◼ Wrestler Robin Reed, gold medalist at the 1924 Olympics, retired undefeated.

◼ Mark Spitz was perfect at the 1972 Summer Olympics: he entered seven swimming events (four individuals, three relays), won seven gold medals, and set seven world records. Eric Heiden entered five speedskating races in the 1980 Winter Games, became the first person in Olympic history to win five individual gold medals in one Games, and set an Olympic record in each event.

◼ At the U.S. Olympic trials in Chicago in 1972, diver Michael Finneran was awarded perfect 10s by all seven judges for a backward 1½ somersault, 2½ twist (free) from the 10-meter platform. Greg Louganis matched this feat in 1982. They are the only two divers in international competition to receive straight 10s from all the judges.

◼ The only major professional football team besides the 1972 Miami Dolphins to record an unbeaten, untied season was the 1948 Cleveland Browns, who were 15-0 in winning the All-America Football Conference title.

◼ In international competition, Japanese wrestler Osamu Watanabe won the 1964 Olympic freestyle featherweight championship without giving up a point in his six matches.

■ In the Olympic equestrian jumping competition, a perfect score—for a run with no faults—has been awarded twice: to Frantisek Ventura of Czechoslovakia riding Eliot in 1928, and by Alwin Schockemohle of West Germany, riding Warwick Rex in 1976.

■ Aleksandr Dityatin of the U.S.S.R., the first person to win eight medals in one Olympics, was also the first male gymnast to receive a perfect 10 for the vault, in 1980.

■ American weightlifter John Davis was never defeated in Olympic competition in the press, snatch, or jerk.

■ Kickers Ray Wersching and Danny Villaneuva are tied for the NFL record for most PATs made in a season, 56, without a miss.

■ Pitching for the 1946 Peekskill (New York) Highlanders of the Class D, North Atlantic League, Tony Napoles was 18-0 in the regular season and 4-0 in the playoffs.

■ Laurie Doherty of Great Britain is the only man in tennis history never to lose in a challenge round in Davis Cup. He was 7-0 in singles and 5-0 in doubles.

■ Dan Patch, a great turn-of-the-century pacer, never lost a final heat.

■ Pitcher Michele Broussard of the Vanderbilt (Louisiana) Catholic High School girl's softball team was 88-0 for her career (including 32-0 as a sophomore, 27-0 as a junior, 27-0 as a senior) and helped to lead Vanderbilt to four consecutive state titles.

■ Sybil Bauer held the world record in every backstroke event when she captured the 100m Olympic backstroke gold medal in 1924. She was undefeated when she died of intestinal cancer on January 31, 1927, at age 23.

■ In 1926, his rookie year for the Philadelphia Athletics, relief pitcher Joe Pate won all nine of his decisions.

■ Major league pitcher J. R. Richard had an 0.00 ERA in his senior season at Ruston Lincoln High School in 1969.

■ In the second half of Super Bowl XXI, New York Giants quarterback Phil Simms threw 10 passes and completed all 10 (for 166 yards).

■ National Leaguer Steve Garvey was 10-0 in All-Star games.

■ Maureen Connolly was never beaten in a Grand Slam singles event. She won three U.S. titles, three Wimbledons, two French, and one Australian.

10 OF THE MOST UTTERLY DOMINATING INDIVIDUALS IN SPORTS HISTORY

■ Squash player Heather McKay lost only two games, and no matches, from 1961–80.

■ In the 1910s, Fanny Durack of Australia once held every world record in women's swimming from 50 yards to one mile.

■ Chiquito de Cambo was rated as the world's best

jai alai player from the beginning of the century through 1938.

■ In women's figure skating, no one was greater than Sonja Henie. She won the Norwegian figure skating championships at age 10, first competed in the Olympics at 11, captured 10 consecutive world championships from 1927 to 1936, and the Olympic gold medals in 1928, 1932, and 1936. Her reported earnings at the time of her death were $45 million.

■ The most famous ancient Olympian was Milo of Croton, who won the boys' wrestling event in 540 B.C., six successive senior Olympiads, and more than two dozen crowns in other Panhellenic festivals.

■ Kelso was named Horse of the Year five times, from 1960 through 1964.

■ Oscar Robertson averaged a triple double with the Cincinnati Royals in the 1961–62 basketball season.

■ Between 1972 and 1980, Soviet Vassily Alexeyev broke 80 official world weightlifting records. He won two Olympic golds, eight world titles, and nine European championships.

■ In 1889, Boston pitcher John Clarkson led the National League in wins, ERA, strikeouts, shutouts, complete games, innings pitched, games, and winning percentage.

■ In 1988, West German tennis star Steffi Graf pulled off an unprecedented "Golden Slam" by winning the Grand Slam and the Olympic tennis gold medal.

IT SHOULD HAVE BEEN ENOUGH: GREAT PERFORMANCES OVERSHADOWED BY EVEN BETTER PERFORMANCES

On March 2, 1962, New York Knick Cleveland Buckner, a career 6.4 points-per-game scorer, had a career night, scoring 33 points against the Philadelphia Warriors. Reporters should have surrounded him after the game. It did not matter that teammate Richie Guerin also scored over 30 points; he was one of the NBA's top scorers, so that kind of performance was expected. And it did not matter that teammate Willie Naulls also scored over 30 points; he, too, was a top scorer.

It *did* matter, however, that Wilt Chamberlain of the Warriors scored 100 points that night, the all-time NBA record.

Too bad for Buckner.

Here are a collection of fine performances that would have received more recognition had it not been for someone else who outperformed them.

◼ Lou Gehrig's season slugging percentage of .765 in 1927 was the fourth best of all time but only the second best on the team that year, behind Babe Ruth's .772, third-best all-time.

◼ Jack Nicklaus had the second-lowest total score in British Open history, 269, in 1977. Unfortunately for Nicklaus, that was the same year that Tom Watson shot a 268, the lowest British Open score ever, to beat Nicklaus by a stroke.

◼ Charlie Borah equaled the then-Olympic 200m record (21.6 seconds) in the 1928 quarterfinal heat but was still eliminated.

◼ In 1971, Oakland Athletic Vida Blue became the only pitcher in the modern era to strike out 300 or more batters in a season and not lead the league in strikeouts. His total of 301 lost to the 308 of Detroit Tiger Mickey Lolich.

■ USC's 1971–72 basketball team had only two losses (24-2), but they did not go to the NCAA tournament because of the one school per conference rule. Their two defeats were both to conference mate UCLA, the eventual national champion.

■ Mickey Mantle's 54 home runs in 1961 are the most a player has ever hit without winning a home run title. Roger Maris, his teammate, beat him by seven home runs.

■ Ty Cobb and Joe Jackson are the only two players with a .400 season average in baseball's modern era not to win the batting title.

■ In the Olympic 800m finals in 1976, Anita Weiss of East Germany broke the world record but did not even win a medal, as three other runners broke the record more resoundingly.

■ The 1942 Brooklyn Dodgers won 104 games but finished 2 games behind the St. Louis Cardinals. The 1909 Chicago Cubs won 104 games and finished 6½ games behind the Pittsburgh Pirates.

■ Pittsburgh Pirate Omar Moreno stole a dazzling 96 bases in 1980 but finished second in the league to Montreal Expo Ron LeFlore, who stole 97.

■ In the 1960 Olympic speedskating 10,000m race, Viktor Kosichkin of the U.S.S.R. broke the world record by more than 43 seconds—and earned the silver medal. His time was more than two seconds slower than that of Knut Johannesen of Norway.

■ In 1930, Chuck Klein had 250 hits, the seventh-best ever, and 170 RBIs, 10th-best ever, and won neither a hits nor an RBI title. Bill Terry had a National League record 254 hits that year and Hack Wilson set the all-time record for RBIs with 190.

THE HOMAGES THAT RUTH BUILT

Babe Ruth was known as much for the larger-than-life way in which he did things as the things themselves. A home run of "Ruthian" proportions is one that will long be remembered, and to be nicknamed "Babe" is often a testament to both an athlete's charisma and great skill. More than two dozen major leaguers have been nicknamed "Babe" (though several preceded Ruth: Jay Towne and Charles Adams, both of whom began playing in 1906, are the earliest-known "Babes") but none approached Ruth's reputation.

To be compared to Babe Ruth is the ultimate compliment to a baseball player—or to any athlete, for that matter.

▪ John Beckman, captain of the Original Celtics and his sport's first great gate attraction, was called "The Babe Ruth of Basketball."

▪ Billy Gonsalves, member of the United States World Cup teams in 1930 and 1934, was called "The Babe Ruth of Soccer." He is considered the greatest American player ever.

▪ Moses Solomon, a slugger who played at the end of the 1923 season for the New York Giants, was known as

"The Jewish Babe Ruth." Before being called up to the majors, he hit 49 home runs for Hutchinson of the Southwestern (Class C) League. He was also called "The Rabbi of Swat."

■ Howie Morenz, the swift and great scorer for the Montreal Canadiens in the 1920s and 1930s, was called "hockey's answer to Babe Ruth."

■ Joe Bauman, who hit 72 home runs for the 1954 Roswell (New Mexico) Rockets in the Class C Longhorn League, a professional baseball record for one season, was known as "The Babe Ruth of the Minors." He later became manager of a beer distributorship in Albuquerque, where he was known as "The Sultan of Schlitz."

■ Josh Gibson, who hit 89 home runs in one Negro League season and 75 in another, was called "The black Babe Ruth."

■ Sadaharu Oh, the great Japanese player who launched 868 home runs in 22 years, was called "The Babe Ruth of Japan."

■ Enrico Rastelli is considered "The Babe Ruth of Juggling."

■ Billy Haughton, winner of 4,910 races in his career, was considered "The Babe Ruth of Harness Racing."

■ While at Columbia University, Lou Gehrig, Ruth's future New York Yankee teammate, was called "The College Babe Ruth."

■ Outfielder Sammy Byrd, the New York Yankees defensive replacement from 1929–34, was known as "Babe Ruth's Legs."

THE BEST INNOVATORS AND PIONEERS IN SPORTS

■ The origin for the "high-five" is claimed by Derek Smith of the 1980 NCAA champion University of Louisville basketball team. Smith was quoted in *The New York Times*, *The Sporting News*, and other publications as saying that he and teammates Wiley Brown and Daryle Cleveland wanted something "a little odd." The high-five was created and fine-tuned during preseason practice and introduced to the nation on TV in 1979.

■ Elston Howard invented the warm-up donut.

■ In the 1930s, U.S. swimmers in the breaststroke began bringing their arms back above the surface of the water. In 1952, this stroke was officially recognized as the butterfly and added to the Olympics as a separate event.

■ Arch Ward, sports editor for *The Chicago Tribune*, came up with the idea of a baseball All-Star Game in 1933.

■ Montreal Canadien Jacques Plante introduced the goalie mask on November 1, 1959.

■ Stanford's Hank Luisetti helped to revolutionize the game of basketball when he pioneered the one-handed jump shot on the run, at a time when players scored only with lay-ups or two-handed set shots. Luisetti, along with Seton Hall's Bob Davies, also helped popularize the behind-the-back dribble in the early 1940s.

■ In 1948, Los Angeles Rams halfback Fred Gehrke painted blue Rams logos on 70 of the team's plain leather football helmets, leading to colorful insignias on helmets for the league's other teams.

■ Pitcher Jim Brosnan's book, *The Long Season*, published in 1960, paved the way for sports "tell-all" biographies, including Jim Bouton's controversial account, *Ball Four*.

■ Arnold Lunn organized the first downhill ski race in Switzerland in 1911, and invented the modern slalom in 1922.

■ René Lacoste had the first tennis ball–throwing machine constructed to his design. He also analyzed his own game by using slow-motion photography, and developed the round-headed, open-throated racket.

■ The baseball warning track was inspired by Brooklyn Dodger Pete Reiser, who was seriously injured in 1947 crashing into the outfield wall at Ebbets Field.

■ Harry Miller designed the front-wheel-drive car in 1925.

■ Arthur Howie Ross, for whom the Ross Trophy (given to the NHL's leading scorer) is named, designed the modern hockey puck and nets.

■ Joe Pepitone was the first player to use a blow-drier in the locker room.

■ Dick Young was the first sportswriter to get postgame locker-room quotes for his story.

■ Charlie Waitt wore the first baseball glove in 1875.

■ Kid Gavilan gave the world the bolo punch.

■ In the 1890s, American jockey Todhunter "Tod" Sloan popularized the technique of crouching forward while riding, rather than sitting upright, for better weight distribution. He also helped to popularize the use of stirrups and short reins.

■ German figure skaters Ernst Baier and Maxi Herber pioneered "shadow skating," in which partners perform the same moves without touching.

■ The valve-free, hidden-lace basketball was developed by Walter Meanwell, coach at Wisconsin and Missouri.

■ Tommy McCarthy and Hugh Duffy developed the hit-and-run play.

■ Fred Perry introduced the short-sleeved, knitted white tennis shirt.

■ James Van Alen was the originator of the tie-break scoring system in tennis.

■ Alvin Kraenzlein of the United States, gold medalist in the 120-yard hurdles in 1900, introduced the leg-extended style of hurdling.

■ Marie Provaznikova of the 1948 Czech gymnastics team refused to return to her native country, becoming the first Olympic athlete to defect.

■ Cincinnati Reds shortstop Dave Concepcion was the first to bounce a throw, intentionally, on Astroturf from deep in the hole.

■ Florence Griffith Joyner unveiled her wildly colored, one-legged body suit at the Olympic trials at Indianapolis in 1988. Evelyn Ashford is acknowledged to have first popularized the full body suit.

■ R. C. Owens, San Francisco 49er receiver, is credited

with originating the "Alley Oop" play while he was a rookie in 1957. He would outjump defenders for passes lofted by quarterback Y. A. Tittle.

INNOVATIONS NAMED FOR THEIR INNOVATORS

■ Sweden's Ulrich Salchow, men's world figure skating champion from 1901–05 and 1907–11, originated the figure skating jump now called a "salchow," in which a skater takes off from the back inside edge of one skate, makes a complete turn in the air, and lands on the back outside edge of the opposite skate. Norwegian figure skater Axel Paulsen gave his name to the "axel," Alois Lutz his name to the "lutz," and American Dorothy Hamill her name to the "Hamill camel."

■ Along with figure skating, no sport so honors its own the way gymnastics does. American gymnast Bart Conner developed the "Conner spin" on the parallel bars, and Kurt Thomas the "Thomas flair" on the pommel horse. Japanese gymnast Mitsuo Tsukahara first performed the "Suk" vault—a backward 1½ somersault—in the 1972 Olympics. Haruhiro Yamashita executed the first handspring in a piked position off the vault in the 1964 Olympics, for which he received a perfect 10 from the Swiss judge. The move became known as a "yamashita."

■ Dick Fosbury introduced the "Fosbury Flop" high jump internationally at the 1968 Olympics, where he won the gold medal. His technique—jumping headfirst, and back to the ground—would become favored by most highjumpers in the world.

■ Pole vaulter Dave Volz was the first to steady the

bar with his hand as he went over, a technique now known as "volzing."

■ Heavyweight champion Muhammad Ali developed the "Ali shuffle," copied by a generation of quick-footed boxers.

JUST A FEW OF WAYNE GRETZKY'S NHL RECORDS

There is debate among fans of at least two of the four major sports over who was the best ever to play the game. In baseball, some argue for Babe, some for Ty, or Willie, or Shoeless Joe, if only he'd been allowed to play longer; and that doesn't even address the issue of who the best pitcher was (some might say Babe again, end of argument). In basketball, legitimate cases may be made for Russell, Wilt, Magic, Larry, Kareem, Jordan. In football, no one can really entertain a serious who's-the-best, no-if's-and's-or-but's discussion because each player's role is so specialized.

In hockey, no such ambiguity exists. The best player who ever picked up a stick and skated onto the ice is Wayne Gretzky. This is not to be dogmatic: Orr, Richard, Howe, Hull, Lemieux—all great, true. But Gretzky is without question the greatest: not only do the statistics bear this out, but in none of the other major sports is there a comparable case of a player who combined winning (both games and championships) and durability with individual statistics that were so profoundly out of kilter with anything that had gone before.

In honor of the man, just a few of the records that he holds or co-holds (through 1988–89):

Regular Season: (through November 13, 1989)

Most points, career:	1,872
Most assists, career:	1,225
Most three-or-more-goal games, career:	46
Most points, season:	215, in 1985–86
Most goals, season:	92, in 1981–82
Most assists, season:	163, in 1985–86
Most consecutive 40-or-more-goal seasons:	10
Most consecutive 100-or-more-point seasons:	10
Most shorthanded goals, season:	12, in 1983–84
Most assists, game:	7, accomplished three times (ties record)
Most goals in 50 games, from the start of a season:	61, in 1981–82
Longest consecutive point-scoring streak, from the start of a season:	51 games, 1983–84

Playoffs: (through 1988–89 playoffs)

Most points, career	274
Most goals, career:	86
Most assists, career:	188
Most three-goal-or-more games, career:	7
Most points, one year:	47, in 1985
Most assists, one year:	31, in 1988
Most shorthanded goals, one year:	3, in 1983
Most assists, one series:	14, in 1985
Most points, final series:	13, in 1988
Most goals, final series:	7, in 1985 (ties record)
Most assists, final series:	10, in 1988
Most assists, game:	6, in 1987
Most shorthanded goals, game:	2, accomplished twice (ties record)
Most points, period:	4, in 1987 (ties record)
Most assists, period:	3, accomplished five times (ties record)

Gretzky has also won the following coveted trophies and awards multiple times (through the 1988–89 season):

Art Ross (regular season scoring champion): 7 times

Hart (regular season MVP): 9 times

Conn Smythe (Stanley Cup MVP): 2 times

Lester B. Pearson (NHL's outstanding player

as selected by the players) 5 times

THE GREATEST MULTISPORT TALENTS

Bo Jackson is a multitalented athlete, starring as a slugger and outfielder for baseball's Kansas City Royals and as a running back for football's L.A. Raiders. But others have had such success in two, and even more, sports.

■ Althea Gibson, #1 in the world in tennis in 1957–58, later played on the women's golf tour. Ellsworth Vines became one of the top 15 golfers in America after leaving the tennis tour in 1939.

■ Amos Alonzo Stagg is the only man in both the Pro Football and Basketball Halls of Fame. Besides his many contributions to football, he played in the first public basketball game on March 11, 1892, organized the University of Chicago National Interscholastic Basketball Tournament in 1917, and established basketball at the University of Chicago.

■ Cal Hubbard is the only man in both the Baseball and Pro Football Halls of Fame. He was a star NFL lineman (1927–33, 1935–36) and an American League umpire (1936–51).

■ Lottie Dod, five-time Wimbledon singles champion, represented England in field hockey in 1899, won the British Ladies Golf Championship in 1904, and won an Olympic silver medal for archery in 1908.

■ Mildred "Babe" Didrickson Zaharias was an All-America basketball player, took the silver medal in the high jump and gold medals in the javelin throw and 80m hurdles in the 1932 Olympics (in track and field, she held or tied world records in the javelin, the 80m hurdles, the high jump, and the long jump), won 31 golf championships, including 10 majors, and held the women's world record for the longest throw of a baseball (296 feet). She got her nickname for hitting five home runs in a baseball game. She was also a superior diver, roller skater, boxer, bowler, and tennis player.

■ Jim Thorpe starred in pro football, played major league baseball, and won the decathlon and pentathlon gold medals at the 1912 Olympics. If that wasn't enough, he won the 1912 intercollegiate ballroom dancing championship.

■ Three years after winning the U.S. Amateur golf title in 1909, Robert Gardner broke the world pole vault record, becoming the first man to clear 13 feet.

■ Vic Janowicz, 1950 Heisman Trophy winner, played major league baseball, as did 1953 Heisman runner-up Paul Giel.

■ In 1976, Sheila Young held world titles simultaneously in two sports: she won the Olympic 500m speedskating gold medal (as well as a speedskating silver and bronze) and a world title in cycling.

■ Golfing great Jack Nicklaus, fishing off the Australian coast in the early 1980s, caught what was then the fourth-largest blue marlin ever taken, weighing 1,358 pounds.

■ Michael Carter, All-Pro nose guard for the San Francisco 49ers, won the silver medal in the 1984 Olympic shot put.

■ Edward Eagan won the light-heavyweight boxing gold medal in 1920, and the four-man bobsled gold in 1932. He is the only person to win gold medals in both the Summer and Winter Olympics.

■ Earl Quigley coached 18 consecutive boys' state high school track titles in Arkansas. His football teams were 134-61-12 and won seven state titles. His basketball teams won 306, lost 95, and won six state titles. His baseball teams were 207-37 and won nine state titles. He won 40 state titles overall.

■ Seven Pro Football Hall of Famers played in the major leagues, including Ernie Nevers and George Halas.

■ Tennis star Jaroslav Drobny won a silver medal as a member of Czechoslovakia's 1948 Olympic hockey team.

■ Oregon State's Terry Baker, 1962 Heisman Trophy winner and #1 pick in the 1963 NFL draft, played starting guard in the NCAA basketball Final Four in 1963.

■ Baltimore Orioles outfielder Phil Bradley was the Big Eight passing leader for three years, 1978 through 1980, while at the University of Missouri.

■ Olympic heptathlete and long-jumper Jackie Joyner-Kersee was a starter on UCLA's basketball team. Olympic swimmer Matt Biondi was co-captain of the University of California's water polo team.

■ Major league pitchers Bob Gibson and Ferguson Jenkins both played for the Harlem Globetrotters.

■ NFL tight end Russ Francis's high school javelin record (254'11") lasted from 1971 to 1988.

■ Golfer Hale Irwin was an All–Big Eight defensive back in football for Colorado in 1965 and 1966.

■ On November 8, 1968, Don Gullett, future major league pitcher, scored 72 points in a football game for South Shore (McKell, Kentucky) High School—seventh all-time scoring performance in high school history.

■ Former major league player and manager Alvin Dark led LSU in passing and rushing in 1942. His play pushed Steve Van Buren, a future star running back in the NFL, into the role of blocking back.

■ As a youngster, major leaguer Lee Mazzilli won eight national speedskating championships.

■ Dallas Cowboys defensive lineman Ed "Too Tall" Jones was 6-0 as a professional boxer in 1979.

■ Deion Sanders scored an NFL touchdown and hit a major league home run in the same week, in September 1989. Jim Thorpe accomplished the same feat in both 1917 and 1919.

■ Football legend Jim Brown is considered one of the greatest lacrosse players of all time.

STAYING POWER

Some examples of extraordinary stamina and conditioning in sports:

■ For the 1961–62 season, Wilt Chamberlain averaged 48.5 minutes per game—*more* than a full regulation game per game. That year, he played in 79 complete games (including overtime games). For his career, Chamberlain averaged 45.8 minutes per game.

■ Baltimore Orioles shortstop Cal Ripken's 8,243 consecutive-innings streak is the longest in major league history. It started on June 5, 1982, and ended September 14, 1987.

■ For each of the seven seasons from 1955–56 through 1961–62, goalie Glenn Hall played 4,200 minutes—every minute of every game.

■ Jack Taylor of the Chicago Cubs and St. Louis Cardinals threw 188 consecutive complete games from 1901–06. He also made 15 relief appearances during the streak, finishing each game; thus, he went 203 consecutive appearances without being relieved. The Brooklyn Dodgers finally knocked him out in the third inning of a game on August 12, 1906.

■ Pitcher George Zabel of the 1915 Chicago Cubs finished one game with 18⅓ innings of relief.

Chief Bender completed all but one of his 10 World Series starts.

■ The New York Rens, an all-black basketball team that was formed in 1922, were renowned for their stamina and never called a time-out.

■ In a 1909 fight in Paris, heavyweight Joe Jeannette was knocked down 27 times but still beat Sam McVey in the 49th round.

STAYING POWER II: SPORTS FIGURES WHO EXCELLED WHEN THEY WERE YOUNG AND EXCELLED WHEN THEY WERE NOT SO YOUNG

■ In 1972, 16-year-old Ulrike Meyfarth of West Germany won the Olympic high jump to become the youngest individual track gold medal winner ever. Twelve years later, in 1984, she won the gold again to become the oldest Olympic high jump winner ever.

■ C. Alphonso Smith won the U.S. National Boys tennis title in Chicago on August 14, 1924. Fifty-five years later, in August of 1979, he won the National 70-and-over title, in Santa Barbara, California.

■ Ty Cobb and Rusty Staub both hit homers as teenagers and in their forties.

■ Gene Upshaw played in Super Bowls in three decades— II, in 1968; XI, in 1977; and XV, in 1981.

■ Al Unser, Sr. first won the Indianapolis 500 in 1970 and, most recently, in 1987.

■ Bucky Harris managed World Series winners 23 years apart.

■ Willie Mays has the longest stretch between MVP seasons, 11 years, winning the award in 1954 and 1965. He also hit 50 home runs in a season 10 years apart.

■ Ken Rosewall won his two U.S. championship singles titles 14 years apart, and his first and last Australian Championships 19 years apart.

■ Gary Player won golf tournaments in the 1950s, 1960s, 1970s, and 1980s.

■ Texas lineman K. L. Berry lettered in 1912, 1914, and 1915. He left school for military service, then returned to win All-SWC honors in 1924, at age 31.

■ Betty Richey was a U.S. Women's Lacrosse Association All-America for 22 straight years, from 1933 to 1954.

■ Dick Weber is the first professional bowler to win major championships in four decades.

■ Pete Sheehy was the New York Yankees clubhouse man for 60 years, from Babe Ruth through Don Mattingly.

THAT MISSING SOMETHING: 22 GREATS AND THE MILESTONES THEY NEVER ACHIEVED THAT YOU'D THINK THEY WOULD HAVE

■ Kathy Whitworth, the winningest golfer on the LPGA Tour, never won the U.S. Open.

■ Ken Rosewall never won Wimbledon, and neither did Pancho Gonzales.

■ Jim Ryun, nine-time holder of the world record in the mile, never won an Olympic gold medal. Mary Decker never won an Olympic medal.

■ Man O' War never ran in the Kentucky Derby.

■ Maurice Richard never led the NHL in scoring.

■ Willie Mays never led the league in runs batted in.

■ Pelé was never the leading goal scorer in a given World Cup.

■ Hall of Famers Nap Lajoie, Ernie Banks, Luke Appling, Harry Heilmann, George Sisler, and Ralph Kiner never played in a World Series game.

■ Tom Watson and Arnold Palmer never won the PGA.

■ Sam Snead never won the U.S. Open.

■ Nolan Ryan has never won a Cy Young Award.

■ Neither Bjorn Borg nor Evonne Goolagong ever won the U.S. Open, losing four finals each.

■ Joe Namath was never an All-America.

LIVING LEGENDS

The following athletes have been honored in ways usually reserved for athletes who have passed away, or at least were very ill.

■ Tennis player Billie Jean King has a mountain in the Catskills named for her.

■ Former Negro League legend James "Cool Papa" Bell lived on James Cool Papa Bell Avenue in St. Louis, Missouri.

■ The name of the tournament played on Sam Snead's home course in White Sulphur Springs, West Virginia, was eventually changed from the Greenbrier Open to the Sam Snead Festival.

■ After Pelé's great debut at age 17 in the 1958 World Cup, in which he scored two goals against Sweden in the finals to help his country to victory, European clubs offered the Brazilian star huge sums to play for them. However, the Congress of Brazil stepped in and declared Pelé an official national treasure and forbade his sale or trade.

■ Boston Celtic and native Hoosier Larry Bird has not one but two streets named for him in Indiana: Larry Bird Avenue in Terre Haute, and Larry Bird Boulevard in French Lick, his hometown.

■ Special "living legend" commendation to a dead person: Athletic superstar Jim Thorpe was buried in a Pennsylvania town, Mauch Chunk, that agreed to change its name to Jim Thorpe in exchange for his body.

BEYOND 60 + 714:
SOME LESSER-KNOWN FACTS ABOUT, AND RECORDS HELD BY BABE RUTH

■ He is the only starting pitcher in World Series history to bat anywhere but ninth in the order.

■ On May 6, 1915, he hit his first major league home run. On May 7, 1915, a German submarine sank the *Lusitania*.

■ Until 1931, or for the first 17 years of his career, a ball that bounced over the fence—what would today be a ground-rule double—counted as a home run. Although none of his record 60 home runs in 1927 is believed to have bounced over the fence, there is no way of telling how many of his career total were of this variety. To his credit, however, sluggers of his era, until 1920, were disadvantaged by a now-defunct rule that stated that any ball that cleared the fence fair but landed in the stands in foul ground was considered foul. Today, such a hit would be ruled a home run.

■ He pitched the longest complete game, 14 innings, in World Series history, in 1916.

■ Despite popular belief, he was not an orphan. His parents felt that he needed guidance and discipline, and in 1902 enrolled him in St. Mary's Industrial School for Boys, a reform school.

■ Along with fellow Yankee Bob Meusel, he was fined his World Series share of $3,500 and suspended in the fall of 1921 by baseball commissioner Kenesaw Landis for barnstorming after the World Series over Landis's objections. The two players were reinstated on May 20, 1922.

■ He was the first major athlete to endorse Jockey, famed today for Jim Palmer's underwear ads.

■ He won his last nine decisions as a pitcher, spread out over 15 years. His last pitching appearance was a 1933 complete-game victory over the Boston Red Sox.

■ The "Baby Ruth" candy bar, which made its appearance in 1917, was named *not* after him but after Ruth Cleveland, the daughter of President Grover Cleveland.

■ On September 5, 1914, he hit his first and only minor

league home run, for Providence of the International League.

■ In 1923, he stole 17 bases but was caught stealing 21 times.

■ In 1918, he hit all 11 of his home runs on the road.

■ He co-holds the record for shutouts in a season by an American League left-hander with nine, in 1916.

■ He pitched in 10 seasons, and had a winning record in every one of them.

■ The last man to pinch-hit for him was Ben Paschal in the 1927 season opener. Babe had been 0-for-3 that day, with two strikeouts. Paschal singled.

■ In his final major league at-bat, he grounded out to Philadelphia Phillies first baseman Dolf Camilli. The pitcher was Jim Bivin, the date May 30, 1935, the place Baker Bowl.

■ Of all pitchers in history with 15 or more wins over the New York Yankees, the one with the best won-lost percentage against them, with a sparkling 17 victories and just 5 defeats, is, of course, Babe Ruth.

CHRONIC WINNERS: RIDICULOUSLY SUCCESSFUL SPORTS FIGURES

Professional and Olympic athletes are, by definition, winners; they got where they are by beating out many others for the privilege. But some athletes, to paraphrase Orwell, are more victorious than others.

This list includes those who are addicted to winning—wherever they go, and often.

■ Ken Morrow went straight from the 1980 Olympic gold medal–winning hockey team to four straight Stanley Cup titles with the New York Islanders, from 1980 to 1983.

■ Bill Bradley was a Rhodes Scholar, a College Player of the Year, a Final Four MVP, a first-round draft pick, a two-time NBA world champion, a best-selling author, and victorious on the only two occasions that he has run for public office, the U.S. Senate.

■ Otto Graham was the first player chosen by the new AAFC pro football league, played on all four championship Cleveland Brown teams during the league's four-year tenure, then joined the NFL, where he led his team to the title game six out of their first six years, winning it all in his first year (and in two later years), and was elected to the Pro Football Hall of Fame. He was also a basketball All-America and played in the NBL (precursor to the NBA).

■ Lew Alcindor, later Kareem Abdul-Jabbar, led his Power Memorial (New York) High School team to a 79-2 record, his UCLA freshman team to a 21-0 record, the UCLA varsity to three consecutive NCAA titles, the Milwaukee Bucks to their first and only NBA championship, and the Los Angeles Lakers to five more NBA titles. He was the most sought-after player out of high school, twice College Player of the Year, the #1 draft choice out of college, and he won six NBA MVP Awards and two NBA playoff MVP Awards.

■ Anyone associated with the New York Yankees in their glory years was bound to find himself on at least one winner. Some of the timelier Yankees include Yogi Berra, who played on a record 10 championship teams; Casey Stengel, who managed 10 pennant-winning teams, also a record; Billy Martin, whose first six years with the team led to the American League pennant; and Joe DiMaggio, each of whose first four years with the Yankees resulted in a World Series ring.

◾ Bill Russell played on two national championship teams at the University of San Francisco, where he led a 55-game winning streak, played on the U.S. Olympic gold medal basketball team, and won 11 titles in 13 years with the Boston Celtics, including eight straight from 1959–66.

Magic Johnson, Billy Thompson, and Henry Bibby also went straight from NCAA title teams to NBA championships.

◾ The three biggest medal winners at the Olympics (for events that are still contested today) are Russian gymnast Larissa Latynina, with nine golds, five silvers, and four bronzes, the most in history; Finnish runner Paavo Nurmi, with nine golds and three silvers between 1920–28; and American swimmer Mark Spitz, with nine golds, one silver, and one bronze.

◾ Wide receiver Lynn Swann played in the Rose Bowl with USC in 1973 and 1974, then in the Super Bowl with the Pittsburgh Steelers in 1975 and 1976 (as well as in 1979 and 1980).

◾ Bobby Knight played on the 1960 Ohio State NCAA championship team, coached Indiana to the NCAA title in 1976, 1981, and 1987, the NIT title in 1979, and coached the U.S. Olympic team to gold in 1984.

◾ In 1989, 12-year-old Chris Drury starred for the Greater Bridgeport (Connecticut) Youth Hockey Team, which won the U.S. Amateur American Hockey Championship in April. Five months later he pitched a complete-game victory to lead his Trumbull baseball team to an upset over Taiwan in the Little League World Series.

◾ Henri Richard played on 11 Stanley Cup champions with the Montreal Canadiens. Jean Beliveau played on 10.

◾ Gene Conley played for the 1957 World Series champion Milwaukee Braves and the 1959, 1960, and 1961 NBA champion Boston Celtics.

OVERSHADOWED: THE 23 MOST PROMINENT— THAT IS, NEGLECTED— SECOND BANANAS OF ALL TIME

This list is dedicated to the second most-watched basketball team in history, the Washington Generals. With that kind of exposure, they should be household names, but they have the honor of having played—and lost— thousands of games all over the world and almost anonymously to the *most*-watched and colorful basketball team in history, the Harlem Globetrotters.

■ Notre Dame of Louisiana.

■ Wrigley Field in Los Angeles, torn down in 1966.

■ Harry Steinfeldt, the third baseman in the Chicago Cub's Tinker-to-Evers-to-Chance infield.

■ The London Prize Ring Rules, the principles that guided boxing before they were replaced by the Marquis of Queensberry Rules in 1865.

■ Indiana University of Pennsylvania, located in Indiana, Pennsylvania.

■ Klaus Beer's 26'10½" Olympic silver medal–winning long jump in 1968.

■ Dallas Smith, the main Boston Bruin defensive mate of Bobby Orr.

◪ Chicago Cub Bob Hendley's beautiful one-hitter on September 9, 1965, which was just good enough to lose to the perfect game of Los Angeles Dodgers pitcher Sandy Koufax.

◪ Parry O'Brien's May 1954 track and field world record (becoming the first to break 60 feet in the shot put), which was overshadowed by Roger Bannister's May 1954 track and field world record two days earlier (becoming the first to break the four-minute mile).

◪ The travel article that's always included in the *Sports Illustrated* swimsuit issue.

◪ The four at-bats that Cleveland Indian Vic Wertz had in Game 1 of the 1954 World Series—two singles, a double, and a triple—which were overshadowed by his other at-bat, a long fly ball that New York Giants centerfielder Willie Mays turned into a spectacular, over-the-shoulder out.

◪ 1970s Montreal Canadien goalie Bunny Larocque, co–Vezina Trophy winner with, and backup to, Ken Dryden, co–Vezina Trophy winner and starting Canadien goalie.

◪ Roger Maris's national high school record for most touchdowns scored on kickoff returns in a game (four, for Shanley High School in Fargo, North Dakota, in 1951), a record somewhat overshadowed by the single season home run record that he set with the New York Yankees.

◪ The 1959 NFL title game between the Baltimore Colts and the New York Giants, a rematch of their 1958 NFL title clash, the sudden-death contest that has been called "the most exciting football game ever played."

◪ The RBI single that New York Yankee Thurman Munson had nullified because there was pine tar too far up his bat handle, which is overshadowed by the home run that Kansas City Royal George Brett did—and then did not—have taken away for the same reason eight years later.

■ The 1981 Cincinnati Reds, who won more games than anyone in the National League that year but did not go to the playoffs because of the strike-format system for the postseason.

■ The two home runs, including the game-winner, hit by New York Yankee Lou Gehrig in a 1932 World Series game against the Chicago Cubs, forgotten in the wake of another home run hit that day, teammate Babe Ruth's "called shot."

■ Chicago Black Hawk Gus Bodnar's record for the fastest three assists in NHL history (21 seconds) at 6:09, 6:20, and 6:30 of the third period, March 23, 1952, against the New York Rangers. This record is overshadowed because with those three assists, Bodnar helped linemate Bill Mosienko to set a more prominent record, the fastest hat trick in NHL history.

■ The steroid-related disqualification and nullified world record of one Ben—American discus thrower Plucknett, who was banned indefinitely by the International Amateur Athletic Federation on July 13, 1981, when traces of anabolic steroids were found in his system—are overshadowed by those of another Ben—Canadian sprinter Johnson, whose 100m world record at the 1988 Olympics was nullified when he tested positive for Stanozolol, a steroid.

■ Larry Doby, the second black player in baseball's modern era after Jackie Robinson, and the second black manager after Frank Robinson.

■ Bernie Carbo's three-run, score-tying home run in Game 6 of the 1975 World Series, that enabled his Boston Red Sox teammate Carlton Fisk to hit his more famous extra-inning home run.

■ Catfish Metkovich, major league infielder, 1943–54.

■ UCLA's Brad Holland, the Los Angeles Lakers' *other* first-round pick in 1979.

10 GREAT COACHES AND MENTORS

■ Angelo Dundee trained nine world boxing champions: Carmen Basilio (welterweight), Willie Pastrano (light heavyweight), Ralph Dupas (light middleweight), Luis Rodriguez (welterweight), Sugar Ramos (featherweight), Muhammad Ali (heavyweight), Jimmy Ellis (heavyweight), José Napoles (welterweight), and Sugar Ray Leonard (welterweight).

■ At one time, Paul "Tony" Hinkle, a 49-year man at Indiana's Butler University as basketball coach and athletic director, had 55 protégés coaching basketball in the state.

■ Harry Hopman was the non-playing captain of the Australia Davis Cup team that won 16 Cups between 1939–67. (The Cup was not contested from 1940–45.)

■ Romanian gymnastics coach Bela Karolyi coached Nadia Comaneci to seven perfect 10s and a gold medal–winning performance at the 1976 Olympics. Karolyi later defected to the United States and fashioned another gold medal–winning performer out of Mary Lou Retton, at the 1984 Olympics.

■ Charlie Lau, a marginal major leaguer with a lifetime .255 batting average, was the hitting guru for George Brett.
    Walt Hriniak, who played for just two years in the majors, was instrumental in the success of perennial American League batting champion Wade Boggs.

■ Italian Carlo Fassi coached Peggy Fleming, as well as both Dorothy Hamill and John Curry, the women's and men's figure skating champions at the 1976 Innsbruck Olympics.

■ In the 1980s, Aaron Krickstein, Andre Agassi, Carling Bassett, Jimmy Arias, and Monica Seles were all products of Nick Bollettieri's tennis academy in Florida.

■ In 27 years as UCLA's basketball coach, John Wooden compiled a 620-147 record and won 10 national titles, including seven in a row from 1967–73. He coached 24 first-team All-Americas and presided over UCLA's NCAA record 88-game winning streak. In Wooden's last 12 years, the Bruins were 335-22.

■ Horse trainer Michael Dickson saddled the first five finishers in the 1985 Cheltenham Gold Cup.

And two great coaching chains:
Curly Lambeau, who later bought the Green Bay Packers, was the high school football coach of Jim Crowley, who became one of the "Four Horsemen" at Notre Dame under Knute Rockne. Later, as the football coach at Fordham, Crowley would coach "The Seven Blocks of Granite," including Vince Lombardi, who would, in turn, go on to become a coaching legend at Green Bay.

In the autumn of 1890 in Springfield, Massachusetts, James Naismith, the founder of basketball, played center on the first organized football team under Amos Alonzo Stagg, the founder of football.

15
CURIOSITIES

ONE DOZEN OF THE STUPIDEST IDEAS IN SPORTS

■ *Color-coordinated uniforms.* In 1882, the color of a baseball player's cap and shirt signified his position: pitchers wore blue, catchers scarlet, shortstops maroon, leftfielders white, rightfielders gray, and the other positions a combination of two colors. A team could only be told apart by its socks. The idea fizzled when someone realized that you could tell a player's position by where he stood on the field.

■ *Using reverse psychology.* Already behind 28-0 to Georgia Tech in a 1916 game, Cumberland College opted to kick off instead of receive in the hope that its defense could pin Tech deep in its own territory. Tech returned the ensuing kickoff 70 yards to the Cumberland 10, scored yet again, and continued on its way to registering the worst rout in the history of college football, 222-0.

■ *Messing with tradition.* The NBA tried a 12-foot basket in a March 7, 1954 game between Minneapolis and Milwaukee, and just as soon abandoned that for the traditional 10-foot basket. This desire to change the scope of the game had precedent. For the first Olympic basketball competition, in 1936, the International Basketball Federation passed a rule banning all players taller than 6'3". The United States objected and the rule was withdrawn.

■ *Eyeglasses for horses.* Legendary horse owner Colonel Edward Riley Bradley tried to fit eyeglass blinkers on a nearsighted racehorse. When the blinkers were fitted over the horse's head, the horse panicked, tossed the rider, and ran off.

■ *Overdoing a good thing*. From 1959–62, baseball held two All-Star games a year.

■ *Overzealousness*. In 1923, the town of Shelby, Montana guaranteed to put up $300,000 to stage a fight between heavyweight Jack Dempsey and Tommy Gibbons. The fight attracted only 7,202 paid customers and the town went bankrupt.

■ *Strange baseballs*. Because of the rubber shortage during World War II, the major leagues experimented in 1943 with Balata, a rubber substitute around the core of the baseball (the same material that covers most golf balls). Balata substantially reduced the ball's resiliency: by April 29, the entire American League had hit just two home runs. By May 9, Balata balls were no longer shipped. The major leagues also tried yellow baseballs for one game, an August 2, 1938 contest between the Brooklyn Dodgers and the St. Louis Cardinals, and that was that.

■ *Ice hockey in Florida*. The World Hockey Association awarded a franchise to Miami, the Screaming Eagles, and the team even held a press conference in February 1972 to introduce goalie Bernie Parent. But the team failed to obtain a building permit for a suitable arena and never actually played a game.

■ *Overextending yourself*. Dave Rowe, an outfielder in the 1870s and 1880s, tried pitching a game in 1882. He went the distance, giving up 29 hits and 35 runs.

■ *Coaching by committee*. In 1961 and 1962, the Chicago Cubs' experimental "Council of Coaches," in which several coaches rotated as manager, produced no geniuses. In 1961, the winningest coach had a percentage of .442. In 1962, coach Lou Klein, who managed wins in 40 percent of his games, was the most successful.

■ *Consolation prizes*. From 1960 to 1970, the losers of the NFL conference finals played in the NFL Playoff Bowl—known colloquially as the "Third Place Bowl." The consolation game to determine third place at the NCAA basketball Final Four was abolished in 1981.

■ *Marine life as part of a fashion statement*. Former Pittsburgh Steelers running back John "Frenchy" Fuqua, a noted clotheshorse, once wore platform shoes with see-through heels. The heels were filled with water and goldfish.

THE MOST NOTABLE DRAFT ODDITIES

■ The Boston Celtics drafted former University of Indiana star Landon Turner in the 10th round of the 1982 NBA draft. Turner had been paralyzed in a car accident eight months before but had expressed a lifelong dream to be drafted by the Celtics.

■ In 1983, the Philadelphia 76ers used their 10th-round pick to select Norman Horvitz, a 50-ish doctor who worked for 76ers owner Harold Katz's Nutri-Systems, Inc.

■ At the player draft for the short-lived National Bowling League in July 1960, New York Yankees Mickey Mantle and Yogi Berra were selected.

■ In 1986, Bo Jackson was the #1 pick of the NFL Tampa Bay Buccaneers, the fourth-round pick of baseball's Kansas City Royals, and the fifth-round pick of the Continental Basketball Association's Savannah Spirits.

■ In 1977, Lucille Harris of Delta State was drafted in the seventh round by the New Orleans Jazz, the only woman ever drafted in NBA history.

■ In 1981, the Chicago Bulls spent their 10th-round pick on Ken Easley, a UCLA defensive back with only one year of JV basketball experience and a future star for the NFL Seattle Seahawks. In 1984, the Bulls drafted track star Carl Lewis in the 10th round.

■ In 1977, the NBA's Kansas City Kings drafted Bruce Jenner in the seventh round.

■ The Atlanta Hawks apparently have scouts with a sense of humor. In 1987, the Hawks drafted Song Tao of China in the third round; Theo Christodoulou of Greece in the fourth round; Jose-Antonio Montero of Spain in the fifth round; Ricardo Morandoti of Italy in the sixth round; and Franjo Arapovic of Yugoslavia in the seventh round. The Hawks did not sign any of them.

■ The Pittsburgh Steeler team that won the NFL championship in 1980 is the only Super Bowl squad made up entirely of players who had never played for another team: thirty-nine of the players had been Steeler draft picks, and six others had been free agents right out of school.

■ In 1955, the Los Angeles Rams drafted K. C. Jones of the University of San Francisco in the 30th round. Jones was also drafted by the Boston Celtics and opted for a basketball career. In 1983, Jones became coach of the Celtics. His counterpart on the opposing sidelines for several NBA Finals, Los Angeles Lakers coach Pat Riley, had also opted for a career playing and coaching basketball, not football. Riley had been drafted out of the University of Kentucky by the Dallas Cowboys in the 11th round in 1967.

■ In 1989, soccer player Simon Keith was the first player chosen overall in the Major Indoor Soccer League draft, by the Cleveland Crunch, three years and a day after undergoing a heart transplant.

■ In 1987, the MISL's Tacoma Stars drafted University of Oklahoma linebacker Brian Bosworth.

■ The 1966 Michigan State University football team produced four of the first eight picks in the 1967 NFL-AFL draft. Five players from the University of Southern California were taken in the first round of the 1968 NFL-AFL draft. In 1984, 17 University of Texas players were chosen in the NFL draft.

■ In 1981, Vic Sison was drafted by the New Jersey Nets in the 10th round. He was the head student-manager at UCLA when Nets coach Larry Brown was there.

13 EXAMPLES OF BAD TIMING, ROTTEN LUCK, AND GENERALLY BAD KARMA

■ Harriet Quimby was the first woman to fly across the English Channel but she received virtually no publicity for the achievement. She had taken off on April 16, 1912, at 5:00 A.M. Soon after, the details of another event—the April 14th sinking of the *Titanic*—reached the world, obscuring Quimby's accomplishment.

■ Because of a sore arm, Philadelphia Phillies starting pitcher Wayne LaMaster left his May 5, 1938 game against the Chicago Cubs after making just three pitches, for a 2-1 count on Stan Hacker, the leadoff batter. Relief pitcher Tommy Reis walked Hacker, the walk was charged to LaMaster, as was the run that he scored, as was the loss, a 21-2 wipeout by the Cubs.

■ Javelin thrower Bruce Kennedy was kept out of the 1972 and 1976 Olympics when his country, Rhodesia—now Zimbabwe—was banned. In 1977, Kennedy became a U.S. citizen, qualified for the 1980 Olympic team, and was kept out for a third time by the U.S. Olympic boycott. In 1980, Zimbabwe was allowed to compete.

■ Bill Bevens, Al Gionfriddo, and Cookie Lavagetto—three of the pivotal performers in the 1947 World Series between the New York Yankees and the Brooklyn Dodgers—never played in a major league game after that Series.

■ Here is what has happened to just a few members of the 1969 "Miracle" New York Mets: first baseman Donn Clendenon pleaded guilty to a charge of cocaine possession, catcher Jerry Grote served time in jail for cattle-sale fraud, outfielder Cleon Jones received a suspended sentence for forging checks, and reliever Jack DiLauro joined a California commune in 1970 and has not been heard from since.

■ In 1985, Johnnie LeMaster played for three last-place teams—the San Francisco Giants, the Pittsburgh Pirates, and the Cleveland Indians.

■ Jim Perry was the losing pitcher in three of the four no-hitters pitched in the American League from the 1970 All-Star Game through the 1973 All-Star Game.

■ Three members of the U.S. gold medal–winning four-man bobsled team in 1932 died within a one-year period starting in 1940.

■ In 1978, California Angels outfielder Lyman Bostock was accidentally shot to death in Gary, Indiana, while riding in a car with a childhood friend, among others. The friend's estranged husband had been shooting at her. (He was later found not responsible by reason of insanity.)

■ Ron Hansen is the only man to play in the last game in the history of both the original and the second Washington Senator franchises, in 1960 and 1971. (In both cases, Hansen played against the Senators.)

■ Gary Davidson was involved in the formation of the WFL, the ABA, and the WHA—all defunct leagues.

■ Jim Weaver pitched for the 1931 New York Yankees and was then demoted to the minors. In 1932, the Yankees won the pennant. In 1934, Weaver pitched for the Chicago Cubs. After the season, he was traded to the Pirates; in 1935, the Cubs won the pennant. In 1939, Weaver pitched early in the year for the Cincinnati Reds before being let go. That season, the Reds won the pennant.

■ Heavyweight Jack Johnson, financially strained, finally landed a profitable fight to defend his title against Frank Moran in Paris. Johnson triumphed in the June 27, 1914 bout. The following day, news of the assassination of Austrian archduke Francis Ferdinand—the catalyst for the outbreak of World War I—reached Paris. In the ensuing chaos, Johnson never collected his purse.

7 SPORTS SUPERSTITIONS AND JINXES

■ Starting on April 15, 1952, when a Detroit fan flung an octopus onto the ice and the Red Wings went on to win the Stanley Cup, an octopus has been tossed onto the ice during every Detroit Red Wings playoff series.

■ For every game for three years, a man named Charles "Victory" Faust warmed up for the New York Giants baseball team because manager John McGraw thought Faust brought luck.

■ A prevailing theory states that when one of the original

NFL teams wins the Super Bowl, the stock market will be up for the year, and when a team from the old AFL wins, the stock market will be down. This theory has held true 23 years in a row.

■ Another stock market theory holds that, on a daily basis, when the New York Mets win, the stock market falls; when they lose, it goes up.

■ Under Connie Mack, the 1911–14 Philadelphia Athletic mascot was a good luck hunchback named Louis Van Zelst.

■ A baseball superstition says that whichever World Series team has the most ex–Chicago Cubs on its roster will lose the Series.

■ Perhaps the most renowned superstition in sports is the "*Sports Illustrated* cover jinx," which suggests that to appear on the cover of the magazine is to be doomed to disaster. While it is true that no one makes note of the numerous cases in which a cover boy or girl does *not* run into bad luck, it is also true that, to cite just a few cases, skier Jill Kinmont, the January 31, 1955 cover girl, broke her back and was paralyzed in an accident that week in the Snow Cup Giant Slalom race in Alta, Utah; that the Chicago Cubs began perhaps their most famous collapse after third baseman Ron Santo appeared on the June 30, 1969 cover; and that after Magic Johnson appeared on the June 4, 1984 cover, the Los Angeles Lakers not only lost in the NBA Finals to the Boston Celtics in seven games, but did so after they had a one game to none lead, and the lead and the ball with only 15 seconds left in Game 2 (which they lost); and a five-point lead with 56 seconds left in Game 4 (which they lost). Even the series MVP, Larry Bird, was surprised by the turn of events. "To be honest, they should have swept," he said.

HUH?:
A DOZEN SPORTS THINGS WE SIMPLY
DON'T UNDERSTAND

Certain profound mysteries in sports baffle us—why, for example, pitchers who have runners on first and third base fake a throw to third and then wheel around to try to catch the runner on first napping. We have never seen this ploy work in hundreds of attempts, and if you have, we'd rather not know about it.

Why do many major league hitters check their swing on 3-0?

Why do sportswriters think they should tell us who in football to bet on—and who to BEST BET on—when their records against the spread are always under .500?

What kind of a doctor *is* Jerry Buss, anyway?

Why do defensive linemen taunt quarterbacks whom they have just sacked when the lineman's team is losing 45-7 with three minutes to go?

Why do people compete in triathlons?

What follows is a collection of sports questions that mystify us. We don't understand, for example:

■ Why, on August 6, 1941, Al Benton became the only player ever to sacrifice-bunt twice in one inning—an inning in which the Detroit Tigers scored 11 runs.

■ Why the fittingly christened boxer, John Badman, lightweight fighter in the 1840s, changed his given name to Johnny Walker.

■ Why Cincinnati Red and Brooklyn Dodger catcher Bill Bergen, a .170 lifetime hitter, had an 11-year career.

■ Why the 1980 Olympic women's pair-oared shell (without coxswain) competition had two elimination heats and a repechage (a second-chance round) to trim the original field of six crews to five for the finals.

■ Why golfer Tommy Armour, who had just shot—or so everyone thought—a 22 on one hole at the 1927 Shawnee Open, claimed that it was really a 23.

■ Why infielder Larry Gardner of the Cleveland Indians continued to try to steal bases during the 1920 season, during which he was successful three times and was thrown out 20 times.

■ Why Harvey Johnson, who had coached the Buffalo Bills to a 1-10-1 record as interim coach in 1968, was rehired as interim coach in 1971. This time he went 1-13.

■ How the University of Michigan football team beat Ohio State, 9-3, in 1950 without making a first down.

■ Why pitcher Bill Gray of the Washington Senators was left in long enough to walk eight batters in one inning in a 1909 game.

■ Why the national high school record for the longest field goal is 68 yards (by Dirk Borgognone, Reno, Nevada, 1985), and the NFL record is only 63 yards (by Tom Dempsey, New Orleans Saints, 1970).

■ Why certain people in 1954 felt it necessary to honor basketball star Bobby McDermott, who had been voted nine years earlier "the greatest pro basketball player of all time," as "the greatest Fort Wayne Zollner Piston player of all time."

■ Steve Garvey Junior High School, in Lindsay, California.

400

10 GREAT SPORTS IRONIES

Isn't it ironic...

... that George S. Patton, the future U.S. Army general who placed fifth in the 1912 modern pentathlon, might have won had he not finished 21st out of 32 in the shooting competition?

... that Al Campanis, the shortstop for the Brooklyn Dodgers' Montreal farm team in 1946, the same year that Jackie Robinson made his professional debut as the team's second baseman, and who was one of Robinson's leading supporters and best friends on the team, should lose his job over his racist remarks in 1987 on "Nightline"?

... that Jim Thorpe, probably the greatest American athlete of the century, should be stripped of his Olympic 1912 decathlon and pentathlon gold medals for having played professionally the one sport at which he was truly mediocre—baseball? Thorpe, who played off and on from 1913–19, apparently could not hit the curveball and had a lifetime average of .252.

... that Ted Williams served for nearly two years and 39 missions in the Korean War without getting seriously injured, and then broke his collarbone on the first day of spring training after he came back?

... that Hank Aaron, first in career home runs—perhaps the most cherished of all baseball records—is the first player alphabetically in major league history?... and isn't it ironic that Kareem Abdul-Jabbar, first in career points—perhaps the most cherished of all basketball records—is second alphabetically in NBA history (behind Zaid Abdul-Aziz)? (As Lew Alcindor, he would have been 18th).

... that the 1972 Munich Olympic marathon champion, American Frank Shorter, was born in Munich? (His father had been a U.S. Army doctor there).

... that American Helen Stephens, who beat Stella Walsh in the 1936 Olympic 100m, was accused by a Polish journalist—falsely—of being a man, while Walsh, upon her death, was discovered to be a man?

... that Dickie Kerr, one of the clean Chicago White Sox players in 1919, should be suspended for three years (1923–25) for pitching against an outlaw team during a contract dispute?

... that running author and guru James Fixx, whose books helped fuel the jogging craze, died in Vermont on July 21, 1984, of a heart attack while jogging?

24 FACTS THAT YOU MIGHT EASILY HAVE FORGOTTEN OR NEVER KNEW

■ The jury in the 1919 Black Sox case found the players *not* guilty. It was baseball commissioner Judge Kenesaw Mountain Landis who decided to ban the accused players for life.

■ Soviet gymnast Olga Korbut finished seventh in the all-around competition at the 1972 Olympics.

■ Except for the 1925 Rose Bowl, Notre Dame did not play in bowl games until the 1969 Cotton Bowl.

■ Roger Maris was the American League MVP in 1960, the year *before* he hit his record 61 home runs (when he again won the MVP).

■ Pete Rozelle, the powerful former NFL commissioner who found great popularity among the owners, was not elected to that post until the 23rd ballot on January 26, 1960. At that time, Rozelle, 33 years old and the general manager of the Los Angeles Rams, emerged as the compromise candidate when owners became deadlocked between choosing acting commissioner Austin Gunsel or attorney Marshall Leahy.

▣ Jackie Robinson's first position with the Brooklyn Dodgers was first base. He played all of his 151 games there in 1947. The next year he moved to second base.

▣ Keith Jackson was in the booth for ABC Monday Night Football's first season, before Frank Gifford replaced him the next year.

▣ Lew Alcindor passed up the 1968 Olympics in support of the threatened black boycott of the Games.

▣ O. J. Simpson started his collegiate career at City College of San Francisco, a two-year college, before transferring to USC.

▣ Joe Theismann spent the first three seasons of his professional football career in the Canadian Football League, with the Toronto Argonauts.

▣ Mark Spitz was once considered an Olympic disappointment because he was predicted to win several gold medals in the 1968 Olympics and won only two, both in relays.

▣ For more than half of the Miami Dolphins' perfect 1972 season, quarterback Bob Griese was on the bench with a broken leg, and backup QB Earl Morrall led the team.

▣ The Celtics basketball team was founded not in Boston but in New York, in 1914. When the team was reorganized after World War I, they continued to be based in New York but called themselves the Original Celtics.

▣ Wayne Gretzky began his professional hockey career in 1978 with the Indianapolis Racers of the WHA.

▣ From 1966–72, Whitey Herzog, the former manager and heart and soul of the St. Louis Cardinals, was a vital part of the New York Mets organization, his major nemesis. Herzog served as third-base coach and special assistant to the general manager before being promoted to director of player development in September of 1967.

■ Tom Watson, the Los Angeles Lakers, and Ivan Lendl all used to be as well-known for their inability to win in the clutch as they were for their talent. Each shed their "choke" label and soon came to be known as much for their *ability* to win in the clutch as for their talent: Watson by capturing eight majors, several with magnificent charges on the final holes; the Lakers by dominating the 1980s with five NBA titles, including victories the last two times they faced their perennial rivals, the Boston Celtics; and Lendl by winning two Australian Opens, three French Opens, and three U.S. Opens (through the beginning of 1990).

■ Sandy Koufax was mediocre for the first half of his career.

■ The current New York Mets are the second major league incarnation of that club. The New York Metropolitans, or Mets, of the American Association played their first game in the original Polo Grounds and appeared in what was an early version of the World Series, in 1884.

■ Although Jerry West of the Los Angeles Lakers made that spectacular half-court, buzzer-beating, game-tying shot against the New York Knicks in Game 3 of the 1970 NBA Finals, the Knicks won the game in overtime.

■ Dick Vitale, the motor-mouthed announcer, was coach of the Detroit Pistons for the 1978–79 season and part of the following season, during which time he was 34-60.

■ Roger Bannister did not break the four-minute mile in an actual race. On May 6, 1954, he ran 3:59.4 while being carefully paced by rabbits Chris Brasher and Chris Chataway.

■ The jockey with the longest losing streak (110 straight defeats) in the history of American horse racing is Steve Cauthen.

10 THINGS IN SPORT THAT
YOU'LL RARELY, IF EVER, SEE

■ *A false start in the marathon.*

■ *A white heavyweight boxing champion.* Gerrie Coetzee, who held the WBA title from September 1983 through December 1984, is the only white champion in the last 30 years; Ingemar Johansson held the title from 1959–60.

■ *A black hockey player.* There have been half a dozen blacks in the NHL, the first of whom, Willie O'Ree, played in 1957–58 and the most prominent of whom is Edmonton Oilers goalie Grant Fuhr.

■ *The Cleveland Indians in a pennant race.* They have not finished within 10 games of first place in a nonstrike season since 1959, when they were second, five games behind the Chicago White Sox. They have finished first just three times since the turn of the century.

■ *A triple steal.* The last major league triple steal occurred on May 3, 1980, when Oakland Athletics Dwayne Murphy, Mitchell Page, and Wayne Gross accomplished it. There have been only five triple steals in the last 20 years.

■ *A southpaw catcher.* Since 1902, the major leagues have seen just three—the Chicago Cubs' Dale Long in 1958, the Chicago White Sox's Mike Squires in 1980, and the Pittsburgh Pirates' Benny Distefano in 1989.

■ *A goaltender score a goal.* Only three times in NHL history has a goalie been credited with a goal. Billy Smith of the New York Islanders had the first, in 1979, and Ron Hextall of the Philadelphia Flyers had the other two, one in 1987 and one in 1989, during the playoffs.

■ *A golfer miss a tournament because of a groin injury.*

■ *An American League pitcher hit a grand slam.* The last

to do so was Steve Dunning of the Cleveland Indians in 1971.

■ *A left-throwing, right-hitting baseball player.* Since 1876, approximately 35 such non-pitchers, including Rickey Henderson, have played in the major leagues.

20 OF THE MOST UNUSUAL COLLEGE MASCOTS

The most common team mascot in America is the Tigers. Next on the list are Bulldogs and Wildcats.

It is unlikely that the popularity of these team names will be challenged any time soon by the ones favored by the following colleges and universities.

Santa Cruz (California) Banana Slugs
Trinity Christian (Illinois) Trolls (and the Lady Trolls)
Evergreen State (Washington) College Geoducks
Alaska Southeast Humpback Whales (and the Lady Whales)
Southern Illinois Salukis
Washburn (Kansas) Ichabods
Simon Fraser (Burnaby, B.C., Canada) Clansmen
Pittsburgh State (Kansas) Gorillas (and the Gussies)
Coastal Carolina (S.C.) Chanticleers
South Dakota Tech Hardrockers
Hawaii-Loa Mongoose
Pomona Pitzer (California) Sagehens
Elon (North Carolina) Fightin' Christians (and the Lady Fightin' Christians)
Southeastern Oklahoma Savages (and the Savagettes)
Albany State (New York) Great Danes
Irvine (California) Anteaters
Southern Arkansas Muleriders (and the Riderettes)

Arkansas-Monticello Boll Weevils (and the Cotton
   Blossoms)
University of Tennessee-Chattanooga Moccasins
Oglethorpe (Georgia) Stormy Petrels

THE MOST INGRAINED MISNOMERS
IN SPORTS

The following names are unsuitable to the things
named, not that our pointing this out will stop anyone
from continuing to call them that.

■ *Foul pole*. A ball that hits the foul pole is fair.

■ *Boxing ring*. The traditional boxing stage is square, and
experiments on this standard have been infrequent and
unsuccessful. A circular ring was used in England in 1912
and in San Francisco in 1944 but did not catch on.

■ *Los Angeles Lakers*. There are no natural lakes in the
city of Los Angeles. The franchise name *was* appropriate
when the team, originally the Minneapolis Lakers, was
based in Minnesota, "Land of 10,000 Lakes."

■ *Madison Square Garden*. The latest and fourth version
of the New York City sports mecca is a good half mile
from Madison Square. MSG I was built at Madison Square—
26th Street and Madison Avenue—but was demolished in
1889. The current Garden is on Seventh Avenue, between
31st and 33rd Streets.

■ *Charley Winner*. Winner, a football coach, was 9-14 in
one-plus seasons as the New York Jet head coach in

1974–75, and 35-30-5 in five seasons as coach of the St. Louis Cardinals in 1966–70. His total was 44-44-5.

■ *The All-England championships*. The official name for Wimbledon belies not only the tournament's international field but also the infrequency of an English champion. An Englishman has not won the men's singles draw since Fred Perry did it in 1936, and only three Englishwomen have won the Wimbledon singles crown in the last half-century.

■ *Polo Grounds*. Polo was never played in the defunct stadium that opened in July of 1889 and became home to baseball and football's New York Giants and, for various and brief periods, the early New York Yankees and the New York Mets. Polo *had* been played at the original Polo Grounds at 110th Street and Sixth Avenue, which served as home park for the old New York Metropolitans and Giants from 1880–88.

■ *Utah Jazz*. Again, as with the Lakers, the name once fit—when the franchise was based in New Orleans, home of Dixie, incubator of jazz. The name was preserved even after the team relocated before the 1979–80 season to one of the most conservative states in the Union.

■ *Yankee Sullivan*. The bareknuckles heavyweight in the 1850s was actually a British fighter who toured America.

■ *The Bagel Twins*. The nickname for the pair of top-ranked diminutive American tennis players in the 1970s— Harold Solomon and Eddie Dibbs—was only half-wrong. Solomon is Jewish but Dibbs is of Lebanese descent.

■ The NBA *lifetime ban* for drug abusers. By lifetime, the league means two years, the period after which a multiple drug offender can apply for reinstatement.

NOTABLE LEAGUE COMMISSIONERS AND ASSORTED EXECUTIVES

■ Henry Kissinger became Chairman of the Board of the North American Soccer League (NASL) after the 1978 season.

■ In 1987, Hamilton Jordan, White House Chief of Staff under Jimmy Carter, was elected executive director for the Association of Tennis Professionals (ATP).

■ In 1951, General Douglas MacArthur was nominated to be commissioner of baseball but declined the candidacy.

■ It is not unusual to select former stars to head new leagues. Jim Thorpe was the first president of pro football's first league, the American Professional Football Association. (The APFA eventually became the NFL.)

■ Former Minneapolis Lakers great George Mikan was the first commissioner of the American Basketball Association (ABA).

■ The president of the Argentine World Cup organizing committee, retired general Omar Actis, was assassinated by left-wing guerillas on August 19, 1976.

■ Former basketball star Wilt Chamberlain was the commissioner of the International Volleyball Association in the late 1970s.

■ Former Los Angeles Rams quarterback Roman Gabriel is general manager of the Charlotte Knights in baseball's AA Southern League.

■ Former University of Michigan athletic director and football coach Bo Schembechler is president of baseball's Detroit Tigers.

■ Richard Nixon was chosen in October of 1985 to arbitrate a dispute between the Major League Umpires Association and the owners. Nixon ultimately decided to award umpires a 40 percent pay increase.

■ The NFL Los Angeles Rams advisory board includes Bob Hope, Henry Mancini, Maureen Reagan, Lord David Westbury, and Danny Thomas.

INTRIGUING TEAM OWNERS

■ Bing Crosby was a Pittsburgh Pirates minority owner from 1946 until his death in 1977.

■ Danny Kaye was one of a group of six that purchased the Seattle Mariners in 1976, and was involved with the team until 1981.

■ David Letterman became a Seattle Mariners minority owner in 1989.

■ Soccer player Giorgio Chinaglia, once a New York Cosmo, took controlling interest in the Cosmos by purchasing 60 percent of the team in July 1984, and held it until the team suspended operations in June 1985.

■ Pete Rose was part owner of the Major Indoor Soccer League's Cincinnati Kids. On December 22, 1978, he kicked out the first ball in the team's history.

■ Bob Hope, a Cleveland Indians minority owner, sold his interest in December of 1986. He was also part owner of the Los Angeles Rams in the 1950s and early 1960s before Dan Reeves purchased full interest in 1962.

■ George W. Bush, son of the President, became managing partner of the Texas Rangers in 1989.

■ Kansas City Royal George Brett and his brothers Ken, Bobby, and John have owned the Spokane Indians (minor league baseball team) of the Northwest League since 1986, and the Riverside Red Wave of the California League since 1988.

■ In 1975, Elton John became a part-owner of the Los Angeles Aztecs of the North American Soccer League. He was also part-owner of the Philadelphia Freedom of World Team Tennis.

SERIOUS TRIVIA:
39 THINGS WORTH KNOWING, LATE AT NIGHT, IN A BAR

■ The first Super Bowl was covered by CBS *and* NBC. They fought over who should cover it—CBS had rights to the NFC, NBC to the AFC—and finally decided that they would both do it.

■ In rhythmic gymnastics, exposure of bra straps is an automatic deduction.

■ Blacks played in the NFL from 1920–33, then not at all from 1934–45.

■ A false start in the 1904 Olympics resulted in a two-yard penalty.

■ Until 1938, records were not counted in hurdle events if any hurdles were knocked over.

■ In early auto races, including the Indianapolis 500, two people rode in the car: a driver and a mechanic. Also, relief drivers were routine at Indy.

411

■ Winners at the first modern Olympics in 1896 were presented with olive branches and *silver* medals, while runners-up received laurel boughs and bronze medals. Gold medals for winners were first awarded in 1900.

■ In the 1908 Olympic marathon in London, the route was the 26 miles from Windsor Castle to the Olympic Stadium, concluding with 385 yards around the stadium track so that the finish would be directly in front of the royal box of Queen Alexandra. The distance of 26 miles, 385 yards became standard for the marathon.

■ The first modern Olympic swimming competition was held outdoors in open water, in 1896, in the Bay of Zea, Greece.

■ There were no written rules forbidding blacks from playing professional baseball. In the last two decades of the 19th century, approximately 30 blacks played organized ball. In this century, the first one is Jimmy Claxton, who pitched briefly in 1916 for the Oakland Oaks in the Pacific Coast League.

■ Foul balls were not counted as strikes until 1901 in the National League and 1903 in the American League, except for foul bunts and foul tips.

■ Figure skating was part of the Summer Olympics until 1924, when the first Winter Olympics were staged.

■ During the Los Angeles Olympics in 1932, when the U.S. was in the midst of Prohibition, French team members were given special permission to drink wine because they argued that it was an essential part of their diet.

■ Former Minnesota Vikings coach Bud Grant, who led his team to four Super Bowls without winning, played on the NBA championship 1949–50 Minneapolis Lakers.

■ The Houston Astrodome had natural grass during its first season in 1965. In 1966, an Astroturf infield was put in, and later that year the outfield surface was changed.

■ Roger Maris received no intentional walks in 1961, the year that he hit a record 61 home runs. Batting behind him was Mickey Mantle, who hit 54 home runs that season.

■ In tennis doubles, if the server hits either opponent with a serve on the fly, the serving team gets the point.

■ There is a World Elephant Polo Association.

■ Bing Crosby is one of only seven golfers to get a hole-in-one at the 16th hole at Cypress Point, acing it in 1948. The hole is 180 yards across the Pacific Ocean.

■ In 1890, two legs of horse-racing's Triple Crown—the Belmont and the Preakness—were run on the same track, New York's Morris Park, on the same day, June 10.

■ The distance from home plate to second base is 127 feet 3⅜ inches.

■ The men's tennis tour has traveling chair umpires. The women's tour does not.

■ The Tour de France bicycle race used to include several legs of night riding.

■ The official baseball rulebook requires that a major league stadium built after June 1, 1958 must be a minimum distance of 325 feet from home to the nearest fence and a minimum of 400 feet from home to the center-field fence.

■ There was an Olympics in 1906, in between the 1904 and 1908 Games, called the Intercalated or Interim Games.

■ In 1952, all three medalists in the Olympic individual foil competition were left-handed.

■ If a greyhound catches the mechanical rabbit (because of mechanical failure), it's considered a "no race."

■ The maximum number of clubs that you are allowed to carry during a golf match is 14.

■ Jack Nicklaus played for Upper Arlington High School, whose nickname is the Golden Bears.

■ Before the institution of the NHL player draft, the Montreal Canadiens had the rights to sign any French-speaking player before any other team.

■ Boston Red Sox slugger Jim Rice once broke his bat in two on a checked swing.

■ On September 4, 1916, Mordecai Brown and Christy Mathewson, both future Hall of Famers, pitched against each other in what was the final major league game for each.

■ The first televised sporting event was of a college baseball game, in Japan in 1931.

■ In 1975, Houston Astros first baseman Bob Watson scored the one millionth run in major league history.

■ The winner of the second Boston Marathon, in 1898, was named Ronald McDonald.

■ The wind reading for Bob Beamon's world record long jump at the 1968 Olympics was 2.0 miles per second, the exact legal maximum.

■ David Thompson's 73 points in a 1978 game are the most scored in one NBA game by anyone not named Wilt Chamberlain.

■ The original suggested name for basketball was Naismith Ball.

■ In Auckland, New Zealand, on April 16, 1983, Kenya's Mike Boit ran the fastest mile ever—3:28.36, about 20 seconds faster than the world record. His time was not official because the course was downhill all the way.

16
THE ENDS

MEMORABLE VICTORY CELEBRATIONS

Victories—especially pennant-clinching, gold medal–winning, title belt–capturing victories—are followed by celebrations that have become familiar to all fans. Some of these images remain vivid and particular, others gather to form a tableau in the mind's eye: we have seen catchers jumping into pitchers' arms (Yogi Berra and Don Larsen after the latter's perfect game in the 1956 World Series), pitchers jumping into catchers' arms (Jerry Koosman and Jerry Grote after the New York Mets captured the 1969 World Series), countless football coaches raised on players' shoulders, Bjorn Borg dropping to his knees and looking heavenward after winning Wimbledon, the young Ali in half-snarl, standing over Sonny Liston after conquering him for the second time, the train snaking around the hockey rink with the Stanley Cup aloft, and an ocean of champagne, flowing in locker rooms of all kinds.

The following is a collection of the most memorable celebrations of sporting triumphs.

■ Jeff Float, an American swimmer who contracted viral meningitis at 13 months and lost 80 percent of the hearing in his right ear and 60 percent in his left ear, signed "I love you" on the victory stand at the 1984 Los Angeles Olympics after winning the gold medal for the 4x200m freestyle relay. During the relay final, the roar of the crowd was so great that he heard it for the first time in his life.

■ New York City has staged many ticker-tape parades for victorious athletes. The only parade ever given for a golfer honored Bobby Jones on his return from England after winning the 1930 British Open. New York also gave a ticker-tape parade in 1926 for 19-year-old Gertrude Ederle, the first woman to swim the English Channel.

■ After winning the Tournament Players Championship in 1982, golfer Jerry Pate took a dive into the lake at the 18th hole, after first pushing in PGA commissioner Deane Beaman and course architect Pete Dye.

■ After Luciano Giovannetti of Italy won the 1980 trap-shooting gold, he tossed his cap into the air and shot a hole through it.

■ Fathers and sons have been involved in many memorable celebrations. Captured in photographs that made newspapers all over the world, Australian tennis player Pat Cash ran into the crowd to hug his father after beating Ivan Lendl to win Wimbledon in 1987.

When swimmer Jean Boiteux of France won the 400m freestyle at the 1952 Olympics, his father leaped fully clothed into the water to embrace him.

Captured in a lasting television image right after the United States beat Finland to clinch the 1980 Olympic hockey gold medal, American goalie Jim Craig was seen skating around the Lake Placid rink and beyond the bedlam of his celebrating teammates to search out his father.

And after winning a gold medal at the 1984 Olympics, American cyclist Mark Gorski took his 13-month-old son Alexander on a victory lap.

■ Gabriella Dorio received a bath in wine from her husband after winning the Olympic 1,500m race in 1984.

■ After each New York Giants win in the 1986 season, including their culminating Super Bowl XXI victory over the Denver Broncos, several members of the Giants, led by linebacker Harry Carson, poured a bucket of Gatorade over head coach Bill Parcells. The ritual would be repeated countless times by countless other teams.

■ After knocking out Benny Paret, welterweight Emile Griffith did a headstand. Valerio Arri did three cartwheels after crossing the finish line to take third place in the 1920 Olympic marathon. Don Bragg let out a Tarzan yell after winning the 1960 pole vault.

■ Boxer Evander Holyfield was disqualified in the 1984 Olympics for throwing a late punch that knocked out his opponent. At the awards ceremony, gold medal winner Anton Josipovic of Yugoslavia pulled Holyfield up onto the gold medal platform with him.

■ In 1952, four women were allowed to participate in the equestrian dressage competition for the first time in Olympic history. One of them, Lis Hartel of Denmark, had to be helped on and off of her horse because she had been paralyzed below the knees from polio. She won the silver medal, and in a poignant scene, gold medalist Henri Saint Cyr of Sweden helped her up onto the victory platform. (Hartel won the silver again in 1956.)

THE MOST NOTABLE AND UNUSUAL RETIRED NUMBERS

One of the highest honors bestowed upon an athlete, outside of electing him to his sport's hall of fame, is retiring his number. Retiring numbers is an art more than a science, and unusual honorees and circumstances have marked these occasions.

■ The minor league Williamsport Bills retired the #59 that was worn by catcher Dave Bresnahan in 1988 to commemorate his most famous act as a player—firing a previously concealed potato past third base to trick a runner into coming home. "He's probably the only .149 hitter in baseball to ever have his jersey retired," said a team spokesman.

■ The Boston Celtics have retired the most numbers in basketball, 15. The New York Yankees have retired more numbers, 12, than any major league team, including every single-digit number except for 2 and 6, and several two-digit numbers. The Chicago Bears lead the NFL with 10 numbers, as well as "GSH" for the late founder and owner George Halas, and the Boston Bruins have retired seven numbers to lead the NHL. The Montreal Canadiens have eight players with retired numbers, but only six retired numbers: Jean Beliveau and Aurel Joliat both had their #4 retired, and Henri Richard and Elmer Lach both had their #16 retired.

■ Henri and Maurice Richard of the Montreal Canadiens are the only brothers in sports to have their numbers retired.

■ The Cincinnati Reds retired #5 for star catcher Johnny Bench in August of 1984. The Reds had also retired #5 when their backup catcher, Willard Hershberger, committed suicide in 1940. Apparently, it was not a permanent honor.

■ The Cleveland Browns retired #45, the number that 1961 Heisman Trophy winner and #1 draft choice Ernie Davis was supposed to wear for them but never did. He died of leukemia in 1963.

■ Several athletes have had their numbers retired by two teams:
   Casey Stengel's #37 by the New York Yankees and Mets
   Hank Aaron's #44 by the Atlanta Braves and the Milwaukee Brewers

418

Rod Carew's #29 by the Minnesota Twins and the California Angels

Julius Erving's #32 by the New Jersey Nets, and his #6 by the Philadelphia 76ers

Oscar Robertson's #14 by the Cincinnati Royals, and his #1 by the Milwaukee Bucks

Nate Thurmond's #42 by the Golden State Warriors and the Cleveland Cavaliers

Gordie Howe's #9 by the Detroit Red Wings and the Hartford Whalers

Bobby Hull's #9 by the Chicago Black Hawks and the Winnipeg Jets

No NFL player has had his number retired by more than one team.

▨ The NFL's Seattle Seahawks retired #12 to honor "The Twelfth Man," their fans. The NBA's Sacramento Kings retired #6 for their fans, "The Sixth Man."

▨ The New York Yankees retired #8, honoring at once Yogi Berra and Bill Dickey, their two greatest catchers.

▨ In 1939, the #4 worn by Lou Gehrig became the first number in the major leagues ever retired when the New York Yankees accorded him the honor.

▨ The Boston Celtics have retired #2 for mastermind and former coach Red Auerbach, #1 for Celtics founder Walter Brown, and the name "Loscy" for former player Jim Loscutoff.

▨ Baseball's San Francisco Giants retired the jerseys of pitcher Christy Mathewson and manager John McGraw, both of whom were major leaguers before numbers were worn.

▨ The NBA's Philadelphia 76ers retired the microphone of announcer Dave Zinkoff.

419

ENDING WITH A FLOURISH, CLOSING WITH A RUSH: THE GREATEST FINALES

Here are the best examples of athletes and teams who ended their careers, or the season, or a game, in a way that they would cherish.

■ In his last regular season college game, Syracuse running back Jim Brown totaled 43 points, a record for most points scored in a major college game.

■ Gary Cowan won the 1971 U.S. Amateur tournament with an eagle two on the 18th hole.

■ California Angel Mike Witt pitched a perfect game on the last day of the 1984 season.

■ Future Hall of Famer Ted Williams could have sat out the last day of the 1941 season and been credited with a .400 average—he was hitting .39955 at the time—but he chose to play the first game of a doubleheader. He went 4-for-5. He could have sat out the second game to make sure he protected his average (now .4039), but he played that one, too, went 2-for-3, and finished at .406 (.4057).

Williams also finished his career dramatically in 1960, as he homered in his final at-bat, at Fenway Park.

■ Phil Niekro won his 300th major league victory on the last day of the 1985 baseball season.

■ The most consecutive games won at the end of an NBA season is 15, by the 1950 Rochester Royals.

■ Johnny Miller shot a final round 63 to win the 1973 U.S. Open.

■ On January 22, 1983, the Portland Trail Blazers outscored the Houston Rockets 17-0 in overtime to win 113-96.

■ New York Yankee Roger Maris hit his record 61st home run on the final day of the 1961 season.

■ The Chicago Cubs captured the 1935 National League pennant with one of the greatest stretch runs ever, winning 21 consecutive games from September 4 to September 27.

■ In his last start of the 1973 season, California Angel Nolan Ryan struck out 16 batters (in 11 innings), giving him 383 for the year, to beat Sandy Koufax's single season record of 382.

■ In the last game of the 1985 NFL season, Kansas City Chiefs wide receiver Stephone Paige caught passes totaling 309 yards, breaking a 40-year-old record for receiving yardage.

■ In the 1957 World Series, Milwaukee Braves pitcher Lew Burdette was unscored upon in his final 24 innings.

■ Mike Scott pitched a no-hitter to clinch the 1986 National League West title for the Houston Astros.
    In 1951, New York Yankees pitcher Allie Reynolds pitched a no-hitter to beat the Boston Red Sox 8-0 and clinch a tie for the American League pennant.

■ American cyclist Greg LeMond won the 1989 Tour de France on the final day of the race by overcoming what was considered an impossible margin, 50 seconds, with the fastest time trial in Tour history.

■ The last game Babe Pinelli umpired behind the plate before retiring was Don Larsen's perfect game in the 1956 World Series.

GOING OUT WITH A THUD:
THE SORRIEST FINISHES IN SPORT

◪ On September 30, 1962, in his last major league at-bat, New York Mets catcher Joe Pignatano hit into a triple play.

◪ In December of 1965, in his last regular season game in football, Cleveland Browns running back Jim Brown was ejected for fighting with St. Louis Cardinal Joe Robb just before halftime, the only time in Brown's career that he was thrown out of a game.

◪ The Los Angeles Dodgers were shut out in the final three games of the 1966 World Series.

◪ In the final game of his college career—the 1986 Rose Bowl against UCLA—University of Iowa running back Ron Harmon fumbled four times in the first half and dropped a touchdown pass. Before that day, he had fumbled once all season.

◪ In 1899, baseball's Cleveland Spiders, managed by an Australian undertaker, lost 40 of their final 41 games.

◪ On October 10, 1904, the last day of the regular season, the New York Highlanders (later the Yankees) sent their ace, Jack Chesbro, to the mound to help win the pennant over the Boston Red Sox. Chesbro was 41-11, a major league record for wins, and had an ERA under 2.00. But he threw a wild pitch in the ninth inning, allowing the Red Sox to score the winning run and clinch the pennant.

◪ The final-season average for Harmon Killebrew was .199 (in 1975); for Babe Ruth, .181 (1935); for Brooks Robinson, .149 (1977); for Ernie Banks, .193 (1971); and for Bill Mazeroski, .188 (1972). Willie Mays hit .211 in his last year and fell down in the outfield in the 1973 World Series. He said, "Growing old is just a helpless hurt."

◪ In the last regular season game of his career, Wilt

Chamberlain scored one point on a free throw. (In his next-to-last game, he did not even attempt a shot from the field.)

■ As a three-year-old in 1948, Citation won 19 of 20 races, including the Triple Crown, and earned $865,150. His owner wanted him to be the first million-dollar winner and kept him racing despite the fact that Citation was suffering from an osselet, a bony growth on the ankle which put the horse out for a year. Citation lost races to horses vastly inferior. He finally surpassed the million-dollar mark in 1951 and retired.

■ On October 6, 1911, in the last game of his career, future Hall of Famer Cy Young, pitching for the Boston Braves against the Brooklyn Dodgers, went 6⅓ innings, gave up 11 hits and 11 runs, and lost, 13-3.

■ In 1925, Roger Peckinpaugh, the Washington Senator shortstop and the American League MVP, led his team to the pennant. In the seven-game World Series against Pittsburgh, Peckinpaugh committed eight errors, a Series record.

IF AT FIRST...:
ATHLETES WHOSE PERSEVERANCE
HAPPILY PAID OFF

■ Jockey Gordon Richards, aboard Pinza, won the 1953 Epsom Derby on his 28th and last attempt.

■ After crashing at 270 mph while attempting to set a new motorcycle world speed record at the Bonneville Salt Flats in September of 1975, Don Vesco tried again and became the first man to exceed 300 mph.

■ In his eighth and final playoff year, Montreal Canadiens defenseman Jack Portland scored the only playoff goal of his career in his last series.

■ Satchel Paige was the oldest rookie in baseball history at 42. Diomedes Olivo broke into the major leagues at 41.

■ Tom Gullikson won his first professional singles tennis title, the 1985 Volvo Hall of Fame at Newport, Rhode Island, when he was 35.

■ As a freshman running back at the University of Georgia, Herschel Walker was third in the Heisman Trophy voting. As a sophomore, he was second. As a junior, he won the Trophy.

■ Boxer Archie Moore won his first title at either 36 or 39—depending on whether you believe the birth date he gave or the one his mother gave—in a 1952 decision over Joey Maxim.

■ Brooklyn Dodger Pee Wee Reese played on five consecutive World Series losers before winning one.

■ Casey Stengel did not lead a pennant winner until his 10th year as manager. (Perhaps we should also mention that his 10th year was also his first year managing the New York Yankees.)

■ Pitcher Joe Niekro appeared in his first World Series game in his 21st major league season.

■ Simone Mathieu lost the French singles finals six times, then won it twice.

■ In 1964, owner Charlie Finley's proposal to move his Athletics from Kansas City to Louisville was rejected by the other American League owners. Four years later, Finley tried to move the team to Oakland, and succeeded.

1 ATHLETE WHOSE PERSEVERANCE UNHAPPILY PAID OFF

■ While trying to set a land speed record at Daytona Beach in February 1928, driver Frank Lockhart crashed on the sand, flipped into the sea, and almost drowned. Two months later, he went back to Daytona, crashed again and, this time, died.

1 ATHLETE WHO SIMPLY WAITED LONG ENOUGH

■ In the 1924 Olympic 90m hill ski jumping competition, Thorleif Haug won the bronze medal. In 1974, a scoring error was discovered that demoted Haug, dead for 48 years, to fourth. Norwegian-born American Anders Haugen, now 83, was moved up to third and awarded the bronze medal in a special ceremony in Oslo. Fifty years after the competition, Haugen officially became the only American ever to win an Olympic ski jumping medal.

I SHOULDA STOOD IN BED: AT LEAST 5 REASONS TO STAY RETIRED

■ Bud Wilkinson, the University of Oklahoma coaching

legend who led the Sooners to a 47-game winning streak in the 1950s, came out of retirement to coach the NFL's St. Louis Cardinals in 1978 and was fired in 1979 after compiling a 9-20 record.

■ Heavyweight Joe Louis retired as an unbeaten champion in 1949, then came back and lost to Ezzard Charles and Rocky Marciano. Muhammad Ali came out of retirement to fight and lose to Larry Holmes (1980) and Trevor Berbick (1981). In 1981, Joe Frazier tried a comeback after a five-year retirement and drew with a journeyman named Jumbo Cummings. Larry Holmes unretired to try and outshine Marciano's record, and lost to Michael Spinks and Mike Tyson.

■ Tight end Jackie Smith came out of retirement in 1978 to play one more season with the Dallas Cowboys. During the 1979 Super Bowl, Smith was wide open in the end zone when he dropped a touchdown pass that cost the Cowboys a chance to tie at the end of the third quarter. The Cowboys lost, 35-31, to the Pittsburgh Steelers, and the dropped pass would become perhaps Smith's most renowned moment as a pro.

■ The 1987 exhibition matches scheduled between former tennis stars Bjorn Borg and Vitas Gerulaitis were canceled because of low ticket sales.

■ Jim Thorpe, who had starred for the 1916 Canton Bulldogs, considered one of the greatest teams in the history of pro football, came back to play for a new version of the team in 1926. This time they went 1-12.

THE MOST MEMORABLE FAREWELLS

Whether they like it or not, great athletes are seen as heroes, and the heroic acts that they perform are what we remember best. Then the day comes when they are finished performing and we bid them farewell, and sometimes we remember these moments, too.

■ On the night of December 3, 1987, in a ceremony honoring Phil Esposito, Boston Bruin captain and All-Star defenseman Ray Bourque surprised Esposito and the Boston crowd by pulling off his own jersey—the #7 that he had worn for eight years—so that Esposito's old #7 could be retired by the Bruins. Underneath Bourque's old jersey was another one that displayed his new number, 77.

■ When Man O' War, age 30, died on November 1, 1947, he became the first thoroughbred to be embalmed in preparation for his funeral. Two thousand people turned out for the ceremony, which was broadcast nationwide on radio. He was extolled by nine speakers, and many who filed by his open casket reached down to touch his flesh. Local merchants draped their storefronts in black.

(When the horse retired in 1920, the Lexington, Kentucky Chamber of Commerce announced that school children would throw flowers in his path during a parade through town. Owner Samuel Riddle rejected the idea. "He's only a horse," he said via telegraph.)

■ After the Los Angeles Lakers lost the fourth and final game of the 1989 NBA Finals to the Detroit Pistons, which was also the final game in the career of Laker center and legend Kareem Abdul-Jabbar, Lakers coach Pat Riley took Abdul-Jabbar's sweaty jersey home with him as a memento. Magic Johnson took Abdul-Jabbar's warm-up jacket, Byron Scott his shoes, and PR director Josh Rosenfeld his shorts.

■ On July 4, 1939, Lou Gehrig Day at Yankee Stadium, the great first baseman gave his farewell speech and uttered one of the most famous lines in sports history: "Today, I consider myself the luckiest man on the face of the earth." At the time, Gehrig was in the advanced stages of amyotrophic lateral sclerosis, the disease that would kill him a year later.

■ In 1974, in Brazilian soccer immortal Pelé's supposed final game after 18 years with Santos, he trotted around the stadium with tears streaming down his face, before leaving the field at halftime as the fans chanted, "Stay! Stay! Stay!" A year later, he signed with the NASL's New York Cosmos.

During a pregame ceremony before his final professional game on October 1, 1977, Pelé led the crowd of 75,646 at the Meadowlands in a chant of "Love! Love! Love!" He played the first half with the Cosmos and at halftime removed his #10 Cosmos jersey and gave it to his father. Pelé then donned his old #10 for Santos, the Cosmos' opponent, and played the second half with them. After the game, he gave his Santos jersey to his first coach and took a lap around the field. Cosmos goalies Shep Messing and Erol Yasin then carried him off on their shoulders.

■ Three days after distance runner Steve Prefontaine's death at age 24 in a May 1975 car accident, a hearse carrying his body took a lap around the Marshfield High School track in his hometown of Coos Bay, Oregon. A crowd of 2,500 attended.

■ On "Yaz Day" in 1983, the day before his final game with the Boston Red Sox, outfielder Carl Yastrzemski grounded into the last out of the game. After reaching first base, he ran to the stands, then circled the field counterclockwise, shaking hands with fans and saluting the crowd.

■ An unexpectedly poignant twist was put on Chris Evert's farewell to major tournament tennis when she hugged and consoled Zina Garrison, who had just conquered Evert in the 1989 U.S. Open quarterfinals and could not contain her tears over what she herself had just done.

■ On May 7, 1959, 93,103 fans, an all-time major league record, turned out at the Los Angeles Coliseum for an exhibition game between the Dodgers and the New York Yankees to honor Roy Campanella. At the end of the fifth inning, Campanella, the former Dodger All-Star catcher who had been crippled in an automobile accident in

January of 1958, was wheeled to the center of the infield. The stadium lights were turned out, and for a full minute fans stood, each holding up a lighted match or cigarette lighter.

IT AIN'T OVER ... IT AIN'T OVER ...

Yogi warned us that "It ain't over till it's over." He was right—he usually is—but, amazingly, people still forget. Here are a few examples of finishes and done deals that turned out not to be.

■ With the bases empty of New York Mets and two outs in the bottom of the 10th inning of Game 6 of the 1986 World Series, New York's Shea Stadium scoreboard flashed the message, "Congratulations, Red Sox."

■ In a United States–Africa meet in North Carolina in 1971, Miruts Yifter sprinted to an apparent win over Steve Prefontaine in the 5,000m, but he had miscounted and quit running one lap too soon.

■ 1960 pole vault Olympian Ron Morris failed to clear the height necessary to qualify for the finals. But because only 10 vaulters had cleared the height, and rules stated that 12 had to compete in the finals, the three next-best vaulters, one of whom was Morris, were duly advanced. Morris won the silver medal.

■ On September 22, 1927, in the famous "Long Count" fight, Jack Dempsey knocked down Gene Tunney in the seventh round. The referee did not start the count right away because Dempsey was standing over Tunney and did not at first heed the ref's warning to go to a neutral corner. Tunney, up at the count of nine, actually had at least 14 seconds of rest, and went on to win in a 10-round decision.

■ On June 15, 1976, Oakland Athletics owner Charlie Finley sold Vida Blue to the New York Yankees for $1.5 million, and Joe Rudi and Rollie Fingers to the Boston Red Sox for $1 million each. On the night of the sale, the Red Sox were in Oakland, and Rudi and Fingers changed clubhouses and donned their new Red Sox uniforms, though neither player was used in the game. The next day, baseball commissioner Bowie Kuhn ordered the Red Sox and the Yankees to refrain from using any of the three players while he investigated the deal. On June 18, Kuhn voided the trades, saying that they were not in the best interests of baseball.

■ In the 1984 Olympics, Daley Thompson apparently finished a point away from equaling the decathlon world record. Two years later, the IAAF announced that his time in the 110m hurdles was actually 14.33 seconds and not 14.34, and a point was added, allowing him to tie the world record.

■ In the 1957 Kentucky Derby, jockey Willie Shoemaker, leading on Gallant Man, mistakenly pulled up 110 yards before the finish line, and was passed by Iron Liege.

■ Jockey Ralph Neves was declared dead by doctors after he fell at Bay Meadows Racetrack on May 8, 1936. They were wrong. Neves came back to race.

■ On October 8, 1981, Bobby Unser was finally declared the winner of the Indianapolis 500, held 4½ months earlier on May 24. Unser had crossed the finish line first but a protest was filed claiming that he had violated the no-pass rule under a yellow caution. The next day, the protest was upheld and Mario Andretti was declared the winner. A USAC appeals panel eventually restored Unser's victory.

■ In a steeplechase race on December 29, 1945, Never Mind II balked at the fourth hurdle, and horse and rider eventually returned to the paddock without completing the course. The jockey was then informed that all of the other horses had fallen. He and Never Mind II returned to the course and won the race in a time of over 11 minutes, almost three times the expected clocking.

IT'S OVER! IT'S OVER!

For those who have been too often burned by not heeding Yogi's dictum, here are five examples of competitions that went on even *after* they were over.

▪ In an August 8, 1903 Eastern League (now International League) game, Rochester and Providence went into extra innings before someone discovered that Providence had already won the game, 1-0. No one on the visiting Providence bench had kept score, and the scoreboard boy had forgotten to tally their run in the fifth inning. In the bottom of the 10th inning, someone finally showed an official scorecard to the umpire, and he awarded the game to Providence, 1-0 winners in nine innings.

▪ On May 25, 1965, in his second loss to Muhammad Ali, Sonny Liston went down at 1:42 of the first round. The knockdown timekeeper had counted all the way to 22 when Liston finally got to his feet. He and Ali began to throw punches but referee Jersey Joe Walcott, responding to shouts that Liston had not gotten up in time, separated the men and declared Ali the winner at 2:12.

▪ In the 1932 Olympic steeplechase, the runners took an extra lap because the lap checker forgot to change the lap count after their first circuit. During the extra lap, Thomas Evenson passed Joseph McCluskey for second.

▪ In 1973, Australian Steve Holland, in his first international race, beat Rick DeMont and Brad Cooper in the 1,500m freestyle in world record time, and kept on swimming even after the distance was covered. The more experienced DeMont and Cooper, skeptical that their lap count was wrong, followed anyway for 100 more meters. Holland made the turn for his third extra lap before officials could stop him.

■ With Dartmouth leading Cornell 3-0 late in the fourth quarter of their November 18, 1940 football game, Cornell drove to the six-yard line, where they had first down. The Big Red ran three rushing plays to the one-yard line, then were moved back five yards after a penalty was called. They then threw an incomplete pass on what should have been fourth down. But Red Friesell, an official, miscalculated and on fifth down Cornell threw for a touchdown and won, 7-3. When the mistake was later discovered, Cornell relinquished the victory. Ivy League commissioner Asa Bushnell sent Friesell a telegram that read, "Don't let it get you down, down, down, down, down."

LET'S PRETEND IT NEVER HAPPENED: 22 GREATS WHO FINISHED THEIR CAREERS ON UNHOLY GROUND

Few men have the integrity that Jackie Robinson showed in 1956. When the lifelong Brooklyn Dodger was traded, at age 37, to the New York Giants, he retired rather than play for the hated crosstown rivals. But he is the exception. Too often, athletes cannot bring themselves to retire even though their skills are fast deteriorating—and, sadly, this is more true of great athletes, since their careers usually last longer than those of lesser competitors. The team on which the fading star flourished no longer wants him, so he takes his act elsewhere. The experience can be as jarring for fans as it is for the player. We try to hold fast to the memory of pitcher Steve Carlton's brilliant 21-plus seasons with the St. Louis Cardinals and the Philadelphia Phillies, all the while looking askance at his pathetic showings, in his last year and a half, with the San Francisco Giants (1986), the Chicago White Sox (1986), the Cleveland Indians (1987), and finally, briefly—mercifully—the Minnesota Twins (1987).

The following is a list of great athletes and the teams with which they finished their careers—*not* the one (or two) with which they will forever be associated.

We'll just pretend none of it ever happened.

■ Hank Aaron as a Milwaukee Brewer (1975–76)

■ Yogi Berra as a New York Met (1965)

■ Bob Cousy as a Cincinnati Royal (1969–70)

■ Dave Cowens as a Milwaukee Buck (1982–83)

■ Dizzy and Paul Dean as St. Louis Browns (1947 and 1943, respectively)

■ Jimmie Foxx as a Chicago Cub (1942, 1944) and a Philadelphia Phillie (1945)

■ Walt Frazier as a Cleveland Cavalier (1977–79)

■ Franco Harris as a Seattle Seahawk (1984)

■ Harmon Killebrew as a Kansas City Royal (1975)

■ Ralph Kiner as a Chicago Cub (1953–54) and a Cleveland Indian (1955)

■ Vince Lombardi as coach of the Washington Redskins (1969)

■ Christy Mathewson as a Cincinnati Red (1916—for one game)

■ Willie Mays as a New York Met (1972–73)

■ Joe Namath as a Los Angeles Ram (1977)

433

- Bobby Orr as a Chicago Blackhawk (1976–77, 1978–79)

- Babe Ruth as a Boston Brave (1935)

- O. J. Simpson as a San Francisco 49er (1978–79)

- Duke Snider as a New York Met (1963) and a San Francisco Giant (1964)

- Warren Spahn as a New York Met (1965) and a San Francisco Giant (1965)

- Johnny Unitas as a San Diego Charger (1973)

- Paul Waner as a Brooklyn Dodger (1941), a Boston Brave (1941–42), a Brooklyn Dodger again (1943–44), and a New York Yankee (1944–45)

ATHLETIC CAREERS THAT WERE CUT SHORT

- Toronto Maple Leaf Ace Bailey was checked from behind by Boston's Eddie Shore in 1933 and his head struck the ice. Bailey was carried off with a cerebral concussion and teetered on the brink of death for several days. He recovered but never played hockey again.

- New England Patriots wide receiver Darryl Stingley was paralyzed and confined to a wheelchair after a notorious hit that he received from Oakland Raider Jack Tatum in a 1978 preseason game.

- While horseback riding at age 19, Maureen "Mo" Connolly, the youngest woman to win the tennis Grand Slam, broke her leg when a truck hit her. She never played competitive tennis again. She died of cancer in 1969, at age 34.

◼ In March of 1958, 24-year-old Cincinnati Royal Maurice Stokes, a three-time NBA All-Star, hit his head on the floor while scrambling for a loose ball, and was knocked unconscious. Stokes revived and continued to play but three days later, he collapsed while in a plane and went into a six-month coma, apparently caused by swelling on the brain from his collision. He suffered permanent paralysis and died in 1970, at 36.

◼ After six years in which he drove in more runs than anyone in the American League, including Mickey Mantle, outfielder Jackie Jensen of the Boston Red Sox quit baseball in his prime, mainly because of his fear of flying. He retired after the 1959 season, in which he hit 28 home runs and drove in 112. Hypnotism failed to cure him. He came back to play in 1961, then retired again.

◼ Bill Carr, Olympic 400m champion in 1932, broke both his ankles and fractured his pelvis in a car accident on March 17, 1933, ending his career.

◼ Talented Detroit Tigers righthander Mark "The Bird" Fidrych went 19-9 his rookie year, then "blew" his arm and only won 10 more games in the majors.

◼ Brazil's Joao Carlos de Oliveira, a triple jump world record holder and third at both the 1976 and 1980 Olympics, had to have his right leg amputated below the knee after a car accident in January of 1982.

◼ The career of tennis player Tracy Austin was substantially shortened by various injuries including sciatic nerve damage, a stress fracture in her back, and a shoulder injury.

◼ The repeated punishment that NFL running backs absorb each week has hastened the end of several brilliant careers, notably Chicago Bears halfback Gale Sayers, who retired with knee injuries after only seven years (1965–71) in the league (though he was great enough in those years to become the youngest inductee into the Pro Football Hall of Fame); and Detroit Lions running back Billy Sims, who also retired with knee injuries, after just five seasons (1980–84), rushing for over a thousand yards in three of them.

■ The athletic careers of Australian James Carlton, world record holder in the 200m and the favorite for an Olympic gold medal in 1932, and of American John Mostyn, a world-class sprinter, were abbreviated when each, still in his twenties, became a monk.

AND ONE *RACE* THAT WAS CUT SHORT

■ The 1916 Indianapolis 500 was actually the Indianapolis 300. The race was shortened because World War I had limited European entries and curtailed American car-making. Carl Fisher, the Indy president, did not think that older cars would survive 500 miles.

PERFECTION UNDONE

■ On November 21, 1982, University of Washington placekicker Chuck Nelson was a perfect 30-for-30 in field goals for the season. Late in the fourth quarter of the final regular season game of the year, Nelson missed a field goal from 30 yards that would have given Washington the lead. Washington State went on to win, 24-20. A Washington victory would have put the Huskies in the Rose Bowl.

■ In his sophomore, junior, and senior years playing for St. John's University, Chris Mullin scored in double figures in every game but his last, the 1985 Final Four semifinal against Georgetown. Mullin had eight points in the game.

■ On September 2, 1972, Chicago Cubs pitcher Milt Pappas had a perfect game going for 8⅔ innings. He went to a 3-2 count on the 27th batter before walking him.

■ The Duke Blue Devils were unbeaten, untied, and unscored upon going into the 1939 Rose Bowl. They led USC 3-0 in the last quarter when fourth-string Trojan quarterback Doyle Nave threw a touchdown pass to second-string receiver Al Krueger with 41 seconds left in the game to win 7-3 and destroy Duke's visions of perfection.

■ Majestic Prince's only defeat was in his last race, the 1969 Belmont. His trainer did not want to run him because the horse was tired, but he relented to pressure by racing officials and the press. Majestic Prince finished second to Arts and Letters, developed leg trouble, and never raced again.

■ The Chicago Bears finished with perfect regular season records twice, in 1934 and again in 1942, but in both years lost in the championship game.

■ In 1964, Ara Parseghian's first year as head coach, Notre Dame was unbeaten in nine games and ranked #1. In their final game, they were leading USC 17-0 at halftime but lost the game, 20-17, and their top ranking.

■ Cleveland Indians pitcher Johnny Allen lost his last start of 1937, making his season's final record 15-1.

■ Olympic wrestling champion Dan Gable was 64-0 at West High School in Waterloo, Iowa, and won his first 117 matches in college at Iowa State, then lost his final college match to Larry Owings of Washington in the NCAA finals, 13-11.

■ Mickey Wright won three legs of the women's golf Grand Slam in 1961—the LPGA, the U.S. Open, and the Titleholders tournament—but finished second to Mary Lena Faulk in the final leg, the Western Open.

■ Chic Harley, Ohio State's All-America halfback, played on two undefeated teams in 1916–17, then left for military service. He returned in 1919, and Ohio State again went undefeated up to the final game against Illinois. Harley had never played on a losing side in college, and Ohio State led 7-6 late in the fourth quarter. In the last 10 seconds of the game, Illinois' Bob Fletcher kicked a field goal for a 9-7 win.

■ Lew Hoad won the first three legs of the tennis Grand Slam in 1956. In the last leg, the U.S. championships, he lost in the final to Ken Rosewall.

■ For the three-year span from 1948–50, the University of California went 29-0-1 during the regular season. After each of those three undefeated seasons, the Golden Bears lost in the Rose Bowl.

■ The Oakland Raiders lost the first 13 games of the 1962 AFL season but ruined their spotless record by winning the final game of the season.

GOING OUT ON TOP: SPORTS FIGURES WHO GOT OUT BEFORE THE CHEERS TURNED TO BOOS

■ Philadelphia Eagles quarterback Norm Van Brocklin led a fourth-quarter drive that culminated in the winning touchdown in the 1960 NFL title game, to beat the Green

Bay Packers and give Vince Lombardi his only title game loss as coach. Van Brocklin quit football after the season.

■ In his last five years in the big leagues, Los Angeles Dodgers pitcher Sandy Koufax led the National League in ERA every season. In his final season, 1966, he was 27-9, with a 1.73 ERA and 317 strikeouts. Only 30 years old, Koufax retired because of arm trouble.

■ Bruce Jenner did not even take his vaulting poles with him after winning the 1976 Olympic decathlon because he knew that he would not compete again.

■ Despite injuring his right front ankle during the Belmont race, Count Fleet won the Triple Crown in 1943 and then retired to stud.

■ Aleksandr Tikhonov won his fourth straight Olympic team biathlon gold medal in 1980, then announced his retirement.

■ Cleveland Browns running back Jim Brown retired in 1965 at age 29, at the peak of his career, to make movies. He was the NFL's rushing champion for eight of his nine years, including his last three.

■ San Francisco 49ers coach Bill Walsh retired after winning his third Super Bowl.

■ East German Katarina Witt won her fourth figure skating world championship and then retired.

■ Although he was just 28 years old, Bobby Jones retired after winning the golfing Grand Slam in 1930.

■ Frank Hadow won the second Wimbledon tournament in 1878 and then never played in it again.

■ Ray Harroun, the winner of the first Indianapolis 500, retired from driving after the race. (His car, a single-seater, was banned from the race.)

■ Middleweight champion Carlos Monzon retired in 1977, going undefeated in his last 13 years.

THE 11 MOST UNFULFILLING
CELEBRATIONS

To the victor go the spoils—and on each of the following occasions, the victor's celebration was indeed spoiled.

■ Abebe Bikila of Ethiopia won his second Olympic marathon gold medal at the 1964 Tokyo Games. At the awards ceremony, no one in the band knew the Ethiopian national anthem, so they played the Japanese anthem instead.

■ On the day that the Detroit Pistons were to visit the White House to be honored for their 1989 NBA championship, starting forward Rick Mahorn, left unprotected in the expansion draft, was chosen by the Minnesota Timberwolves.

■ During the medal ceremony for the 200m backstroke in 1984, American gold medal winner Rick Carey hung his head in disappointment because he had not broken the world record.

■ At the 1972 Munich Games, Americans Vincent Matthews and Wayne Collett finished 1-2 in the 400m run. While the National Anthem played, Matthews and Collett talked and fidgeted. The West German crowd booed them and the International Olympic Committee banned the runners from further competition.

■ After the Philadelphia Phillies won the World Series in 1980, the team's first Series victory ever, star pitcher Steve Carlton, known for his aversion to the media, hid in the Phillies training room rather than celebrate with the team. He drank from his own bottle of champagne while teammates sprayed each other with theirs.

■ In the 5,000m final at the 1932 Los Angeles Olympic Games, American Ralph Hill tried to pass Lauri Lehtinen of Finland. Lehtinen swerved twice to block Hill and crossed the finish line first by three inches. The crowd booed until public-address announcer Bill Henry uttered what would become a renowned admonition: "Please remember, folks, that these people are our guests." Lehtinen tried to lift Hill onto the first-place platform, but Hill refused.

■ After being drafted as the #1 pick by the Boston Celtics on June 17, 1986, and then spending time in New York and Boston for media coverage, basketball star Len Bias returned to his University of Maryland dormitory to celebrate with friends. He collapsed into convulsions on Thursday morning, June 19, and died of intoxication from cocaine.

■ In 1976, the victory lap by the three Olympic medalists in the 200m was delayed 10 minutes for the awards ceremony in the javelin.

■ Fairfield University basketball coach Mitch Buonaguro, certain that his team had wrapped up a 1988 Metro Atlantic Athletic Conference tournament win over St. Peter's, bolted joyously across the court with two seconds left to hug Harold Brantley, whose lay-up had just given Fairfield a 60-59 lead. Buonaguro was assessed a two-shot technical foul for leaving the coaching box. St. Peter's made both shots, as well as two more after a foul on the ensuing inbounds pass, to win 63-60.

■ Czech Vera Caslavska won the all-around gymnastics gold in 1968, two months after her country had been occupied by Russian troops. In the floor exercise, she tied for first with Russian Larissa Petrik, requiring that the two stand together on the top platform during the ceremony. Caslavska bowed her head and turned away during the Soviet anthem.

■ In 490 B.C., a Greek courier, perhaps named Pheidippides and the unwitting father of the marathon race, ran from the Plain of Marathon to Athens, to announce the Greek victory over the larger Persian army. The story has it that upon covering the great distance and parting with his news—"Rejoice! We have won."—the courier died of exhaustion.

A LIST OF 10 EMPTY LISTS

■ Major leaguers who have hit grand slams off of Baltimore Orioles pitcher Jim Palmer.

■ NBA games—regular season, All-Star, or playoff—in which Wilt Chamberlain fouled out.

■ Holders of the 11th master (*dan*) grade in judo.

■ Pitchers who threw no-hitters in the 61-year history of Pittsburgh's Forbes Field.

■ Non-English speaking men who have won golf's U.S. Open.

■ Boston Celtics who have led the NBA in scoring.

■ Times that heavyweight boxer George Chuvalo was knocked down in his career.

■ Fair catches made by the Dallas Cowboys during the 1982 NFL season.

■ Major league parks where they play only day games.

■ Lists that follow this one.